P9-DJV-285

Early Childhood Education 10/11

Thirty-First Edition

EDITOR

Karen Menke Paciorek
Eastern Michigan University

Karen Menke Paciorek is a professor of early childhood education at Eastern Michigan University in Ypsilanti. Her degrees in early childhood education include a BA from the University of Pittsburgh, an MA from George Washington University, and a PhD from Peabody College of Vanderbilt University. She is the editor of *Taking Sides: Clashing Views in Early Childhood Education* (2nd Ed.), also published by McGraw-Hill. She has served as president of the Michigan Association for the Education of Young Children, the Michigan Early Childhood Education Consortium, and the Northville School Board. She presents at local, state, and national conferences on curriculum planning, guiding behavior, preparing the learning environment, and working with families. She has served as a member of the Board of Education for the Northville Public Schools, Northville, Michigan, since 2002 and is on the Board of Directors for Wolverine Human Services, which serves over 700 abused and delinquent youth in Michigan. Dr. Paciorek is a recipient of the Eastern Michigan University Distinguished Faculty Award for Service.

McGraw-Hill

Connect Learn Succeed™

Mc Graw Hill

Connect
Learn
Succeed™

ANNUAL EDITIONS: EARLY CHILDHOOD EDUCATION, THIRTY-FIRST EDITION

Published by McGraw-Hill, a business unit of The McGraw-Hill Companies, Inc., 1221 Avenue of the Americas, New York, NY 10020. Copyright © 2011 by The McGraw-Hill Companies, Inc. All rights reserved. Previous edition(s) 2008, 2009, 2010. No part of this publication may be reproduced or distributed in any form or by any means, or stored in a database or retrieval system, without the prior written consent of The McGraw-Hill Companies, Inc., including, but not limited to, in any network or other electronic storage or transmission, or broadcast for distance learning.

Some ancillaries, including electronic and print components, may not be available to customers outside the United States.

Annual Editions® is a registered trademark of The McGraw-Hill Companies, Inc.

Annual Editions is published by the **Contemporary Learning Series** group within The McGraw-Hill Higher Education division.

1 2 3 4 5 6 7 8 9 0 WDQ/WDQ 1 0 9 8 7 6 5 4 3 2 1 0

ISBN 978–0–07–805067–1
MHID 0–07–805067–7
ISSN 0270–4456

Managing Editor: *Larry Loeppke*
Developmental Editor: *Dave Welsh*
Editorial Coordinator: *Mary Foust*
Editorial Assistant: *Cindy Hedley*
Production Service Assistant: *Rita Hingtgen*
Permissions Coordinator: *Shirley Lanners*
Senior Marketing Manager: *Julie Keck*
Senior Marketing Communications Specialist: *Mary Klein*
Marketing Coordinator: *Alice Link*
Director Specialized Production: *Faye Schilling*
Senior Project Manager: *Joyce Watters*
Design Specialist: *Margarite Reynolds*
Production Supervisor: *Sue Culbertson*
Cover Graphics: *Kristine Jubeck*

Compositor: Laserwords Private Limited
Cover Images: © Rachael M. Stork (inset); Dean Muz/Agefotostock (background)

Library in Congress Cataloging-in-Publication Data
Main entry under title: Annual Editions: Early Childhood Education 2010/2011.
 1. Early Childhood Education—I. Menke Paciorek, Karen, *comp.* II. Title: Early Childhood Education.
658'.05

Editors/Academic Advisory Board

Members of the Academic Advisory Board are instrumental in the final selection of articles for each edition of ANNUAL EDITIONS. Their review of articles for content, level, and appropriateness provides critical direction to the editors and staff. We think that you will find their careful consideration well reflected in this volume.

ANNUAL EDITIONS: Early Childhood 10/11
31st Edition

EDITOR

Karen Menke Paciorek
Eastern Michigan University

Preface

In publishing ANNUAL EDITIONS we recognize the enormous role played by the magazines, newspapers, and journals of the public press in providing current, first-rate educational information in a broad spectrum of interest areas. Many of these articles are appropriate for students, researchers, and professionals seeking accurate, current material to help bridge the gap between principles and theories and the real world These articles, however, become more useful for study when those of lasting value are carefully collected, organized, indexed, and reproduced in a low-cost format, which provides easy and permanent access when the material is needed. That is the role played by ANNUAL EDITIONS.

Annual Editions: Early Childhood Education has evolved during the over 30 years it has been in existence to become one of the most used texts for students in early childhood education. This annual reader is used today at over 550 colleges and universities. In addition, it may be found in public libraries, pediatricians' offices, and teacher reference sections of school libraries. As the editor for twenty-five years, I work diligently throughout the year to find articles and bring you the best and most significant readings in the field. I realize this is a tremendous responsibility to provide a thorough review of the current literature—a responsibility I take very seriously. I am always on the lookout for possible articles for the next *Annual Editions: Early Childhood Education.* My goal is to provide the reader with a snapshot of the critical issues facing professionals in early childhood education.

Early childhood education is an interdisciplinary field that includes child development, family issues, educational practices, behavior guidance, and curriculum. *Annual Editions: Early Childhood Education 10/11* brings you the latest information in the field from a wide variety of recent journals, newspapers, and magazines. There are four themes found in the readings chosen for this thirty-first edition of *Annual Editions: Early Childhood Education.* They are (1) the importance of the federal, state, and local governments in investing in early childhood programs; (2) the strong focus on early learning standards and the need for teachers to align their curriculum and learning experiences to meet the standards while still providing a classroom setting that is engaging and meaningful; (3) the lifelong benefits of children participating in freely chosen play experiences both inside and outside; and (4) the need for inclusive classrooms that meet the needs of all learners, including those with developmental and medical issues as well as children from diverse family environments.

It is especially gratifying to see issues affecting children and families addressed in magazines other than professional association journals. The general public needs to be aware of the impact of positive early learning and family experiences on the growth and development of children.

Continuing in this edition of *Annual Editions: Early Childhood Education* are selected World Wide Websites that can be used to further explore topics addressed in the articles. I have chosen to include only a few high-quality sites. Readers are encouraged to explore these sites on their own or in collaboration with others for extended learning opportunities.

Given the wide range of topics; *Annual Editions: Early Childhood Education 10/11* may be used by several groups—undergraduate or graduate students, professionals, parents, or administrators who want to develop an understanding of the critical issues in the field.

The cover photo of this edition was taken by photographer Rachael Stork as she watched young Deyana crawl up and snuggle onto the lap of Clay, the young man talking to her mother. Thank you to Rachael, Clay, and Deyana for sharing the touching moment. It is my hope that Deyana and all young children will receive outstanding care and education that will prepare them for a lifetime of learning.

I appreciate the time the advisory board members take to provide suggestions for improvement and possible articles for consideration. The production and editorial staff of McGraw-Hill, led by Larry Loeppke and David Welsh, ably support and coordinate my efforts.

To the instructor or reader interested in current issues professionals in the field deal with on a day-to-day basis, I encourage you to check out *Taking Sides: Clashing Views in Early Childhood Education,* 2nd edition (2008), which contains eighteen critical issues. The book can be used in a seminar or issues course and opens the door to rich discussion.

I look forward to hearing from you about the selection and organization of this edition and especially value correspondence from students who take the time to share their thoughts on the profession or articles selected. Comments and articles sent for consideration are welcomed and will serve to modify future volumes. Take time to fill out and return the postage-paid article rating form on the last page. You may also contact me at kpaciorek@emich.edu.

Karen Menke Paciorek

Karen Menke Paciorek
Editor

Contents

Preface   iv

Correlation Guide   xiii

Topic Guide   xiv

Internet References   xvii

UNIT 1
Perspectives

Unit Overview   xx

1. **Invest in Early Childhood Education,** Sharon Lynn Kagan and
   Jeanne L. Reid, *Phi Delta Kappan,* April 2009
   In her succinct and informative style, Kagan, joined by Reid, outlines a number of
   recommendations for moving forward with early childhood education in this country. The roles of the *federal government,* states, local communities, and families
   are described. The article is a must-read for anyone interested in ensuring quality
   programs are available for all young children. The authors contend that *universal
   preschool* should be available, but not required.   3

2. **A Foundation for Success,** Sara Mead, *American School Board
   Journal,* November 2008
   Legislators throughout the country recognize the long-lasting educational and economic *cost* benefits of *pre-kindergarten* programs. School leaders are beginning
   to see how quality early childhood programs can reduce the *achievement* gap and
   provide a strong foundation for future learning.   8

3. **Joy in School,** Steven Wolk, *Educational Leadership,* September
   2008
   With the focus on academic *achievement,* teachers are feeling the pressure to
   teach so that students learn. For many teachers that means an academic approach where the joy and passion for learning is lacking. Wolk reminds educators
   to plan *developmentally appropriate* activities that encourage children to develop
   lifelong learning habits.   12

4. **Early Education, Later Success,** Susan Black, *American School
   Board Journal,* September 22, 2008
   What used to be called K-12 education has dipped down to include the very critical
   preschool years. School districts are beginning to *align* their PK-third grades into
   an ECE PK-3 unit. Schools committed to *achievement* and *best practices* find a
   cohesive approach to education for their youngest learners most effective.   17

5. **The Changing Culture of Childhood: A Perfect Storm,** Joe L.
   Frost, *Childhood Education,* Summer 2007
   Joe L. Frost was a keynote speaker at the 2006 Annual Conference for the Association for Childhood Education International. Included is an expanded version
   of his address focusing on the decrease of *play,* the increase of *academics,* the
   effects of *poverty,* and other issues affecting young children.   19

6. **No Child Left Behind: Who's Accountable?,** Lisa A. DuBois,
   Peabody Reflector, Summer 2007
   No Child Left Behind (NCLB) is halfway to the year 2014, when the *federal* law
   requires that 100 percent of public school students *achieve* proficiency in reading,
   math, and science. *Accountability* and *best practices* of NCLB are discussed by
   researchers at Peabody College of Vanderbilt University.   25

The concepts in bold italics are developed in the article. For further expansion, please refer to the Topic Guide.

7. **Preschool Comes of Age: The National Debate on Education for Young Children Intensifies,** Michael Lester, *Edutopia,* June 2007

Close to two-thirds of *preschool* children have a school experience prior to entering kindergarten. The data on *achievement* levels and *readiness* for future learning of children who attend preschool programs is well documented. Data on the long-term *cost effectiveness* of preschool programs for *at-risk children* is also striking, yet, there are children without access to quality preschool programs. Michael Lester questions why more young children do not attend preschool.　　　**29**

UNIT 2
Young Children, Their Families, and Communities

Unit Overview　　　**32**

8. **Class Matters—In and Out of School,** Jayne Boyd-Zaharias and Helen Pate-Bain, *Phi Delta Kappan,* September 2008

The effects of *poverty* on school *achievement* can be abated by *collaboration* between school administrators and community leaders. Quality instruction starting in the *preschool* years and *lower class sizes* are effective practices.　　　**34**

9. **Early Childhood School Success: Recognizing Families as Integral Partners,** Janet S. Arndt and Mary Ellen McGuire-Schwartz, *Childhood Education,* Annual Theme 2008

Understanding that even though all *families* are different, they all have the common goal of wanting the best for their children. Involving *parents* from the beginning in the education of their children will help form a successful partnership.　　　**39**

10. **Meeting of the Minds,** Laura Pappano, *Harvard Education Letter,* July/August 2007

Making *parent-teacher* conferences a win-win situation for the *teacher, family,* and student is the key for developing positive relationships. Pappano provides strategies that teachers can use to take full advantage of the opportunity available for parents and teachers to meet.　　　**44**

11. **Making Long-Term Separations Easier for Children and Families,** Amy M. Kim and Julia Yeary, *Young Children,* September 2008

The numbers of children separated from family members by military deployment are staggering. Long deployments, injuries, and death of a *family* member have an impact on the *social, emotional,* and *cognitive development* of children. *Teachers* can work with the family to help alleviate the *stress* children are experiencing.　　　**47**

12. **Fast Times,** Deborah Swaney, *Family Circle,* November 29, 2008

The pressures young girls face to dress and act older than they are can affect many aspects of their *development.* Boys are not under the same pressures as girls but still face *social and emotional stress.* Suggestions for *parents* include decreasing their children's television viewing, monitoring their use of the Internet, helping children to make age-appropriate choices in clothing and play materials, and getting children involved in physical activities.　　　**52**

The concepts in bold italics are developed in the article. For further expansion, please refer to the Topic Guide.

UNIT 3
Diverse Learners

Unit Overview   **56**

13. **Whose Problem Is Poverty?,** Richard Rothstein, *Educational Leadership,* April 2008

There has been much focus on how best to close the **achievement gap** found in children living in **poverty.** Rothstein argues that schools alone will not solve the problem. **Collaboration** between **families,** educators, **health** professionals, the **federal government,** and community agencies is needed.   **58**

14. **How to Support Bilingualism in Early Childhood,** M. Victoria Rodríguez, *Texas Child Care Quarterly,* Winter 2008

The **diverse** home experiences young children bring to their school setting vary in so many ways. None is more challenging for the teacher than children for whom English is not the primary language spoken in the home. These **English language learners** and their **families** have unique needs, and knowledgeable and caring teachers can do much to support and encourage children's language experiences.   **62**

15. **Learning in an Inclusive Community,** Mara Sapon-Shevin, *Educational Leadership,* September 2008

Moving to develop an **inclusive** learning community that meets the needs of all students is the focus of this article. Included are ten suggestions for **teachers** to consider when designing classrooms that support the **diversity** of the children.   **66**

16. **Young Children with Autism Spectrum Disorder: Strategies That Work,** Clarissa Willis, *Young Children,* January 2009

Willis describes some of the characteristics of **autism spectrum disorder,** which is diagnosed in one in every 150 babies. **Teachers** have many questions related to behavior, needs, and specific strategies that will best reach these children in an **inclusive** setting. Suggestions for classroom routines are included.   **71**

17. **Including Children with Disabilities in Early Childhood Education Programs: Individualizing Developmentally Appropriate Practices,** John Filler and Yaoying Xu, *Childhood Education,* Winter 2006/2007

Integrating young children with **disabilities** in early childhood programs requires **teachers** who work closely with **families** to accommodate the special needs of each child. **Teachers** skilled in **differentiating** will be best able to make the practice of **inclusion** successful and a positive learning experience for all children in the classroom.   **77**

UNIT 4
Supporting Young Children's Development

Unit Overview   **84**

18. **Play and Social Interaction in Middle Childhood,** Doris Bergen and Doris Pronin Fromberg, *Phi Delta Kappan,* February 2009

At a time when **recess** and free **play** are disappearing from early childhood programs, Bergen and Fromberg discuss the importance of play during the middle childhood years. **Social, emotional, physical, cognitive** and **creative development** are enhanced through play.   **87**

The concepts in bold italics are developed in the article. For further expansion, please refer to the Topic Guide.

19. **Twelve Characteristics of Effective Early Childhood Teachers,** Laura J. Colker, *Young Children,* March 2008

Colker provides 12 characteristics or dispositions found in skilled early childhood *teachers.* The author describes the characteristics: passion, perseverance, flexibility, and love of learning. All teachers should assess the effectiveness of their own teaching characteristics. 91

20. **Health = Performance,** Ginny Ehrlich, *American School Board Journal,* October 2008

Ehrlich links students' *academic achievement* to their overall *health* and wellness. A strong physical presence and a strong body make one better able to acquire *cognitive* skills. School administrators who focus on offering healthy *food and nutrition,* providing ample opportunities for *physical development,* and partner with staff and *families* to be positive role models will see progress in moving to overall healthy students. 95

21. **Which Hand?: Brains, Fine Motor Skills, and Holding a Pencil,** Louise Parks, *Texas Child Care Quartely,* Spring 2007

Helping *parents* understand the needs of their child when developing *physical skills,* specifically related to handedness, is an important job for teachers. Strategies for helping children feel competent and comfortable with their choice to use either their left or right hand for fine motor skills are included. 97

22. **Keeping Children Active: What You Can Do to Fight Childhood Obesity,** Rae Pica, *Exchange,* May/June 2009

Instilling a love for leading a *healthy* active lifestyle starts when children are young. Pica provides strategies for adults to incorporate *physical* activity and *recess* into each day which will help prevent *obesity* as children age. 101

23. **The Truth about ADHD,** Jeannette Moninger, *Parents,* November 2008

Attention-deficit/hyperactivity disorder (ADHD) affects approximately 4 million children in the United States yet it often is a challenge for the teachers who serve the children with the disorder. The author includes eight facts about ADHD all *teachers* and parents should know. 104

24. **When Girls and Boys Play: What Research Tells Us,** Jeanetta G. Riley and Rose B. Jones, *Childhood Education,* Fall 2007

As many teachers and administrators are deciding to eliminate *play* and *recess,* there is strong evidence supporting the many benefits of child-initiated, free-choice play. Children specifically benefit *physically, socially,* and creatively when given an opportunity to engage in free play. 107

UNIT 5
Educational Practices

Unit Overview 112

25. **Enhancing Development and Learning through Teacher-Child Relationships,** Kathleen Cranley Gallagher and Kelley Mayer, *Young Children,* November 2008

When *teachers* take the time to develop warm and nurturing relationships with each child, they take the first step toward the total education of all children in their classroom. A secure attachment is important for *infants and toddlers* and continues throughout the early childhood years. Research on *best practices* to foster *social and emotional development* are outlined in this article. 115

The concepts in bold italics are developed in the article. For further expansion, please refer to the Topic Guide.

26. **Developmentally Appropriate Practice in the Age of Testing,** David McKay Wilson, *Harvard Education Letter,* May/June 2009

Wilson's message to all teachers is to hold strong to principle of child *development* and provide an environment that is *developmentally appropriate* for all young children to learn. Pressure to use *scripted curriculum* and deny children the opportunity for *inquiry-based learning* is forcing many teachers to not follow what they know to be best practice. Four key foundations of development are described.   **122**

27. **What Research Says about . . . Grade Retention,** Jane L. David, *Educational Leadership,* March 2008

Retention, or repeating a grade, has been increasing as schools work to meet Adequate Yearly Progress (AYP). There is a great difference between countries such as Great Britain, Denmark, Japan, and Sweden with zero children retained each year and the United States with over two million K-12 grade children retained each year. Significant research studies have found retention to not be a positive experience that doesn't lead to successful results in *achievement.* Additional strategies for educators to help struggling students are included.   **125**

28. **Back to Basics: Play in Early Childhood,** Jill Englebright Fox, *Earlychildhood NEWS,* March/April 2006

The basics to which Englebright refers are the benefits of a variety of *developmentally appropriate play* experiences for young children. Freely chosen and supported by a knowledgeable staff, children who are allowed to engage in a variety of play will experience benefits in their cognitive, social, creative, physical, and emotional *development.*   **127**

29. **Scripted Curriculum: Is It a Prescription for Success?,** Anita Ede, *Childhood Education,* Fall 2006

In light of the *NCLB* requirements that students are to achieve by 2014, many school districts have adopted *scripted curriculum* programs for *teachers* to use when teaching reading specifically. The use of these programs is most prevalent with *at-risk learners.*   **130**

30. **Using Brain-Based Teaching Strategies to Create Supportive Early Childhood Environments That Address Learning Standards,** Pam Schiller and Clarissa A. Willis, *Young Children,* July 2008

Creative *primary teachers* can provide quality *inquiry-based* learning experiences where students can achieve content *standards.* Good teachers *differentiate* activities. The authors provide many suggestions for *brain-based* learning activities.   **134**

31. **Successful Transition to Kindergarten: The Role of Teachers and Parents,** Pam Deyell-Gingold *Earlychildhood NEWS,* May/June 2006

Helping young children make a smooth transition to *kindergarten* is a goal of every preschool teacher and parent. When kindergarten teachers prepare environments that are *ready* to accept a variety of *developmental* levels, children can be successful. A *play*-based setting with a focus on the *social and emotional development* of young children will allow them to be successful, lifelong learners.   **138**

32. **The Looping Classroom: Benefits for Children, Families, and Teachers,** Mary M. Hitz, Mary Catherine Somers, and Christee L. Jenlink, *Young Children,* March 2007

Educators often try different practices with improving academic *achievement* as their ultimate goal. The benefits of *teachers* moving up to the next grade with their class of children are many. Skilled teachers are able to provide *developmentally appropriate environments* and best serve *English Language Learners* and other *diverse learners. Families* often like the consistency that comes from their children having the same teacher for two or more years. *Retention* can be decreased when children have the opportunity to continue for another year with the same teacher in the next grade level.   **142**

The concepts in bold italics are developed in the article. For further expansion, please refer to the Topic Guide.

33. **Beyond *The Lorax?*: The Greening of the American Curriculum,** Clare Lowell, *Phi Delta Kappan,* November 2008

Young children are spending fewer hours *playing* outside enjoying nature and spending more time inside using technology. The long-term consequences of this nature deprivation will be a generation of children not familiar and invested with their natural surroundings and everything living outside. The author discusses a number of key issues addressed in this edition including *ADHD* and *obesity*, as well as *physical and creative development.*   **146**

UNIT 6
Helping Children to Thrive in School

Unit Overview   **150**

34. **Play: Ten Power Boosts for Children's Early Learning,** Alice Sterling Honig, *Young Children,* September 2007

Dr. Honig, an icon in the early childhood field, provides ten reasons why *play* is critical for young children. The reasons cover all areas of development and are very appropriate to share with *parents* and administrators questioning the benefit of play for young children's development.   **153**

35. **Ready or Not, Here We Come: What It Means to Be a Ready School,** Paula M. Dowker, with Larry Schweinhart and Marijata Daniel-Echols, *Young Children,* March 2007

For years good early childhood educators have known that we don't get children ready for school, we get schools ready for children. School *readiness* takes on a whole new meaning when it is viewed from the perspective of how all learners will be accepted and accommodated. *Developmentally appropriate practices* that best serve all children are necessary for positive learning experiences to occur.   **158**

36. **"Stop Picking on Me!": What You Need to Know about Bullying,** Barbara A. Langham, *Texas Child Care Quarterly,* Spring 2008

Teachers have a responsibility to educate children about *bullying.* Risk factors as well as protective factors for aggressive behavior are provided along with strategies for teachers to use in preventing bullying.   **160**

37. **Developmentally Appropriate Child Guidance: Helping Children Gain Self-Control,** Will Mosier, *Texas Child Care Quarterly,* Spring 2009

Our ultimate goal for *guiding* children's behavior is to have children express their emotions in *socially* acceptable ways as they learn to develop internal control. *Teachers* who employ natural consequences for inappropriate behavior help children develop the skills they will need throughout their life.   **165**

38. **Fostering Positive Transitions for School Success,** Jayma Ferguson McGann and Patricia Clark, *Young Children,* November 2007

Colleges and universities have, for years, provided well-organized transition programs for incoming students. *Preschools* and elementary schools are just beginning to see the importance of helping children transit to their first or next school experience. The benefits of *social and emotional development* as well as establishing a positive connection with *families* are some of the results seen with an organized transition program.   **168**

The concepts in bold italics are developed in the article. For further expansion, please refer to the Topic Guide.

39. **A Multinational Study Supports Child-Initiated Learning: Using the Findings in Your Classroom,** Jeanne E. Montie, Jill Claxton, and Shannon D. Lockhart, *Young Children,* November 2007

A result from a study in 15 countries of over 5,000 preschoolers provides striking findings for educators everywhere. Applying four key findings can lead to increased *achievement.* Education of the teachers, opportunities to make choices, minimal time spent in large group activities, and classrooms with a variety of materials all led to higher language and/or cognitive achievement.   170

40. **The Power of Documentation in the Early Childhood Classroom,** Hilary Seitz, *Young Children,* March 2008

Documentation takes many forms and should be collected throughout the year. It allows others to gain an understanding of the many learning opportunities in a classroom and shows specific ways in which children benefited from participation in various learning experiences.   175

UNIT 7
Curricular Issues

Unit Overview   180

41. **Preschool Curricula: Finding One That Fits,** Vivian Baxter and Karen Petty, *Texas Child Care Quarterly,* Fall 2008

There are many different *curriculum* approaches used in *preschool* programs. Some are models or packages adopted or purchased and others are an eclectic approach incorporating practices from a number of approaches or theories. This article describes six popular curriculum models and presents the role of the child and *teacher* for each approach.   183

42. **Got Standards?: Don't Give up on Engaged Learning!,** Judy Harris Helm, *Young Children,* March 2006

Judy Harris Helm walks teachers through a planning process where early learning *standards* can be integrated into a child-initiated, *inquiry-based* approach to learning.   187

43. **The Plan: Building on Children's Interests,** Hilary Jo Seitz, *Young Children,* March 2006

Teachers who carefully listen and observe the children will find a wealth of possibilities for the development of an *emergent curriculum.* When the *curriculum* is based on the interests of the children and allows for extended *projects,* there are many rich discoveries waiting for both the children and the teacher.   193

44. **Constructive Play: A Value-Added Strategy for Meeting Early Learning Standards,** Walter F. Drew et al., *Young Children,* July 2008

Constructive *play* is play in which children work to make an original creation or show an understanding of a concept. *Creativity,* imagination, and *inquiry* are all parts of constructive play. Teachers have found that early learning *standards* can be achieved by fostering constructive play in their classrooms.   197

45. **Using Picture Books to Support Young Children's Literacy,** Janis Strasser and Holly Seplocha, *Childhood Education,* Summer 2007

Getting great picture books into the hands of young children and *reading* the stories to them is a critical part of the job for any early childhood educator. *Early literacy* experiences are best fostered in a supportive *environment* that is well stocked with appropriate picture books.   203

The concepts in bold italics are developed in the article. For further expansion, please refer to the Topic Guide.

46. Calendar Time for Young Children: Good Intentions Gone Awry, Sallee J. Beneke, Michaelene M. Ostrosky, and Lilian G. Katz, *Young Children,* May 2008

When *teachers* develop more experience and an understanding of young children's development, they begin to examine traditional classroom practices. The authors explore calendar time and provide suggestions for making the experience more *developmentally appropriate* and authentic for young children.   **208**

Test-Your-Knowledge Form   **212**

Article Rating Form   **213**

The concepts in bold italics are developed in the article. For further expansion, please refer to the Topic Guide.

Correlation Guide

The *Annual Editions* series provides students with convenient, inexpensive access to current, carefully selected articles from the public press. **Annual Editions: Early Childhood Education 10/11** is an easy-to-use reader that presents articles on important topics such as *young children and their families, diverse learners, educational practices,* and many more. For more information on *Annual Editions* and other *McGraw-Hill Contemporary Learning Series* titles, visit www.mhhe.com/cls.

This convenient guide matches the units in **Annual Editions: Early Childhood Education 10/11** with the corresponding chapters in two of our best-selling McGraw-Hill Early Childhood Education textbooks by Gonzalez-Mena and Casper/Theilheimer.

Annual Editions: Early Childhood Education 10/11	Foundations of Early Childhood Education: Teaching Children in a Diverse Setting, 5/e by Gonzalez-Mena	Early Childhood Education: Learning Together by Casper/Theilheimer
Unit 1: Perspectives	**Chapter 4:** Facilitating Young Children's Work and Play **Chapter 8:** Setting Up the Physical Environment **Chapter 13:** Language and Emergent Literacy	**Chapter 1:** Working with Young Children **Chapter 12:** Preschoolers and Kindergartners
Unit 2: Young Children, Their Families and Communities	**Chapter 2:** First Things First: Health and Safety through Observation and Supervision **Chapter 5:** Guiding Young Children's Behavior **Chapter 7:** Modeling Adult Relationships in Early Childhood Settings **Chapter 9:** Creating a Social-Emotional Environment **Chapter 10:** Routines	**Chapter 2:** Children and the Worlds They Inhabit **Chapter 4:** Children Understanding the World through Play **Chapter 8:** Children, Development, and Culture **Chapter 14:** Partnering with Twenty-First-Century Families
Unit 3: Diverse Learners	**Chapter 10:** Routines **Chapter 11:** Developmental Tasks as the Curriculum: How to Support Children at Each Stage	**Chapter 13:** First, Second, and Third Graders **Chapter 14:** Partnering with Twenty-First Century Families
Unit 4: Supporting Young Children's Development	**Chapter 1:** Early Childhood Education as a Profession **Chapter 4:** Facilitating Young Children's Work and Play **Chapter 8:** Setting Up the Physical Environment **Chapter 11:** Developmental Tasks as the Curriculum: How to Support Children at Each Stage	**Chapter 1:** Working with Young Children **Chapter 8:** Children, Development, and Culture **Chapter 14:** Partnering with Twenty-First-Century Families **Chapter 15:** Policy Issues and Early Childhood Practice
Unit 5: Educational Practices	**Chapter 4:** Facilitating Young Children's Work and Play **Chapter 6:** The Teacher as Model **Chapter 8:** Setting Up the Physical Environment **Chapter 12:** Observing, Recording, and Assessing	**Chapter 1:** Working with Young Children **Chapter 7:** Early Childhood Programming **Chapter 15:** Policy Issues and Early Childhood Practice
Unit 6: Helping Children to Thrive in School	**Chapter 3:** Communicating with Young Children **Chapter 13:** Language and Emergent Literacy	**Chapter 1:** Working with Young Children **Chapter 15:** Policy Issues and Early Childhood Practice
Unit 7: Curricular Issues	**Chapter 13:** Language and Emergent Literacy **Chapter 14:** Providing Developmentally Appropriate Experiences in Math and Science **Chapter 15:** Integrating Art, Music, and Social Studies into a Holistic Curriculum	**Chapter 10:** Early Childhood Assessment

Topic Guide

This topic guide suggests how the selections in this book relate to the subjects covered in your course. You may want to use the topics listed on these pages to search the Web more easily.

On the following pages a number of websites have been gathered specifically for this book. They are arranged to reflect the units of this Annual Editions reader. You can link to these sites by going to *http://www.mhhe.com/cls*.

All the articles that relate to each topic are listed below the bold-faced term.

Accountability
6. No Child Left Behind: Who's Accountable?

Achievement/academic achievement
2. A Foundation for Success
3. Joy in School
4. Early Education, Later Success
5. The Changing Culture of Childhood: A Perfect Storm
7. Preschool Comes of Age: The National Debate on Education for Young Children Intensifies
8. Class Matters—In and Out of School
13. Whose Problem Is Poverty?
20. Health = Performance
27. What Research Says about . . . Grade Retention
32. The Looping Classroom: Benefits for Children, Families, and Teachers
39. A Multinational Study Supports Child-Initiated Learning: Using the Findings in Your Classroom

Alignment
4. Early Education, Later Success

Attention-deficit/hyperactivity disorder (ADHD)
23. The Truth about ADHD
33. Beyond *The Lorax?*: The Greening of the American Curriculum

At-risk children
5. The Changing Culture of Childhood: A Perfect Storm
6. No Child Left Behind: Who's Accountable?
7. Preschool Comes of Age: The National Debate on Education for Young Children Intensifies
29. Scripted Curriculum: Is It a Prescription for Success?

Autism spectrum disorder
16. Young Children with Autism Spectrum Disorder: Strategies That Work

Best practices
4. Early Education, Later Success
6. No Child Left Behind: Who's Accountable?
25. Enhancing Development and Learning through Teacher-Child Relationships

Brain development and brain-based learning
30. Using Brain-Based Teaching Strategies to Create Supportive Early Childhood Environments That Address Learning Standards

Bullying
36. "Stop Picking on Me!": What You Need to Know about Bullying

Cognitive development
18. Play and Social Interaction in Middle Childhood
20. Health = Performance
39. A Multinational Study Supports Child-Initiated Learning: Using the Findings in Your Classroom

Collaboration
8. Class Matters—In and Out of School
13. Whose Problem Is Poverty?

Cost, educational
2. A Foundation for Success
7. Preschool Comes of Age: The National Debate on Education for Young Children Intensifies

Creativity
44. Constructive Play: A Value-Added Strategy for Meeting Early Learning Standards

Curriculum
41. Preschool Curricula: Finding One That Fits
43. The Plan: Building on Children's Interests

Development
12. Fast Times
26. Developmentally Appropriate Practice in the Age of Testing
28. Back to Basics: Play in Early Childhood
31. Successful Transition to Kindergarten: The Role of Teachers and Parents

Developmentally appropriate practice
3. Joy in School
26. Developmentally Appropriate Practice in the Age of Testing
28. Back to Basics: Play in Early Childhood
32. The Looping Classroom: Benefits for Children, Families, and Teachers
35. Ready or Not, Here We Come: What It Means to Be a Ready School
46. Calendar Time for Young Children: Good Intentions Gone Awry

Differentiation
17. Including Children with Disabilities in Early Childhood Education Programs: Individualizing Developmentally Appropriate Practices
30. Using Brain-Based Teaching Strategies to Create Supportive Early Childhood Environments That Address Learning Standards

Disabilities
17. Including Children with Disabilities in Early Childhood Education Programs: Individualizing Developmentally Appropriate Practices

Diverse learners/diversity
15. Learning in an Inclusive Community
17. Including Children with Disabilities in Early Childhood Education Programs: Individualizing Developmentally Appropriate Practices
32. The Looping Classroom: Benefits for Children, Families, and Teachers

Documentation
40. The Power of Documentation in the Early Childhood Classroom

Emergent curriculum

43. The Plan: Building on Children's Interests

English language learners

14. How to Support Bilingualism in Early Childhood
32. The Looping Classroom: Benefits for Children, Families, and Teachers

Environment

32. The Looping Classroom: Benefits for Children, Families, and Teachers
45. Using Picture Books to Support Young Children's Literacy

Families

9. Early Childhood School Success: Recognizing Families as Integral Partners
10. Meeting of the Minds
13. Whose Problem Is Poverty?
14. How to Support Bilingualism in Early Childhood
17. Including Children with Disabilities in Early Childhood Education Programs: Individualizing Developmentally Appropriate Practices
20. Health = Performance
22. Keeping Children Active: What You Can Do to Fight Childhood Obesity
32. The Looping Classroom: Benefits for Children, Families, and Teachers
38. Fostering Positive Transitions for School Success

Federal government

1. Invest in Early Childhood Education
6. No Child Left Behind: Who's Accountable?
13. Whose Problem Is Poverty?

Food

20. Health = Performance

Guidance

37. Developmentally Appropriate Child Guidance: Helping Children Gain Self-Control

Health/Safety

13. Whose Problem Is Poverty?
20. Health = Performance
22. Keeping Children Active: What You Can Do to Fight Childhood Obesity

Inclusive education

15. Learning in an Inclusive Community
16. Young Children with Autism Spectrum Disorder: Strategies That Work
17. Including Children with Disabilities in Early Childhood Education Programs: Individualizing Developmentally Appropriate Practices

Infants and toddlers

25. Enhancing Development and Learning through Teacher-Child Relationships

Inquiry-based learning

26. Developmentally Appropriate Practice in the Age of Testing
30. Using Brain-Based Teaching Strategies to Create Supportive Early Childhood Environments That Address Learning Standards
42. Got Standards?: Don't Give up on Engaged Learning!
44. Constructive Play: A Value-Added Strategy for Meeting Early Learning Standards

Kindergarten

31. Successful Transition to Kindergarten: The Role of Teachers and Parents

Literacy

45. Using Picture Books to Support Young Children's Literacy

Lower class size

8. Class Matters—In and Out of School

No Child Left Behind (NCLB)

6. No Child Left Behind: Who's Accountable?
29. Scripted Curriculum: Is It a Prescription for Success?

Obesity

22. Keeping Children Active: What You Can Do to Fight Childhood Obesity
33. Beyond *The Lorax*?: The Greening of the American Curriculum

Parenting/parents

9. Early Childhood School Success: Recognizing Families as Integral Partners
12. Fast Times
21. Which Hand?: Brains, Fine Motor Skills, and Holding a Pencil
34. Play: Ten Power Boosts for Children's Early Learning

Physical development

18. Play and Social Interaction in Middle Childhood
20. Health = Performance
21. Which Hand?: Brains, Fine Motor Skills, and Holding a Pencil
22. Keeping Children Active: What You Can Do to Fight Childhood Obesity
24. When Girls and Boys Play: What Research Tells Us
33. Beyond *The Lorax*?: The Greening of the American Curriculum

Play

5. The Changing Culture of Childhood: A Perfect Storm
10. Meeting of the Minds
18. Play and Social Interaction in Middle Childhood
24. When Girls and Boys Play: What Research Tells Us
28. Back to Basics: Play in Early Childhood
31. Successful Transition to Kindergarten: The Role of Teachers and Parents
33. Beyond *The Lorax*?: The Greening of the American Curriculum
34. Play: Ten Power Boosts for Children's Early Learning
44. Constructive Play: A Value-Added Strategy for Meeting Early Learning Standards

Playgrounds

24. When Girls and Boys Play: What Research Tells Us

Poverty

5. The Changing Culture of Childhood: A Perfect Storm
8. Class Matters—In and Out of School
13. Whose Problem Is Poverty?

Preschool

2. A Foundation for Success
4. Early Education, Later Success
7. Preschool Comes of Age: The National Debate on Education for Young Children Intensifies
8. Class Matters—In and Out of School
38. Fostering Positive Transitions for School Success
41. Preschool Curricula: Finding One That Fits

Primary grades

30. Using Brain-Based Teaching Strategies to Create Supportive Early Childhood Environments That Address Learning Standards

Project approach

43. The Plan: Building on Children's Interests

Reading

45. Using Picture Books to Support Young Children's Literacy

Readiness

7. Preschool Comes of Age: The National Debate on Education for Young Children Intensifies
31. Successful Transition to Kindergarten: The Role of Teachers and Parents
35. Ready or Not, Here We Come: What It Means to Be a Ready School

Recess

18. Play and Social Interaction in Middle Childhood
24. When Girls and Boys Play: What Research Tells Us

Research

24. When Girls and Boys Play: What Research Tells Us
27. What Research Says about . . . Grade Retention

Retention/red-shirting

27. What Research Says about . . . Grade Retention
32. The Looping Classroom: Benefits for Children, Families, and Teachers

Scripted curriculum

26. Developmentally Appropriate Practice in the Age of Testing
29. Scripted Curriculum: Is It a Prescription for Success?

Social/emotional development

12. Fast Times
18. Play and Social Interaction in Middle Childhood
24. When Girls and Boys Play: What Research Tells Us
31. Successful Transition to Kindergarten: The Role of Teachers and Parents
37. Developmentally Appropriate Child Guidance: Helping Children Gain Self-Control
38. Fostering Positive Transitions for School Success

Standards

30. Using Brain-Based Teaching Strategies to Create Supportive Early Childhood Environments That Address Learning Standards
42. Got Standards?: Don't Give up on Engaged Learning!
44. Constructive Play: A Value-Added Strategy for Meeting Early Learning Standards

Stress

12. Fast Times
36. "Stop Picking on Me!": What You Need to Know about Bullying

Teachers/teaching

10. Meeting of the Minds
15. Learning in an Inclusive Community
16. Young Children with Autism Spectrum Disorder: Strategies That Work
17. Including Children with Disabilities in Early Childhood Education Programs: Individualizing Developmentally Appropriate Practices
19. Twelve Characteristics of Effective Early Childhood Teachers
23. The Truth about ADHD
29. Scripted Curriculum: Is It a Prescription for Success?
30. Using Brain-Based Teaching Strategies to Create Supportive Early Childhood Environments That Address Learning Standards
36. "Stop Picking on Me!": What You Need to Know about Bullying
41. Preschool Curricula: Finding One That Fits
43. The Plan: Building on Children's Interests
46. Calendar Time for Young Children: Good Intentions Gone Awry

Universal preschool

1. Invest in Early Childhood Education

Internet References

The following Internet sites have been selected to support the articles found in this reader. These sites were available at the time of publication. However, because websites often change their structure and content, the information listed may no longer be available. We invite you to visit http://www.mhhe.com/cls for easy access to these sites.

Annual Editions: Early Childhood Education 10/11

General Sources

Children's Defense Fund (CDF)
http://www.childrensdefense.org

At this site of the CDF, an organization that seeks to ensure that every child is treated fairly, there are reports and resources regarding current issues facing today's youth, along with national statistics on various subjects.

Connect for Kids
http://www.connectforkids.org

This nonprofit site provides news and information on issues affecting children and families, with over 1,500 helpful links to national and local resources.

National Association for the Education of Young Children
http://www.naeyc.org

The NAEYC website is a valuable tool for anyone working with young children. Also see the National Education Association site: http://www.nea.org.

U.S. Department of Education
http://www.ed.gov/pubs/TeachersGuide

Government goals, projects, grants, and other educational programs are listed here as well as many links to teacher services and resources.

Unit 1: Perspectives

Child Care and Early Education Research Connections
www.researchconnections.org

This site offers excellent help for anyone looking for research based data related to early childhood education. Full text articles and other reference materials are available.

Child Care Directory: Care Guide
http://www.care.com

Find licensed/registered child care by zip code at this site. See prescreened profiles and get free background checks on providers. Pages for parents along with additional links are also included.

Early Childhood Care and Development
http://www.ecdgroup.com

This site concerns international resources in support of children to age eight and their families. It includes research and evaluation, policy matters, programming matters, and related websites.

Global SchoolNet Foundation
http://www.gsn.org

Access this site for multicultural education information. The site includes news for teachers and students as well as chat rooms, links to educational resources, programs, and contests and competitions. Helpful site for teachers serving diverse populations.

Harvard Family Research Project
http://www.hfrp.org

For twenty-five years the Harvard Family Research Project has provided quality information on families, education, and young children. There are many resources and areas of research presented on this useful site.

Mid-Continent Research for Education and Learning
http://www.mcrel.org/standards-benchmarks

This site provides a listing of standards and benchmarks that include content descriptions from 112 significant subject areas and documents from across 14 content areas.

The National Association of State Boards of Education
http://www.nasbo.org

Included on this site is an extensive overview of the No Child Left Behind Act. There are links to specific state's plans.

Unit 2: Young Children, Their Families and Communities

The AARP Grandparent Information Center
http://www.aarp.org/grandparents

The center offers tips for raising grandchildren, activities, health and safety, visitations, and other resources to assist grandparents.

Administration for Children and Families
http://www.dhhs.gov

This site provides information on federally funded programs that promote the economic and social well-being of families, children, and communities.

All About Asthma
http://pbskids.org/arthur/parentsteachers/lesson/health/#asthma

This is a fact sheet/activity book featuring the popular TV character Arthur who has asthma. The site gives statistics and helps parents, teachers, and children understand asthma as well as many other issues affecting young children. It gives tips on how to decrease asthma triggers. It has English, Spanish, Chinese, Vietnamese, and Tagalog versions of some of the materials.

Allergy Kids
http://allergykids.com

Developed by Robyn O'Brien, a mother committed to helping children and families everywhere deal with allergies, this site is extremely valuable for all families and school personnel. Tip sheets are provided that can be shared with teachers and families as well as items for purchase to support allergic children.

Changing the Scene on Nutrition
http://www.fns.usda.gov/tn/Healthy/changing.html

This is a free toolkit for parents, school administrators, and teachers to help change the attitudes toward health and nutrition in their schools.

Internet References

Children, Youth and Families Education and Research Network
www.cyfernet.org

This excellent site contains useful links to research from key universities and institutions. The categories include early childhood, school age, teens, parents and family, and community.

National Network for Child Care
www.nncc.org

This network brings together the expertise of many land grant universities through their cooperative extension programs. These are the programs taped back in early 1965 to train the 41,000 teachers needed for the first Head Start programs that summer. The site contains information on over 1,000 publications and resources related to child care. Resources for local conferences in early childhood education are included.

National Safe Kids Campaign
http://www.babycenter.com

This site includes an easy-to-follow milestone chart and advice on when to call the doctor.

The National Academy for Child Development
http://www.nacd.org

The National Association for Child Development . . . has, over its twenty-nine years of existence and work with over 30,000 clients, developed a unique and effective view of and approach to enhancing the development and function of children and adults.

Zero to Three
http://www.zerotothree.org

Find here developmental information on the first three years of life—an excellent site for both parents and professionals.

Unit 3: Diverse Learners

American Academy of Pediatrics
www.aap.org

Pediatricians provide trusted advice for parents and teachers. The AAP official site includes position statements on a variety of topics related to the health and safety of young children.

Child Welfare League of America (CWLA)
http://www.cwla.org

The CWLA is the United States' oldest and largest organization devoted entirely to the well-being of vulnerable children and their families. Its website provides links to information about issues related to morality and values in education.

Classroom Connect
http://www.classroom.com/login/home.jhtml

A major website for K-12 teachers and students, this site provides links to schools, teachers, and resources online. It includes discussion of the use of technology in the classroom.

The Council for Exceptional Children
http://www.cec.sped.org/index.html

Information on identifying and teaching children with a variety of disabilities. The Council for Exceptional Children is the largest professional organization for special educators.

Early Learning Standards: Full Report
http://www.naeyc.org/positionstatements/learning_standards

This site provides the full joint position statement by the National Association for the Education of Young Children (NAEYC) and The National Association of Early Childhood Specialists in the State Department of Education (NAECS/SDE) on early learning standards.

Make Your Own Web Page
http://www.teacherweb.com

Easy step-by-step directions for teachers at all levels to construct their own web page. Parents can log on and check out what is going on in their child's classroom.

National Resource Center for Health and Safety in Child Care
http://nrc.uchsc.edu

Search through this site's extensive links to find information on health and safety in child care. Health and safety tips are provided, as are other child-care information resources.

Online Innovation Institute
http://oii.org

A collaborative project among Internet-using educators, proponents of systemic reform, content-area experts, and teachers who desire professional growth, this site provides a learning environment for integrating the Internet into educators' individual teaching styles.

Unit 4: Supporting Young Children's Development

Action for Healthy Kids
www.actionforhealthykids.org

This organization works to assist the ever-increasing numbers of students who are overweight, undernourished, and sedentary. They feature a campaign for school wellness.

American Academy of Pediatrics
www.aap.org

Pediatricians provide trusted advice for parents and teachers. The AAP official site includes position statements on a variety of issues related to the health and safety of young children.

Unit 5: Educational Practices

Association for Childhood Education International (ACEI)
http://www.acei.org

This site, established by the oldest professional early childhood education organization, describes the association, its programs, and the services it offers to both teachers and families. Standards for elementary education are included.

Early Childhood Education Online
http://www.umaine.edu/eceol

The Early Childhood Education On Line LISTSERV community offers support and opportunities for information exchange to all educators: families, teachers, caregivers, and others interested in providing quality care and learning situations for young children birth through 8 years.

Reggio Emilia
http://www.ericdigests.org/2001-3/reggio.htm

Through ERIC, link to publications related to the Reggio Emilia approach and to resources, videos, and contact information.

Unit 6: Helping Children in School

Busy Teacher's Cafe
http://www.busyteacherscafe.com

This is a website for early childhood educators with resource pages for everything from worksheets to classroom management.

Internet References

Future of Children
http://www.futureofchildren.org

Produced by the David and Lucille Packard Foundation, the primary purpose of this page is to disseminate timely information on major issues related to children's well-being.

You Can Handle Them All
http://www.disciplinehelp.com

This site describes different types of behavioral problems and offers suggestions for managing these problems.

Unit 7: Curricular Issues

Action for Healthy Kids
www.actionforhealthykids.org

This organization works to assist the ever increasing numbers of students who are overweight, undernourished, and sedentary. It features a campaign for school wellness.

Awesome Library for Teachers
http://www.awesomelibrary.org/teacher.html

Open this page for links and access to teacher information on everything from educational assessment to general child development topics.

The Educators' Network
http://www.theeducatorsnetwork.com

A very useful site for teachers at every level in every subject area. Includes lesson plans, theme units, teacher tools, rubrics, books, educational news, and much more.

The Family Involvement Storybook Corner
http://www.gse.harvard.edu/hfrp/projects/fine.html

In partnership with Reading is Fundamental (RIF) the Family Involvement Storybook Corner is a place to find compilations of family involvement, children's storybooks, and related tools and information.

Grade Level Reading Lists
http://www.gradelevelreadinglists.org

Recommended reading lists for grades kindergarten–eight can be downloaded through this site.

Idea Box
http://theideabox.com

This site is geared toward parents and has many good activities for creating, playing, and singing. The activities are creative and educational and can be done at home or in a classroom.

International Reading Association
http://www.reading.org

This organization for professionals who are interested in literacy contains information about the reading process and assists teachers in dealing with literacy issues.

Kid Fit
http://www.kid-fit.com

A preschool physical education program designed to instill healthy lifestyle habits for young children. Includes some free physical educational activities.

The Perpetual Preschool
http://www.perpetualpreschool.com

This site provides teachers with possibilities for learning activities and offers chats with other teachers and resources on a variety of topics. The theme ideas are a list of possibilities and should not be used in whole, but used as a starting point for building areas of investigation that are relevant and offer firsthand experiences for young children.

Phi Delta Kappa
http://www.pdkintl.org

This important organization publishes articles about all facets of education. By clicking on the links in this site, for example, you can check out the journal's online archive, which has resources such as articles having to do with assessment.

Teacher Quick Source
http://www.teacherquicksource.com

Originally designed to help Head Start teachers meet the child outcomes, this site can be useful to all preschool teachers. Domains can be linked to developmentally appropriate activities for classroom use.

Teachers Helping Teachers
http://www.pacificnet.net/~mandel

Free lesson plans, educational resources, and resources to improve test scores are included. Access is free and material on the site is updated weekly during the school year.

Technology Help
http://www.apples4theteacher.com

This site helps teachers incorporate technology into the classroom. Full of interactive activities children can do alone, with a partner, or for full group instruction in all subject areas. Teachers can sign up for an email newsletter.

UNIT 1
Perspectives

Unit Selections

1. **Invest in Early Childhood Education,** Sharon Lynn Kagan and Jeanne L. Reid
2. **A Foundation for Success,** Sara Mead
3. **Joy in School,** Steven Wolk
4. **Early Education, Later Success,** Susan Black
5. **The Changing Culture of Childhood: A Perfect Storm,** Joe L. Frost
6. **No Child Left Behind: Who's Accountable?,** Lisa A. DuBois
7. **Preschool Comes of Age: The National Debate on Education for Young Children Intensifies,** Michael Lester

Key Points to Consider

- What are some of the key challenges affecting the early care and education profession?

- What is the appropriate mix of standards for accountability and experiences that allow children to appreciate and enjoy learning?

- If our nation wants to make high-quality preschool education a priority, what are some of the steps we must take?

- How much emphasis should be placed on academics in a preschool program?

- What are the long-term benefits of attending a quality preschool program?

- How are social disadvantage and poverty related to low achievement of young children?

- How can teachers become more involved in advocacy issues related to the care and education of young children?

- How has the introduction of early learning standards affected the profession?

Student Website
www.mhhe.com/cls

Internet References

Child Care and Early Education Research Connections
www.researchconnections.org

Child Care Directory: Care Guide
http://www.care.com

Early Childhood Care and Development
http://www.ecdgroup.com

Global SchoolNet Foundation
http://www.gsn.org

Harvard Family Research Project
http://www.hfrp.org

Mid-Continent Research for Education and Learning
http://www.mcrel.org/standards-benchmarks

The National Association of State Boards of Education
http://www.nasbe.org

This unit starts with the message that even in these challenging financial times, it is most important to have a clear plan for early education that is articulated at many levels and within many different venues. "Invest in Early Childhood Education" by Kagan and Reid outlines the critical importance of preschool programs being available for all children whose families choose to take advantage of the program. The message that a strong pre-K foundation can translate to significant learning gains down the road should be communicated to all families. President Obama repeatedly calls for a focus on early childhood education when addressing questions about his plan for improving education in the United States. He recognizes that no improvement in educational achievement can be reached without starting with our youngest learners. This does not mean that early childhood education is viewed as a panacea or a solution to all problems, but it does mean that early childhood educators, and the work they do, are an integral part of the team that will work to improve learning experiences for all children while working to help students meet standards in all areas.

The increasing high-stakes pressure of the past few years on accountability has caused many educators to suck the joy and passion out of learning. The prize has become higher test scores instead of learning for life-long benefits. Many teachers are afraid that children are becoming turned off to school at a young age, and classrooms where children are required to sit all day in desks and complete endless piles of worksheets and workbooks are commonplace in many parts of the country. These types of joyless learning places are especially prevalent in inner cities and charter schools where high test scores may translate into higher enrollment. Steven Wolk shares many ways joyful learning can flourish in school alongside high achievement and provides suggestions for educators of all levels of learners in his article, "Joy in School."

Two articles, Sara Mead's "A Foundation for Success" and Susan Black's "Early Education, Later Success," are aimed at leaders in school districts seeking a way to improve their K–12 education. Both Mead and Black encourage school leaders to look down to the preschool years, where a strong pre-K foundation can translate to significant learning gains down the road. Your job as an early educator is to send the message to your local school board to strongly consider offering a preschool program in the district to provide the foundation for later school success.

Generations of adults have reflected back on their own childhood experiences and schooling and made comparisons to those of current children. Except for childhoods affected by war or the Great Depression, there has not been a greater change in one generation than is occurring now. In his article, "The Changing Culture of Childhood: A Perfect Storm," Joe L. Frost outlines the dramatic changes children are experiencing today on all fronts. The pressure for high-stakes achievement at an early age, the decreasing time allocated for spontaneous creative play, and the deep and lasting impact of poverty are all discussed by Frost.

I always feel good when I realize that others outside of the field of early childhood education recognize that quality care

© Laurence Mouton/Photoalto/PictureQuest RF

and education for young children can have tremendous financial benefits as well as educational benefits for society. Of course, I would always welcome the interest from more people outside of the profession, but the field is receiving increased attention from others for a number of reasons. The nation is learning that high-quality programs are beneficial for young children's long-term development. Much of this interest is in part due to some state legislators allocating resources for state-operated preschool programs. Coupled with the knowledge of the importance of ECE programs is a realization that the quality of these programs should be of utmost importance. Another reason is the compelling evidence from brain research that children are born learning. Yet, despite new information on the importance of early childhood, we still tend to hold onto cultural traditions about who young children are and how to care for them. This dichotomy between information and tradition results in an impasse when it comes to creating national policy related to young children.

For over 135 years, Peabody College of Vanderbilt University has been recognized as a leader in preparing future teachers, administrators, and professors for the field of education.

The article "No Child Left Behind: Who's Accountable?" with the word *accountable* in the title provides insight from key researchers and policymakers at this Nashville, TN, institution. They examine how the No Child Left Behind (NCLB) bill signed in 2001, and expected to show full results in 2014, has affected our education system. The next few years will be critical for NCLB and what will come for the future of this, at times, controversial law. Lisa A. DuBois sends a powerful message about the way others view our profession and what we do. I am reminded of one of the more popular perceptions of early care and education held by those outside of the profession. For the past fifty years, "early childhood education was viewed as a panacea the solution to all social ills in society" (Paciorek, 2008, p. xvii). This is huge pressure to put on one profession, especially one that is grossly underpaid. We do have outside forces carefully watching how early education practices affect long-term development and learning. Early childhood professionals must be accountable for practices they implement in their classrooms and how children spend their time interacting with materials. Appropriate early learning standards are the norm in the profession, and knowledgeable caregivers and teachers must be informed of the importance of developing quality experiences that align with the standards. Teachers can no longer plan cute activities that fill the child's days and backpacks with pictures to hang on the refrigerator. Teachers must be intentional in their planning to adapt learning experiences so that all children can achieve standards that are based on knowledge of developmental abilities.

As the editor, I hope you benefit from reading the articles and reflecting on the important issues facing early childhood education today. Your job is to share the message with others not familiar with our field and the impact of attending a quality preschool program can have on young children throughout their life.

Invest in Early Childhood Education

We need expanded federal leadership in early education to develop an excellent, coherent, and equitable system. The authors recommend 13 ways for the government to develop a universal and sustained approach to early childhood education.

SHARON LYNN KAGAN AND JEANNE L. REID

The federal government's role in early education has a long and contentious history. While the nature and amount of federal engagement has shifted in response to changing social, political, and economic needs, the lack of long-term planning or coordination has yielded an array of programs, dispersed across federal agencies and legislative committees, which begs for greater excellence, coherence, and equity in early childhood education.

The history of American early education is one of changing roles and goals. From the privately funded Infant Schools for indigent families in the earliest days of the republic, to the federal government's foray into early childhood with Depression-era nursery schools, to more recent investments in Head Start, federal early education policies can best be understood as a series of responses to shifting social, economic, and political phenomena (Beatty 1981; Cahan 1989; Cohen 1996). Amid these changes, four durable polemics have shaped the federal response.

First, American society has long questioned whether young children should be served outside their homes at all. From the nation's birth, the primacy and the privacy of the home were ideological mantras, forcing early education programs to legitimate their existence; such programs have never been considered an entitlement akin to K-12 education.

Federal support for early education grew during times of national crises and declined as the crises ebbed.

Second, because public values haven't generally supported out-of-home, nonmaternal care, federal support for early education grew during times of national crises and declined as the crises ebbed, leaving early education bereft of three essential mainstays: vision, permanence, and infrastructure.

Third, there has been an enduring ambivalence regarding which children should be served and how. Most public programs have targeted children from low-income families, while the private sector has served children from middle- and upper-income families. Leaving a legacy of services segregated by income, which often translates into quality differences, early education policy defies deeply held American values regarding the equal opportunity that all young children need in order to thrive and learn.

Fourth, there is no consistent agreement about the mission of early education. Should early education focus on care as the day nurseries did? Should it focus on socialization and education as nursery schools purported to do? Although increasingly regarded as a false dichotomy because good early education does both, federal and state policy makers still must tussle with the question as they debate early education's departmental jurisdictions and funding amounts.

5 Cornerstones

Recognizing this historical context and building on the past, we first recommend five cornerstones for American early education:

- Keep early education voluntary before kindergarten.
- Maintain a diverse delivery system with both public and private providers for both fiscal prudence and choice for parents.
- Foster developmentally oriented pedagogy that stresses cognitive, language, social, emotional, and physical development for all children.

- Honor linguistic, cultural, and programmatic diversity.
- Conceptualize early education as a partnership among families, programs, and communities.

Second, we see a need for expanded federal leadership and investments in early education. However, such investments must be guided by clearly defined roles for federal and state governments. These roles must frame and bound the public early childhood policy agenda. In addition to role clarity, the goals of federal intervention must be clear. Early education efforts should focus on advancing excellence, coherence, and equity.

Third, at the community and family level, we seek a combination of demand- and supply-side strategies for direct provision, noting that a focus on demandside policy alone seriously erodes excellence, coherence, and equity. A mixed delivery system will encourage myriad providers of early education and care and encourage higher quality, irrespective of funding mechanisms. In particular, we encourage the development of high-quality choices for low- and middle-income families—two aspects of early education that the current market fails to address effectively.

Early childhood services should be regarded as a fundamental right of all American children, from birth to age five, whose parents wish to enroll them.

Fourth, we would reposition the debate over universal versus targeted services. Early childhood services should be regarded as a fundamental right of all American children, from birth to age five, whose parents wish to enroll them. Even on a sliding-scale fee basis, this goal will not be achieved for years. But a universal goal would enable us to systematically expand high-quality early education services. This means abandoning the program-of-the-year approach to early education and substituting a clear and steady agenda for reform; it means converting the policy zeitgeist from one that permits multiple idiosyncratic department-by-department and state-by-state efforts and moving to thoughtful, evidence-based policy efforts that fit within a conceptually coherent scheme for universality.

Early education is valuable for all children, but parents should be able to choose whether their children will participate.

Our recommendations address the polemics of early care and education by asserting that early education is valuable for all children, but parents should be able to choose whether

The Role of the Federal Government

- Provide the coordinated long-term vision and leadership for the development of a comprehensive, integrated, early childhood system that makes high-quality early education available to all preschool-age children on a voluntary basis.
- Establish research-driven standards regarding the expectations for children, the skills and competencies their teachers require, the provision of programs that serve children, and the requirements for states regarding their duties in advancing the early childhood system.
- Foster building an infrastructure at the state and local levels as a prerequisite for quality and an integral component of all early education efforts by advancing:

  a. teacher quality and workforce enhancements and credentialing;
  b. governance;
  c. the development of assessment tools and the collection of usable data;
  d. preschool to K-12 school linkage/transition efforts;
  e. parental and public engagement; and
  f. research.

- Fund, in conjunction with the states, essential direct services for children at high risk of school failure and children of the working poor as a first step toward fulfilling the mission of universality.
- Promote a spirit of innovation and the development and use of new knowledge regarding early childhood development, pedagogy, curriculum, assessment, and program effectiveness. This includes the funding and effective dissemination of basic research, longitudinal studies, program evaluations, and a series of research and demonstration efforts to guide policy and practice.

their children will participate. Those who remain ideologically opposed to early education do not have to participate. The universal goal would encourage policies that would not, by design, segregate children by family income. We assume high-quality early education programs would offer both care and education, with the paramount goal of readiness for school and life. Finally, we recognize that federal, state, and local governments have specific roles in relation to early childhood education. (See the box "The Role of the Federal Government," "The Role of State Governments," "The Role of Local Communities".)

Recognizing the special role that the federal government plays in early childhood education, we offer 13 specific recommendations for federal action in the next three years. For some, these recommendations may seem too modest. Advancing a fiscally and operationally prudent policy agenda, we take a steady incremental approach that addresses significant and simultaneous increases in direct services and in the early childhood infrastructure.

Recommendation #1
Establish and Fund a Federal Early Learning Council

Composed of representatives from diverse federal agencies, states, and philanthropic organizations, the council will develop a 10-year plan for the federal government's role in advancing early childhood education. This plan would address government roles and responsibilities to young children and their families and determine how best to handle diverse federal funding streams and ensure that all early education efforts meet standards of excellence, coherence, and equity.

Recommendation #2
Establish Federal Guidelines for Children, Teachers, and Programs

To promote greater consistency across states, guidelines should be established that specify what children should know and be able to do, how teachers should be qualified to teach young children, and what foundational elements of quality should characterize early childhood programs. Developed by three national task forces over a two-year period, the guidelines would not be mandated, but would guide states as they develop and modify their own standards.

Recommendation #3
Modify the NCLB Successor

To promote a continuity of experience for children as they transition from early childhood settings into schools, modify the successor to NCLB to ensure that states align their standards, curricula, and assessments across these age groups and that elementary schools are ready for young children and their families.

Recommendation #4
Set Aside an Additional 10% of All New Federal Early Education Funds

Regardless of funding streams, all new federal direct service dollars for children should have a 10% earmark (on top of all new federal dollars invested in early education) for infrastructure and quality enhancement. States would use these funds to enhance personnel preparation, development, compensation, and credentialing services and systems; standards development and implementation; coordinated assessment, monitoring, and accountability systems; coordinated governance efforts; and program quality enhancement systems.

The Role of State Governments

- Ensure equitable access to early education for all children in ways that do not segregate children along socioeconomic lines.
- Create and monitor long-range state plans so that early education services, irrespective of departments, are coordinated and cohesive.
- Review federal standards; set and monitor state standards for children, programs, and personnel. Inherent in this function is the establishment of state accountability systems that capture young children's access to services and their progress over time.
- Fund and monitor direct services for young children.
- Fund and monitor infrastructure advancements.

Recommendation #5
Enhance Early Childhood Teacher Preparation and Credentialing

Given the importance of teacher quality to early childhood program quality and child outcomes, funding must be considered over and above what is currently provided by the Higher Education Act reauthorization and the infrastructure recommendation above. Increase the Higher Education Act budget by 1% and sustain that increase in each of the three years, with these funds targeted to preparing and credentialing early education personnel.

Recommendation #6
Support Parents with Young Children

Parents are their children's first and most important teachers, but many young low-income women become parents without the requisite supports and knowledge to advance their children's development. In the next fiscal year, the federal government should provide parenting education and support to 100,000 low-income mothers with infants or toddlers. For each of the two subsequent fiscal years, an additional 100,000 mothers should be added. Each mother should be served for two years.

Recommendation #7
Expand Services to Low-Income Infants and Toddlers through Early Head Start

Quadruple funding for Early Head Start in year one, and sustain this increase in subsequent years, so that its services can reach more children and families and its quality can be enhanced.

The Role of Local Communities

- Implement state mandates and reporting requirements.
- Provide funding for programs to reflect a local commitment to young children.
- Engage parents and community leaders in the design and distribution of services.

Recommendation #8
Expand Services to Low-Income Children through Head Start and the Child Care and Development Block Grant (CCDBG)

To enhance the availability of services to preschool-age children, expand Head Start funding by 5% annually. The CCDBG budget should also experience a 5% annual increase with the goal of expanding its direct services to low-income children from birth to age five.

Recommendation #9
Expand the Child and Dependent Care Tax Credit

Increase the value of the credit by 25% for families whose annual incomes are below $40,000.

Recommendation #10
Support States as they Develop Pre-kindergarten and Other Early Education Efforts

For the next three years, provide states 25 cents on each additional dollar the states invest to launch or expand their current enrollments in preK, with first priority accorded to children from low-income families, children for whom English is not the home language, or those at high risk of school failure. Eligibility for these funds is contingent on states having a long-term plan to provide universal preschool for three- and four-year-old children.

Recommendation #11
Expand and Coordinate Federal Research on Young Children and their Families

Dedicate $100 million in new funds for research on young children and sustain this increase in each of the three years. Such funds would be distributed between education and health and human services and would ensure the funding of two early childhood research centers and the continuation of the Early Childhood Longitudinal Studies.

Recommendation #12
Establish an Electronic National Clearinghouse on Early Education Innovations

Given that early educators are experimenting with innovative pedagogical and systems-infrastructure approaches, the federal government should oversee the review of such efforts and make the results widely available through a national clearinghouse. Such a clearinghouse should include results from and links to high-quality research efforts that could affect policy and practice.

Recommendation #13
Award Challenge Grants to States to Promote Innovation and Quality

The federal government should award competitive challenge grants, which require a state match, to 10 states in the amount of $10 million each in the first year; such grants should be sustained for three years. The challenge grants should select highly promising cross-funding stream (public and private sector) efforts that will significantly enhance early education excellence, coherence, and equity, and that offer strong promise of replicability.

Clear and pointed, these recommendations convey the urgent action required to enact an effective federal commitment to young children. In no other field is the evidence of efficacy so compelling, and in no other field is the potential for future investment so promising. Advancing a piecemeal approach would only perpetuate the fragmentation and lack of quality and equity that has characterized American early education to date. To that end, we recommend finally that the new President and new Congress avoid viewing these recommendations as a menu and instead regard them as an integrated package.

We urge federal policy makers to build an infrastructure, as outlined above, that will strengthen current efforts to expand access to early education and increase the return on a sustained early childhood investment. Only by providing the leadership for both direct services and a durable infrastructure will early childhood education finally square with the excellence, coherence, and equity that it—and this nation—have deserved for so long.

References

Beatty, Barbara R. "A Vocation from on High: Preschool Advocacy and Teaching as an Occupation for Women in 19th-Century Boston." Doctoral dissertation, Harvard Graduate School of Education, 1981.

Cahan, Emily D. *Past Caring: A History of U.S. Preschool Care and Education for the Poor, 1820–1965.* New York: National Center for Children in Poverty, 1989.

Cohen, Abby J. "A Brief History of Federal Financing for Child Care in the United States." *The Future of Children* 6, no. 2 (1996): 26–40.

SHARON LYNN KAGAN is the Virginia and Leonard Marx Professor of Early Childhood and Family Policy, associate dean for policy, and co-director of the National Center for Children and Families at Teachers College, Columbia University, New York. **JEANNE L. REID,** is a graduate research fellow at the National Center for Children and Families at Teachers College, Columbia University.

This article is based on a paper commissioned by the Center on Education Policy (CEP). The complete paper, with citations to individual studies and evaluations, is available at www.cep-dc.org.

A Foundation for Success

High-quality pre-k programs can narrow achievement gaps and improve students' chances in elementary school.

SARA MEAD

As school districts work to improve student learning and narrow achievement gaps, it's abundantly clear that starting in kindergarten is too late. Many students, particularly low-income and minority children, arrive in kindergarten and first-grade classrooms already far behind their peers. And while this problem is particularly serious for disadvantaged youngsters, plenty of middle-class children—especially boys—also come to school with poor language, literacy, and social-emotional skills.

That's a big challenge for districts seeking to improve student achievement, but there's also good news: High-quality prekindergarten (pre-k) programs that start building children's academic and social skills can help narrow gaps and build a foundation for success in early elementary school.

Thirty-nine states now invest in programs that provide a publicly funded education to 3- and 4-year-old children. Spending on these programs has risen by more than 50 percent—from $2.4 billion in 2001–02 to $3.7 billion in 2006–07—in just six years. This growth far exceeds growth in K-12 spending, and has continued even as states face increasingly tight budgetary environments.

Today, state pre-k programs serve more than 1 million children, including nearly one in four 4-year-olds in the nation. School districts operate programs that directly serve 55 percent of these students, and play a key role in mediating or overseeing community-based programs run by Head Start or private child care providers.

As these programs continue to grow, it is increasingly important that school board members, superintendents, and other building-level and district leaders view providing quality pre-k as a core part of their educational mission.

Some are rising to this challenge and making high-quality pre-k programs central to their plans to improve student achievement. Others, however, know little about pre-k, or view it as tangential to their mission. As states move toward making these programs a standard part of the public education system, just as kindergarten is today, school leaders must understand the role that early education and high-quality pre-k can play in supporting larger improvement agendas.

The Quest for Quality

When it comes to pre-k programs, quality is the operative word. All of the research showing positive effects from pre-k focuses on programs that are of very high quality. Lower-quality programs do not achieve the same results, and research suggests that extremely poor programs actually may be harmful to students.

So, what does quality pre-k entail? As a school leader, how can you ensure that the pre-k programs your district operates or contracts with offer high-quality services?

It's important to understand that quality pre-k programs aren't just about "extending elementary school down" to 4-year-olds. Quality pre-k programs don't look the same as quality elementary school programs. Some activities, goals, and teaching techniques that are appropriate for older children—such as pencil-and-paper assessments, or heavy use of teacher-led whole-group instruction—aren't appropriate with preschool-aged youngsters.

At the same time, quality pre-k is not just child care. Things that are important in quality child care, such as instructors who love children and can provide a warm, nurturing environment, are also important in pre-k. But it's just as critical to have a strong educational focus that can develop children's emerging academic and cognitive skills.

In K-12 education, teacher quality is the most important in-school factor that determines how well your students are learning. That's equally true in pre-k classrooms. Research shows that the quality of interactions between teachers and children in the pre-k classroom is the primary determinant of pre-k quality. It's also the strongest predictor of how much children will learn in pre-k.

What does it mean to have good teacher-child interactions in a pre-k classroom? Researchers at the National Center for Early Development and Learning (NCEDL) have identified a set of teacher behaviors that are connected to better learning outcomes for children in the pre-k setting. These include: explicit instruction in key skills, sensitive and emotionally warm interactions, responsive feedback, verbal engagement and stimulation, and a classroom setting that is not overly regimented.

These behaviors are what we mean when we talk about high-quality interactions between pre-k teachers and their students.

Most states require pre-k teachers working in public-school-based programs to hold a bachelor's degree and certification in early childhood education—although teachers in community-based settings may not be held to the same standards. Research suggests that these qualifications may enhance a teacher's ability to create quality learning environments for children, but they are no guarantee of quality.

The quality of interactions between adults and children in the classroom is a better predictor of student outcomes than teacher education or certification. As a result, school districts must ensure that effective strategies are in place to evaluate the quality of emotional and instructional support that current and prospective pre-k teachers provide to children in the classroom. Districts also must provide ongoing professional development that helps teachers improve the quality of their interactions with children, and adopt research-based behaviors that support student learning.

In some ways, the pre-k field is more advanced than the K-12 field when it comes to thinking about teacher quality, evaluation, and professional development. NCEDL researchers have developed a tool, the Classroom Assessment Scoring System, which allows trained observers to reliably evaluate the quality of teachers' interactions with children in three areas: instructional support, emotional support, and classroom organization.

These evaluations can be used to provide individual feedback and coaching to help teachers improve classroom interactions. Such strategies have the potential to improve pre-k teaching, and serve as models for new ways of thinking about teacher quality and evaluation in elementary and secondary education as well.

Class Size and Curriculum

In addition to talented teachers, high-quality prekindergarten programs also should have small class sizes (no more than 20 students in 4-year-old classrooms, with smaller class sizes for 3-year-olds), and low ratios of children to adults (no more than 10 children for every adult in the classroom).

Most quality pre-k programs have multiple adults in each classroom, either a lead teacher working with one or more trainees or teachers' aides, or a team-teaching approach.

Quality programs also must have a clearly articulated curriculum, whether it's an "off-the-shelf" model such as Opening the World of Learning or Creative Curriculum, or one developed by the district and/or pre-k provider. Which is better? We are not sure, because relatively little research is available on the most effective early education curriculum.

We do know, however, that a pre-k curriculum should address multiple areas that are important to the development of preschool children. These include language, literacy, emerging math skills, and social and emotional development.

Schools often focus on academic skills, but research suggests that the social and emotional development that occurs—learning self-control, sticking with difficult tasks, resolving conflicts verbally rather than by force—is just as important, if not more important, to future school achievement as academic content.

In addition, quality curricula are aligned with state and district standards and expectations for what prekindergarteners will learn and be able to do. Those standards should be aligned with kindergarten curriculum, so that what children learn in pre-k feeds seamlessly into what they will study the following year.

Part of a Broader Vision

To have a lasting impact on learning, pre-k programs must be aligned with equally high-quality kindergarten and early elementary school programs. Research consistently shows that quality pre-k programs have long-term effects in reducing special education placement, grade retention, and school dropout rates. But other academic effects tend to fade out by the end of third grade, because too many pre-k graduates enter public elementary schools that are ill-equipped to build on their pre-k learning gains.

To reap the full benefits of quality pre-k, district leaders must make it the first step in an aligned system of high-quality early education that runs through third grade. This system, with a goal of having all children at or above grade-level proficiency by the end of third grade, requires an aligned curriculum, assessments, professional development, common planning time, and collaboration between teachers across grade levels.

In a recent report, *Principals Lead the Way for PK-3*, the National Association of Elementary School Principals profiled dozens of schools and districts across the country that are using this PK-3 reform approach. An example used was Deep Creek Elementary School, which serves predominantly low-income and minority students in Baltimore County, Md.

New Report Looks at Pre-K in the Future

What do researchers know about early childhood and preschool programs? And what does this mean for the future?

W. Steven Barnett, director of the National Institute for Early Education Research at Rutgers University, recently completed a comprehensive review of research on pre-k. His conclusions, along with a number of recommendations for school districts, are published in a report released in mid-September by Arizona State University and the University of Colorado.

Among Barnett's conclusions:

- Many preschool programs have been shown to produce positive effects on children's learning and development, but those effects vary in size and persistence by type of program.
- Well-designed programs produce long-term improvements in school success, including higher test scores, lower rates of grade repetition and special education, and higher educational attainment. Some programs also are associated with reduced delinquency and crime in childhood and adulthood.
- The strongest evidence suggests economically disadvantaged children reap long-term benefits from preschool, but students from all other socioeconomic backgrounds benefit as well.
- Current policies for child care, Head Start, and state pre-k do not ensure that most children will attend highly effective pre-k programs. Some have no pre-k options, while others are in educationally weak programs. Middle-income children have the least access, but preschool experiences were found lacking for many in poverty.
- Increasing child care subsidies under current federal and state policies likely will produce mild negative consequences for learning and development, not meaningful improvements. The reason? "The poor quality of child care."
- Increasing investment in effective preschool programs for all children can produce substantial educational, social, and economic benefits. State and local pre-k programs with high standards are the most effective. Public schools, Head Start, and private child care programs have produced similar results when operating with the same resources and standards as part of the same state pre-k program.
- Publicly funded pre-k for all might produce a paradoxical but worthwhile effect. While disadvantaged children benefit (compared to their gains with targeted programs), so do more-advantaged children. This means universal programs may result in higher levels of achievement for the disadvantaged, but a larger achievement gap. Universal programs that substantially increase the enrollment might reduce the gap.

Here are some of the report's recommendations:

- Policymakers should not depart from preschool models that have proven highly effective. These models typically have reasonably small class sizes and well-educated teachers with adequate pay.
- Preschool teachers should receive intensive supervision and coaching, and they should be involved in a continuous improvement process for teaching and learning.
- Programs should regularly assess learning and development to monitor how well children are accomplishing their goals.
- Whole-child development is critical to produce positive effects on children's behavior and later reductions in crime and delinquency. This includes social and emotional development and self-regulation.
- Policies expanding preschool access should give priority to disadvantaged children, who are likely to benefit most. More broadly, preschool policy should be developed in the context of comprehensive public policies and programs that support child development from birth to age 5 and beyond.

For a copy of the full report, visit http://nieer.org/resources/research/PreschoolLastingfects.pdf

In 2001, Deep Creek was one of the county's worst elementary schools, with its third-graders reading at a first-grade level. But today, after a new principal expanded collaboration and professional development for teachers, implemented an aligned reading and math curriculum from pre-k through third grade, and offered summer learning and after-school programs for struggling students, nearly three-quarters of its students read on grade level.

The key to Deep Creek's transformation: a clear vision of high-quality early education, starting in pre-k and continuing through third grade.

Unfortunately, examples like this remain relatively rare, even though the evidence is stark in districts that do not have pre-k programs. Meredith Phillips, a researcher at the University of California at Los Angeles, estimates that as much as half of the achievement gap between black and white students at high school graduation already exists by the time these students enter kindergarten.

Economic research shows that quality pre-k programs return benefits to taxpayers.

Today, new developments in neuroscience and child development research demonstrate that young children can learn far more than we previously realized. Economic research shows that quality pre-k programs return benefits to taxpayers—such as reductions in crime, special education placements, and high school dropouts—that outweigh their costs. And in today's economy, there is an increasing demand for high-quality child care programs to help support our working families.

So why isn't pre-k integrated into more districts' broader school improvement visions? It's a huge missed opportunity, but it's one that district leaders can correct. Take some time to educate yourself about quality pre-k. Reach across traditional boundaries that separate early childhood from K-12 education, and community-based providers from public schools.

State pre-k expansion has tremendous promise to improve student achievement and help narrow achievement gaps—but only if districts do their part.

SARA MEAD (mead@newamerica.net) is director of the Early Education Initiative for the New America Foundation in Washington, D.C. She also writes a blog (www.earlyedwatch.org) on early education issues.

Joy in School

Joyful learning can flourish in school—if you give joy a chance.

STEVEN WOLK

Two quotes about schooling particularly resonate with me. The first is from John Dewey's *Experience and Education* (1938): "What avail is it to win prescribed amounts of information about geography and history, to win the ability to read and write, if in the process the individual loses his own soul?" (p. 49). If the experience of "doing school" destroys children's spirit to learn, their sense of wonder, their curiosity about the world, and their willingness to care for the human condition, have we succeeded as educators, no matter how well our students do on standardized tests?

The second quote comes from John Goodlad's *A Place Called School* (1984). After finding an "extraordinary sameness" in our schools, Goodlad wrote, "Boredom is a disease of epidemic proportions. . . . Why are our schools not places of joy?" (p. 242). Now, a generation later, if you were to ask students for a list of adjectives that describe school, I doubt that *joyful* would make the list. The hearts and minds of children and young adults are wide open to the wonders of learning and the fascinating complexities of life. But school still manages to turn that into a joyless experience.

So what can schools and teachers do to bring some joy into children's formal education? Children typically spend from six to seven hours each day in school for nearly 10 months each year. During the school year, children generally spend more time interacting with their teachers than with their parents. What happens inside schools has a deep and lasting effect on the mind-sets that children develop toward lifelong learning.

Dewey's point about the destructive power of our schools should make us ask ourselves some fundamental questions: What is the purpose of school? What dispositions about learning, reading, school, the world, and the self do we want to cultivate? Ask young adults why they go to school. You will hear nothing about joy.

I am not using the word joy as a synonym for *fun*. For many children, having fun is hanging out at the mall, watching TV, text-messaging their friends, or zipping down a roller-coaster. Having fun certainly brings us joy, but students don't need to be having fun in school to experience joy. According to my Random House dictionary, *joy* means, "The emotion of great delight or happiness caused by something good or satisfying." Surely our schools can do some of that. Joy and learning—including school content—are not mutually exclusive. Many of our greatest joys in life are related to our learning. Unfortunately, most of that joyful learning takes place outside school.

As educators, we have the responsibility to educate and inspire the whole child—mind, heart, and soul.

As educators, we have the responsibility to educate and inspire the whole child—mind, heart, and soul. By focusing on the following essentials, we can put more joy into students' experience of going to school and get more joy out of working inside one.

JOY 1:
Find the Pleasure in Learning

Why do people learn? I don't mean inside school—I mean learning as a part of life. Surely a large part of our learning is necessary for survival and a basic quality of life.

But there is another, entirely different, reason to learn. Learning gives us pleasure. This kind of learning is often (but not always) motivated from within, and no outside forces or coercions are needed. We also don't mind the possible difficulties in this learning. We often expect the challenges we encounter; we tend to see them as a natural part of the learning process, so we are far more open to taking risks. Some love to learn about cars, others love to learn about history, and some find great joy in learning how to dance. According to Mihaly Csikszentmihalyi (1990), such learning is an example of *flow,* which he defines as

> the state in which people are so involved in an activity that nothing else seems to matter; the experience itself is so enjoyable that people will do it at even great cost, for the sheer sake of doing it. (p. 4)

By helping students find the pleasure in learning, we can make that learning infinitely more successful.

If we want students to experience more flow in school—if we want them to see school and learning as joyful—we need to rethink how and what we teach. No longer can schooling be primarily about creating workers and test takers, but rather about nurturing human beings (Wolk, 2007). By helping students find the pleasure in learning, we can make that learning infinitely more successful.

JOY 2:
Give Students Choice

Outside of school, children are free to pursue their interests, and they do so with gusto. They learn how to play baseball or the drums; they learn how to ice skate or play video games; they read comic books, graphic novels, skateboard magazines, and Harry Potter.

But during a typical six-hour school day, how much ownership do students have of their learning? Practically none. It's not surprising that their interest in learning dissipates and that teachers complain of unmotivated students.

Joy in learning usually requires some ownership on the part of the learner. Students can own some of their school learning in several ways. They can choose the books they want to read through independent reading. In writing workshop, we can inspire them to be real writers and choose for themselves what genres to write in. During units in math, science, art, and social studies, they can choose specific subtopics to study; then, as "experts," they can share their learning with the class. Students can also choose which products they want to create to demonstrate their learning. What brings more joy—studying the civil rights movement in the United States through a textbook and lectures or creating comic books, writing and performing plays, interviewing people to create podcasts, and proposing your own ideas? Which would *you* rather do?

I advocate giving students one hour each day to study topics of their choice in what I call "Exploratory" (Wolk, 2001). In Exploratory, teachers collaborate with students to help shape student-initiated ideas into purposeful, inquiry-based investigations. During this time, students are scattered around the room, absorbed in an endless variety of topics that matter to them. While one student is studying the life of ants, a second is researching the workings of the FBI, and a third is exploring the life of Frida Kahlo. While two students work together to investigate the history of soccer, another is engrossed in surveying adults on their opinions of video games. Exploratory can teach students that school can be a place that nurtures curiosity, inspires them to ask questions, and helps them find the joy in learning.

JOY 3:
Let Students Create Things

People like to make stuff. Having control of our work and using our minds and hands to create something original give us a tremendous sense of agency. There is a special pride in bringing an original idea to fruition. It empowers us and encourages us; it helps us appreciate the demanding process of creating something from nothing.

The list of what students can create across the curriculum is virtually limitless: newspapers and magazines, brochures, stories, picture books, posters, murals, websites, podcasts, PowerPoint presentations, interviews, oral histories, models, diagrams, blueprints and floor plans, plays and role-plays, mock trials, photographs, paintings, songs, surveys, graphs, documentary videos—the list goes on and on. At its best, school should help and inspire students to bring their own ideas and creations to life.

JOY 4:
Show Off Student Work

Our schools and classrooms should be brimming with wonderful, original student work. School spaces that are devoid of student work perpetuate a sterile and joyless environment. I tell my teacher education students that the walls of their classrooms should speak to people; they should say exactly what goes on in that space throughout the school day. I can tell what teachers value by simply walking into their classrooms and looking at the walls.

The same is true for a school building. My son, Max, is in 4th grade, and his school, Augustus H. Burley School in Chicago, is a joyous place to visit. The hallways and classrooms are filled with remarkable student work, and there is rarely a worksheet in sight. The teachers also show off the students themselves. There are photographs of students next to their favorite books, above their posted work from writing workshop, and next to the doors of some classrooms.

JOY 5:
Take Time to Tinker

Gever Tulley has started a unique summer school in California called the Tinkering School. His blog describes it this way:

The Tinkering School offers an exploratory curriculum designed to help kids—ages 7 to 17—learn how to build things. By providing a collaborative environment in which to explore basic and advanced building techniques and principles, we strive to create a school where we all learn by fooling around. All activities are hands-on, supervised, and at least partly improvisational. Grand schemes, wild ideas, crazy notions, and intuitive leaps of imagination are, of course, encouraged and fertilized (Tulley, 2005).

At Tinkering School, students are allowed to dream. They come up with their own ideas for an object, and the faculty and staff help them sketch, design, and build it. When have you seen a public school that encouraged students to come up with "grand schemes, wild ideas, crazy notions, and intuitive leaps of imagination"? In fact, schools actually work to prevent this from happening.

Our school days are too planned, leaving no room for spontaneity and happenstance. Kindergarten is the last refuge in school for letting kids tinker. Once they enter 1st grade, students must banish the joy of "fooling around" with objects and ideas and, instead, sit at their desks most of the day listening to lectures, reading textbooks, and filling out worksheets.

Sometimes the best ideas come from tinkering—and teachers, not just students, should be doing more of it. We must push beyond the teacher-proof curriculum the textbook industry has created, which tries to plan every subject for every hour of the day. Far from being think tanks or workshops, our schools continue to be assembly lines. We need to free teachers to take risks, experiment, play with the art of pedagogy, and feel the joy that comes from tinkering with their teaching.

JOY 6:
Make School Spaces Inviting

Why do classrooms need to look so much like, well, *classrooms,* with desks in rows or arranged in groups, with a chalkboard or whiteboard at the front? When I walk into a classroom in my son's school, I usually see a space that looks a lot like a family room. There's a large rug, a class library with the best in children's and young adult literature, bean bags, couches, comfortable chairs, pillows, colorful curtains, fabric hung over the ceiling lights, and lamps scattered about the classroom. In fact, sometimes the ceiling lights are off, and the lamps warmly light the room.

And what about the public spaces inside and outside the school—the hallways, foyers, meeting areas, and school grounds? Anyone who has spent time at a university knows how integral these spaces are to the learning and social dynamics of the campus. The same can be true for a school. Why not transform these often unused and sterile spots into places for small groups of students to work or cozy nooks for kids to read or write? How about filling a foyer with plants and flowers? Why not give a large wall to the students to create and paint a mural? One colorful mural can transform a barren hallway or entrance into a vibrant and joyful sight. And schools can turn outdoor spaces into gardens, sculpture parks, walking paths, and quiet reading areas.

JOY 7:
Get Outside

I am bewildered by how much time students spend inside schools. I don't mean that the school day should be shorter; I mean that more of the school day should be outside. We adults know all too well how much we like to get outside for a respite during the workday, and the same applies to students and teachers in school. They need a break from being confined inside a classroom all day. Fresh air, trees, and a sunny day can do miracles for the human spirit.

Interacting with nature brings a unique joy. Gavin Pretor-Pinney (2006) writes, "I have always loved looking at clouds. Nothing in nature rivals their variety and drama; nothing matches their sublime, ephemeral beauty" (p. 9). Naturalist and artist David Carroll (2004) describes his childhood enthrallment of seeking out turtles as he walked the ponds and marshes:

> The sheer joy of being there, of simply bearing witness, continued to be paramount. I went out neither to heal my heartbreaks nor to celebrate my happiness, but to be in nature and outside myself. Turtles, spotted turtles most significantly, were a living text moving upon an endless turning of the pages of the natural world. (p. 27)

The easiest way to get students outside is simply to have recess. There is a special joy in standing amidst the students as they burst from the school and spread out like a swarm of hungry ants. Kids say that recess is their favorite time in school. Recess was also one of my favorite times of the day as a teacher because I was outside and surrounded by children having fun. Tragically, recess has become a rare sight, which may say more about our schools today than anything else. Why do so many schools find it so difficult to allow children 20 minutes each day to play?

As a teacher, I would often take my students outside to read, write, or have a class meeting. It is delightful for a student to sit under a tree and read or for a class to sit in a circle on the grass and talk. Much of our science curriculums could directly include the outdoors. A school does not have to be near a forest or the ocean for students and teachers to explore nature. Ecosystems are all around us. Have students dig a hole in a patch of dirt, and they will witness the flourishing life in the soil beneath their feet. Don't underestimate the power of sheer joy that children—and adults—can experience from tipping over a large rock and seeing the ground teeming with life.

JOY 8:
Read Good Books

Everyone loves a good story. We all know that if you have a 5-year-old sitting on your lap and a good book in your hands, you will soon experience the magic of stories. And what amazing stories there are! We are living in an astonishing time of children's and young adult literature. Immerse students in a culture of good books, and you surround them with joy.

For the past few years, I've been working on a grant with a Chicago public school, in part to help teachers make literature an important feature of their classrooms. I have brought loads of good books into the school. As I did book talks in 4th and 8th grade classrooms about dozens of new titles we ordered, the room was abuzz with students who could not wait to get their hands on the books. When I walk into a classroom now, I am met with the excited voices of the students telling me what books they're reading.

Of course, if we want joy in schools, then sometimes students should read books that aren't so "serious." I believe that books with important themes can make a better world, but we must also sometimes allow—even encourage—students to experience books for sheer pleasure. Have 3rd graders read Dav Pilkey's *Captain Underpants and the Perilous Plot of Professor Poopypants* (Scholastic, 2000). Have 5th graders read Jeff Kinney's *Diary of a Wimpy Kid* (Amulet, 2007). Have young adults read Sherman Alexie's very funny (and serious) *The Absolutely True Diary of a Part-Time Indian* (Little Brown, 2007). Encourage students to read thrillers; romance novels; action-adventure books; stories about sports, animals, and pop culture; graphic novels and manga; and nonfiction on topics they love. You will see plenty of joy.

JOY 9:
Offer More Gym and Arts Classes

In recent years, with our zeal for increasing test scores, "specials" in school have become nearly as rare as recess. It is not uncommon, especially in more impoverished schools, for students to have no art, music, and drama at all, and gym only once or twice a week. In my son's previous school in Chicago, he did not have gym until January.

With his work on multiple intelligences, Howard Gardner has helped us better appreciate the uniqueness of children and has spoken to the need to give students opportunities to use their varied strengths and interests in school. For the legions of children who have a special affinity for the visual arts, theater, music, or sports, classes in these subjects are golden times for them to experience joy in school. But how much joy can they experience when it's limited to 45 minutes each week?

JOY 10:
Transform Assessment

When I was a kid, I dreaded report card time. When I was a teacher, many of my students were anxious about their grades. For far too many students, assessment in its dominant forms—tests, quizzes, letter grades, number grades, and standardized tests—is a dark cloud that never seems to leave. Must it be this way?

The idea of assessment in school is not inherently bad; children assess themselves all the time. When they're busy doing something they love outside school, such as tae kwon do, baking, or playing the saxophone—when they're experiencing *flow*—they don't mind assessment at all. In fact, they see it as an important part of the process. But for most students, assessment in school is the enemy.

We can, however, make it a more positive experience. We need to help students understand the value of assessment. We also need to rethink "failure." Our schools see failure as a bad thing. But adults know that failure is a vital part of learning. Portraying failure as a bad thing teaches a child to avoid risk taking and bold ideas. Imagine if we graded toddlers on their walking skills. We would be living in a nation of crawlers.

We should limit how we use quantitative assessments and make more use of narrative assessments and report cards,

portfolios of authentic work, and student presentations and performances. In addition, parent conferences should not only include students, but also encourage the students to do much of the talking, using the conference as an opportunity to present their work and discuss their strengths and areas to focus on for growth.

As a teacher, I had my students regularly do self-assessments. This gave them some real power over the process. They assessed most of their schoolwork before I did my own assessment. And during report card time, I passed out photocopies of a blank report card and had my students complete it, for both grades and behavior, before I filled it out. I don't recall a student ever abusing this opportunity. At another school in which I taught, I redesigned our report card to include space for a photograph of the student inside; the cover was left blank so students could either draw a picture or write something meaningful there.

JOY 11:
Have Some Fun Together

Recently, when I was visiting a school, I was standing in the hallway talking to a teacher when a tall 8th grade boy from another classroom exuberantly walked up to that teacher. They began some good-natured ribbing. Back and forth it went for a few minutes with smiles and laughter. What was this about? The teacher-student basketball game held earlier that week. Here were two people—an 8th grader and his teacher—having a joyous good time.

Schools need to find ways for students, teachers, and administrators to take a break from the sometimes emotional, tense, and serious school day and have some fun together. Sporting events, outdoor field days, movie nights, school sleep-ins, potluck meals, visits to restaurants, schoolwide T-shirt days, and talent shows can help everyone get to know one another better, tear down the personal walls that often get built inside schools, form more caring relationships, and simply have a wonderful time together.

Teaching as a Joyful Experience

Recently, I visited a former graduate student in her classroom. It is her third year as a teacher, and I was excited to see her creative and thoughtful teaching. But she said to me, "I never imagined this job would be so hard. I'm tired all the time."

Yes, teaching is hard. John Dewey's quote—about school sapping our souls—can be as true for teachers as it is for students. Considering the staggering turnover of new teachers in urban schools, it is in everyone's interest to help teachers find joy in their work. So teachers must strive in whatever ways they can to *own their teaching* so that each morning they can enter their classrooms knowing there will be golden opportunities for them—as well as for their students—to experience the joy in school.

References

Carroll, D. (2004). *Self-portrait with turtles.* Boston: Houghton Mifflin.

Csikszentmihalyi, M. (1990). *Flow.* New York: Harper Perennial.

Dewey, J. (1938). *Experience and education.* New York: Collier.

Goodlad, J. (1984). *A place called school.* New York: McGraw-Hill.

Pretor-Pinney, G. (2006). *The cloudspotter's guide.* New York: Perigee.

Tulley, G. (2005, May 4). About. *Tinkering School.* Available: www.tinkeringschool.com/blog/?p= 11

Wolk, S. (2001). The benefits of exploratory time. *Educational Leadership,* 59(2), 56–59.

Wolk, S. (2007). Why go to school? *Phi Delta Kappan,* 88(9), 648–658.

STEVEN WOLK is Assistant Professor of Teacher Education at Northeastern Illinois University, 5500 N. St. Louis Ave., Chicago, IL 60625; s-wolk@neiu.edu

From *Educational Leadership,* September 2008. Copyright © 2008 by ASCD. Reprinted by permission. The Association for Supervision and Curriculum Development is a worldwide community of educators advocating sound policies and sharing best practices to achieve the success of each learner. To learn more, visit ASCD at www.ascd.org

Early Education, Later Success

How do you sustain the momentum generated by your prekindergarten and full-day kindergarten programs? Start by considering an aligned and unified PK-3 unit.

SUSAN BLACK

D oes your district offer high-quality prekindergarten and full-day kindergarten programs? If so, your youngest students are off to a good start.

Research confirms that children in good prekindergartens are eager and successful learners in kindergarten. And children who attend good full-day kindergartens stand a better chance of succeeding in first grade. That's the encouraging news.

But there's a worrisome downside. Prekindergarten children's gains in language, literacy, and math often fade out by the end of first grade. The gains children make in kindergarten, whether they attend half-day or full-day, often fade out by third grade.

Don't give up hope. There are steps you can take to ensure that prekindergarten and kindergarten pay off in the long run.

What's Needed?

PK-3 units are a "promising solution" to the fade-out problem, says Kristie Kaurez, director of early learning at the Education Commission of the States.

In an issue brief for the New America Foundation, a nonprofit public policy institute, Kaurez says success requires more than high-quality programs at each grade. The first five grades, she says, must provide similar instruction, curriculum alignment, well-managed transitions between grades, smaller class sizes, parent involvement, and top-quality teaching.

Kaurez envisions a five-step ladder—a "succession of sturdy rungs"—that children climb with confidence during their first five years of schooling. At each rung, children gain and maintain a "strong foothold" in language, literacy, and math.

Studies show it can be done, and children can profit immeasurably.

An evaluation of New Jersey's Union City School District's PK-3 "base camp," a program which links standards, curriculum, and assessments, showed significant gains: When the youngsters reached fourth grade, they nearly doubled their proficiency on state tests in language arts and math.

Multi-year studies of the Chicago Child-Parent Centers, a PK-3 program established by the Chicago Board of Education, show long-lasting effects. Students had higher achievement and, in later years, were less involved in juvenile crime.

Arthur Reynolds, with the University of Minnesota's Institute for Child Development, reports two "striking effects" for children in high-quality PK-3 units: By third grade, they're far less likely to be retained or to be placed in special education. While it's unproven that PK-3 units alone cause higher achievement, Reynolds stands by the "wisdom of high quality PK-3 programs."

Taking a Long View

Well-planned PK-3 programs help children master reading and math, according to researchers with the University of Michigan's Inter-University Consortium for Political and Social Research (ICPSR). Equally important, five-grade units help children develop "social, self-regulating, and motivating traits," attributes considered essential to learning.

PK-3 programs take a long view of children's learning and development, and they give children more time to succeed, ICPSR points out. Compared to school readiness programs, PK-3 programs provide a "richer, more detailed understanding and a better prediction of children's development outcomes," ICPSR says.

Success depends on getting PK-3 units right, and that can take time and effort.

Success depends on getting PK-3 units right, and that can take time and effort. ICPSR says these components are essential:

- School organization that supports PK-3 units
- Strong principal leadership
- Qualified teacher
- Classrooms designed as learning centers
- Curriculum and instruction that is aligned and coordinated across five grades
- Assessment and accountability systems for teachers and administrators
- Family and community engagement and support

An even longer view, beginning with infants and toddlers, adds to the benefits of PK-3.

A 2006 study in *Pediatrics* describes a 36-month health and educational program of home visits and parent support groups provided to families with low birth weight and premature infants. A follow-up study shows that, as teens, the children had higher achievement in math and reading; less tobacco, marijuana, and alcohol use; and less antisocial behavior and suicidal tendencies or attempts.

Citing such effects, some states have expanded early childhood education to include the years preceeding prekindergarten.

New York State's Board of Regents' early childhood education policy covers birth through fourth grade. It begins with prenatal care and extends to health services and educational programs for infants and toddlers. School districts are expected to "ensure that families have access to needed services," particularly families at or below the poverty level and those with children who speak limited English and whose children have disabilities.

Georgia's Department of Early Care and Learning oversees a statewide system that coordinates services for children from birth through age 4. Washington State's Department of Early Learning coordinates Head Start, child care, early reading programs, and prekindergarten.

All in the Family

How important are families? Linda Espinosa, with the University of Missouri-Columbia, says social-emotional development during an infant's first year contributes to learning language. By age 5, a child should have a large vocabulary, narrative skills, and the ability to verbalize thoughts, ideas, emotions, and observations.

Espinosa says children are more likely to succeed in school if they have these experiences during their first five years:

- Close, supportive relationships at home, in day care, and in nursery school
- Opportunities to describe and express feelings
- Opportunities to make choices and to develop self-control and self-regulated learning
- Enrichment, such as field trips to zoos, parks, and museums
- Playtime that includes role play and opportunities to be expressive and imaginative

A child's first relationships are the "prism through which they learn about the world," says Ross Thompson with the University of Nebraska. Social interactions during a child's early years have a greater effect on learning than educational toys, brain-stimulating activities, and nursery school lessons, he claims.

Thompson says infants and toddlers are more likely to succeed if they develop three types of skills: intellectual, including using simple numbers and clearly expressing ideas; motivational, including curiosity and confidence in learning; and social-emotional, including participating in groups, cooperating with others, and exerting self-discipline.

Family engagement is essential to "develop and sustain effective PK-3 programs," says Richard Weissbourd, co-chair of Pre-K to 3 Education: Promoting Early Success, Harvard University's new institute for school leaders. Superintendents, principals, and teachers enrolled in the institute study early childhood literacy, and they learn the importance of helping parents provide reading, math, and rich conversations during daily home activities; involving parents in literacy activities at school; and strengthening teacher-parent partnerships through home visits.

Creating a Good Program

A suburban school district administrator told me it takes "perseverance and pushiness" to create a high-quality PK-3 unit. She's been at it for three years, but progress is slow-going.

So far she's secured board approval for PK-3, found space for new prekindergarten classrooms, and provided teachers with training and supplies. But problems persist. An elementary principal is half-hearted about the PK-3 concept, and some teachers refuse to try new strategies, plan as a team, or conduct home visits.

Still, I'm pinning my hopes on this dedicated administrator and the teachers who have stepped forward and are willing to do all they can to help their youngest students.

Here's why.

A *Washington Post* story describes Johnny, a 5-year-old child of immigrants who entered kindergarten in Maryland's Montgomery County Public Schools. Education writer Jay Mathews says Johnny is part of an "unnerving language gap" that contributes to a wide achievement gap. (Most children from affluent families enter school knowing 13,000 English words, a sharp contrast to many children from poor and immigrant families who know a meager 500 English words.)

Operation Johnny began soon after the school year started. Working as a team, the little boy's kindergarten teacher, his parents, an interpreter, a speech pathologist, a special education consultant, and a social worker designed a year-long plan to help Johnny learn. The teacher was pivotal to the plan, agreeing to sit close to the boy, teach him new vocabulary through games and activities, and videotape classroom lessons for Johnny's parents to reinforce at home.

The district is determined to rescue Johnny and others like him. MCPS's board of education authorized Superintendent Jerry Weast to spend more than $21 million for an Early Success Performance Plan that's reduced class sizes and created full-day kindergartens in all 123 primary schools. The plan is paying off: In three years, the percentage of low-income 5-year-olds attaining grade-level goals has risen from 44 percent to 70 percent. Their fourth-grade passing rate on state tests is 86 percent.

Johnny is off to a good start. He's eager to learn, due in part to the district's plan and in part to his kindergarten teacher's determination and extra effort. Operation Johnny illustrates what all school leaders and teachers can and should do to help struggling students succeed at every step on the five-step ladder.

SUSAN BLACK, an *ASBJ* contributing editor, is an education researcher and writer in Hammondsport, N.Y.

The Changing Culture of Childhood
A Perfect Storm

JOE L. FROST

A kind of "perfect storm" is now brewing in the education and development of children in the United States. Those who have not lived or explored the history of education in the United States; have not experienced both poverty and abundance, have lived lives sheltered from the barrios, slums, homeless shelters, and epidemics; or those unfamiliar with the rich legacy of history and child development scholarship on the nature of learning and relevance of culture are repeating the mistakes to be found in the history of U.S. education.

A combination of interrelated elements is currently changing the face of the civilizing traditions of U.S. education and forming a new culture of childhood. These include: 1) the standardization of education; 2) the dissolution of traditional spontaneous play; and 3) the growing specter of poverty in the United States and around the world.

The Standardization of Schooling

The standardization of schooling began as a state effort to improve achievement and reduce drop-outs by implementing the high-stakes testing movement, later known as No Child Left Behind. From the beginning, a fundamental fault of ignoring individual differences in all dimensions of education and child development spelled failure for this program. Well before the advent of the testing mania, educators learned the lessons of such folly from the scholarly research of the child study movement in the early 1900s, which was influenced by such philosophers as Rousseau, Pestalozzi, Froebel, Hall, and Dewey, and later Piaget and Vygotsky. Throughout the first half of the 20th century, U.S. educators and child development professionals framed their work around conclusions from extensive research at major universities throughout the nation and refined their work through ever-growing research during the second half of the 20th century. I search in vain for the scholarly underpinnings for high-stakes testing.

Historically, scholarship led to emphasis on individuality, creativity, cooperative learning, community involvement, and balancing academics, arts, and outdoor play. Assessment of young children became an ongoing process, involving intensive study of children, testing for diagnostic purposes, individualized assessment, and teacher observation and judgment. A mechanized model of education focuses on one-size-fits all testing and instruction and was never accepted or recommended by national professional organizations, never supported by research, and never embraced by educators and child development professionals.

In the No Child Left Behind program, high-stakes testing was to be the motor driving the standardization movement. Widely implemented in Texas, this movement was called the "Texas Miracle," because of early reported dramatic improvement in test scores—a promise to be dashed as evidence showed that the "improvements" were confounded by cheating and political deals with publishing companies (CNN, 2005). In 2004, the Dallas Morning News (*Austin American-Statesman*, 2004) found evidence of cheating in Houston and Dallas, and suspicious scores in dozens of other Texas cities. For example, 4th-graders in one large city elementary school scored in the bottom 2 percent in the state while the 5th-graders in that school ended up with the highest math scores in the state, with more than 90 percent of the students getting perfect or near-perfect scores. No other school ever came close to that performance. The U.S. Department of Education named this school a Blue Ribbon School and the superintendent of the district was named U.S. Secretary of Education.

In September 2005, the Education Policy Studies Laboratory of Arizona State University (Nichols, Glass, & Berliner, 2005) published yet another study concluding that "pressure created by high-stakes testing has had almost no important influence on student academic performance" (p. 4). This study, conducted in 25 states, found a negative effect on minority students and illuminated the performance gap between white and minority students and between students from middle- and upper-income families and those from low-income homes. Such gaps come as no surprise to those who have studied the research on class, race, and educational achievement over the past half-century.

The prominent Latino authors in Angela Valenzuela's book *Leaving Children Behind: How "Texas-style" Accountability Fails Latino Youth* (2005) reveal the same kind of creeping, hidden discrimination that led to the civil rights struggle in the United States and the recent riots by disenfranchised minority youth in France and other European countries. The state's methods of collecting and reporting high-stakes test scores "hide as much as they reveal. . . . When skyrocketing dropout and projected retention rates are factored in, the state's 'miracle' looks more like a mirage" (p. 1). These Latino scholars contend that high-stakes testing is harmful to all children, but especially poor, minority, non English-speaking children; they state that children have a right to be assessed in a fair, impartial manner, using multiple assessment criteria.

Daily teaching and practicing the test has become the norm. Recess, arts, physical education, and creative inquiry are replaced with pizza parties, pep rallies, mock test practice, and teaching the test. Teachers, administrators, children, and parents face ever-growing pressure from threats of failure, retention, and demotion. As the schools focus ever more on bringing low-performing students up to grade-level standards, the most brilliant, most creative students, already performing well beyond their grade level, are left to languish in mediocrity and sameness. "In recent years the percentage of California students scoring in the 'advanced' math range has declined by as much as half between second and fifth grade" (Goodkin, 2005, p. A-15). It makes little difference in this draconian system whether a child merely meets the grade level standard or far exceeds it.

Politicians, not educators, are framing the U.S. education system and radically changing the culture of education, and standardized tests are becoming the curriculum of the schools. As the testing movement spreads across the nation, the Texas miracle is recognized by educators, professional organizations, and a growing number of politicians as bureaucratic bungling.

High-stakes testing is damaging to children and teachers—emotionally, physically, and intellectually. Around the country, children are wetting their pants, crying, acting out, becoming depressed, and taking their parents' pills on the day of testing to help them cope. In 2005, several children doped out and were taken to hospitals on the day of testing. In this same city, a high school that received a "School for Excellence Award" in 2002 was declared "low performing" in 2004 because a small group of children with disabilities did not perform well on a test designed for typical children.

Creative approaches to teaching value the souls and intellects of children and reveal and complement the wonderful creative powers of the best teachers. While teaching to the test may falsely guide the poorest teachers who struggle for direction, the best teachers are bound to a humdrum existence, divorced from teaching to interests, talents, and abilities; bound to endless regimented paperwork, meaningless workshops and repetition; and reduced to stress and mediocrity. Standardized tests tell good teachers what they already know and take an awesome toll on their teaching effectiveness, health, and creative powers.

In many states around the country, kindergartens and preschools are no longer a place for play, singing, and art; no longer a place for lessons on cooperation and sharing, or learning to love compelling literature and telling stories. They are no longer a place of fun and joy. Now, 3- to 5-year-olds, some still wetting their pants, not knowing how to stand in line, sit in a circle, or follow simple instructions, spend much of their time drilling skills and prepping for tests. We teach little kids to walk and talk and play together, then we tell them to sit down, shut up, and take the test. Yet learning by rote—by memory without thought of meaning—has never been a sound educational process.

The Dissolution of Traditional Spontaneous Children's Play

The early 20th century was a period of unparalleled interest in children's play and playgrounds. The U.S. play movement saw the promotion of spontaneous play and playgrounds in schools nationwide. The report of the 1940 White House Conference on Children and Youth (U.S. Superintendent of Documents, 1940, p. 191) stated, "All persons require types of experiences through which the elemental desire for friendship, recognition, adventure, creative expression, and group acceptance may be realized. . . . Favorable conditions of play . . . contribute much toward meeting these basic emotional needs." Play, the report stated, also supplies the growth and development of the child, and promotes motor, manual, and artistic skills—all conclusions supported by research and experience throughout the latter half of the 20th century.

Traditional spontaneous play is declining in U.S. neighborhoods and schools, and school recess is declining (Pica, 2003, 2005). The Atlanta school system built schools without playgrounds to demonstrate their devotion to high academic standards (Ohanian, 2002). Across the United States, school districts are abolishing recess or denying recess to children who score poorly on tests (Ohanian, 2002, p. 12). The International Play Association reports that 40 percent of U.S. elementary schools are deleting recess or reducing recess time to prepare for tests. *Psychology Today* reports that 40,000 schools no longer have play times.

Spontaneous play is also disappearing from the streets of cities throughout the industrialized world. In 1979, Keiki Haginoya began his intended life's work of preparing photo documentaries of children at play on the streets of Tokyo. In 1996, he wrote a sad conclusion to his career. Children's laughter and spontaneous play, which once filled the streets, alleys, and vacant lots of the city, had vanished. His photos show the rapid loss of play space, the separation of children from natural outdoor activities, traditional games, and creative play—indeed, the transformation of children's culture.

Haginoya's photos represent a sociological/psychological history of the cultural transformation—the construction of buildings and fences, the increase in cars, mass-produced toys, video game machines, and school entrance examinations. He mourns the demise of children's play and the end of his work:

> If I look back over the past seventeen years, it appears that
> I have taken the last record of children at play in the city,
> and that makes me deeply sad. . . . Children have learned
> enormous things through play. . . . The mere thought of

growing into a social person without the experience of outdoor play makes me shudder. (Haginoya, 1996, p. 4)

Kid pagers, instant messaging, video games, and chat rooms are replacing free, natural play in the fields and forests, a phenomenon Louv (2005) describes as "nature-deficit disorder." Even summer camps, only recently places for hiking in the woods, learning about plants and animals, and telling firelight stories, are now becoming computer camps, weight loss camps, and places where nature is something to watch, wear, consume, or ignore—places where attendance is linked to comfort and entertainment. If the present trends continue, summer camps may well become places to ditch children for tutoring on testing (Louv, 2005). In response, we have been transforming the playgrounds at our research site of three decades—Redeemer Lutheran School in Austin, Texas—into an integrated outdoor learning environment of playgrounds, natural habitats, and gardens. We see such work growing in acceptance, especially at child care centers where NCLB has only limited impact.

What is it like to bond with the wilderness? Having managed to survive the hazards of a childhood in the hillside farms and wilderness of the Ouachita Mountains of Arkansas more than half a century ago, I offer a personal glimpse of a childhood among the creeks and rivers, hills and valleys, and among domesticated and wild animals on the farm and in the wilderness. I never understood why kinfolk visiting from cities would ask, "Don't you get lonely down here?" The word "lonely "was not in my vocabulary or experience, because the days were filled with plowing and digging in the earth, wondering about the arrowheads found there; drinking from cool springs on hot days; swimming in the creeks and rivers at the end of long, sweaty days; riding horses and playing rodeo in the barn lots on weekends; feeding the cows, pigs, and chickens; building tree houses and hideouts in the woods; hunting raccoons at night and squirrels and deer in the daytime; cutting trees and chopping wood; taking pride in baling hay with the grown men; exploring fields and woods while eating watermelon and muscadines; building fires and cooking fish on the river bank; scanning the forest ahead for thorn bushes, snakes, and wild game; lying on the creek bank in the springtime, watching the creative movements of clouds; and all the while reveling in a sense of deep satisfaction and appreciation of the ever-changing natural wilderness.

We gathered along the gravel road before daylight during the winter to ride the back of a pick-up truck to school, stopping every half-mile or so to pick up other children who forded the river in boats or walked down out of the hills and valleys. We sat on sacks of mail, for the driver was also our mail carrier. We had five recess periods—before school and after school while waiting for the old truck to make runs over muddy road, and mid-morning, noon, and mid-afternoon. There was a level area in front of the school for organized games, most created by the children themselves, a creek along the back of the school for hunting frogs and building dams, and beyond that a pine-covered hillside. Here, we played war, built forts, and attacked the enemy with dead tree limb projectiles created by hitting the limb across a tree, breaking off the ends, which would fly

through the air, creating disarray and, sometimes, a bloody arm or nose. All of this constituted, as it turned out, a rather complete yet formidable playground. Play was truly free, for teachers stayed indoors. We stationed a kid at the edge of the woods to alert the group when the teacher rang the bell and it was time for "books." The ragged army then trooped indoors barefoot, muddy, and winded, but ready to sit down and pay attention. ADHD and obesity were unknown in that school and I never saw an injury that led to long-term consequences. What a difference six decades makes in the work and play of children!

The standardization of U.S. education extends well beyond the classroom curriculum into the playgrounds. Since the inception of national playground safety standards in 1981, constant revision has led to a 55-page standard of growing complexity, internal inconsistency, and estrangement from creativity. The "modern playground" is, in the main, an assemblage of steel and plastic structures, differing little from place to place, and devoid of natural habitats. Litigation replaces common sense and personal responsibility, and competition from testing and technology and careless parenting are producing a generation of obese kids with growing health and behavior problems. Safety standards are needed, but they should be consistent across state and national agencies, simple and clear in their expectations, and addressed to hazards in consumer products that threaten disability and death. Living is fraught with risks— emotional risks, financial risks, physical risks. Risk is essential for physical development. Overweight children with limited physical skills are unsafe on any playground. The issue is not merely how to make playgrounds safe for children, but how to make children safe for playgrounds.

In failing to cultivate the inherent play tendencies of children in the outdoor world, we fail to plant the early seeds of passionate exploration, artistic vision, creative reflection, and good health. Childhood is the time when, and playgrounds and natural habitats are the special places where, the culture, arising from tradition, knowledge, and skills, is readily and rapidly assimilated into the growing brain and psyche.

The Impact of Poverty on the Culture of Childhood

Poverty has powerful associations with school performance and exerts severe limits on what high-stakes testing can accomplish. Thousands of studies show positive correlations between poverty and achievement for children of all ethnic groups (Berliner, 2005). We don't need No Child Left Behind to tell us where failing schools are located—we have known for over a half century. The childhood poverty rate in the United States is greater than that of 25 wealthy countries, and poverty in the United States is clustered among minorities (UNICEF, 2005). As a group, African American and Hispanic American 15-year-olds rank 26th among 27 developed countries in reading, mathematics, and science literacy (Lemke et al., 2001).

More than half of all children born during this decade in developing countries will live their childhoods in urban slums. A quarter of those living in the United States will start their lives in urban slums (Nabhan & Trimble, 1996). Such children will have precious little opportunity to smell the flowers, sift clean dirt between their fingers, build a private hut in the wilds, walk in the morning dew, hear the quiet sounds of small animals at dusk, or see the heavens and the Milky Way in their full glory. Such seemingly insignificant experiences are the stuff that bond children to the natural world, introduce them to beauty and belonging, and surround them with opportunities to sharpen their growing minds with emerging concepts of geology, botany, physics, mathematics, and language.

For two decades, Annette Lareau (2003) and her team of researchers studied the differences in child rearing in upper middle-class versus working-class homes. The parenting styles and the results are dramatic, not good versus bad, but radically different in ways that prepare children to be successful in school. Upper middle-class families are more deeply involved in all aspects of their children's lives—providing a wide range of learning experiences, engaging in a lot of talk, reasoning with them, scheduling activities and getting them there, fighting over homework. In working-class homes, play is seen as inconsequential—a child's activity, not for adults. There was less talk, orders were brusque but whining was less. Parents offered fewer explanations and children, like their parents, were more likely to be intimidated by teachers and others in positions of authority. Working-class children had more intimate contact with extended families, they were taught right from wrong, and in many respects they were raised in the healthier environment. However, as adults, the working-class children are not doing well. They were not prepared for a world valuing verbal skills and an ability to thrive in organizations. They are picking up the same menial jobs their parents held, while the upper middle-class children are attending good colleges and preparing for professional careers.

The first White House Conference on Children in a Democracy was called by President Franklin D. Roosevelt in 1940, just after the onset of world war and during a time of exploitation of minorities and political patronage threatening the democratic process. The conference report (U.S. Superintendent of Documents, 1940, pp. 192–193) concluded that families of low-income children, minority children, slum children, and children with disabilities were deprived of toys, books, recreational areas, artistic events, and community recreation and playgrounds—in many respects, mirror images of what we see today.

The 2003 Census Report shows a steady rise in the number of families in poverty each year since 1999. When power and wealth rule a political structure, education itself is discriminatory (Wallis, 2005). We have known for decades that poverty is a key factor in school failure, yet both state and national governing bodies accommodate lobbyists and corporations while neglecting health care, housing, and living standards for the poor. Promises that the federal No Child Left Behind program would be accompanied by funds to make it work have gone unfulfilled, and children of the poor, especially minorities, are again stuffed into poverty-area schools rated "low performing" and "unacceptable." Now, public schools are threatened as students failing the tests are shifted to charter schools of questionable credentials and results, thus depriving public schools of desperately needed funds.

We see a growing storm for America's poorest children, with shrinking resources for school books, health insurance, affordable housing, health care, and food stamps. One in six U.S. children is poor; four million Americans are hungry and skipping meals; 45 million have no health insurance; 14 million have critical housing needs (Wallis, 2005, p. 223). With funding cuts in education and social services, the growing cost of war, tax cuts for the wealthy, natural disasters, and political cronyism, we now have a crisis among the poorest children.

The plight of the poor and minorities is nowhere more apparent than in the inequity of concern for the residents of New Orleans, both before and after Hurricane Katrina. Even before Katrina, the New Orleans schools were a failing system (Gray, 2005): already $45 million in debt; plagued by leadership crises (four superintendents in four years), scandals, and a squabbling school board; and strapped for resources. A majority of the students failed mandatory tests. After Katrina, we see a crisis of major proportions among displaced people striving to put their lives back together and a school system $300 million in debt.

Poverty-plagued and overlooked schools exist through the United States, especially in the slums and barrios of the cities. In Chicago, students from poor neighborhoods fail to receive their fair share of school funding and attend schools with tattered textbooks, decrepit buildings, overcrowded classrooms, and poorly qualified teachers (Loftus, 2005). Frustrated, stressed-out teachers desert the profession or pray for the day they can retire. Teachers in a growing number of schools must teach only one way. Policymakers must decide whether they want skillful, creative teachers or robots. If they want the former, they must put their money into supporting educators in developing curricula and sharpening their teaching skills.

Kozol (2005) tells stories about the dedication of teachers and the generosity in spirit of the children in the South Bronx; yet, in one school, only 65 of the 1,200 ninth-graders are likely to graduate. He points out that Mississippi spends $4,000 per pupil, inner-city Philadelphia schools get $6,000 per pupil, New York middle-class suburbs get $12,000 per pupil, and some very wealthy suburbs get $24,000 per pupil. Yet all are held to the same standards and all students take the same standardized exams. What history and research have always shown, but what policymakers ignore, is that poverty and hopelessness are fundamental causes of illiteracy and school failure in the United States. Regimented schooling does not address the problem of poverty.

Countering the Growing Storm

Author and poet Robert Louis Stevenson, sickly and in bed as a child, once watched the lamplighter move from place to place lighting the oil street lamps. He commented to his mother, "A man is coming down the street making holes in the darkness." We can all make little holes in the darkness and these holes can grow to illuminate entire neighborhoods, towns, and cities. Peaceful, informed dissent is a cornerstone of democracy and Americans are stepping up to protest the growing storm of elements that are eroding the culture of childhood. In April 2005, the Associated Press reported that the National Education Association (NEA) and school districts in Vermont, Michigan, and Texas, along with NEA chapters, were suing the federal administration for failing to provide support for the No Child Left Behind Act. In 2005, the Utah state legislature filed a lawsuit challenging the No Child Left Behind law, arguing that it is illegal to require expensive standardized testing for which it does not pay (Gillespie, 2005, p. A-10). Also in 2005, the NEA filed a lawsuit on behalf of local school districts and 20 state union chapters. A glimmer of hope emerged in November 2005, when the U.S. Secretary of Education, under fire from governors of several states, proposed allowing schools in some states to use children's progress on tests as evidence of success.

Who opposes high-stakes testing? Is it merely a handful of disgruntled parents, teachers, school boards, and professional organizations? Hardly. More than 70, and counting, professional organizations are in opposition, including such groups as the International Reading Association, the National Association for the Education of Young Children, American Educational Research Association, the American Psychiatric Association, the National Parent Teacher Association, the National Association for Elementary School Principals, the American Association of School Administrators, Students Against Testing, the National Association of School Psychologists, the American School Counselor Association, the National Council of Teachers of Mathematics, and the Association for Childhood Education International.

None of these organizations opposes meaningful testing or high academic expectations, nor do they hold that accountability is unnecessary. They simply contend that the system is deeply flawed. They promote assessments based on decades of research and experience; both formative and summative assessment, making decisions from multiple forms of assessment, not on a single test, adjusted for special needs and culturally different children; involving classroom teachers in assessment; and rejecting the use of test scores for punishing or rewarding administrators, teachers, and children.

Fortunately, private preschools remain relatively untouched by NCLB, although Head Start and other tax-supported early programs are under pressure to conform. Yes, professional standards and guidelines are essential, but look to those developed by such century-old organizations as NAEYC and ACEI-standards built by top researchers and successful practitioners worldwide, tied to the voluminous research of the past century, and refined by decades of experience.

High-stakes testing is not only wrong—it doesn't work. We are cultivating a culture of mediocrity and sameness and abandoning traditional ideas of creativity, ingenuity, ethical behavior, and imagination that make cultures and countries great. The most powerful policy for improving school achievement is reducing poverty. Focusing public policy on neighborhoods and families is an infinitely better strategy than focusing on testing to determine what we already know.

A reasonable substitute for the ill-founded emphasis on drill and testing for the very young would be to focus on encouraging parents to turn off the televisions, video games, and cell phones, and instead engage their children in conversation, take them to places of educational interest, read to them, teach them about the world beyond cartoons and video games, and teach them the value of giving over taking. Public policy should be directed toward rebuilding poverty-stricken neighborhoods, ensuring good jobs, medical care, and superior schools for all children, but especially for the very poor.

The impact of poverty, the demise of play, and high-stakes testing collectively are like the perfect storm. Each element contributes its destructive force, creating enormous potential for failure and damage to children—a sociopolitical system out of control. We must replace reactive, standardized learning with creative, thoughtful, introspective, interactive learning. We cannot allow the present generation of children to be the last to taste the joy of creative teaching and learning or to experience the delights of living with nature; the last children to know the collective inspiration of free, spontaneous play, and the separate peace of nature with all its fantasy, beauty, and freedom; the last to know the teachers and classrooms that molded people from all over the world into a fruitful, generous, and creative society. The engine that drives high-stakes testing, dismisses the value of children's play, and ignores the poor is a political engine. If we speak out, we can prevail; the storm will pass and good sense and a confluence of cultural creativity will return to the classrooms.

References

Austin American-Statesman. (2004, December 20). Signs of fraud found in study of TAKS results.

Berliner, D. C. (2005, August 2). *Teachers College Record,* www.tcrecord.org ID Number 12106.

CNN. (2005, May 8). *CNN Presents—High Stakes: No Child Left Behind.* Available on videotape.

Gillespie, N. (2005, August 23). Connecticut sues over No Child Left Behind. Associated Press in *Austin American Statesman,* p. A-10.

Goodkin, S. (2005, December 28). We should leave no gifted child behind. *Austin American-Statesman* from *Washington Post,* p. A-15.

Gray, C. (2005). Even before the hurricane: A failed system. *Philadelphia Inquirer,* www.parentdirectededucation.org

Haginoya, K. (1996). Children's play has disappeared from the city. *PlayRights,* 18(1). Raleigh, NC: International Association for the Child's Right to Play.

Kozol, J. (2005). *Hypocrisy in testing craze.* Retrieved August 17, 2005, from www.weac.rg/news/2000-01/kozol.htm

Lareau, A. (2003). *Unequal childhoods: Class, race, and family life.* Berkeley, CA: University of California Press.

Lemke, M., Lippman, C., Jocelyn, L., Kastberg, D., Liu, Y. Y., Roey, S., Williams, T., Kruger, T., & Bairu, G. (2001). *Outcomes of learning: Results from the 2000 program for international student assessment of 15-year-olds in reading, mathematics, and science literacy.* Washington, DC: U.S. Department of Education, National Center for Education Statistics.

Loftus, K. P. (2005). *Katrina inequities already a reality for poor kids.* Retrieved March 23, 2006, from www.parentdirectededucation.org

Louv, R. (2005). *Last child in the woods: Saving our children from nature-deficit disorder.* Chapel Hill, NC: Algonquin Books.

Nabhan, G. P., & Trimble, S. (1996). *The geography of childhood: Why children need wild places.* Boston: Beacon Press.

Nichols, S. L., Glass, G. V., & Berliner, D. C. (2005). *High stakes testing and student achievement: Problems for the No Child Left Behind Act.* Tempe, AZ: Arizona State University, Education Policy Studies Laboratory.

Ohanian, S. (2002). *What happened to recess and why are our children struggling in kindergarten?* New York: McGraw-Hill.

Pica, R. (2003). *Your active child: How to boost physical, emotional, and cognitive development through age-appropriate activity.* New York: McGraw-Hill.

Pica, R. (2005). Reading, writing, 'rithmetic—and recess! *Linkup Parents Newsletter.* Retrieved August 8, 2005, from www.linkup-parents.com/education.html

UNICEF. (2005). *Child poverty in rich countries, Innocenti Report Card No. 6.* Florence, Italy: UNICEF Innocenti Research Centre, www.unicef.org/irc

U.S. Superintendent of Documents. (1940). *White House conference on children in a democracy.* Washington, DC: Author.

Valenzuela, A. (Ed.). (2005). *Leaving children behind: How "Texas-style" accountability fails Latino youth.* Albany, NY: State University of New York Press.

Wallis, J. (2005). *God's politics.* San Francisco: HarperCollins.

JOE L. FROST is Parker Centennial Professor Emeritus, University of Texas, Austin.

From *Childhood Education*, Summer 2007, pp. 225–230. Copyright © 2007 by the Association for Childhood Education International. Reprinted by permission of Joe L. Frost and the Association for Childhood Education International, 17904 Georgia Avenue, Suite 215, Olney, MD 20832.

No Child Left Behind

Who's Accountable?

Lisa A. DuBois

To many federal legislators, No Child Left Behind is like the cavalry sent to rescue the American educational system. To many teachers, the federal mandate is simply another shackle, more paperwork and red tape, as they try to stimulate and expand the minds of the young. But to many involved in educational research, No Child Left Behind is akin to the leg of an elephant. The information they are gathering about that leg is helpful and important, but it is also becoming increasingly clear that the animal resting on the appendage is far more gargantuan and complex than originally imagined. Still, many look forward to embarking on a quest, albeit imperfect and unpredictable, to unravel the mysteries of the beast.

Certainly, experts and non-experts across the nation do not dispute that the American system of education is not where it needs to be. Right now, for example, the United States is tied with Zimbabwe for achievement in 8th grade mathematics. Today, over 80 percent of African American and Latino 8th graders say they plan to attend a two- or four-year college. Yet, once there, many are not prepared for a rigorous postsecondary education. Between 40 and 60 percent of college students need remedial work to catch up, and between 25 and 50 percent of these students drop out after their first year. These data imply that although the existing K–12 system is graduating students, it is not necessarily preparing them for life beyond high school.

The Bush Administration's answer to this conundrum has been to rigidly implement the No Child Left Behind (NCLB) law. Enacted during the president's first term and up for reauthorization in 2007, NCLB requires that 100 percent of American public school students reach set proficiency standards in reading and math (and as of 2008, in science, as well) by the year 2014. Individual states set their own standards and all students, regardless of family income, race, ethnicity, or disability must comply. Schools whose students fail to achieve these goals face increasingly onerous penalties and sanctions.

> **"NCLB makes a lot of sense if it would work. It's saying to schools, you can't ignore some of your kids just because they're tough to teach." —Andrew Porter**

Academicians are studying NCLB's impact on a number of fronts. Andrew Porter, Patricia and Rodes Hart Professor of Educational Leadership and Policy, believes that NCLB, while flawed, is in many ways "a beautiful thing," because it has beamed a spotlight on the need for equity, opportunity and accountability from all schools. "You can't just forget about your poor kids, or forget about your English language learners, or your special ed kids, or your black or Hispanic kids, or your boys. You've got to do well by everybody. . . . NCLB is better than anything we've ever had in the past on that score," he says. "Think about a kid from a low-income family. NCLB makes a lot of sense if it would work. It's saying to schools, you can't ignore some of your kids just because they're tough to teach."

Also, Porter adds, deliberations have now effectively shifted from input and process to what teachers are teaching (content) and what students are accomplishing (proficiency), which he considers a healthy change from past educational reform movements. NCLB approaches the problems of the education system from the perspective of the students matriculating through it. Every public school student must take a state-designed reading and math assessment every year in grades 3 to 8, and also during one high school year, usually grade 10. These assessments hold schools accountable for student proficiency by requiring them to reach the stated benchmarks, known as Adequate Yearly Progress (AYP). Students in those schools that fail to meet AYP goals for two consecutive years are given "an escape hatch," meaning they can choose to attend a different school. Schools that fail three years in a row are given a carrot in the form of supplemental services like funds for tutoring and enhanced teaching materials. After five years of a school's failing to meet targets, the measures become more punitive—that school can be taken over by the state, reconstituted, restructured or shut down.

As with any nationally mandated reform that imposes sanctions for noncompliance, NCLB has generated angst and hand-wringing among those in the trenches—teachers, principals, parents and superintendents—particularly concerning issues of accountability. In fact, accountability debates crop up at every turn: Is it fair to hold schools accountable? Are these standardized tests valid measures of content and proficiency? And are sanctions the best way to address accountability issues?

Is It Fair to Hold Schools Accountable?

Porter, for one, favors school accountability, because it addresses the educational framework on a very specific local level. However, he also is pressing for "symmetry in accountability," meaning that teachers and students should likewise be held responsible for achieving certain benchmarks. "If you're going to have accountability for schools, then you should also have accountability for students. You don't want schools to be left hanging out to dry for students who don't try," he says. "When education is successful, students, teachers and administrators roll up their sleeves and work together." NCLB does not currently address this existing accountability gap.

By the same token, Porter is bothered that NCLB was set into motion with an endpoint that guarantees failure. The goal of having 100 percent of students achieve 100 percent proficiency by 2014 is so unattainable that even countries with the most proficient educational systems in the world would not use that as a target.

"Demanding 100 percent proficiency is the only way we could have gotten started," counters Stephen Elliott, Peabody professor of special education and the Dunn Family Professor of Educational and Psychological Assessment. Elliott is an international expert on testing accommodations and alternate assessments for children with disabilities. When NCLB was being formed, disability advocacy groups wanted schools to be held accountable for the inclusion of their children, realizing that every disabled child certainly would not be able to meet the national standards. Yet they also didn't want disabled children to be given short shrift or for the bar to be set inappropriately low just so schools could slide into compliance. The resounding consensus, says Elliott, was that these groups had to advocate for 100 percent proficiency, pushing the limits so that disabled students can get the educational tools and services they need. NCLB opens a window for them to design a criterion, set expectations, see if students can reach them, and then readjust them as necessary.

"This is an experiment and we're learning as we go," Elliott says, acknowledging that some schools have failed to meet AYP goals because their special needs students were unable to pass the assessment tests.

Are Standardized Tests Valid Measures of Content and Proficiency?

Porter believes that the testing industry, which is making a mint from the explosion in demand for more standardized tests from pre-school through graduate school, is actually pretty good at what it does. The validity of the content of these tests is a less critical issue than our nation's tendency to water down curricula and have teachers in charge of courses they were never trained to teach. Teachers, meanwhile, complain that they have to "teach to the test."

"That's cheating," claims Elliott. "They should be teaching to the standards the tests are aligned to. Curriculum, testing and standards are all being aligned, which is the backbone of the accountability issue. The finger-wagging should be on the instruction. Our tests today are far better than they were a decade ago because of this legislation."

Ironically, two of the biggest drivers forcing the refinement of standardized testing are children with disabilities and low-income gifted students. Because special needs children are included in AYP, researchers have been studying which kinds of multiple-choice questions, for example, are best at illuminating a child's mastery of content without being skewed by that child's decision-making and reading challenges. Most standard multiple-choice tests give the taker four or five options; but according to Michael Rodriguez of the University of Minnesota (*Educational Measurement: Issues and Practice*, Summer 2005), the best format for truly gauging knowledge is one that presents three multiple-choice options. It turns out that this format is the best determinant of content mastery for non-disabled students, as well.

Elliott and his colleagues have also been examining testing accommodations and their influence on the scores of students with special needs. They discovered some unsettling data. As expected, children with Individualized Education Programs (IEPs) tested better when given special accommodations, such as private settings, reading support and extra time. However, children with no perceived special needs also scored higher on standardized tests when given these same accommodations. Surprisingly, the highest functioning children were the only ones who actually used the extra time they'd been given. But all groups of students reported feeling a psychological edge and believed they performed better with the opportunity to have extra time if they needed it.

Teachers, meanwhile, complain that they have to "teach to the test."

For low-income, minority and English-language learners, NCLB has yanked the veil off the ever pervasive "achievement gap" in American education. Simply put, affluent children are receiving a better public education than those whose families are struggling. After studying this dilemma for years, Porter and others have found that the achievement gap between preschoolers who come from wealthy families versus those from impoverished families is enormous, as big as it will ever be—before these children ever go to school.

Once they reach school age, the gap does not increase during the school year. Minority and poor youngsters make achievement gains parallel to their more affluent peers. Unfortunately, says Porter, "Minority and poor kids lose more achievement in the summer than do white and more affluent kids. All the spread in the achievement gap happens when they're not in school in the summer time."

These two factors—that the achievement gap is greatest among preschoolers and that the gap widens every summer while children are not in school—means that schools are being asked to fix a societal problem that extends beyond the confines of the classroom. Donna Y. Ford, Betts Professor of Education and Human Development in the department of special education, and Gilman W. Whiting, director of Vanderbilt African American Diaspora Studies, have initiated the Vanderbilt Achievement Gap Project to bring about large-scale change by addressing contributing factors on a local level. Ford believes that a major obstacle to closing the achievement gap is that schools that serve large numbers of underprivileged children are not offering them the kinds of rigorous curricula that will enable them to excel. In other words, expectations for disadvantaged populations have been set too low.

Ford says, "If we don't put more poor kids in gifted programs in K–6, how are we going to get them into AP classes in high school? They've had nine years of not being challenged, so how can they survive? The ability is there and the potential is there, if given the opportunity."

The data support her argument. Researchers from the private Center for Performance Assessment identified schools in which 90 percent of the students are poor, 90 percent are members of ethnic minority groups, and 90 percent also meet high academic standards. Some of the common characteristics these schools share include a strong focus on academic achievement and frequent assessment of student progress with multiple opportunities for improvement (*Challenge Journal: The Journal of the Annenberg Challenge*, Winter 2001/02).

One approach for more accurately evaluating achievement, again being driven by advocates of students with disabilities, is to offer more formative assessments. Rather than giving students a single "do-or-die" test at the end of the school year to measure their progress, Elliott and others are promoting the idea of delivering shorter, lower stakes assessments, delivered two or three times during the school year. They're finding that good formative tests are predictive of how proficient students will be by the end of the year.

Elliott explains, "The lowest functioning kids can make progress, even if they may never be proficient."

"Across the nation, one of the fastest spreading reforms is interim assessment," Porter says. "The upside to interim assessment is that teachers find out how well students are performing all along. The downside is what do you do when you find out they're not doing so well? Nobody's answering that question."

In 2005, NCLB asked states to compete for the opportunity to replace AYP with improved performance plans, considered by some researchers to be a superior index of proficiency, but, out of all the submissions, only North Carolina and Tennessee had the models and infrastructure to execute such a plan. "One of the most fragile areas of NCLB is the ability of states to manage the data," Elliott says. "Many statistical experts are going to work in the lower pressure, higher paying testing industry. So we're leaving people in the states who don't have the technical skills to manage the information."

One solution to this conundrum is to completely nationalize NCLB assessments, both in terms of content and proficiency. Porter is an avid proponent of this idea. Right now, each state has invested in its own content standards for math and reading. Unfortunately, a child from, say, Colorado, who moves to a new school in Georgia, may suddenly face an entirely different curriculum in the same school year. Concentrating all the energy that is now being used to develop materials, standards and assessments for 50 different states into the creation of one voluntary national standard, says Porter, "would mean enormous efficiency and would undoubtedly result in tremendous improvements in quality. If you're sinking all your resources into building one really great test, you can do a great job."

One approach for more accurately evaluating achievement, again being driven by advocates of students with disabilities, is to offer more formative assessments.

While national content standards may receive some level of support, Porter is also advocating for voluntary national proficiency standards, considered a less popular option. Right now, there are far-flung variances between states in benchmarks for achievement, and in most cases, a larger percentage of students reach proficiency on the state tests than on a comparable nationwide instrument, the National Assessment of Educational Progress (NAEP).

"In some states, the difference is enormous," Porter says, "like the difference between 30 percent and 90 percent."

Are Sanctions the Best Way to Address Accountability Issues?

In its current form, one of NCLB's most glaring glitches is its inability to impose the kinds of sanctions that result in student achievement. After a school fails for three consecutive years, students are supposed to receive the benefits of tutoring and supplemental services.

"Supplemental services haven't worked as well as we hoped they would," Porter says. Some districts aren't receiving the funding for these services in time to help the students, but more crucially, schools don't know what services they need until after their students have taken and failed the AYP assessment. So, they are faced with constantly moving targets.

Once a school misses its benchmarks two years in a row, students are allowed to transfer to schools that have not been identified as needing improvement. This has not panned out for a variety of reasons, Porter says. First, the better performing schools don't want to risk their AYP status by accepting an influx of students who've failed to meet the benchmarks. Second, in some cases, every school in the district is failing to reach NCLB guidelines. The sanction becomes irrelevant, because students have no place to go. Finally, poor and non-English speaking parents may find the logistics of transferring their children out of a neighborhood school to be too overwhelming to be worth the ordeal.

According to Ford, the solution will not be a band-aid or a simple promise to move kids to a new school. Instead it will require an intrinsic, primordial transformation across the education network. "If you move a child from an economically disadvantaged background and from a school that isn't rigorous into a school with a more rigorous curriculum, that child is going to need a lot of support not just to catch up, but to keep up," she says. "That's an equity issue. You can't just put children in a new school to frustrate them and make them fail. You have to believe in them and support them."

Now that NCLB is entering its first phase of reconstituting low-performing schools, the Bush administration is pushing to have private school vouchers added to the law, a proposal opposed by the National Education Association and others involved in collective-bargaining agreements.

Today, the achievement gap between underserved children and children of privilege stands at a full standard deviation, which in raw terms means that vast numbers of kids are undereducated.

The Next Wave Will Be NCLB's Effect on Higher Education

Today, the achievement gap between underserved children and children of privilege stands at a full standard deviation, which in raw terms means that vast numbers of kids are undereducated. Closing that gap by one standard deviation would, for example, bring a child at the 50th percentile up to the 84th percentile, a phenomenal gain. Porter contends that such a jump can happen if America improves the quality of its teaching.

"If we could get every kid to have a good teacher every year and if the effects of having a good teacher had a shelf life and were cumulative, it wouldn't take much of a change per year to add up to a standard deviation," he says. "We've got 12 years. If students could move up a tenth of a standard deviation every year, we'd get up to 1.2 standard deviations."

The onus, says Ford, is on the nation's universities to step up and prepare highly qualified teachers with high expectations who will enter the field and teach our children. To accomplish that, she thinks universities should revamp their courses so that student teachers start their practica earlier in college and spend more of their training out in the field gaining experience in a range of educational settings.

For all its many flaws and pitfalls, Porter, Elliott and Ford agree that NCLB has served the public well by forcing the conversation about education in the U.S. It has sparked new energy and directed attention to equity issues that have long been swept under the rug. NCLB obligates Americans to acknowledge the inadequacies in our school systems.

"That's the best thing NCLB could have done," says Ford. "The numbers are so dismal that we couldn't ignore them any longer. NCLB showed us the numbers. That's why I appreciate it. I don't blame NCLB solely for the problems we're having. It could have been any other piece of education legislation, and we still would have had to face these numbers."

Preschool Comes of Age
The National Debate on Education for Young Children Intensifies

Educators rave about the benefits of early-childhood schooling. So, why don't we support it more?

MICHAEL LESTER

Early this year, two dissimilar governors delivered two similar messages.

"Effective preschool education can help make all children ready to learn the day they start school and, more importantly, help close the enormous gap facing children in poverty," announced New York's Eliot Spitzer. He boldly promised to make a high-quality prekindergarten program "available to every child who needs it within the next four years."

Across the continent, California governor Arnold Schwarzenegger signed legislation expanding preschool opportunities in low-performing school districts and providing additional state dollars for building and improving preschool facilities. "Preschool gives our kids the strong foundation they need to be successful in school and in life," said Schwarzenegger.

Spitzer (a Democrat) and Schwarzenegger (a Republican) may not agree about a lot of things, but here's one area where they concur: Preschool education can perform miracles. Children who attend prekindergarten programs have bigger vocabularies and increased math skills, know more letters and more letter-sound associations, and are more familiar with words and book concepts, according to a number of studies.

Nationwide, almost two-thirds (64 percent) of children attend a preschool center in the year prior to kindergarten, typically at age four. On any given day, more than 5 million American youngsters attend some prekindergarten program.

And a preschool day is not just advanced babysitting for busy parents. Kids also practice many key components of the school day, including the importance of routine. That's key for early learners. "They understand carpet time, clean-up procedures, how to share crayons, or even getting their pants on and off without the teacher's help; that's big," says Steve Malton, kindergarten and first-grade teacher at Parkmead Elementary School, in Walnut Creek, California. "Little kids have only a

certain amount of what's called 'active working memory.' If a large portion of their brain is figuring out what they're going to do next, there's less room there to spend on learning." Result: Preschool has a huge impact on their ability to keep up in class.

Too Much, Too Soon?

So, what's not to love about preschool? Plenty, say critics. "Young children are better off at home," says Michael Smith, president of the Home School Legal Defense Association. "We are in danger of overinstitutionalizing them. A child will develop naturally if the parents give the child what he or she needs most in the formative years—plenty of love and attention. In this way, the brain can develop freely."

As soon as the subject of schooling before K-12 comes up, another concept quickly follows: testing. That gives some parents the jitters. "The only way for school programs, including preschool programs, to show accountability of public funding for education is through testing," says Diane Flynn Keith, founder of Universal Preschool. "The only way to prepare children for standardized testing is to teach a standardized curriculum. Standardized preschool curriculum includes reading, writing, math, science, and social sciences at a time when children are developmentally vulnerable and may be irreparably harmed by such a strategy."

That's part of a broader test-them-sooner move across many grades. One pushdown from No Child Left Behind, for instance, is that highstakes testing now begins as early as the second grade. "It's not the same kindergarten we went to," says Don Owens, director of public affairs for the National Association for the Education of Young Children (NAEYP). "It's not the same kindergarten it was ten years ago. Kindergarten used to be preparation for school, but now it *is* school. That's why school districts and boards of education are paying attention to what happens before the kids arrive at school."

America is forcing its parents to decide between paying for early education and saving for college.

The result is a desperate tug-of-war between prekindergarten advocates and critics, with the under-six set placed squarely in the middle. In 2006, for instance, the Massachusetts legislature passed, by unanimous vote, an increase in state-funded high-quality prekindergarten programs. Governor Mitt Romney promptly vetoed the bill, calling preschool an "expensive new entitlement."

On the national stage, Oklahoma is the only state to offer publicly funded preschool education to virtually all children (about 90 percent) at age four. But twelve states—Alaska, Hawaii, Idaho, Indiana, Mississippi, Montana, New Hampshire, North Dakota, Rhode Island, South Dakota, Utah, and Wyoming—provide no preschool services at all. "There is not enough support for preschool," explains David Kass, executive director of Fight Crime: Invest in Kids. "It's very expensive, and most parents cannot afford it."

The three costliest states for private preschool are Massachusetts (where preschool runs an average of $9,628 per year), New Jersey ($8,985), and Minnesota ($8,832). In Rhode Island, the average yearly tab for preschool ($7,800) represents 45 percent of the median single-parent-family income. In California, part-time private preschool and child-care programs cost families on average $4,022 statewide. By comparison, the average full-time tuition at a California State University campus was $3,164.

"America is forcing its parents to decide between paying for early education for their kids and saving for their college education," says the NAEYP's Don Owens.

That's when the subject of state-sponsored preschool comes up. Over the past two years, the total state prekindergarten funding increased by a billion dollars to exceed $4.2 billion. But those numbers are often inadequate. After Florida voters approved a preschool-for-all initiative similar to a voucher program, the state legislature appropriated about $390 million—or roughly $2,500 per child served. Reasonable budgeting for preschool, however, should parallel that for K-12 schools. "If you're a state like Florida spending $9,000 per student on a yearly full-day program of K-12, your costs for a half day of prekindergarten should be somewhere around $4,500, not $2,500," complains Steve Barnett, director of the National Institute for Early Education Research.

That pattern is true nationwide. In 2002, average state spending was at $4,171 per enrolled child, but that figure fell to $3,482 in 2006, according to the NIEER's 2006 *State Preschool Yearbook*. Some states spend even less: New Mexico provides $2,269 per child, and Ohio budgets just $2,345. Compare those amounts with the national average of $10,643 for each child enrolled in K-12 schools.

Barnett says Florida and other states are creating a dual system consisting of high-quality, expensive preschools in private settings and underfunded public schools for low-income families.

The Survey Says . . .

While the battle over funding continues, it's difficult to dispute the positive effects of preschool not only in better learning in kindergarten but also in long-term educational value. Furthermore, key research findings indicate that those who go through prekindergarten programs are more likely to graduate from high school and make higher wages as adults.

The research recited in support of preschool education usually comes from three long-term studies of low-income families. In the Abecedarian Project, launched in 1972 in rural North Carolina, 57 infants from low-income, African American, primarily single-mother families were randomly assigned to receive early intervention in a high-quality child-care setting; 54 children were assigned to a control group. Each child had an individualized prescription of educational activities, which consisted of "games" incorporated into the child's day and emphasized language skills. The child care and preschool were provided on a full-day, year-round basis.

Initially, all children tested comparably on mental and motor tests; however, as they moved through the child-care program, preschoolers had much higher scores on mental tests. Follow-up assessments completed at ages twelve, fifteen, and twenty-one showed that the preschoolers continued to have higher average scores on mental tests. More than one-third of the children who attended preschool went to a four-year college or university; only about 14 percent of the control group did.

Another important research effort was the High/Scope Perry Preschool study, which began in Ypsilanti, Michigan. From 1962 to 1967, 123 three- and four-year-olds—African American children born into poverty and at high risk of failing school—were randomly divided into one group that received a high-quality preschool program and a comparison group that received no preschool.

These children were evaluated every year, ages 3–11, and again three times during their teens and twice in adulthood. The latest results of this High/Scope study were released in 2004. By the time members of the preschool-provided group reached age forty, they had fewer criminal arrests, displayed higher levels of social functioning, and were more likely to have graduated from high school.

Meanwhile, Chicago's Child-Parent Centers (CPC) have been around for forty years, and more than 100,000 families have gone through the federally funded program, which still operates in twenty-four centers. Parents are drawn into the program with classes, activities, and their own resource room at each school site.

A longitudinal study by Arthur Reynolds, a researcher at the University of Wisconsin at Madison, looked at 1,539 Chicago students enrolled in CPCs in 1985 and 1986 and tracked their progress through 1999. He found they were much more likely to finish high school and less likely to be held back a grade, be placed in special education, or drop out than 389 youngsters who participated in alternative programs. Intervening early improves student achievement and has a cumulative effect: The longer students were in the CPC programs, the higher their level of school success.

Quantifying Quality

The National Institute for Early Education Research has compiled ten generally accepted benchmarks for what constitutes high-quality prekindergarten education. The list follows:

- Lead teacher has a bachelor's degree, or higher
- Teacher has specialized training in prekindergarten
- Teacher has at least fifteen in-service hours per year
- Assistant teacher has a child-development associate (CDA) degree, or equivalent
- Early-learning standards are comprehensive
- Maximum class size is twenty
- Staff/child ratio is one to ten, or lower
- Children are screened for vision, hearing, and health
- Meals are provided at least once a day
- Monitoring takes place through on-site visits

Unfortunately, almost half the states do not meet the degree benchmark for all lead teachers. Not one state meets all ten benchmarks.

Other shorter-term studies—and there are many—argue these kinds of benefits are not limited to at-risk children but extend to middle income kids as well. But when a family's budget is tight, preschool becomes unaffordable. Less than half of low-income toddlers attend preschool, but half of middle-class four-year-olds and three-quarters from high-income families (earning $75,000 or more) attend preschool.

That enrollment gap can have immediate academic consequences, say educators, who note that the lower the family income, the more pronounced the benefits of preschool. "I've worked with a lot of kids and know the achievement gap starts before kids are even in kindergarten," says Kimberly Oliver, a kindergarten teacher from Silver Springs, Maryland, and 2006 National Teacher of the Year.

Learning While Playing

Many educators appreciate the wide range of positive influences preschool seems to germinate. Debra King, a preschool teacher for thirty-five years, has run the Debra King School, in San Francisco, for nearly half that time. "There's been a big push lately to make preschoolers ready for academic learning, to teach children the alphabet and how to write their names," King says. "Many children are developmentally ready to learn these things, but I think socialization skills are more important. I believe that playing with blocks, dolls, and toys, scribbling with crayons, painting, communicating, storytelling, and music—that's readiness for school. There are a lot of different things to learn to be successful in the world."

That's an important insight. "The original preschool was a place for socialization, but, increasingly, today it has become necessary because of working and single parents," explains David Elkind, professor of child development at Tufts University and author of *The Hurried Child* and *The Power of Play*. "And that's muddied the waters, because people think it needs to be an educational thing. We got it turned around and are learning the academic things before we learn the social skills that are prerequisites for formal education."

Elkind believes phonics, math, and book reading are inappropriate for young children. "There is no research supporting the effectiveness of early academic training and a great deal of evidence that points against it," he says. "The age of six is called the age of reason because children actually develop those abilities to do *concrete* operations; brain research substantiates this. Take reading: A child needs to be at the age of reason to understand that one letter of the alphabet can sound different ways. That age might be four or it might be seven. They all get it; they just get it at different ages."

Elkind argues that toddlers need to learn only three things before entering kindergarten, and they're all socialization skills: listen to adults and follow instructions, complete simple tasks on their own, and work cooperatively with other children. "Children need to learn the language of things before they learn the language of words," he adds. "They are foreigners in a strange land, and they need to learn about the physical world, they need to explore colors, shape, and time, they need to find out about water and the sky and the stars, and they need to learn about human relations. Much of this learning comes from direct experience."

Sharon Bergen, senior vice president of Education and Training for the Knowledge Learning Corporation, counters that curriculum and fun are not mutually exclusive: "Children are capable of a lot of development earlier than we thought," she says. "But we don't want their time to be overly structured. We still want kids to have a good, fun, joyful childhood." With prekindergarten education, many people think, we can have it both ways.

MICHAEL LESTER is a writer and editor. He recently launched a site about fatherhood, *Dad Magazine Online,* at www.dadmagazineonline .com.

From *Edutopia,* June 2007, pp. 41–44. Copyright © 2007 by George Lucas Educational Foundation (GLEF). All Rights Reserved. www.edutopia.org

UNIT 2

Young Children, Their Families, and Communities

Unit Selections

8. **Class Matters—In and Out of School,** Jayne Boyd-Zaharias and Helen Pate-Bain
9. **Early Childhood School Success: Recognizing Families as Integral Partners,** Janet S. Arndt and Mary Ellen McGuire-Schwartz
10. **Meeting of the Minds,** Laura Pappano
11. **Making Long-Term Separations Easier for Children and Families,** Amy M. Kim and Julia Yeary
12. **Fast Times,** Deborah Swaney

Key Points to Consider

- How are social disadvantages and poverty related to low academic achievement of young children?

- What role do families play in ensuring their children have a successful school experience?

- How can teachers develop strong working relationships with parents of children in their class?

- What can teachers and school administrators do to help families dealing with long-term separations for a variety of reasons such as military service or job requirements?

- Reflect on the pressures you may see young girls and boys face as they deal with development in our age of media and fast-paced technology.

Student Website
www.mhhe.com/cls

Internet References

The AARP Grandparent Information Center
   http://www.aarp.org/grandparents
Administration for Children and Families
   http://www.dhhs.gov
All About Asthma
   http://pbskids.org/arthur/parentsteachers/lesson/health/#asthma
Allergy Kids
   http://allergykids.com
Changing the Scene on Nutrition
   http://www.fns.usda.gov/tn/Healthy/changing.html
Children, Youth and Families Education and Research Network
   www.cyfernet.org

The National Academy for Child Development
   http://www.nacd.org
National Network for Child Care
   www.nncc.org
National Safe Kids Campaign
   http://www.babycenter.com
Zero to Three
   http://www.zerotothree.org

Many of the articles read for possible inclusion in this edition focused on the effects of poverty on young children. There is increased attention to narrowing the achievement gap among minorities and children living in poverty. Some say the best way for children to achieve higher test scores is for teachers to teach better. Others say higher achievement among minorities and children living in poverty cannot be possible without attention to the living conditions and the support families receive. Jayne Boyd-Zaharias and Helen Pate-Bain discuss this most important issue in "Class Matters—In and Out of School." They focus on the needs of affordable housing and access to health care and early childhood education, along with improved instruction from teachers in class sizes that have proved to support education, especially for children in poverty. There is substantial research indicating that high-quality pre-kindergarten programs can help narrow the achievement gap. The research is so solid that thirty-nine states now provide publicly funded preschool education of some form that serves more than one million preschoolers.

One of the benefits of working with young children is having opportunities to interact with family members and to get to know what life is like at home for the children in our classes. The chance to interact with family diminishes as the learner gets older until it is almost nonexistent at the secondary level. Early childhood educators who recognize and fully embrace the rich contributions families can make as partners in the education process will benefit and so will the children. Janet S. Arndt and Mary Ellen McGuire-Schwartz in "Early Childhood School Success: Recognizing Families as Integral Partners" and Laura Pappano in "Meeting of the Minds" provide strategies for developing warm supportive relationships and then ways to build on those relationships to engage families. Transitioning from the traditional teacher-dominated conference to a two-way conference is just one example Pappano outlines. Sharing between the parents and teachers about the strengths and needs of the child becomes the path to student success.

As the United States continues to send soldiers on long deployments overseas, some for multiple tours of duty, there are ramifications for the over 700,000 children with a parent serving in the U.S. military. Educators are also finding that the challenging economic times mean families are separated for long periods of time while one parent works in a distant city just to have a secure job. Recognizing that the child may go through

© Getty Images/Digital Vision RF

various stages of separation is important for teachers to understand. Suggestions for teachers working with children living in a stressful family situation are included. Support from the teacher and consistent communication with family members can help to ease the separation anxiety that children face. Educators living in areas with a high number of military families will especially benefit from reading "Making Long-Term Separations Easier for Children and Families" by Amy M. Kim and Julia Yeary.

The unit ends with Deborah Swaney's look at "Fast Times." This articles is from *Parents* and is aimed at that group; however, early educators can also gain a great deal from understanding the pressures children of both sexes face. Teachers will want to develop stress-relieving strategies to implement in their classrooms. Involving children in physical activities is an excellent stress reliever mentioned in the article.

Families can provide a wealth of information about their child, and teachers who develop strong relationships with families are beneficiaries of this knowledge. Get to know the families of your children. Share a bit about yourself and your interests, and you may be rewarded with information from families about the children in your class. Build on this information to provide learning experiences that are relevant and meaningful to your children.

Class Matters—In and Out of School

Closing gaps requires attention to issues of race and poverty.

JAYNE BOYD-ZAHARIAS AND HELEN PATE-BAIN

Low achievement and high dropout rates among poor and minority students continue to plague U.S. society. And we say "plague" purposefully, because these children are all our children, and our nation will profit by or pay for whatever they become. While much attention over the past quarter century has focused on reforming the schools these students attend, little or no progress has been made in actually closing the achievement gaps or reducing the number of dropouts.

Why? Aren't Americans a "can-do" people? We eradicated the childhood scourge of polio, built the best road system since the Romans, put men on the moon, outlasted the Soviet Union, and created universities that are the envy of the world.

But the problem of underachievement by poor and minority students has confounded us. High-level commissions issue warnings, governors hold summits, think tanks produce reports, scholars write books, and Congress passes laws. But the U.S. has failed to deliver on its promise to provide a high-quality education to every child.

In the 1960s, Martin Luther King, Jr., forced our nation to face the inequities of race, poverty, and war. But today, these three inequities still exist in this country.

Rethinking the Problem

Surely schools need to be improved, especially the schools that serve poor and minority children. But school improvement alone will not suffice. We believe in the power of good teaching, but educators alone cannot do a job so large. We can inspire individual students to break through the boundaries of social class, but we cannot lift a whole social class of students to a higher level of achievement. Low achievement and dropping out are problems rooted in social and economic inequality—a force more powerful than curricula, teaching practices, standardized tests, or other school-related policies. Richard Rothstein summed it up best:

> For nearly half a century, the association of social and economic disadvantage with the student achievement gap has been well known to economists, sociologists, and educators. Most, however, have avoided the obvious implication of this understanding—raising the achievement of lower-class children requires amelioration of the social and economic conditions of their lives, not just school reform.[1]

Once acknowledged, this truth has profound implications for educators and policy makers alike.

If all efforts to close achievement gaps concentrate exclusively on schools and school reform, they will fail, leaving schools and teachers to shoulder the blame. In turn, good administrators and teachers, who are doing their best under difficult circumstances, will be driven *out* of the profession, a prospect that can only make matters worse. As Gary Orfield sums it up: "Doing educational reform while ignoring the fundamental cleavages in society is profoundly counterproductive."[2]

A useful way of visualizing the remedy for the chronic problem of low achievement of poor and minority students is to return to Abraham Maslow's 1954 hierarchy of needs for self-actualization. We have patterned a hierarchy of needs for a self-actualized society after Maslow's (see Figure 1).

Affordable Housing in Stable Neighborhoods

Nearly one-third of the nation's poorest children have attended three different schools by third grade. Such high mobility depresses achievement. One study found that reducing the mobility of low-income students to that of other students would eliminate 7% of the test-score gap by income and 14% of the

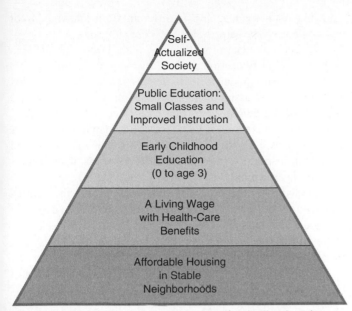

Figure 1 A hierarchy of needs for a self-actualized society.

black/white test score gap.[3] Other studies have shown that low-income families and children benefit when integrated into middle-class neighborhoods. This integration requires housing subsidies for poor families.[4]

After *Brown* v. *Board of Education,* "white flight" became common across the country. Middle-income white families moved to the suburbs, leaving only poor families in the inner cities. The challenge today is to integrate low- and middle-income families into stable neighborhoods. Margery Turner and Susan Popkin have identified several ways to afford this mix of income groups: 1) low-income housing tax credits, 2) housing choice vouchers, 3) HOPE VI (a public housing plan that has been successful in Seattle and Kansas City), 4) new communities, and 5) linking supportive services to affordable housing.[5] The most effective integrated communities will include:

- elected local committees to keep residents informed and active;
- public schools with small classes, teachers who make home visits, family resource centers with health-care services available to the community, active parent/teacher organizations, and after-school care and summer programs;
- support services: adult education, job training, and financial and budgeting classes.

A Living Wage with Health-Care Benefits

One in four American workers today earns poverty-level hourly wages. What's more, 33% of black and 39.3% of Hispanic workers earn poverty-level hourly wages.[6] These are appalling numbers, and they have a profound impact on poor and minority

children. Poverty, especially long-term, chronic poverty, takes a terrible toll on children's health and their readiness for school.

In 1968, 12.8% of America's children lived in poverty. In 2006, that proportion had risen to 17.4%—an increase of 1.2 million children.[7] Raising the minimum wage, protecting workers' rights to organize and join unions, and implementing living wage ordinances will certainly benefit poor children and families.

Early Childhood Education

There is no question that those poor and minority children who participate in prekindergarten programs are better prepared for school, especially in terms of letter/word recognition, pattern recognition, and ability to work with others. As Clive Belfield has noted, "Model pre-K programs show extremely powerful effects over the long term. There are significant reductions in special educational placement and grade retention. Pre-K participation reduces high school dropout rates dramatically."[8]

Arthur Rolnick and Rob Grunewald conclude that the case in favor of investing in early childhood education is closed. "Now," they continue, "it is time to design and implement a system that will help society realize on a large scale the extraordinary returns that high-quality early childhood programs have shown they can deliver."[9]

Today, we are indebted to researchers in education and to economists for providing us with proof that early childhood education saves money and children. By acting on their findings, we can improve the lives of the 13 million children living in poverty.

Public Education: Small Classes

Teachers have long known intuitively that small classes allow them to devote more attention to individual students. Hence, class size has been one of the most researched topics in education. But studies prior to Tennessee's Project STAR, with which we have both been intimately involved, were found to be inconclusive because of weak methodologies. STAR was independently reviewed by Frederick Mosteller of Harvard University, and he declared it to be "one of the most important educational investigations ever carried out and illustrates the kind and magnitude of research needed in the field of education to strengthen schools."[10]

Because of STAR's strong research design, there is widespread confidence in its major finding that small classes in K-3 provide extraordinary academic benefits to students, especially low-income and minority students. STAR is where intuition met empirical proof. And since STAR, other studies (SAGE, Success Starts Small, Burke County, etc.) have shown the positive impact of small classes in the primary grades.[11]

Small classes in the early grades also provide long-term positive outcomes. STAR students have been followed through high school and beyond. Research from follow-up studies indicates that students who entered small classes in kindergarten or first grade and had three or more consecutive years of small classes showed gains in academic achievement through at least eighth grade.[12]

Attending small classes in K-3 reduces the black/white gap in the rate at which students take college entrance exams by an estimated 60%

In addition, Alan Krueger and Diane Whitmore found that attending small classes in K-3 reduces the black/white gap in the rate at which students take college entrance exams by an estimated 60%. Their research also showed that attending small classes raised the average score on the exams by 0.15–0.20 of a standard deviation for black students and by 0.04 of a standard deviation for white students.[13]

But cost is the bottom line when education budgets are developed. When the value of reducing class size was first introduced, the initial response of policy makers was that it would cost too much. However, recent research provides evidence that small classes produce long-term savings.

Follow-up data from STAR have shown that criminal conviction rates were 20% lower for black males assigned to small classes than for those assigned to regular size classes. Maximum sentence rates were also 25% lower for black males from small classes. Teen birth rates were shown to be one-third less for white females assigned to small classes than for their peers assigned to regular size classes, and the fatherhood rate for black teenage males from small classes was 40% lower than for those from regular size classes.[14]

Small K-3 classes have been identified as a cost-effective educational intervention that reduces high school dropout rates. They are a wise investment.

> From a societal perspective (incorporating earnings and health outcomes), class-size reduction would generate a net cost savings of approximately $168,000 and a net gain of 1.7 quality-adjusted life-years for each high school graduate produced by small classes. When targeted to low-income students, the estimated savings would increase to $196,000 per additional graduate.[15]

Although research related to small classes in later grades is somewhat scarce, new findings suggest that class size reduction at the middle-school level will also provide substantial benefits to students.[16] More studies need to be conducted to determine the impact of class size reduction beyond the primary grades.

Public Education: Improved Instruction

Most school improvement efforts don't focus sufficiently on instruction. It is time that policy makers recognize that teaching, which is at the very core of education, involves complex tasks that require specialized skills and knowledge. It is not enough, for example, for a teacher of mathematics to know mathematics.

Knowing math for teaching is different from knowing it for one's own use. The same holds for other subjects.

"Teachers can't learn for students," notes Deborah Ball, dean of the School of Education at the University of Michigan.[17] No matter the instructional format—lecture, small-group activity, or individualized assignment—students make their own sense of what they're taught. Ideas don't fly directly from teachers' minds into learners' minds. Effective teaching requires teachers to be able to assess what students are taking from instruction and adapt their instruction to meet the differing needs of students.

There is an old but wise saying in teaching, "If my students can't learn the way I teach, then I must teach the way they learn." This requires teachers to ask probing questions, listen carefully to student answers, and create assignments to provide appropriate help. Moreover, teachers today must do all of this with an ever-increasing variety of students, spanning gulfs of social class, language, and culture, to ensure that each student learns.

Confronting Three Inconvenient Truths

To achieve a high quality education for every child, policy makers in Washington, D.C., and in state capitals must confront three inconvenient truths.

Inconvenient truth #1. Our nation's social class inequalities are vast and growing. If we are serious about providing equal educational opportunity for every child, we must address these inequalities. They are not immutable. Barack Obama has addressed such inequalities directly and vowed:

> This time we want to talk about the crumbling schools that are stealing the future of black children and white children and Asian children and Hispanic children and Native American children. This time we want to reject the cynicism that tells us that these kids can't learn; that those kids who don't look like us are somebody else's problem. The children of Americans are not those kids, they are our kids, and we will not let them fall behind in a 21st century economy.[18]

Inconvenient truth #2. Schools alone cannot close the achievement gap or solve the dropout problem. The renowned sociologist James Coleman has written, "Inequalities imposed on children by their home, neighborhood, and peer environment are carried along to become the inequalities with which they confront adult life at the end of school."[19]

According to Thomas Bellamy and John Goodlad:

> Collaborative decision making and collective actions depend on leaders who can cross boundaries within and among various groups involved in setting school priorities. The ability to frame issues in ways that support broad participation, bridge communication gaps across groups, and facilitate local deliberation is critical, but often missing. Consequently one important way to support local renewal is by identifying individuals who are attempting such cross-sector leadership, connecting them with one another, and offering learning experiences related to local challenges.[20]

Inconvenient truth number #3. It is going to cost a lot of money to ameliorate the achievement-depressing social and economic conditions of lower-class children's lives and to improve the public schools they attend. But the costs of allowing another generation of children from lower-income groups to grow up undereducated, unhealthy, and unconnected with our economy or society will be even greater.

A black boy born in 2001 has one chance in three of going to prison in his lifetime. A Hispanic boy born in the same year has one chance in six of going to prison in his lifetime.[21] Faced with such stunning indicators of things gone wrong, one can only conclude that a serious course of correction is in order.

Advocating for Transformational Change

Educators have a special insight into the damage that deprivation does to children's learning. We and the organizations that represent us must speak up and keep the policy makers on task. It won't be easy. They are pushed and pulled in many different directions, so that even the more sympathetic ones are easily distracted. We will have to stop being so defensive and go on the offense. We will have to be bold without being belligerent. The stakes are high, but we must be heard.

In the words of David Labaree, "In a democratic society, everyone is affected by what schools accomplish as they educate the majority of each generation's voters, jurors, and taxpayers. So all have reasons to stay involved in the public conversation about school quality."[22]

As advocates for equal opportunity, we must insist on transformational change. Incremental change that merely nibbles around the edges of long-term problems will fall woefully short—again. When a swimmer is drowning 50 feet offshore, it does no good to throw a 10-foot rope. Yet that is precisely what we do, year after year, when it comes to poor and minority children.

The federal government can start by living up to its promises. It promised to cover 40% of the cost of educating disadvantaged students under Title I of the Elementary and Secondary Education Act (ESEA), and it has never done so. Since 2002, for example, when ESEA became No Child Left Behind, the federal government has shortchanged states and school districts by $54.7 billion.[23] School districts and states need fewer mandates and more monetary support.

We need a self-actualized society. We need massive public investments in our children, in their schools, and in our future. It has been more than half a century since *Brown* v. *Board of Education,* but if Linda Brown were a girl today, we still could not guarantee her a high-quality education. It's time we heed the words of Dr. Martin Luther King, Jr., "Save us from that patience that makes us patient with anything less than freedom and justice."[24]

Notes

1. Richard Rothstein, *Class and Schools: Using Social, Economic, and Educational Reform to Close the Black-White Achievement Gap,* Washington, D.C.: Economic Policy Institute, 2004, p. 11.
2. Gary Orfield, "Race and Schools: The Need for Action," *Visiting Scholars Series,* Spring 2008, National Education Association, Washington, D.C., www.nea.org/achievement/orfield08.html
3. Eric A. Hanushek, John Kain, and Steven G. Rivkin, "Disruptions Versus Tiebout Improvement: The Costs and Benefits of Switching Schools," *Journal of Public Economics,* vol. 88, 2004, pp. 1721–46.
4. Rothstein, pp. 135–38.
5. Margery Austin Turner and Susan J. Popkin, "Affordable Housing in Healthy Neighborhoods: Critical Policy Challenges Facing the Greater New Orleans Region," statement before the Committee on Financial Services, U.S. House of Representatives, 6 February 2007.
6. *The State of Working America 2005–07,* Economic Policy Institute, Washington, D.C., www.epi.org/content.cfm/datazoneindex
7. "CDF Examines Progress Made Since Dr. King's Death," Children's Defense Fund, 25 January 2008, www.childrensdefense.org
8. Clive R. Belfield, "The Promise of Early Childhood Education Interventions," in Clive R. Belfield and Henry M. Levin, eds., *The Price We Pay: Economic and Social Consequences of Inadequate Education* (Washington, D.C.: Brookings Institution Press, 2007), p. 209.
9. Arthur J. Rolnick and Rob Grunewald, "Early Intervention on a Large Scale," Federal Reserve Bank of Minneapolis, 2007, http://woodrow.mpls.frb.fed.us/Research/studies/earlychild/earlyintervention.cfm
10. Frederick Mosteller, "The Tennessee Study of Class Size in the Early School Grades," *The Future of Children: Critical Issues for Children and Youths,* Summer/Fall 1995, p. 113.
11. Student Achievement Guarantee in Education (SAGE), www.weac.org/sage; C. M. Achilles, "Financing Class-Size Reduction," SERVE, University of North Carolina, Greensboro, ERIC ED 419 288; and C. M. Achilles, Patrick Harman, and Paula Egelson, "Using Research Results on Class Size to Improve Pupil Achievement Outcomes," *Research in the Schools,* Fall 1995, pp. 23–31.
12. Jeremy D. Finn et al., "The Enduring Effects of Small Classes," *Teachers College Record,* April 2001, pp. 145–83.
13. Alan B. Krueger and Diane M. Whitmore, "The Effect of Attending a Small Class in the Early Grades on College-Test Taking and Middle School Test Results: Evidence from Project STAR," *Economic Journal,* January 2001, pp. 1–28.
14. Alan B. Krueger and Diane M. Whitmore, "Would Smaller Classes Help Close the Black-White Achievement Gap?" in John E. Chubb and Tom Loveless, *Bridging the Achievement Gap* (Washington, D.C.: Brookings Institution Press, 2002).
15. Peter Muennig and Steven H. Woolf, "Health and Economic Benefits of Reducing the Number of Students per Classroom in U.S. Primary Schools," *American Journal of Public Health,* November 2007, www.ajph.org/cgi/content/abstract/97/11/2020
16. Christopher H. Tienken and C. M. Achilles, "Making Class Size Work in the Middle Grades," paper presented at the annual meeting of the American Educational Research Association, New York City, March 2008.
17. Deborah Loewenberg Ball, "Improving Mathematics Learning by All: A Problem of Instruction?" *Visiting Scholars Series,* Spring 2008, National Education Association, Washington, D.C., p. 5.

18. Remarks of Senator Barack Obama: "A More Perfect Union," Philadelphia, 18 March 2008, www.barackobama .com/2008/03/18/remarks_of_senator_ barack_obam_53.php

19. James S. Coleman et al., *Equal Educational Opportunity* (Washington, D.C.: United States Government Printing Office, 1966), p. 26.

20. G. Thomas Bellamy and John I. Goodlad, "Continuity and Change in the Pursuit of a Democratic Public Mission for Our Schools," *Phi Delta Kappan,* April 2008, p. 570.

21. "CDF Examines Progress Made Since Dr. King's Death."

22. David Labaree, quoted in Bellamy and Goodlad, p. 570.

23. "ESEA Title I-A Grants: Funding Promised in Law vs. Funding Actually Received, FY 2002–09, www.nea.org/lac/ funding/images/title1gap.pdf

24. Martin Luther King, quoted in Michael J. Freedman, "U.S. Marks 50th Anniversary of Montgomery Bus Boycott," International Information Programs, www .america.gov/st/diversity-english/2005/November/ 20080225140519liameruoy0.664715.html

JAYNE BOYD-ZAHARIAS began work on Project STAR in 1986 and was named director of Class Size Studies at Tennessee State University. She is currently executive director of Health & Education Research Operative Services, Inc. where she developed the National Class Size Database and continues her role as a co-principal investigator on STAR Follow-up Studies. **HELEN PATE-BAIN** was one of four original Project STAR principal investigators. She has been a classroom teacher, a professor of educational administration, and is a past president of the National Education Association. The authors wish to express their thanks to David Sheridan of the Human and Civil Rights Division of the National Education Association for his advice and input on this article.

From *Phi Delta Kappan,* by Jayne Boyd-Zaharias and Helen Pate-Bain, September 2008, pp. 40–44. Reprinted with permission of the authors and Phi Delta Kappa International, www.pdkintl.org, 2009. All rights reserved.

Early Childhood School Success
Recognizing Families as Integral Partners

JANET S. ARNDT AND MARY ELLEN MCGUIRE-SCHWARTZ

Much thought must go into preparing children for the transition from home or a child care environment to school. Transition experiences need to consider the whole child, including children's cognitive, socio-emotional, and physical readiness for learning. It is equally vital to explore ways to involve families, who are children's first and most important teachers.

Research highlights the importance of family involvement in children's school success (Epstein, Coates, Salinas, Saunders, & Simon, 1997; Ramey & Ramey, 1999; Snow, Burns, & Griffin, 1998). Most people would agree that families have the greatest knowledge of their children's strengths and challenges. When teachers are able to converse with families, they can collect detailed information about their incoming students so that they are better able to meet the children's needs.

Determining the best ways to involve families in the educational process from the beginning is vital.

A number of theories can influence the manner in which we work with families. For example, early childhood theorist Urie Bronfenbrenner (1979) believed that children should be viewed within the complex systems of their changing environments. Children's development, as well as family development, is shaped by the extended family, religious community, school, friends, organizations, government, and culture. The interaction of these various systems influences family identity. Thus, focusing on how to involve families in the transition to school and school readiness is crucial. And determining the best ways to involve families in the educational process from the beginning is vital. Because of the complexity of families, a comprehensive approach is needed.

Who Are the Families?

Communicating regularly with families helps teachers recognize the variety of backgrounds and experiences that shape families' perceptions of their children's development. As we focus on families, we must remember to listen and appreciate them as they are, not how we think they are or should be. Our intent should be to understand differences in people and improve communication in order to be heard. "To serve children well, we must work with their families. To be effective in this work, we must understand families who are diverse in ways such as culture, sexual orientation, economic status, work, religious beliefs, and composition" (Christian, 2007, p. 4). Family systems theory focuses on family behavior and includes interconnected members and their influences on one another (Christian, 2007). Family systems theory can help us to recognize and understand different parenting styles and family boundaries. It enables us to avoid stereotypes, recognize the different ways that families handle situations, and balance children's activities and curriculum. Family systems theory incorporates individual and group identity, and respects a family's need for control (Christian, 2007).

To build better relationships, both preservice and inservice educators need to understand the values espoused by each child's family. A variety of factors determine the way we approach and interact with families. First, one must consider the culture from which families come. People are often shaped by the times in which they live. Thus, families with adults in their 20s will most likely differ from those with adults in their 30s or 40s. Generational differences influence thinking about family life, balance of work and family, responsibilities, gender roles, lifestyle, culture, and outlook for the future (Rutherford, 2005). Rutherford provides some guidance about several recent generations that may prove useful in helping teachers understand families. Knowing the values and characteristics of the adults parenting the children can provide insight on how to engage them in their children's early school experience.

According to Rutherford, the younger end of the "Baby Boomers," who are in their 40s, may be first-time parents or may be acting as parents to their grandchildren. "Boomers" are often thought of as "workaholics," seeking to move up the career ladder. They value change, hard work, and success, and they often overcommit. Being process-oriented rather than product-oriented, "Boomers" may need reminders to keep them focused on desired outcomes. The Gen-Xers, born between 1965–1982, broadly speaking, value relationships over organizations. For them, the personal touch and immediate feedback are very important. This characteristic complements their spirit of informality, creativity, and desire for a balance of personal and professional lives. "Millennials," or parents who were born beginning in the 1980s, appreciate time spent with family (Howe & Strauss, 2000). They value involvement, have a positive outlook, and embrace technology. E-mail is their preferred way to communicate.

Families from all ethnic and racial groups benefit from early childhood educators who have an understanding of culturally appropriate practice. Cultural competence involves the ability to think, feel, and act in ways that acknowledge, respect, and build on ethnic, sociocultural, and linguistic diversity (Lynch & Hanson, 1998). Early childhood educators should take the time to thoroughly understand the hidden curriculum of each culture in order to connect with families.

As educators, we must understand how culture shapes children's development by recognizing cultural identities and differences in families that are shaped by everything from broad sociocultural influences to unique family influences (Hyun, 2007). Honing cross-cultural communication skills may support teachers' understanding of what each family wants for its children (Gonzalez-Mena, 2005). These communication skills include language, personal space, smiling, eye contact, touch, silence, and time concepts (Gonzalez-Mena, 2005).

Children may be members of homeless families; families headed by a single parent or by gay or lesbian parents; or blended families, adoptive families, foster families, or intergenerational families. Each family unit has issues unique to it. In order to engage families in participation, educators must willingly discern the families' strengths and needs, then communicate in ways that families are able to embrace. For example, findings from one survey done by a preschool director found that lesbian/gay parents "want the same as other parents—that [their] child be nurtured and stimulated to learn" (Clay, 2007, p. 24). These parents deemed important a school environment that supported emotional safety and diversity (e.g., regarding family structure, race and ethnicity, adopted children, and transracial families). Teachers who had experience working with gay- and lesbian-headed households thus were important to this family group (Clay, 2007). Important issues to some other families included adoption issues and ways of relating to other families.

Socioeconomic status is sometimes an overlooked issue when understanding families. Having an awareness of how socioeconomic status affects families can help educators be more responsive. Educators with such awareness will be better able to create and develop appropriate ways to engage these families. As educators teach growing numbers of children who live in poverty, they are challenged to think beyond traditional lines of race and ethnicity (Cuthrell, Ledford, & Stapleton, 2007). It is important to focus on the strengths of children and families, not the deficits, and to develop strategies around such strengths (Cuthrell et al., 2007).

Professionals must examine and determine the influences of their own backgrounds, cultures, attitudes, and experiences before they can understand the needs, experiences, and cultures of individual families. Educators must reflect on how cultural diversity or working with children who have special needs affects the teacher's roles and relationships. Early childhood educators need to ponder these questions thoughtfully to consider and overcome biases in all of these relationships. It is important for families and professionals to form equitable and collaborative partnerships that support and involve families in meaningful ways.

Why should educators invest the time and effort necessary to understand families? Alma Flor Ada (2003) shares the following rationale for why educators and families should work together: "Students live in two worlds: home and school. If these two worlds do not recognize, understand, and respect each other, students are put in a difficult predicament and very little learning can take place" (p. 11).

What Early Childhood Educators Do Best

Early childhood educators have strengths from which to draw when it comes to helping children enter school. Teachers can make connections with children by exploring their interests and engaging them in the classroom, using that information. Relationships based on trust and attachment help build warmth, understanding, and reflective listening. Appropriate nonverbal language, such as teachers communicating at eye level, is also important. Early childhood teachers should foster and encourage children's initiative, and work to extend children's cognitive, social-emotional, and language skills. Early childhood teachers generally handle with ease issues of social adjustment—the concern most parents have about a transition (Dockett & Perry, 2003). We also must recognize that "one size" does not "fit all" and so we must work to promote a variety of high-quality programs, such as Head Start, cooperative preschools, family child care, employer-supported child care, and center-based programs to meet the needs of all families.

What Early Childhood Educators Need to Learn

As Sarah Lawrence-Lightfoot writes, "There is no more complex and tender geography than the borderlands between families and schools" (2003, p. xi). Developing a working relationship with families is key for the early childhood educator. It is a skill that comes naturally for some teachers but is a struggle for others. Some teachers enjoy working with children, but lack confidence in building relationships with adults. Such relationship-building with parents is an area in which preservice teachers receive little training (Nieto, 2004).

The role of supporting and involving families and children is crucial for the early childhood educator. It is important that professionals welcome all families into programs by building mutual understanding and trust through daily communication, listening carefully to parents to understand their goals and preferences for their children, and being respectful of cultural and family differences in order to develop partnerships with parents (Bredekamp & Copple, 1997). We must continue to learn about the cultures in our classrooms by observing, asking questions, and being aware of any discomfort that we or our families may have, in order to develop awareness, tolerance, respect, and appreciation of differences and cultural diversity (Gonzalez-Mena, 2005).

A transition into school is a new beginning, and an opportune time for beginning a partnership, so make sure you have carefully thought out your approach. A partnership calls for teachers and families sharing information about children in order to provide consistency of early education and care. Educators need to reach out to children's prior schools or child care providers to learn about the children's experiences. Often, schools accept children while almost ignoring their prior experiences. Bronfenbrenner (1979) encourages a more global approach. A good example of this global approach may be found in a project undertaken in Massachusetts. The Massachusetts Department of Education, through a federal grant administered by Early Learning Services Program Unit and the Community Partnership for Children Program, provided grants for a summer initiative titled "Increasing the Capacity To Serve Young Children," which gathered child care providers, private and public preschool teachers, and administrators (Massachusetts Department of Education, 2003). The initiative focused on giving all individuals who work with children the same information on preschool standards and on ways to help children with special needs access the curriculum. Teachers from all types of programs learned from each other as well as from special educators. Sharing the preschool standards and ways to teach those standards gave all individuals who cared for and taught the community's children a better understanding of expectations and an opportunity for more equal educational experiences. Consequently, relationships between providers and public schools were strengthened. As the transition time neared, more communication occurred.

Families, children, and teachers are equal participants and must learn from one another during the process of separation and children's entry into early care and education (Balaban, 2006). Some specific activities may pave the way for transition into school for the families, children, and teachers, such as: inviting the family and child to the school, holding a meeting before school opens, providing families with a written description of what to expect as school begins, making home visits, and sending a letter to the child before school starts (Balaban, 2006). These steps may lead to a better understanding of the children and their families.

Teachers may provide support and information to families and children by discussing the entry process. It is important to listen to families and reflect on what is heard so that families know they are understood. Teachers should assure families that they will partner with them in their child's learning process. Supporting and communicating with families daily during the entry process is an effective way to begin that partnership (Balaban, 2006).

To develop a partnership with families, educators need to explore families' cultural backgrounds. One way to discover the information is to define the family and each family member's role. Identifying family traditions, child-rearing practices, and what is most important to them is also important. Recognize that different levels of family participation may be due to their backgrounds rather than their desire. Lack of participation also may be due to families' reduced understanding of how the education system works. Other issues, such as the inability to thoroughly understand the primary language being spoken in the classroom setting, may sometimes prevent involvement. Other factors that may thwart involvement include struggling with such concerns as providing food for their children, working two to three jobs, or managing all of the children's needs. Cultural differences may affect beliefs that influence the concept of teachers and parents being equal partners. In some cultures, educators are revered and families believe that whatever they say or do should be respected. For example, in some Asian cultures, making recommendations to educators seems disrespectful (Hyun & Fowler, 1995). By knowing families' needs and understanding their behaviors, educators can respond appropriately.

A Common Thread

It is interesting to note that research compiled by Henderson and Mapp (2002) shows certain commonalities among families, regardless of their race, ethnicity, income level, or educational background. All of the families surveyed want their children to do well academically. They aspire for their children to achieve a post-secondary degree, for example, and they want their children to regularly attend school. They also desire lower rates of high-risk behavior and increased social competence.

The goals for families are usually the same, but how families interpret those goals and act on them may look different. All families want their children to be successful. Research (Henderson & Mapp, 2002) supports this belief, which gives us the impetus to help families realize their goals. Because research (Souto-Manning & Swick, 2006; Tayler, 2006) also shows the importance of family involvement in that success, early childhood educators must move forward with ways of increasing that participation.

Keys to Engagement

It is important to begin early to make families feel welcome. Provide directions to classrooms or special event areas so that families will be able to navigate the school building. Having a "live person" answer the phone is more welcoming than a series of voice mail prompts requiring the caller to press numerous buttons in the hopes of getting a human being. Schools should invite families for pre-visits about a year before their children make the transition to the school. The visit could be for a brief story time (provide interpreters if necessary). Hold this event two or three times during the year. Remember that some parents are intimidated just by going into the school building. Have a community group sponsor a bus ride for the children, if this is how they will travel to school. Conducting home visits is another option. When parents understand that the purpose of these visits is for their children to meet their future teachers and help them feel more comfortable about their new school placement, parents will see the value of these efforts. Providing a welcome meal at the school and offering child care while adults talk is an alternative way to get parents into school before making

that transition. Outreach is important. Schools must shed the notion that families will come simply because the school asks.

When families feel cared for unconditionally, they will be responsive. When families are responsive, professionals have the opportunity to work with them and provide support. When families feel supported, they become involved and work with professionals for the success of their children.

References

Ada, A. F. (2003). *A magical encounter: Latino children's literature in the classroom.* Boston: Allyn & Bacon.

Balaban, N. (2006). *Everyday goodbyes: Starting school and early care.* New York: Teachers College Press.

Bredekamp, S., & Copple, C. (Eds.). (1997). *Developmentally appropriate practice in early childhood programs.* Washington, DC: National Association for the Education of Young Children.

Bronfenbrenner, U. (1979). *The ecology of human development: Experiments by nature and design.* Cambridge, MA: Harvard University Press.

Christian, L. G. (2007). *Understanding families: Applying family systems theory to early childhood practice. Spotlight on young children and families.* Washington, DC: National Association for the Education of Young Children.

Clay, J. W. (2007). *Creating safe places to learn for children of lesbian and gay parents. Spotlight on young children and families.* Washington, DC: National Association for the Education of Young Children.

Cuthrell, K., Ledford, C., & Stapleton, J. (2007). Empty tissues boxes: Considering poverty in diversity discourse. *Childhood Education, 83,* 273–276.

Dockett, S., & Perry, B. (2003). The transition to school: What's important? *Educational Leadership, 60(7),* 30–33.

Epstein, J., Coates, L., Salinas, K. C., Saunders, M. G., & Simon, B.S. (1997). *School, family, and community partnerships: Your handbook for action.* Thousand Oaks, CA: Corwin.

Gonzalez-Mena, J. (2005). *Diversity in early care and education.* New York: McGraw-Hill.

Henderson, A. T., & Mapp, K. (2002). *A new wave of evidence: The impact of school, family, community connections on school achievement.* Austin, TX: Southwest Educational Laboratory.

Howe, N., & Strauss, W. (2000). *Millennials rising: The next generation.* New York: Vintage.

Hyun, E. (2007). Cultural complexity in early childhood: Images of contemporary young children from a critical perspective. *Childhood Education, 83,* 261–266.

Hyun, J., & Fowler, S. A. (1995). Multicultural consideration in promoting parent participation in developing the IFSP. *Teaching Exceptional Children, 28*(1), 22–18.

Lawrence-Lightfoot, S. (2003). *The essential conversation: What parents and teachers can learn from each other.* New York: Ballantine Books.

Lynch, E., & Hanson, M. (1998). *Developing cross-cultural competency: A guide for working with young children and their families.* Baltimore: Brookes.

Massachusetts Department of Education. (2003). *Increasing the capacity to serve young children.* Fund Code 262-A/216-A. Malden, MA: Author.

Nieto, S. (2004). *Affirming diversity: A socio-political view of multicultural education* (4th ed.). New York: Pearson.

Ramey, C. T., & Ramey, S. L. (1999). Beginning school for children at risk. In R. C. Pianta & M. J. Cox (Eds.), *The transition to kindergarten* (pp. 217–252). Baltimore: Brookes.

Rutherford, P. (2005). *The 21st century mentor's handbook: Creating a culture for learning.* Alexandria, VA: Just ASK Publications.

Snow, C., Burns, S., & Griffin, P. (1998). *Preventing reading difficulties in young children.* Washington, DC: National Academies Press.

Souto-Manning, M., & Swick, K. J. (2006). Teachers' beliefs about parent and family involvement: Rethinking our family involvement paradigm. *Early Childhood Education Journal, 34*(2), 187–193.

Tayler, C. (2006). Challenging partnerships in Australian early childhood education. *Early Years, 26*(3), 249–265.

JANET S. ARNDT is Assistant Professor, Education Department, Gordon College, Wenham, Massachusetts. **MARY ELLEN MCGUIRE-SCHWARTZ** is Assistant Professor, Elementary Education, Rhode Island College, Providence.

Meeting of the Minds

The parent-teacher conference is the cornerstone of school-home relations. How can it work for all families?

LAURA PAPPANO

Agnes Jackson isn't proud to admit it, but last year she didn't attend a single parent-teacher conference for her youngest son, who just completed third grade at the Thomas O'Brien Academy of Science and Technology in Albany, New York.

It's not as if she didn't try. Jackson did respond when the school asked her to select a time for a face-to-face meeting. "They asked me what time could I be there and I told them, but they said, 'Oh, somebody already took that,'" says Jackson, a single mother of three who works nights as a certified nursing assistant. She made several impromptu visits to the school, whose website touts it as a "nationally recognized Blue Ribbon School of Excellence," but each time her son's teacher was unavailable. "They'd say, 'You need to wait until school is over,'" she recalls.

The parent-teacher conference may be the most critical, yet awkward, ritual in the school calendar. It is treated as a key barometer of parental involvement, so important that a Texas lawmaker earlier this year proposed fining parents $500 and charging them with a Class C misdemeanor for skipping one. New York City Mayor Michael R. Bloomberg wants to pay poor families up to $5,000 a year to meet goals, including attending parent-teacher conferences.

Yet, in practice, these conferences can be ill-defined encounters whose very high-pressure design—bringing together a child's two most powerful daily influences for sometimes super-brief meetings about academic and social progress—make them a volatile element in home-school relations. For schools, parent-teacher conferences can be a nightmare to organize and may leave teachers spinning after hours of quick encounters. For parents, sessions can feel more like speed-dating than team-building and may encourage snap judgments.

Surveys of K–8 parent involvement conducted by the National Center for Educational Statistics indicate that a majority of parents attended parent-teacher conferences in 2003. Yet, many are still absent. Those parents who might most need to show often don't or can't. The most involved can now, in a growing number of districts, access their child's homework, grades, and attendance online.

Given the weight that parents and teachers place on these once- or twice-a-year get-togethers, what can schools do to ensure that parent-teacher conferences are effective and productive—and meet the needs of all families?

The "Two-Way" Conference

Kathleen Hoover-Dempsey, associate professor and chair of the department of psychology and human development at Vanderbilt University, who studies home-school communication, says face-to-face conversations are more effective than written notes and e-mails, especially when the teacher has concerns or suggestions to make. For parents, "the heart just leaps a bit at the thought that something is wrong," she says. Conferences should include a chance for parents to share observations or concerns, specifics from the teacher about positive things a child is doing, and thoughts on how the teacher and parent might support a child's performance, Hoover-Dempsey says.

The conference is not for me to give you my judgment, but for us to share experiences and suggestions.

Many schools are rethinking conferences to make them less a complaint session and more a collaborative discussion, she says. "People are really starting to talk about the 'two-way parent-teacher conference' and the 'mutually respectful parent-teacher conference.' The conference is not for me to give you my judgment, but for us to share experiences and suggestions about things we can do to really support this child's education."

Collaborative conferences can be promoted by "bundling" them with other chances for parents and teachers to communicate, according to Karen Mapp, lecturer at the Harvard Graduate School of Education and a coauthor of *Beyond the Bake Sale: The Essential Guide to Family-School Partnerships.* Very effective schools may hold several face-to-face conferences each year, including some in which students present their schoolwork

Laying the Groundwork for Successful Parent-Teacher Conferences

To foster parent-teacher talk—formal or informal—Claire Crane, principal of the Robert L. Ford School in Lynn, Mass., has structured her school to get parents in the building as often as she can. Many are recent immigrants working two or three jobs, so she lures them to school by meeting *their* needs. School is open Monday and Tuesday until 9 P.M., when 250 parents attend English as a Second Language classes and a course on surviving in the U.S. Ford staff members teach the classes and provide babysitting and a chance to connect.

The school also operates like a community center. Parents perform in neighborhood talent shows, raise money, and plant trees to beautify the grounds. They have even volunteered alongside city health officials to try to halt a rat problem by putting out bait.

Crane says the intense level of involvement and communication enhances parent-teacher relationships and, in turn, both the formal and informal conferences that take place. So when it's time for formal parent-teacher conference nights three times a year, Crane says, "I can't handle the crowds."

As a result, when there are difficult conversations to have—and there are plenty in a school in which one-third of students attend summer school in order to be promoted—parents feel they are on the same team with the school.

"I feel so much confidence in the principal, I come and ask her, 'What can I do?'" says Beverly Ellis, a mother of five and Ford School parent for 22 years. Ellis, who has two children at the school now, recently had to speak with teachers when her daughter started throwing erasers in her sixth-grade class. "I like to hear they are doing good. But if things are not going right, you can talk to the teachers."

- In what ways is your child working up to his or her expectations?
- What things at school make your child happiest? Most upset?
- Think of a time when your child dealt with a difficult situation that made you very proud. What did you see as the strengths of your child in that situation?

Chrispeels, who trains teachers in conducting parent conferences, says such questions are important both for the information they provide teachers and because they position parents as partners in their child's schooling. The process also lets parents know that teachers realize children may be acting differently at school than at home.

Teachers should be prepared to show concrete examples of academic expectations, including student papers with names removed. "Teachers need to be able to explain to parents, 'Here is the range of work in this class,'" says Chrispeels. That way, she says, parents can have a better idea of what the teacher will be encouraging students to achieve in the future.

Chrispeels advocates ending conferences with what she calls a "one to grow on" message, to let parents know what the teacher intends to do to address any areas of weakness—and how the parent might help at home. Sometimes that can be as simple as explaining what skills they are working on in school and what resources are available to help students outside of school, like a before-school phonics help session.

Even parents of children who are doing well in school need reassurance that their child is developmentally, socially, and intellectually on track, says Chrispeels. Teachers also have experience and information to relay, for example, about planning high school course loads to meet graduation and college-entrance requirements. This helps parents anticipate a child's stresses and needs.

and share responses to questions they have pondered in advance, says Mapp, former deputy superintendent for family and community engagement for the Boston Public Schools. Others may be times for parents and teachers to meet solo and discuss an agenda agreed upon in advance. The key, says Mapp, is that the school community should shape how conference time is used.

Shifting Dynamics: A Larger Role for Parents

Building a two-way exchange, says Janet Chrispeels, professor of education studies at the University of California at San Diego, also requires shifting the dynamic of the conference from *reporting on* a child to *eliciting from* parents a better understanding of a child's strengths at home, in order to provide clues to helping them at school. Questions that might reveal these clues include:

- What homework habits does your child have that make you proud?

Facilitating Participation

More parent-teacher dialogue means schools must work harder to meet parents on their turf and tailor meetings to suit particular lifestyles and needs. Because their parent populations can vary significantly, school administrators are using different approaches to facilitate parent-teacher conferencing.

At Arlington (Mass.) High School, an upper-middle-class suburb of Boston where 72 percent of graduates go on to four-year colleges, parents can now sign up online for five-minute, face-to-face parent-teacher conferences. It's so popular that when administrators opened up the conference registration at midnight in the fall of 2004, 200 slots were booked in the first 10 minutes. Principal Charles Skidmore says online registration gives parents more choice and control and that, as a result, teachers are drawing more parents to conferences. "We are seeing some of the 'hard-to-reach' parents," Skidmore reports.

The situation is much different at the K–8 Robert L. Ford School in Lynn, Mass., where 90 percent of students are low-income and 58.5 percent speak English as a second language. Principal Claire Crane has created multiple ways for parents and teachers to talk, including holding parent-teacher conferences

Conference Dos and Don'ts

Some teachers dread parent-teacher conferences because no one has taught them what to do—or what not to do, says Todd Whitaker, professor of educational leadership at Indiana State University and author or coauthor of several books, including *Dealing with Difficult Parents.*

His advice for setting a positive tone and dealing with difficult parents:

- Hold the first parent-teacher conference early in the year, before children get into trouble or fall behind. Call parents in advance if there is a problem. Nothing in the conference should be a surprise.
- Sit next to the person. "We are on the same team," says Whitaker.
- Even if parents are angry, keep calm and treat them in a positive manner.
- Speak about "we" and not "you": "What can we do together so your son can be more successful?"
- Focus on the future. Do not treat conferences as a conclusion but as a step along a path.

as early as 7 A.M. and as late as 9 P.M. (see "Laying the Groundwork for Successful Parent-Teacher Conferences"). These conferences are sensitive to parents' needs. They are folded into family evenings that include displays of student work (no babysitters needed, and kids can show off learning). There is food. There are translators. The conferences are never held in the winter (easier for families with babies). Last year, Crane even held a conference in the street because a father with health problems couldn't easily get out of his car.

The formula appears to have worked. Crane, whose school has an attendance rate of 95.5 percent, had 92 percent of families come to an open house in November 2006 and attend parent-teacher conferences later that same night.

Other schools focus on welcoming parents during the school day. At Harriet Gibbons High School in Albany, New York, a new school serving ninth graders in a community in which 40 percent of students qualify for free or reduced-priced lunches, principal Anthony Clement built parent-teacher conference time into the daily school schedule. Team A teachers are available from 12:40 P.M. to 1:40 P.M., and Team B teachers are available from 10:30 A.M. to 11:30 A.M. If parents are not free during the conference hour, teachers will meet at other times, or—as in the case of the mother of a child in math teacher George Benson's class who must pack up three young kids and take two city buses to attend a conference—plan regular phone calls. School social workers will even make home visits. Noting that many of his parents work at jobs with hourly wages, Clement says, "We know when a parent is here, we need to see them."

As a result, Clement says, 80 percent of parents have attended one or two daytime parent-teacher conferences *in addition* to the two districtwide conferences held on two school days in November and January. Clement credits the emphasis on conferencing with increasing school attendance from 63 percent last year to 85 percent this year, more parent involvement in school activities, and a dramatic up-tick in ninth graders earning five or more of the required credits for promotion to tenth grade, from 45 percent last year to almost 70 percent this year.

The school's approach has also helped parents like Agnes Jackson get involved in her middle son's education. Where Jackson has yet to attend a conference at her third grader's school, she sat down more than a dozen times with her ninth-grade son's teachers at Harriet Gibbons—and that doesn't count scores of informal conversations about her son's school progress.

The frequent conferences have given Jackson a better handle on how the school system works and what is expected of her children. "In the past, I was quick to say, 'These people are doing this to my child,'" she says. "Now I ask, 'But what is my child doing that causes this to happen?' I can hear good and bad. But it's all good because I know how to respond to help my child. It helps me to say, 'OK, bud, you've got to do this,'" says Jackson. "It's helped me to grow as a single parent."

The easy access to teachers at Harriet Gibbons has also colored her views about her son's schools. Her third grader's school, she says, "will call if there is a problem," whereas the constant conversation with her ninth grader's teachers has made her more of a partner. "They tell me about his potential; they tell me what he is capable of doing," she says.

LAURA PAPPANO writes about education and is coauthor, with Eileen McDonagh, of *Playing with the Boys: Why Separate Is Not Equal in Sports,* to be published in November 2007 by Oxford University Press.

Making Long-Term Separations Easier for Children and Families

Jenny, a teacher of young toddlers, notices that 18-month-old Kyle is very emotional this week. He cries and clings to his mother each morning, and Jenny has to hold him for quite a while after his mom leaves. Jenny sees that Kyle is eating less than normal, but he will let her spoon-feed him his lunch. Kyle's mom mentions that he is acting this way at home too. Since he has no fever or other symptom of illness, Jenny wonders if Kyle's mood change has to do with his dad leaving three weeks ago for a military deployment. Jenny decides she'll talk with Kyle's mom about this, and to see how she's coping as a "single parent."

AMY M. KIM AND JULIA YEARY

Jenny is very observant and tuned in to Kyle's emotional development. Often adult caregivers minimize or do not recognize the effects of long-term separation on young children. This may be due to a child's limited ability to express his discomfort or insecurity, coupled with the caregiver's assumption that the child is too young to be aware of his or her circumstances. Caregivers may attribute children's challenging behaviors or the return to previous developmental stages (such as wetting the bed after completing toilet training) to something other than a grief reaction to the separation from their parent.

The issues military families face when parents deploy, especially to combat zones, are quite complex; each family's circumstances, challenges, and stressors are unique.

In this article, we explore the importance of early attachments, the effects of separation on infants, toddlers, and 3-year-olds, and ways teachers can support children and families during separations. As difficult as a separation might be for an individual child and family, there are strategies to help them cope with this potentially challenging experience. The issues military families face when parents deploy, especially to combat zones, are quite complex; each family's circumstances, challenges, and stressors are unique. But all caregivers and teachers can learn from the methods used by military families who are very familiar with frequent extended parent-child separations.

Early childhood educators can explore the strategies that professionals supporting military families use to foster stronger parent-child relationships and, as appropriate, implement them in their own settings.

The Importance of Early Attachments

John Bowlby (1988) describes *attachment* as a lasting psychological connectedness between human beings. For young children, secure attachment develops when they know with certainty that a primary caregiver will respond to their emotional needs, such as by providing comfort or a calming presence if they are distressed or frightened, as well as their physical needs. Early relationships are critical, and the responsiveness of a parent is crucial to a child's healthy development. The benefits of a healthy attachment relationship may include the reduction of fear in challenging situations, an increase in self-efficacy, and the ability to build on skills to better manage stress (Shonkoff & Phillips 2000). These benefits extend into adulthood, supporting healthy adult relationships, the ability to maintain employment, and the capacity to care for one's own children (Edelstein et al. 2004; Onunaku 2005).

When a Caregiver Leaves

Bowlby, in referencing his work with researcher John Robertson, states that the effect of separation is considerable for the youngest children, who still rely on caregivers to help them regulate their emotions (Lieberman et al. 2003). Research shows that children who experience a prolonged separation may exhibit anxiety, withdrawal, hyper-vigilance, eating disorders, and possibly anger and aggression (Parke & Clarke-Stewart 2001). Young children may also have trouble sleeping, become clingy or withdrawn, and regress (for example, have a lapse in toilet learning).

It is important to remember that separation is not just a one-time event, but rather something experienced before, during, and after a departure.

It is important to remember that separation is not just a one-time event, but rather something experienced before, during, and after a departure. Often, the effects of separation continue after the reunion. One teacher offers an example from her classroom:

> Three-year-old Bailey had previously experienced separation when her father was deployed to Iraq for six months. For the first couple of weeks after his return, she continually asked, "Who will pick me up today?" Bailey also had difficulty at nap times, often waking up, looking for a teacher, and then closing her eyes as soon as she spotted one. Later, teachers learned that Bailey was afraid that her father would leave again while she was at school, without her knowing.

Offering Parents Support Impacts Family Resiliency

By understanding what military families do to foster resiliency in their children, caregivers and teachers can provide better support and information to the families of young children experiencing a lengthy separation from a parent. There are numerous factors that predict the level of resiliency a family coping with long-term separations will show. However, military families who use active coping styles, receive social and community support, are optimistic and self-reliant, and give meaning to the separation are shown to function more effectively than those who don't (APA 2007).

An active coping style can be as simple as the family planning to have a neighbor watch the children one afternoon a week so the caregiver at home can run errands. A family that participates in a neighborhood play group or attends family activities at their church is receiving support from their community. A parent who believes that he or she can get through the separation and that there will be support if problems arise is self-reliant and optimistic. The military family who feels their service member is deployed to help others or to defend the country is giving meaning to the separation. Adopting these attitudes or following similar actions will foster resiliency in a family, a key to successfully meeting the challenge of separation.

Understanding the Emotional Cycle of Long-term Separation

Pincus and colleagues (2005) developed the Emotional Cycle of Deployment as a model to explain the emotional responses many military families experience during a deployment. While every family will not react to separation in exactly the same way, there are some predictable stages. This model can offer insights into the emotions nonmilitary families may experience when one parent leaves for an extended period of time.

The first stage begins when the family is notified of the deployment. During this stage, families enter a period of anticipatory grief. Though the separation hasn't yet taken place, the thought of the separation can begin the grieving process. Anticipatory grief has been defined as a feeling of loss before a dreaded event occurs (Hodgson 2005). Symptoms can include denial, mood swings, forgetfulness, disorganized and confused behavior, anger, depression, and feeling disconnected and alone. Physical symptoms such as weight loss or gain, sleep problems, nervous behavior, and general fatigue may also be present. At this stage, families are working to strengthen their bonds while letting go at the same time.

The second stage occurs when the individual leaves. During this phase, family members left at home may go through a period of grief or mourning. They may have periods of tearfulness and experience a change in their appetite and sleep patterns. These depression-like symptoms are typical, and they usually lessen after two to four weeks. In some cases, the remaining family members may experience relief at the departure of the military member. This also is a typical reaction, as families have dealt with many of their emotions prior to the departure and are ready to move to the next stage.

About a month after departure, the family typically settles into the third stage: a new family routine that usually lasts until just before the absent parent returns home. Adults and children typically do best if the newly established family routine is similar to what they did prior to separation. Families who take advantage of neighborhood and community support systems report fewer difficulties during a separation.

The fourth stage occurs about four to six weeks prior to reunion, when the family begins anticipating the return of the absent family member. For many families, this reunion stage is more stressful than the other stages (National Military Family Association 2005). Not knowing how each partner in the relationship has changed, how those changes will be accepted, and how children will accept the returning family member can raise many questions and anxieties.

Upon the return of the member who has been away, the family enters the fifth stage, when they must renegotiate the family roles and reestablish their relationships. This stage may begin with a happy, almost honeymoon-like period but can turn stressful quickly if family members do not recognize the need to communicate and work together. Professionals working with military families identify this stage as one of great concern. This time of disequilibrium may contribute to heightened risks for child or spouse abuse due to the increased stress.

Ongoing Communication

Communication is one of the primary concerns of military families coping with family separation (National Military Family Association 2005), and it is the most important aid in minimizing negative effects during every stage experienced during the separation. Communication is important not only between the adults, but also with children (in developmentally appropriate ways). Parents and teachers can help by offering children words for the emotions they might be experiencing. Providing the child with needed vocabulary and simple, factual information will help them begin to make sense of the situation and will make them feel like what they are experiencing is validated (Parke & Clarke-Stewart 2001).

Working to Stay Connected: Co-parenting Alliance

Families who cope successfully with frequent separations are likely to work together as partners in raising their children. Such parents are likely to communicate regularly, using letters, e-mail, or phone calls to discuss *all* aspects of raising their child. One mother shared as much information as possible, so the father, who was in Iraq, was able to ask their 3-year-old son specific questions about his child care friends and activities. Another father, who had been away for 17 months, found resuming his role as father in the home was a great deal easier because he knew about his children's daily routine and accomplishments while he was away.

Military parents demonstrate this co-parenting alliance by working hard to keep the child and absent parent connected. Rather than simply letting an absence take its course, they work to keep the absent parent in the child's mind through a variety of interactive means, and include that parent in all major decisions regarding the child. A teacher can support families experiencing separation. For example, after sharing that a couple's 19-month-old daughter was biting other children in the class and displaying aggressive behaviors, her teacher arranged for her father, in Korea on military assignment, to participate in the parent-teacher conference via Webcam so everyone could strategize together about how to help the toddler learn more appropriate ways to express her frustration and cope with her strong feelings.

For the Classroom

Teachers of young children play an important role in supporting the strong connections between families and children. The strength of these connections begins with the teacher being aware of the circumstances of the children in the classroom and their families.

Support the at-home parent. Simply taking a moment to ask a parent how he or she is doing will help strengthen connections between the parent, caregiver, and child. It is difficult to parent without the support of a second adult in the home.

> **Simply taking a moment to ask a parent how he or she is doing will help strengthen connections between the parent, caregiver, and child.**

It is important that program directors and teachers know of community resources that can provide needed services. Mental health and financial concerns are two issues that may surface when a parent is faced with the long-term absence of his or her partner. It is helpful to have information or resources to discreetly give to parents should the need arise. These positive interactions may encourage parents to reach out to other agencies for assistance.

Maintain a consistent program environment. Although some change is inevitable, try to keep the classroom setting as consistent as possible, including maintaining a predictable daily routine. You may want to reconsider the timing of moving a child to a new class. Provide opportunities for a child to feel more in control of daily activities to help her feel more secure. Be aware of children's need to make choices whenever possible. For example, ask a child if he would like juice or water with his meal, or ask which center he would like to play in first.

Be aware of stages of child development. Separation anxiety is a normal part of development for infants and toddlers. Having a parent leave for an extended period of time adds another layer to the challenge of learning to separate from a parent. Children experiencing long separations from their parent are best supported in an environment that honors their need to stay connected to their parent.

Include parent-child photos. Place pictures of family members at children's eye level to help them feel closer to their parents, no matter the length of a separation. Teachers can have parents help create special memory books with laminated pictures for toddlers and young preschoolers to carry with them in the classroom.

Use video or audio tapes. Invite children's parents to create tape recordings of themselves singing or reading to their children. These tapes can bring the absent parent into the classroom while he or she is away. Such recordings help a child stay in touch with the parent and soothe the child when he or she is missing that parent. If video equipment is available, parents can record themselves playing with or reading to their children. Parents can take the videos home to watch with their child. Teachers can set up special viewing centers in the classroom. These ideas are extremely helpful to the child with an absent parent, but also are helpful for all young children as they learn to separate from their primary caregivers.

Use transitional objects. Transitional objects may help a child cope with strong feelings about a parent's absence. Programs can encourage parents to send their child's favorite cuddly toy to help the child feel more secure. These transitional objects, along with the voice recordings from parents, can be especially soothing for the older infant or young toddler.

To create a special transitional object for a young child, take a T-shirt the parent has worn and make it into a pillow. One mother made a pillow out of her nightgown because her young twins liked to feel the soft fabric while they rested. The scent of the parent adds an additional layer of comfort. Some military parents spray the pillow with the cologne or aftershave the absent parent uses to invoke memories of the parent for the child. Older infants and toddlers may hold onto the pillow and snuggle into it when they are missing their parent. (Note: Infants should not sleep with pillows.)

Teachers can establish a special place in the classroom for quiet reflection. Children can keep their transitional objects in that area and use them as needed.

Reinforce parent-child connections. Books can be a wonderful resource to connect a child with a caring adult. Some titles frequently used to emphasize the parent-child connection are *The Kissing Hand,* by Audrey Penn, *Owl Babies,* by Martine Waddell, and *Are You My Mother?* by P.D. Eastman. After reading books such as these, children can do follow-up activities. For example, after reading *The Kissing Hand* teachers can have young children trace their hands and place a kiss in the center to give to a parent. To extend this activity to home, ask parents to trace their hands and place a kiss in the palm. They can send the hands in with their children. This activity may also be done by a parent who is away.

If possible, mail items directly to the absent parent; this helps the parent know you are remembering to include him or her in the collaborative team caring for the child.

Review communication strategies. Ask yourself, "How can I share information with parents who are away?" Consider incorporating technology such as e-mail or Webcams to allow for conferences. Have the child make two different creations during a project; one to take home and one for the parent who is away. Teachers can make two copies of classroom reports or communications, so one can be mailed to the absent parent. If possible, mail items directly to the absent parent; this helps the parent know you are remembering to include him or her in the collaborative team caring for the child.

For More Resources on Separation

Many parents want to learn more ways to support their child through a period of separation and how to keep parent-child connections strong. The ZERO TO THREE website (www.zerotothree.org) has information to support families of young children and the professionals who work with them. Information specific to helping families cope with parental separation can be found in the Military Families section, under Key Topics. Links to organizations that support military families, including counseling and resource information, can also be found there.

Conclusion

As a teacher or caregiver, you play a very important role in a young child's life while a parent is away. You serve as a valuable resource by supporting the parent at home and helping to foster the relationship between the away parent and the child. Incorporating a few strategies may help families to develop coping skills, build resiliency, and maintain important relationships crucial to the well-being of children and families.

References

APA (American Psychological Association). 2007. *The psychological needs of U.S. military service members and their families: A preliminary report.* www.apa.org/releases/MilitaryDeploymentTaskForceReport.pdf

Bowlby, J. 1988. *A secure base: Parent-child attachment and healthy human development.* New York: Basic Books.

Edelstein, R.S., K.W. Alexander, P.R. Shaver, J.M. Schaaf, J.A. Quas, G.S. Lovas, & G.S. Goodman. 2004. Adult attachment style and parental responsiveness during a stressful event. *Attachment and Human Development* 6(1): 31–52.

Hodgson, H. 2005. Anticipatory grief symptoms: What's the big deal? www.americanhospice.org/index.php?option=com_content&task=view&id=80&Itemid=13

Lieberman, A.F., N.C. Compton, P. Van Horn, & C.G. Ippen. 2003. *Losing a parent to death in the early years: Guidelines for the treatment of traumatic bereavement in infancy and early childhood.* Washington, DC: ZERO TO THREE Press.

National Military Family Association. 2005. *Report on the Cycles of Deployment Survey: An analysis of survey responses from April through September, 2005.* www.nmfa.org/site/DocServer/NMFACyclesofDeployment9.pdf?docID=5401

Onunaku, N. 2005. *Improving maternal and infant mental health: Focus on maternal depression.* Los Angeles, CA: National

Center for Infant and Early Childhood Health Policy at UCLA. www.healthychild.ucla.edu/Publications/Maternal%20Depression%20Report%20Final.pdf

Parke, R., & K.A. Clarke-Stewart. 2001. Effects of parental incarceration on young children. Presented at the National Policy Conference: From Prison to Home: The Effect of Incarceration and Reentry on Children, Families, and Communities, Washington, DC, January 2002. http://aspe.hhs.gov/HSP/prison2home02/parke&stewart.pdf

Pincus, S.H., R. House, J. Christenson, & L.E. Adler. 2005. *The emotional cycle of deployment: A military family perspective.* www.hooah4health.com/deployment/Familymatters/emotionalcycle.htm

Shonkoff, J., & D. Phillips, eds. 2000. *From neurons to neighborhoods: The science of early childhood development.* Washington, DC: National Academy Press.

Amy M. Kim, MEd, is a training and consultation specialist for military projects at ZERO TO THREE, the National Center for Infants, Toddlers, and Families. Amy works on material development and trainings for military professionals and families. akim@zerotothree.org **Julia Yeary,** LCSW, is a senior training and consultation specialist with military projects at ZERO TO THREE, the National Center for Infants, Toddlers, and Families. Julia has worked extensively with military families; she is also a military spouse and mother. jyeary@zerotothree.org

From *Young Children*, September 2008, pp. 32–36. Copyright © 2008 by National Association for the Education of Young Children. Reprinted by permission.

Fast Times

When did 7 become the new 16? For today's young girls, the pressure to look and act hot is greater than ever. Here's help cooling things down.

DEBORAH SWANEY

The job description for parent says you prep yourself for the dicey stuff kids are likely to ask for. So I was ready for the day my daughter would beg for a fashion doll of notoriously unrealistic proportions, or even for one of those skimpily dressed Bratz dolls. Instead, last fall my 7-year-old freaked me out a whole different way—by begging for a bra. "Two girls in my class have them," she argued.

Skeptical that she'd gotten her facts straight, I checked out a local children's store. Yikes! They had a whole assortment of flirty bras and panties perfectly sized for second-graders. Staring at those crazy underthings, and at the body-glitter tubes on the counter, something creepy dawned on me. Today's girls don't just want to *own* a hot-looking doll, they want to *be* one.

Maybe I shouldn't have been so shocked. After all, my daughter and her friends are more likely to worship teen heroes like Troy and Gabriella from the *High School Musical* movies than to expend energy adoring cuddly cartoon characters like the Care Bears. And these same kids are the ones shaking their little booties when the Pussycat Dolls come on the radio, singing, "Don'tcha wish your girlfriend was hot like me?"

Clearly, something's going on, so much so that the American Psychological Association (APA) recently convened a task force on girls' sexualization. "There's a real syndrome happening, and it's picking up speed," says Eileen L. Zurbriggen, PhD, who chaired the APA group. "Even little girls are now feeling they should look and act alluring." Her committee found that this is harmful to girls on several levels.

> **"The core issue is what girls feel valued for. It's as though factors like whether they're smart or kind or talented at something get erased."**
>
> —Eileen L. Zurbriggen

"The core issue is what they feel valued for," Zurbriggen explains. "It's as though factors like whether they're smart or funny or kind or talented at something like sports or art get erased." And their self-esteem suffers for it. "The images their idols present are so idealized, most girls can't attain them. That makes them feel bad about their own bodies, and this can eventually lead to anxiety and depression," Zurbriggen says. Preoccupation with their "hot-o-meter" score can even hurt their school performance. "A girl's mind becomes literally so full of worries about how she looks and what other people are thinking, she doesn't have enough energy left to focus on learning," says Zurbriggen.

How did things get that way, and what can parents do to counteract the situation? For answers, we have to look beyond the kiddie lingerie aisle.

Stay Tuned for Mature Content

The sexy-girl trend didn't start overnight. "I trace it to the mid-1980s, when children's television was deregulated, allowing TV shows to market products to kids," says Diane Levin, PhD, of Wheelock College in Boston and co-author of *So Sexy So Soon* (Ballantine Books). Companies noticed girls' love for ultra-feminine programs and their product tie-ins, and played it to the max. In the flush 1990s the media pushed harder, with the teen dial moving more toward sexy with sitcoms like *Saved by the Bell.*

Nowadays, "programs aimed at my daughter feature kids twice her age," complains Lisa Rinkus, of Newton, Massachusetts, mom of 9-year-old Elizabeth. "There's stuff like *Wizards of Waverly Place*, where girls dress up and go on dates." Even cartoons have become sexier. A recent study released by the Geena Davis Institute on Gender in Media found that female animated characters wear less clothing than male ones. And the current rash of reality TV shows like *America's Next Top Model* and *My Super Sweet 16* also fuel the fire.

The media onslaught extends to cyberspace as well, with an explosion of kids' interactive websites tied to TV shows like *iCarly* and *Hannah Montana.* "They push girls to further identify with these older, more mature girls," says Levin. And that's just the nice sites: One called "Miss Bimbo" gives girls a nearly naked doll to look after and urges them to score points redeemable for plastic surgery and skimpy clothes.

The Action behind the Scenes

Still, sex-tinged kids' TV has been around for a couple of decades. So why are girls today more precocious than just five years ago? Because a whole other pop culture avalanche has hit, experts say. For starters, we've got tons of teen idols now, including Miley Cyrus (the real-life Hannah Montana) and Demi Lovato, star of the Disney TV movie *Camp Rock.* "Even little kids look up to them," says M. Gigi Durham, author of *The Lolita Effect* (Overlook Press).

These teen stars and their characters may seem mild (say, compared with the Britneys, Lindsays and Jessicas in the headlines or even the adolescents on your block), but much of what they do and say is still over the top for tweens. "When younger girls watch them they see ways of behaving, looking, and feeling that would otherwise be outside their world," Levin says.

And now teen idols are also prime paparazzi fodder. As their personal slipups are relentlessly captured and widely publicized, even their littlest fan's consciousness is being raised in ways her parents hoped wouldn't happen for years. Donna Miller of Summit, New Jersey, faced this recently. Her daughter Lucie, 8, loves the show *Zoey 101,* whose star, Jamie Lynn Spears (Britney's sis), gave birth earlier this year at 17. "I tried to explain what was wrong with the whole situation," says Donna. "Lucie's answer was, 'But she and her boyfriend love each other, and you said love is important!' I think I communicated our family values about sex and babies in a way that didn't confuse Lucie. But she's so young. I'm not sure she understood all the nuances."

Parents are still the main influence on their daughters, but kids have got to be confused when bombarded with contradictory messages.

Certainly, fawning coverage of the birth didn't help clarify things for young fans. One tabloid cover featured a glowing picture of the teenage Spears cuddling with her daughter, calling motherhood "the best feeling in the world." Parents are still the main influence on their daughters, but kids have got to be confused when they're bombarded with contradictory messages.

Marketing Madness

If teen idols are a trap for young girls, it's partly because their princess obsession laid the groundwork. In 2007 sales of Disney princess products totaled $4 billion. "To parents, the princesses seem relatively wholesome," says Levin, "but they do convey the message that you should spend a lot of time, energy, and money on looking pretty." What's more insidious is the way girls use them. "Give a girl a princess-type doll and she often doesn't invent ways to play with it," says Levin. "Instead, she'll act out a fairy tale script, having learned that the princess should be beautiful and seductive and catch the prince." The more time a girl plays this way, the more she'll focus on looks and coquettish behavior, and the less time she'll spend doing the open-ended activities kids need. "It puts girls on a conveyor belt to early sexualization," Levin says.

And merchandizing linked to girls' idols doesn't stop with dolls. According to a report by the NPD Group, girls 8 to 12 years old now spend $500 million a year on beauty products of all kinds, including those endorsed by their idols. Then there are the flirty fashions. "Where are the age-appropriate clothes?" asks Marie Ortiz of San Antonio, mom of 8-year-old Karina. "Even the kids' fashions at mass retailers look like they're for mini Paris Hiltons." It's a coast-to-coast lament as mothers of girls shop among racks of child-size swimsuits with padded chests and slinky underwear for 8-year-olds.

Of course, when it comes to the 7-going-on-16 phenomenon, it's easy to point a finger of blame everywhere else, but we also have to take a hard look at ourselves. It's not that parents want to shirk being gatekeepers. "There's just so much sex around, it's easy to stop noticing and drawing the line," Durham explains. But we've got to try.

What's a Mom to Do?

Forget about overreacting. Sending your daughter to school in overalls, clutching your old prairie-skirted Holly Hobbie doll is like putting a giant "L" on her forehead and a "kick me" sign on her back. The idea is to help her live in the real world while preserving her innocence and honoring your family's morals. Try these tactics:

Cut back on the TV consumption. Her shows, your shows—just watch less. A 2005 Kaiser Family Foundation report found that the proportion of programs with sexual content rose from 54% to 70% between 1998 and 2005. And learn what the mysterious ratings at the start of kids' shows mean. Stuff tagged TV-Y or TV-G is the tamest. Other ratings require you to make a judgment call. You can get the scoop at fcc.gov/parents/parent_guide.html.

Teach your daughter how to think like a critic. When she does watch, try to join her. "That way when something questionable pops up, you can point it out," recommends

Where the Boys Are

While girls are getting trapped in a sexual pressure cooker, boys seem to steer clear of the worst of it. "I have 8-year-old boy-girl twins, and I see a huge difference," says Donna Miller of Summit, New Jersey. "My son doesn't feel the need to wear certain clothes like my daughter does." But there are some uncomfortable dynamics emerging. "I notice boys talking about girls being 'hot' earlier than they used to," says Richard Gallagher of the Parenting Institute of NYU. None of which, sadly, surprises him or other experts. "As girls are dressing provocatively at young ages, it's sparking the sexual inquisitiveness of younger boys," says Scott Haltzman, MD, a Brown University psychiatrist who specializes in gender issues.

Diane Levin, PhD, of Wheelock College, also sees negative sexual standards and messages in boys' toys and heroes. "The muscles on action toys have been getting bigger," she says. "It makes boys feel like they have to be rough instead of affectionate or tender. But those gentle qualities are what they'll need for developing good relationships in the future." Furthermore, says Gallagher, a sexually charged kids' culture can make it hard for a young boy to befriend a female classmate. "If he's afraid his buddies and the girl's friends are going to taunt them, saying, 'Ooh, what are you guys up to?' he often decides it's not worth it," he explains.

The solutions? They're not so different from what they are for girls. Tone down the sex-stereotype toys and be selective about what your sons watch on TV. "So many music videos show a guy surrounded by lots of girls, which sends boys the message that sexy equals cool," Haltzman says. And don't automatically assume your son would never hang out with a girl from his class. "At least suggest it and see what he says," advises Gallagher. It could help him like and respect girls as individuals.

Durham. Levin suggests regularly exposing the ridiculous or unrealistic sides of on-screen scenarios. For instance, you could try, "Don't you wonder how London gets her homework done when she spends so much time in front of the mirror?"

Monitor Web choices. Just because a website is linked to a TV show doesn't mean it's healthy or wholesome. Try bookmarking a few quality sites like pbskids.org or starfall.com, which are chockablock with fun learning games. "Be picky," says Maria Bailey, founder of bluesuitmom.com, an advice site for employed moms. "Thirty four percent of children will visit some kind of social networking or vitual-world website this year." One new option about to be launched is the Precious Girls Club social network, where girls can earn points for engaging in kind behavior (preciousgirlsclub.com).

Promote other kinds of idols. Show your daughter women she can admire for what they do, not for how they look, advises Richard Gallagher, PhD, director of the Parenting Institute at the Child Study Center of New York University. You could take her to a community musical and afterward meet the actress whose singing she loved. Or how about attending a local women's basketball game, where she can give the high-scorer postgame congratulations? And even if you aren't a fan of every female on the political scene, point out how cool it is that women are so prominent there.

Help her explore her talents and interests. Whether it's tennis or chess, being good at something gives girls confidence. "Sports especially are great," advises Levin. "They

help girls value their bodies for what they're able to do, not for how pretty they look."

"Sports especially are great. They help girls value their bodies for what they can do, not for how pretty they look."
—Diane Levin

Hold the line on makeup and glittery clothes. "It's not enough to just say no," warns Levin. "Your daughter will be exposed to these things anyway, and if you clamp down entirely, it'll only set the stage for her to rebel later on." Instead she suggests moderation. If your daughter begs for a cropped top, for instance, layer it over a longer tee or tank, or let her wear it only at home.

Mix up her peer group. Invite over a kid from another class in her grade, or sign her up for an activity that isn't school-based (such as karate or art). Spending time with other kids, other ideas, other ways of doing things widens a girl's world and reduces the pressure on her to follow the crowd.

Guide the gift-giving. Tell grandparents and other relatives that you're trying to hold back on the sexy stuff, says Levin. Ideally, they'll shop more sensitively.

Personally, I'm taking all of this advice and using it with my daughter. I've been questioning what we're seeing on her favorite TV shows, as well as her fervent desire, sympathetic though I may feel, to emulate her fashion-forward classmates right down to their underwear.

And in case you're wondering whether I got her that bra, I'll admit I thought about it. But then I said no. "That's for when you're older," I told her. Then I took her to our community rec department and signed her up for our town's soccer league. Five weeks later I stood at the edge of a field, screaming like crazy as she scored her very first goal.

That, not a bra, is the kind of support young girls really need.

Reprinted with permission from *Family Circle Magazine,* November 29, 2008, pp. 44, 46, 48, 50, 55. Copyright © 2008 by Meredith Corporation. All rights reserved.

UNIT 3

Diverse Learners

Unit Selections

13. **Whose Problem Is Poverty?,** Richard Rothstein
14. **How to Support Bilingualism in Early Childhood,** M. Victoria Rodríguez
15. **Learning in an Inclusive Community,** Mara Sapon-Shevin
16. **Young Children with Autism Spectrum Disorder: Strategies That Work,** Clarissa Willis
17. **Including Children with Disabilities in Early Childhood Education Programs: Individualizing Developmentally Appropriate Practices,** John Filler and Yaoying Xu

Key Points to Consider

- What are some strategies that teachers can use to assist English language learners and their families?

- Describe some of the ways in which teachers can include children with disabilities in their classroom.

- What are successful strategies teachers can use to assist children with autism spectrum disorders in their classroom?

- Why is differentiating the learning environment so important when working with children with disabilities?

Student Website

www.mhhe.com/cls

Internet References

American Academy of Pediatrics
   www.aap.org

Child Welfare League of America (CWLA)
   http://www.cwla.org

Classroom Connect
   http://www.classroom.com/login/home.jhtml

The Council for Exceptional Children
   http://www.cec.sped.org/index.html

Early Learning Standards: Full Report
   http://www.naeyc.org/positionstatements/learning_standards

Early Learning Standards: Executive Summary
   http://www.naeyc.org/resources/position_statements/creating_conditions.asp

Make Your Own Web Page
   http://www.teacherweb.com

National Resource Center for Health and Safety in Child Care
   http://nrc.uchsc.edu

Online Innovation Institute
   http://oii.org

This unit focuses on the many diverse learners who are in our early childhood programs and schools. It starts with a continuation of the issue of poverty that was prominent in the previous unit on working with families. "Whose Problem Is Poverty?" by Richard Rothstein explores the need for collaboration between families, educators, and community members to counteract the effects of poverty. This issue is so important that I have included it in more than one unit so that students can revisit the issue and build on discussions as they read the various articles included in this edition.

Another issue with deep implications for the early childhood profession is how we care for and educate children in inclusive environments. Nationwide, college and university programs are adapting to new standards from the National Association for the Education of Young Children (NAEYC) that require programs educating teachers at two- and four-year institutions to include much more on working with special needs children, especially children with disabilities. As teacher preparation institutions adapt to meet the new standards, there will be more teachers out in the field better equipped to meet the needs of special needs children and their families. The new NAEYC standards are all-encompassing in their focus on the diversity and richness in the children and families we serve.

Early childhood educators who are knowledgeable and comfortable working with children and families who come from a variety of cultures, speak world languages, or have a disability will be most successful in meeting the learning needs of the children. In Mara Sapon Shevin's "Learning in an Inclusive Community," the reader will find ten strategies for creating positive, inclusive classrooms to meet the needs of all children. Preservice teachers need many experiences in settings serving diverse learners. This can be challenging for teacher-preparation institutions located in communities lacking diversity. Education students with limited experience traveling to other areas or interacting with children and families who are different from themselves must supplement their own experiences to be successful teachers who are able to meet the needs of all children and families. Assess your prior experiences with children and families and see if you need to volunteer or work in settings different from your past work to better equip yourself with skills needed to work with all families and children. We all tend to gravitate to familiar and comfortable experiences, but a good teacher stretches himor herself to become familiar with the life experiences children in

© Purestock/Getty Images RF

his or her class bring to the learning environment. Spend some time with a family who has a child with a disability. Get to know the stresses that child as well as the parents and other siblings may deal with on a day-to-day basis. If you own a car and many of your families depend on public transportation, take the bus one day to more fully understand the frustrations that can come from depending on a fixed schedule. In short, really get to know the many different life experiences the families you work with face in their daily lives.

In "Young Children with Autism Spectrum Disorder: Strategies That Work" Clarissa Willis helps teachers to recognize some of the characteristics of autism spectrum disorder. As more and more children are receiving this diagnosis, approximately one in every 150, teachers are feeling unprepared to best meet the learning needs of children with autism. The author provides suggestions for teachers to implement in their classrooms.

There are more and more examples of teachers adjusting their image of diverse learners. Only when all educators are accepting of the wide diversity that exists in family structures and among individual children will all children feel welcomed and comfortable to learn at school. The collaboration of families, the community, and school personnel will enable children to benefit from the partnership these three groups bring to the educational setting. The articles in this unit represent many diverse families and children and the issues surrounding young children today.

Whose Problem Is Poverty?

It's no cop-out to acknowledge the effects of socioeconomic disparities on student learning. Rather, it's a vital step to closing the achievement gap.

RICHARD ROTHSTEIN

In my work, I've repeatedly stressed this logical claim: If you send two groups of students to equally high-quality schools, the group with greater socioeconomic disadvantage will necessarily have lower *average* achievement than the more fortunate group.[1]

Why is this so? Because low-income children often have no health insurance and therefore no routine preventive medical and dental care, leading to more school absences as a result of illness. Children in low-income families are more prone to asthma, resulting in more sleeplessness, irritability, and lack of exercise. They experience lower birth weight as well as more lead poisoning and iron-deficiency anemia, each of which leads to diminished cognitive ability and more behavior problems. Their families frequently fall behind in rent and move, so children switch schools more often, losing continuity of instruction.

Poor children are, in general, not read to aloud as often or exposed to complex language and large vocabularies. Their parents have low-wage jobs and are more frequently laid off, causing family stress and more arbitrary discipline. The neighborhoods through which these children walk to school and in which they play have more crime and drugs and fewer adult role models with professional careers. Such children are more often in single-parent families and so get less adult attention. They have fewer cross-country trips, visits to museums and zoos, music or dance lessons, and organized sports leagues to develop their ambition, cultural awareness, and self-confidence.

Each of these disadvantages makes only a small contribution to the achievement gap, but cumulatively, they explain a lot.

I've also noted that no matter how serious their problems, all disadvantaged students can expect to have higher achievement in better schools than in worse ones. And even in the same schools, natural human variability ensures a distribution of achievement in every group. Some high-achieving disadvantaged students always outperform typical middle class students, and some low-achieving middle class students fall behind typical disadvantaged students. The achievement gap is a difference in the *average* achievement of students from disadvantaged and middle class families.

I've drawn a policy conclusion from these observations: Closing or substantially narrowing achievement gaps requires combining school improvement with reforms that narrow the vast socioeconomic inequalities in the United States. Without such a combination, demands (like those of No Child Left Behind) that schools fully close achievement gaps not only will remain unfulfilled, but also will cause us to foolishly and unfairly condemn our schools and teachers.

Closing achievement gaps requires combining school improvement with reforms that narrow the vast socioeconomic inequalities in the United States.

Distorting Disadvantage

Most educators understand how socioeconomic disadvantage lowers average achievement. However, some have resisted this logic, throwing up a variety of defenses. Some find in my explanations the implication that disadvantaged children have a genetic disability, that poor and minority children can't learn. They say that a perspective that highlights the socioeconomic causes of low achievement "blames the victim" and legitimizes racism. Some find my analysis dangerous because it "makes excuses" for poor instruction or because demands for social and economic reform "let schools off the hook" for raising student achievement. And others say it's too difficult to address non-school problems like inadequate incomes, health, or housing, so we should only work on school reform. The way some of these critics see it, those of us who call attention to such non-school issues must want to wait until Utopian economic change (or "socialism") becomes a reality before we begin to improve schools.

Some critics cite schools that enroll disadvantaged students but still get high standardized test scores as proof that greater socioeconomic equality is not essential for closing achievement gaps—because good schools have shown they can do it on their own. And some critics are so single-mindedly committed to a schools-only approach that they can't believe anyone could seriously advocate pursuing *both* school and socioeconomic improvement simultaneously.

Seeing through "No Excuses"

The commonplace "no excuses" ideology implies that educators—were they to realize that their efforts alone were insufficient to raise student achievement—would be too simple-minded then to bring themselves to exert their full effort. The ideology presumes that policymakers with an Olympian perspective can trick teachers into performing at a higher level by making them believe that unrealistically high degrees of success are within reach.

There's a lack of moral, political, and intellectual integrity in this suppression of awareness of how social and economic disadvantage lowers achievement. Our first obligation should be to analyze social problems accurately; only then can we design effective solutions. Presenting a deliberately flawed version of reality, fearing that the truth will lead to excuses, is not only corrupt but also self-defeating.

Mythology cannot, in the long run, inspire better instruction. Teachers see for themselves how poor health or family economic stress impedes students' learning. Teachers may nowadays be intimidated from acknowledging these realities aloud and may, in groupthink obedience, repeat the mantra that "all children can learn." But nobody is fooled. Teachers still know that although all children can learn, some learn less well because of poorer health or less-secure homes. Suppressing such truths leads only to teacher cynicism and disillusion. Talented teachers abandon the profession, willing to shoulder responsibility for their own instructional competence but not for failures beyond their control.

Mythology also prevents educators from properly diagnosing educational failure where it exists. If we expect all disadvantaged students to succeed at levels typical of affluent students, then even the best inner-city teachers seem like failures. If we pretend that achievement gaps are entirely within teachers' control, with claims to the contrary only "excuses," how can we distinguish better from worse classroom practice?

Who's Getting Off the Hook?

Promoters of the myth that schools alone can overcome social and economic causes of low achievement assert that claims to the contrary let schools "off the hook." But their myth itself lets political and corporate officials off a hook. We absolve these leaders from responsibility for narrowing the pervasive inequalities of American society by asserting that good schools alone can overcome these inequalities. Forget about health care gaps, racial segregation, inadequate housing, or income insecurity. If, after successful school reform, all adolescents regardless of background could leave high school fully prepared to earn middle class incomes, there would, indeed, be little reason for concern about contemporary inequality. Opportunities of children from all races and ethnic groups, and of rich and poor, would equalize in the next generation solely as a result of improved schooling. This absurd conclusion follows from the "no excuses" approach.

Some critics urge that educators should not acknowledge socioeconomic disadvantage because their unique responsibility is to improve classroom practices, which they *can* control. According to such reasoning, we should leave to health, housing, and labor experts the challenge of worrying about inequalities in their respective fields. Yet we are all citizens in this democracy, and educators have a special and unique insight into the damage that deprivation does to children's learning potential.

If educators who face this unfortunate state of affairs daily don't speak up about it, who will? Educators and their professional organizations should insist to every politician who will listen (and to those who will not) that social and economic reforms are needed to create an environment in which the most effective teaching can take place.

And yes, we should also call on housing, health, and anti-poverty advocates to take a broader view that integrates school improvement into their advocacy of greater economic and social equality. Instead, however, critical voices for reform have been silenced, told they should stick to their knitting, fearing an accusation that denouncing inequality is tantamount to "making excuses."

What We Can Do

It's a canard that educators advocating socioeconomic reforms wish to postpone school improvement until we have created an impractical economic Utopia. Another canard is the idea that it's impractical to narrow socioeconomic inequalities, so school reform is the only reasonable lever. Modest social and economic reforms, well within our political reach, could have a palpable effect on student achievement. For example, we could

- Ensure good pediatric and dental care for all students, in school-based clinics.
- Expand existing low-income housing subsidy programs to reduce families' involuntary mobility.
- Provide higher-quality early childhood care so that low-income children are not parked before televisions while their parents are working.
- Increase the earned income tax credit, the minimum wage, and collective bargaining rights so that families of low-wage workers are less stressed.
- Promote mixed-income housing development in suburbs and in gentrifying cities to give more low-income students the benefits of integrated educations in neighborhood schools.
- Fund after-school programs so that inner-city children spend fewer nonschool hours in dangerous environments and, instead, develop their cultural, artistic, organizational, and athletic potential.

None of this is Utopian. All is worth doing in itself, with the added benefit of sending children to school more ready to learn. Educators who are unafraid to advocate such policies will finally call the hand of those politicians and business leaders who claim that universal health care is too expensive but simultaneously demand school reform so thcy can posture as defenders of minority children.

In some schools, disadvantaged students are effectively tracked by race, denied the most qualified teachers and the best curriculum. Failure is both expected and accepted. Unfortunately, some educators do use socioeconomic disadvantage as an excuse for failing to teach well under adverse conditions. But we exaggerate the frequency of this excuse. Some teachers excuse poor practice, but others work terribly hard to develop disadvantaged students' talents. Where incompetence does exist, we should insist that school administrators root it out.

But consider this: The National Assessment of Educational Progress (NAEP), administered to a national student sample by the federal government, is generally considered the most reliable measure of U.S. students' achievement. Since 1990, the achievement gap between minority and white students has barely changed, feeding accusations that educators simply ignore the needs of minority youth. Yet average math scores of black 4th graders in 2007 were higher than those of white 4th graders in 1990 (National Center for Education Statistics, 2007, p. 10). If white achievement had been stagnant, the gap would have fully closed. There were also big math gains for black 8th graders (National Center for Education Statistics, 2007, p. 26). The gap stagnated only because white students also gained.

In reading, scores have remained flat. Perhaps this is because math achievement is a more direct result of school instruction, whereas reading ability also reflects students' home literacy environment. Nonetheless, the dramatic gains in math do not suggest that most teachers of disadvantaged students are sitting around making excuses for failing to teach. Quite the contrary.

Reticent about Race

It is puzzling that some find racism implied in explanations of why disadvantaged students typically achieve at lower levels. But to understand that children who've been up at night, wheezing from untreated asthma, will be less attentive in school is not to blame those children for their lower scores. It is to explain that we can enhance those students' capacity to learn with policies that reduce the epidemic incidence of asthma in low-income communities—by enforcing prohibitions on the use of high-sulfur heating oil, for example, or requiring urban buses to substitute natural gas for diesel fuel—or provide pediatric care, including treatment for asthma symptoms. Denying the impact of poor health on learning leads to blaming teachers for circumstances completely beyond their control.

Denying the impact of poor health on learning leads to blaming teachers for circumstances completely beyond their control.

The fact that such conditions affect blacks more than whites reflects racism in the United States. Calling attention to such conditions is not racist. But ignoring them, insisting that they have no effect if teaching is competent, may be.

Some critics lump my analyses of social and economic obstacles with others' claims that "black culture" explains low achievement. Like other overly simplistic explanations of academic failure, cultural explanations can easily be exaggerated. There is, indeed, an apparent black-white test score gap, even when allegedly poor black and white students are compared with one another or even when middle class black and white students are compared with one another. But these deceptively large gaps mostly stem from too-broad definitions of "poor" and "middle class." Typically, low-income white students are compared with blacks who are much poorer, and middle class black students are compared with whites who are much more affluent. If we restricted comparisons to socioeconomically similar students, the residual test-score gap would mostly disappear (see Phillips, Grouse, & Ralph, 1998).

But probably not all of it. Responsible reformers are seeking to help low-income black parents improve child-rearing practices. Others attempt to reduce the influence of gang role models on black adolescents or to raise the status of academic success in black communities. Generally, these reformers are black; white experts avoid such discussions, fearing accusations of racism.

This is too bad. If we're afraid to discuss openly the small contribution that cultural factors make to achievement gaps, we suggest, falsely, that we're hiding something much bigger.

Dancing around the Issue

I am often asked to respond to claims that some schools with disadvantaged students have higher achievement, allegedly proving that schools alone *can* close achievement gaps. Certainly, some schools are superior and should be imitated. But no schools serving disadvantaged students have demonstrated consistent and sustained improvement that closes—not just narrows—achievement gaps. Claims to the contrary are often fraudulent, sometimes based on low-income schools whose parents are unusually well educated; whose admissions policies accept only the most talented disadvantaged students; or whose students, although eligible for subsidized lunches, come from stable working-class and not poor communities.

Some claims are based on schools that concentrate on passing standardized basic skills tests to the exclusion of teaching critical thinking, reasoning, the arts, social studies, or science, or of teaching the "whole child," as middle class schools are more wont to do. Increasingly, such claims are based on high proportions of students scoring above state proficiency standards, defined at a low level. Certainly, if we define proficiency down, we can more easily reduce achievement gaps without addressing social or economic inequality. But responsible analysts have always defined closing the achievement gap as achieving similar score distributions and average scale scores among subgroups. Even No Child Left Behind proclaims a goal of proficiency at "challenging" levels for each subgroup. Only achieving such goals will lead to more equal opportunity for all students in the United States.

Beyond Either/Or

Nobody should be forced to choose between advocating for better schools or speaking out for greater social and economic equality. Both are essential. Each depends on the other. Educators cannot be effective if they make excuses for poor student performance. But they will have little chance for success unless they also join with advocates of social and economic reform to improve the conditions from which children come to school.

Note

1. For further discussion of this issue, see my book *Class and Schools: Using Social, Economic, and Educational Reform to Close the Black-White Achievement Gap* (Economic Policy Institute, 2004) and "The Achievement Gap: A Broader Picture" (*Educational Leadership,* November 2004).

References

National Center for Education Statistics. (2007). *The nation's report card: Mathematics 2007.* Washington, DC: Author. Available: http://nces.ed.gov/nationsreportcard/pdf/main2007/2007494.pdf

Phillips, M., Grouse, J., & Ralph, J. (1998). Does the black-white test score gap widen after children enter school? In C. Jencks & M. Phillips (Eds.), *The black-white test score gap* (pp. 229–272). Washington, DC: Brookings Institution Press.

RICHARD ROTHSTEIN is Research Associate at the Economic Policy Institute; riroth@epi.org

Author's note—For documentation of the specific critiques referenced in this article, readers can contact me at riroth@epi.org

How to Support Bilingualism in Early Childhood

M. Victoria Rodríguez

Increasingly, children come to early childhood centers with the experience of listening and speaking a language other than English at home. Many families, including those who speak only English at home, express strong interest in raising their children to be bilingual.

The reasons vary. They want their children to communicate with parents and other members of the family who do not speak English, or they want to maintain the family's heritage language and culture. They believe bilingualism is valuable for future employment purposes. Finally, they want their children to have the cognitive, academic, and social advantages of being bilingual (King and Mackey 2007).

While few people question the benefits of being bilingual, there are different opinions about the best ways of becoming bilingual. The purpose of this article is two-fold: 1) to suggest ways in which early childhood centers can support the parents' dream of bilingualism for their children; and 2) to give classroom support not only to English language learning but also to the maintenance of the child's native language.

From the Parents' Viewpoint

To decide how to achieve bilingualism for their children, parents may consider several factors. They may decide based on what the family's linguistic characteristics are, what they consider is the best way to provide the support their children need to learn both languages, and what the family thinks is the best way to learn English (Rodríguez 2006).

Families that spoke a language different from English at home in the past, but speak only English now, often look for early childhood centers and schools that offer bilingual programs in a specific language and English. Families that currently speak a language other than English at home may also choose to send their children to early childhood centers that provide bilingual services in the family's native language as well as English.

However, bilingual early childhood centers are not always available in the family's native language or located near their homes. Also, bilingual centers—even if they are available—are usually not affordable for most families.

In any case, bilingual programs, even when available and affordable, are often not the first choice of parents. Here are some reasons:

- Parents that express a strong interest in making sure their children speak the family's native language and English firmly believe that, as long as they speak the native language with their children at home, their children will be fluent in that language.
- Bilingualism for these families is more about being able to speak the native language than about mastering reading and writing in that language.
- Most parents are eager for their children to learn English, the language that guarantees academic and occupational success. These parents may feel, as do many people, including teachers, that the best time to learn a second language is when a child is young. Children are like sponges and quickly absorb the second language, in this case English.

This feeling, combined with the belief that the more you expose children to English, the faster they master the language (Espinosa 2006; Genesee 2006; McLaughlin 1992), lead parents to assume that the right choice is to send their children to preschools in which they are exposed only to English. They don't see the need for sending their children to bilingual programs that are often featured in the media as places where children speak their native language to the detriment of learning English.

Addressing the Linguistic Diversity of Your Center

The National Association for the Education of Young Children (NAEYC 1995), in the position statement on "Responding to Linguistic and Cultural Diversity," discussed the challenges that young children and their families face in negotiating the transition from home to early childhood center.

Often preschools have different rules, values, and expectations from the home and require different behaviors from the children. For many children another obstacle is communicating for the first time in their young lives only in English, a language different from the home language and one they associate mainly with the cartoons and shows they watch on television.

Respect and value the home culture.

To help children navigate the transition to a preschool and to promote children's development and learning, the position paper established that "educators must **accept** the legitimacy of children's home language, **respect** (hold in high regard) and **value** (esteem, appreciate) the home culture, and **promote** and **encourage** the active involvement and support of all families, including extended and nontraditional family units" (NAEYC 1995, p. 2 [bold in text]).

Promote and encourage the active involvement and support of all families.

This is a statement that all educators would consider in line with developmentally appropriate practice. But what does it really mean? How do we show children and parents that "we accept the legitimacy of the child's home language"?

Accept the legitimacy of children's home language.

Supporting the Parents' Dream

Attaining the goal of bilingualism is a difficult task, regardless of the programs available and the early childhood program parents choose for their child. However, many parents are not aware of the challenges their children face, especially in maintaining their native language.

Early childhood centers have an important role to play in promoting not only English but also the native language. Ideally this starts when the parents enroll the child in the program and continues without interruption in individual and group conversations between parents and teachers until the child leaves the center.

At the intake stage, consider these suggestions:

- Get information about the language(s) used at home, including who uses which language(s), and for what purposes.
- Ask for the family's goals for the child, including language(s) they want the child to acquire. This is a prime moment to start an ongoing conversation about language development, bilingualism, and second language acquisition. The child's teacher will continue the conversation based on the child's needs, but it would be a good idea to have materials available in several languages for the parents to read about these issues.

- Prepare the center's philosophy about language, if it is not available, and share it with the family. This includes, but is not limited to, informing the family about the languages spoken in the center by children and personnel, the reasons the center offers or does not offer bilingual programs, and the center's commitment to supporting minority languages.
- Have staff available that are knowledgeable about bilingualism and second language acquisition.

This cannot be done without ongoing and in-depth professional development that includes administrators, teachers, and aides. Based on my conversations with parents and early childhood teachers, I suggest asking the following questions as you prepare for addressing the needs of the linguistically diverse children as well as children whose parents want them to be bilingual.

What Are the Staff's Attitudes toward Language Diversity?

Teachers who firmly believe that children should learn English as soon as possible, without considering the minority language the child speaks, may have difficulty thinking positively about the child's native language and, therefore, accepting the minority languages in the classroom. They may also find it hard to accept and support the parents' wish of bilingualism for the child.

How Do we Help Staff Understand Important Issues Related to Bilingualism?

Training needs to cover at least six issues:

1. a definition of bilingualism and its advantages;
2. misconceptions about a) the best time to acquire two languages, b) time required to become bilingual, c) effects of maintaining the native language on the acquisition of English, and d) impact of birth order in becoming bilingual;
3. different programs available to develop bilingualism;
4. theories of second language acquisition;
5. effects of native language loss on the socio-emotional, academic, and cognitive development of the child and on the well-being of the family; and
6. challenges families encounter when raising children bilingually.

How Do We Inform Parents about Issues of Bilingualism When They Are Set on Beliefs That Are Not Supported by Research?

Parents need to know what the research says about roles played by the individual characteristics of the child, birth order, gender, and the linguistic characteristics of the family in maintaining the minority language (De Houwer 1999; King and Fogle 2006; McLaughlin 1995).

Children's Language Experiences

The acceptance of the minority language of all children needs to be consistent throughout the child's experience in the early childhood center. This is clearly revealed in the child's classroom experience and in the ongoing conversation between parents and the school personnel, especially the teacher.

The suggestions below, many of which are from NAEYC's position statement, need to be explained to parents who often are concerned only about the child's acquisition of English.

On the child's language experiences:

- Show parents and children that your agenda is not to teach the children English while completely disregarding the child's native language.

     This may seem challenging when staff do not speak all the minority languages represented in the school. Actually, it is not. Teachers and children may show interest in learning important words that the children are eager to teach. This is an easy and meaningful way of showing that everybody in the classroom values the children's family language, that all acknowledge a child's expertise in that language, and that all are interested in a child's language.

- Support the children's native language by asking everybody (director, teachers, aides, and support personnel) to speak with the children in the minority language(s) in which they are fluent.

     Often the staff speak at least some of the minority languages represented, but they use the minority language only when they have to talk to non-English-speaking parents or when translating for other staff. When staff speak minority language(s), children become aware that important people in the school also speak the native language and thus have the opportunity to feel proud of it.

- Invite parents to share lullabies, songs, poetry, dances, books, games, toys, and the values they want to transmit to their children.

- Provide materials in the classroom in the languages represented by the children.

- When more than one child in the classroom speaks a minority language, invite them to work together in challenging activities using that language.

For ongoing conversations with parents, plan how you will deal with the following topics:

- The emotional and social cost of losing the native language for the child and the family alike (Chang et al. 2007; Wong Fillmore 1991).

- Ways to support the native language at home. For example, encourage parents, older siblings, and extended family members to teach their children lullabies, songs, and dances in the native language if they don't do it already. Suggest that the parents involve the children in fun community activities in which languages other than English are spoken. Children need to see the utility of the languages they speak.

- The many different ways young children learn languages and the different paces at which they learn them.

- The challenges of bilingualism. Although bilingualism is a valuable goal for children that the school supports, learning two languages takes time and is a complicated enterprise for children and adults alike.

- Maintenance of the native language. In a society in which bilingualism is not fully valued and where the majority language (English) enjoys worldwide prestige, we need to support the first language. Children will learn English because it is around them and it is the "cool" language to speak, but many forget or feel ashamed of the native language unless it is valued by important people in their lives, including their teachers, friends, parents, and grandparents.

- The need for providing input at home in the native language. Often parents who speak in the native language at home think their children get much more input in that language than they really receive.

In fact, let's consider a child who is in a monolingual English preschool for seven to eight hours a day. Then the child may return to a home in which older siblings talk to each other more in English than the native language and the children spend time watching TV in English.

The child in our example listens to and is encouraged to express thoughts and feelings in English much more often than in the native language. Your conversation with the parents probably will lead them to focusing on the native language, the weakest language in our society, and, contrary to popular belief, the one that needs more support.

A Responsibility and an Opportunity

Early childhood centers, regardless of the programs they offer, have the responsibility of responding adequately to the linguistic needs of children who, at home, listen and speak in a language other than English. In addition, centers can encourage and support families whose goal is bilingual education for their children.

Professional development, using topics suggested here, will guide the meaningful and ongoing conversations that families, teachers, and staff initiate at the intake stage and continue all during the child's experience in the center.

References

Chang, F., G. Grawford, D. Early, D. Bryant, C. Howes, M. Burchinal, O. Barbarin, R. Clifford, and R. Pianta. 2007. Spanish-speaking children's social and language development in pre-kindergarten classrooms. *Early Education and Development*, 18 (2): 243–269.

De Houwer, A. 1999. Two or more languages in early childhood: Some general points and practical recommendations. Center for Applied Linguistics. Digest. www.cal.org/resources/digest/early-child.html

Espinosa, L. 2006. Challenging common myths about young English language learners. Foundation for Child Development Policy Brief # 8. Advancing Pre-K-3rd. www.fcd-us.org/usrdoc/MythsOfTeachingELLsEspinosa.pdf

Genesee, F. 2006. Bilingual acquisition. www.ColorinColorado.org/article/12916

King, K. and L. Fogle. 2006. Raising bilingual children: Common parental concerns and current research. Center for Applied Linguistics. Digest. www.cal.org/resources/digest/RaiseBilingChild.html

King, Kendall and Alison Mackey. 2007. The Bilingual Edge. *Why, When, and How to Teach Your Child a Second Language.* New York: HarperCollins.

McLaughlin, B. 1992. Myths and misconceptions about second language learning: What every teacher needs to unlearn. National Center for Research on Cultural Diversity and Second Language Learning. www.ncela.gwu.edu/pubs/ncrcdsll/epr5.htm

McLaughlin, B. 1995. Fostering second language development in young children. National Center for Research on Cultural Diversity and Second Language Learning. www.cal.org/resources/digest/ncrcds04.html

National Association for the Education of Young Children. 1995. Responding to Linguistic and Cultural Diversity: Recommendations for Effective Early Childhood Education. www.naeyc.org

Rodríguez, M.V. 2006. Language and literacy practices in Dominican families in New York City. *Early Child Development and Care,* 176 (2): 171–182.

Wong Fillmore, L. 1991. When learning a second language means losing the first. *Early Childhood Research Quarterly,* 6: 323–346.

M. VICTORIA RODRÍGUEZ, EdD, is an associate professor in the Departments of Early Childhood and Childhood Education as well as Counseling, Literacy, Leadership, and Special Education at Lehman College, the City University of New York. She has worked for 20 years as a preschool and special education teacher in urban settings in Madrid and Barcelona in Spain and in New York City and as a college instructor in New York and Spain.

From *Texas Child Care Quarterly,* Winter 2008, pp. 24–29. Copyright © 2008 by Texas Child Care Quarterly. Reprinted by permission.

Learning in an Inclusive Community

Inclusive classrooms create students who are comfortable with differences, skilled at confronting challenging issues, and aware of their interconnectedness.

MARA SAPON-SHEVIN

Schools are increasingly acknowledging the heterogeneity of their student populations and the need to respond thoughtfully and responsibly to differences in the classroom. It's understandable that educators often feel overwhelmed by growing demands for inclusion, multi-cultural education, multiple intelligences, and differentiated instruction to deal with the growing diversity.

But what if including all students and attending thoughtfully to diversity were part of the solution rather than part of the task overload? What if we put community building and the emotional climate of the classroom back at the center of our organizing values? What if we realized that only inclusive classrooms can fully support the goal of creating thoughtful, engaged citizens for our democratic society?

Redefining the Inclusive Classroom

After years of struggle about the politics and practice of inclusion and multicultural education, it's time we understand that inclusive, diverse classrooms are here to stay. But inclusion is not about disability, and it's not only about schools. Inclusion is about creating a society in which all children and their families feel welcomed and valued.

Inclusion is about creating a society in which all children and their families feel welcomed and valued.

In truly inclusive classrooms, teachers acknowledge the myriad ways in which students differ from one another (class, gender, ethnicity, family background, sexual orientation, language, abilities, size, religion, and so on); value this diversity; and design and implement productive, sensitive responses. Defining inclusion in this way requires us to redefine other classroom practices. For example, *access* can mean, Is there a ramp? But it can also mean, Will letters home to parents be written in a language they can understand?

Differentiated instruction can mean allowing a non-reader to listen to a book on tape. But it can also mean organizing the language arts curriculum using principles of universal design, assuming and planning for diversity from the beginning rather than retrofitting accommodations after the initial design.

Positive behavior management can be a system of providing support to students with diagnosed emotional problems. But it can also mean ongoing community building, classroom meetings, cooperative games, and a culture of appreciation and celebration for all students.

What does it mean to think inclusively, and how can this framework enhance the learning of all children? There are many lessons that inclusive education settings can teach us. Here are just a few.

Comfort with Diversity

In our increasingly diverse world, all people need to be comfortable with diversity. Inclusion benefits all students by helping them understand and appreciate that the world is big, that people are different, and that we can work together to find solutions that work for everyone.

Inclusion teaches us to think about *we* rather than *I*—not to ask, Will there be anything for me to eat? but rather to wonder, How can we make sure there's a snack for everyone? Not, Will I have friends? but rather, How can I be aware of the children here who don't have anyone to play with? When we are surrounded by people who are different from us, we are forced to ask questions that go beyond the individual and address the community. When we have friends who use wheel-chairs, we notice that there are steep stairs and no ramps. When we have friends who wear hearing aids, we listen differently to comments like "What are you, deaf or something?" When we have friends with different skin colors, we become more alert to racist and exclusionary comments. When we have friends from different religious backgrounds, we are more aware that the decorations in the mall are about only one religion.

Inclusion teaches us to think about *we* rather than *I*.

In the absence of diversity, it's hard to learn to be comfortable with difference. The white college-age students I teach are often confounded about how to talk about people of color: "Is the right term *African American* or *black?* What if the person is from Jamaica or Haiti? How do I describe people?" Similarly, many adults are nervous about interacting with people with disabilities, unsure whether they should offer help or refrain, mention the person's disability or not.

The only way to gain fluency, comfort, and ease is through genuine relationships in which we learn how to talk to and about people whom we perceive as different, often learning that many of our initial assumptions or judgments were, in fact, erroneous. The goal is not to make differences invisible ("I don't see color"; "It's such a good inclusive classroom, you can't tell who the kids with disabilities are") but to develop the language and skill to negotiate diversity. Classrooms cannot feel safe to anyone if discussions of difference are avoided, discouraged, or considered inappropriate.

I am always delighted, and a bit stunned, when I see young people easily negotiating conversations about difference that would have been impossible a decade ago and that are still out of reach for many of us. I recently witnessed a discussion of different kinds of families during which children from ages 5 to 8 spoke of adoption, same-sex parents, known and unknown donors, and the many ways they had come to be members of their family.

These students, growing up in an inclusive, diverse community, will not need a book that says, "There are many kinds of families." That understanding is already part of their lived experience.

As a teacher, you can successfully facilitate discussions like this by doing the following:

- Familiarize yourself with the current terminology and debates about what people are called: Do Puerto Ricans call themselves *Latino?* Why is the term *hearing impaired* preferred by some but not all "deaf" people? If there are disagreements about terms—for example, some people prefer the term *Native American* and *some Indian*—find out what that conversation is about. Model appropriate language when discussing differences in the classroom.

- Provide multiple opportunities for talking about diversity. When a news story is about a hurricane in Haiti, pull down the map: Where is that country? What languages do the people there speak? Do we have anyone at our school from Haiti?

- If you hear teasing or inappropriate language being used to discuss differences, don't respond punitively ("I don't ever want to hear that word again!"), but don't let it go. As soon as possible, engage students in a discussion of the power of their language and their assumptions. Teach students the words *stereotype, prejudice,* and *discrimination* and encourage them to identify examples when they see them. "On the commercial on TV last night, I noticed that all the people they identified as 'beautiful' were white."

Inclusion is not a favor we do for students with disabilities, any more than a commitment to multicultural education benefits only students of color. Inclusion is a gift we give ourselves: the gift of understanding, the gift of knowing that we are all members of the human race and that joy comes in building genuine relationships with a wide range of other people.

Honesty about Hard Topics

Inclusion not only makes students better educated about individual differences, but also provides a place to learn about challenging topics. In inclusive classrooms, teachers and students learn to talk about the uncomfortable and the painful.

Often, as adults, we don't know what to do when we are confronted by people and situations that frighten, surprise, or confound us. Children, through their eagerness to engage with the world and seek answers to their questions, can learn important repertoires of communication and interaction in inclusive settings: How can I find out why Michelle wears that scarf on her head without hurting her feelings? How can I play with Jasper if he doesn't talk? Learning how to ask questions respectfully and how to listen well to the answers are skills that will provide a smoother entry into the complexities of adulthood.

In one school, a young boy who required tube feeding provided the opportunity for all the students to learn not only about the digestive system but also about ways to help people while preserving their dignity and autonomy. In another school, a child whose religion kept him from celebrating birthdays and holidays gave other students the opportunity to not only learn about different religions but also brainstorm ways of keeping Jonah a valued and supported member of the classroom. And when a young Muslim child was harassed on the way home from school in the months after the attack on the World Trade Center, the whole class was able to engage in an important discussion of racism and being allies to those experiencing prejudice and oppression.

A student in one classroom was dying of cancer. The teachers, rather than excluding the student and avoiding the subsequent questions, helped all the other students stay informed and involved in his life (and eventually, in his death). With close communication with parents, the teachers talked to students about what was happening to Trevor and how they could support him: "Of course we would miss you if you died." "Yes, it's very, very sad." "No, it's not fair for a 6-year-old to die; it doesn't happen very often." On days when Trevor was in school and feeling weak, the students took turns reading to him. On days when he was not able to come to school, they wrote him notes and made cards. When he died, many of them went to the funeral. Tears were welcomed and tissues were widely used; the teachers were able to show their sadness as well. Teachers had to be thoughtful about discussions of religious beliefs in order to be inclusive: "Yes, some people believe in heaven, and they think that's where Trevor is going."

Although no parents would want their children to have to deal with the death of a classmate, the sensitivity and tenderness of the experience helped bond the class and enabled students to connect to both the fragility and the sacredness of life. When they experience death again later in their lives, they will have some understanding of what it means to offer and receive support and will be able to seek the information and caring they need for their own journeys.

Ten Strategies for Creating a Positive, Inclusive Classroom

1. Make time for community building throughout the year. Time spent building community is never wasted.
2. Proactively teach positive social skills: how to make friends, how to give compliments, what to do if someone teases you or hurts your feelings. Don't wait for negative things to happen.
3. Be explicit in explaining to your students why treating one another well and building a community is important. Use key terms: *community, inclusion, friends, support, caring, kindness.* Don't let those words become empty slogans; give lots of examples of positive behaviors.
4. Adopt a zero-indifference policy. Don't ignore bullying in the hope that it will go away. Don't punish the participants, but be clear about what is acceptable. Say, "I don't want that word used in my classroom. It hurts people's feelings and it's not kind."
5. Share your own learning around issues of diversity and inclusion. When students see that you are also learning (and struggling), they can share their own journeys more easily. Tell them, "You know, when I was growing up, there were some words I heard and used that I don't use anymore, and here's why." "You know, sometimes I'm still a little uncomfortable when I see people with significant physical differences, but here's what I've been learning."
6. Think about what messages you're communicating about community and differences in everything you do, including the books you read to your students, the songs you sing, what you put on the walls, and how you talk about different families and world events.
7. Seize teachable moments for social justice. When students say, "That's so gay," talk about the power of words to hurt people and where such oppressive language can lead. When a student makes fun of another student, talk about different cultures, norms, and experiences.
8. Provide lots of opportunities for students to work together, and teach them how to help one another. End activities with appreciation circles: "What's something you did well today?" "How did Carlos help you today?"
9. Don't set students up to compete with one another. Create an atmosphere in which each student knows that he or she is valued for something.
10. Keep in mind that your students will remember only some of what you taught them but everything about how they felt in your classroom.

In inclusive classrooms, I have seen students learn to support a classmate with cerebral palsy, become allies in the face of homophobic bullying, and help a peer struggling with academic work. All of these were possible because the teachers were willing and able to talk to the students honestly about what was going on, creating a caring, supportive community for all students rather than marginalizing those who were experiencing difficulty.

Mutual Support

Sadly, teasing and exclusion are a typical part of many students' school experience. Bullying is so common that it can become virtually invisible. But inclusive classrooms foster a climate in which individual students know they will not be abandoned when they experience injustice. Inclusion means that we pay careful attention to issues of social justice and inequity, whether they appear at the individual, classroom, or school level or extend into the larger community.

I have used Peggy Moss's wonderful children's book *Say Something* (Tilbury House, 2004) to engage students and teachers in discussions about what we do when we see someone being picked on. In the book, a young girl goes from witnessing and lamenting the mistreatment of her classmates to taking action to change the patterns she observes.

This book and similar materials encourage students to talk about the concept of courage, about opportunities to be brave in both small and large ways, and about how they can make a difference.

Inclusive classrooms give us many opportunities to be our best selves, reaching across our personal borders to ask, Do you want to play? or Can I help you with that? Our lessons about how we treat one another extend beyond the specificity of rules (Don't tease children with disabilities) to broader, more inclusive discussions: How would you like to be treated? What do you think others feel when they're left out? How could we change this activity so more kids could play? How do you want others to deal with your challenges and triumphs, and what would that look like in our classroom?

Teachers in inclusive classrooms consider helping essential. The classroom becomes a more positive place for everyone when multiple forms of peer support—such as peer mentoring and collaborative learning—are ongoing, consistent, and valued. Rather than saying, "I want to know what you can do, not what your neighbor can do," inclusive teachers say, "Molly, why don't you ask Luis to show you how to do that," or "Make sure everyone at your table understands how to color the map code."

Inclusive settings provide multiple opportunities to explore what it means to help one another. By challenging the notion that there are two kinds of people in the world—those who need help and those who give help—we teach all students to see themselves as both givers and receivers. We recognize and honor multiple forms of intelligence and many gifts.

Courage to Change the World

When students develop fluency in addressing differences, are exposed to challenging issues, and view themselves as interconnected, teachers can more easily engage them in discussions about how to improve things.

Having a personal connection profoundly shifts one's perception about who has the problem and who should do something about it. When students have a classmate who comes from Mexico and is undocumented, discussions of immigration rights, border patrols, and fair employment practices become much more real. When students have learned to communicate with a classmate with autism, they understand at a deep level that being unable to talk is not the same as having nothing to say. When a classmate comes from a family with two mothers, reports of gay bashing or debates about marriage rights become more tangible.

A powerful way to combat political apathy is by helping young people make connections between their lives and those of others and giving them opportunities to make a difference in whatever ways they can. Although it's certainly possible to teach a social-justice curriculum in a fairly homogeneous school, inclusive classrooms give us the opportunity to put social-justice principles into action. In inclusive classrooms, students can *live* a social-justice curriculum rather than just study it.

A powerful way to combat political apathy is by helping young people make connections between their lives and those of others.

Inclusive classrooms that pay careful attention to issues of fairness and justice bring to the surface questions that have the potential to shift students' consciousness now and in the future: Who gets into the gifted program, and how are they chosen? How can we find a part in the school play for a classmate who doesn't talk? Why do people make fun of Brian because he likes art and doesn't like sports? How can we make sure everyone gets to go on the field trip that costs $20?

Inclusive classrooms put a premium on how people treat one another. Learning to live together in a democratic society is one of the most important goals and outcomes of inclusive classrooms. How could we want anything less for our children?

MARA SAPON-SHEVIN is Professor of Inclusive Education, Syracuse University, New York; msaponsh@syr.edu. She is the author of *Widening the Circle: The Power of Inclusive Classrooms* (Beacon Press, 2007).

From *Educational Leadership*, September 2008, pp. 49–53. Copyright © 2008 by Mara Sapon-Shevin. Reprinted by permission of the author.

Young Children with Autism Spectrum Disorder
Strategies That Work

Alexis is new to Ms. Roxanne's preschool classroom and spends a lot of time wringing her hands and staring out the window. She has been diagnosed with Asperger's syndrome, one of five conditions classified as an autism spectrum disorder. Roxanne wonders about Asperger's and what she can do to help Alexis adjust to being in the classroom.

CLARISSA WILLIS

Autism spectrum disorder (ASD) affects about one and a half million people in the United States. One in every 150 babies is diagnosed with autism spectrum disorder, and boys are four times more likely than girls to have a form of the neurological disorder (Autism Society of America 2006). Many children with ASD, especially those with Asperger's syndrome, are fully included in regular early childhood classrooms with their typically developing peers (Willis 2009).

> **The term *spectrum* is used because the characteristics of the disorder occur along a continuum, with severe symptoms at one end and very mild behaviors at the other.**

ASD is a broad-based term under which there are five recognized types of autism. The term *spectrum* is used because the characteristics of the disorder occur along a continuum, with severe symptoms at one end and very mild behaviors at the other. Where a child falls on the continuum helps determine how to plan for his education. For example, a child may be at the mild end in his ability to communicate with others, but at the severe end regarding his behavior around others.

ASD is a medical condition usually diagnosed by a developmental pediatrician and/or a team of specialists that may include a speech-language pathologist, occupational therapist, or child psychologist. Early intervention offering behavorial, social, and skill-building training is vital. Most children with ASD have an Individual Family Service Plan (IFSP) or an Individual Education Program (IEP) in place by the time they enter the classroom. These plans are designed with input from the child's family and can serve as a guide for planning activities and making modifications to the curriculum. They outline the broad goals and objectives written with a child's individual strengths and weaknesses in mind.

This article discusses the major characteristics associated with autism and offers some simple strategies for helping children with autism function in preschool settings (see "Characteristics of Autism Spectrum Disorder"). While each child with autism is unique and exhibits characteristic/symptomatic behaviors in varying degrees, most children diagnosed with an autism spectrum disorder have difficulty with communication and social relationships, including interactive play; display behaviors not typical of their peers; and respond to sensory stimuli by screaming or reacting strongly to light, sound, or motion (Sicile-Kira 2004).

> **Families and educators should focus on what the child can learn, rather than what cannot be learned.**

It is important to view a child with autism as a person with talents, strengths, and potential. In other words, families and educators should focus on what the child can learn, rather than what cannot be learned. Remember,

- Always put the child first. He is a "child with autism" not an "autistic child." Use the child's name as often as possible.
- Each child is unique, and no two children with autism have the same strengths and weaknesses.

Characteristics of Autism Spectrum Disorder

Autism	To be diagnosed with autism, a child must exhibit a significant number of the following characteristics: a significant delay in social interaction, such as eye contact or expression; a communication delay; behaviors including stereotypical behavior, such as intense, almost obsessive, preoccupation with objects; the need for nonfunctional and ritualistic routines, such as lining up books or food in a certain manner; and repeated movements, such as finger popping or hand flapping.
Pervasive development disorder not otherwise specified (PDD-NOS)	This classification is used when it is determined that a child has autism, but the characteristics displayed by the child are not like the characteristics of other children with autism. This diagnosis is also used when the onset of the disorder happens after age 3. Of all the autism classifications, this is the most vague and confusing for both families and teachers. However, this classification allows a child with a few, but not all, of the characteristics of autism to be classified as having autism, so that he can receive needed services.
Asperger's syndrome	Children with Asperger's typically behave much like children with other types of autism when they are young. However, as they grow into middle school age or in adolescence, they often learn how to socialize, communicate, and behave in a more socially acceptable manner. Most children with Asperger's have normal or above normal intelligence, so they learn new skills as quickly or in many cases more quickly than their typical peers.
Rett's syndrome	This is a degenerative disorder, meaning it gets worse with time. It begins in the first two years of life and is found almost exclusively in girls. Unlike other types of autism, children with Rett's develop normally prior to the onset of the disorder. Characteristics include loss of motor skills, hand-wringing or repetitive hand washing, and a decrease in head growth. Seizures and sleeping disorders may also develop.
Childhood disintegrative disorder	Sometimes called Heller's syndrome, this is a degenerative condition in which a child may begin to develop normally but start to lose skills or seem to forget how to do things over a few months. Loss of skills usually happens in the area of toilet training, play, language, or problem solving, typically between ages 3 and 4.

Adapted with permission from C. Willis, *Teaching Young Children with Autism Spectrum Disorder* (Beltsville, MD: Gryphon House, 2006).

- Not all information about autism (including what is shown on television and found on the Internet) is accurate.
- While there are several approaches to teaching a child with autism, there is no single method, specific program, or magic cure that can *fix* autism. Many programs and methods are successful with some children, yet may not be successful with others (Willis 2006).

How Might a Child with Autism Behave in My Classroom?

Children with an autism spectrum disorder may display in varying degrees some or all of the following behaviors: obsession with specific objects, such as collecting forks or having an attachment to a piece of cloth; prolonged interest in common occurrences like watching water as it swirls down the drain; adherence to rituals, such as arranging food in a certain order; and repetitive (stereotypic) behaviors like hand flapping or repeating the same phrase over and over.

What Is Stereotypic Behavior?

Stereotypic behavior is usually defined as a behavior carried out repeatedly and involving either movement of the child's body or movement of an object (Edelson 1995). Some of the most common stereotypic behaviors seen in young children with autism include flapping one or both hands, pulling or tapping the ears, rocking back and forth or from side to side, sniffing the air, or sucking on the upper lip.

Stereotypic actions allow the children to move further into their own world and away from reality. While stereotypic behavior is not usually physically harmful, it often interferes with a child's ability to focus on what is going on around her (Lee, Odom, & Loftin 2007). Of course, all children, from time to time, tune out activities they want to avoid. Unlike typically developing children, however, many children with autism learn that by doing a specific thing, such as rocking, they can consistently tune out everything around them.

Knowing the reason for a behavior can often help teachers determine what a child is trying to communicate through his or her actions.

Attempting to understand the function behind the behavior is important. Knowing the reason for a behavior can often help teachers determine what a child is trying to communicate through his or her actions. Behavior specialists and teachers can work together to conduct a functional behavior assessment, which involves observing the child's particular behavior across time to help determine its function.

How Do We Know What a Child with Autism Is Trying to Communicate with a Behavior?

It is very difficult for a teacher to be responsive when she does not know what a child is trying to say. To try to understand the child's communication, ask yourself the following questions:

1. **What was the child doing immediately before the behavior started?** For example, if Aaron is sitting down for small group time and suddenly stands up and screams, his teacher can try to recall what occurred just before his outburst. Perhaps she had stopped interacting with him and is now talking to the group. If Aaron typically has a tantrum during group activities, it may indicate that he is using the tantrum to regain the teacher's attention.

2. **What in the environment might have triggered the behavior, outburst, or tantrum?** Did something make a loud noise? Did the classroom suddenly get brighter? Is there a smell unfamiliar to the child?

3. **What is the child trying to say by his behavior?** Sometimes a child will act a certain way as a protest, while other times she may cry out to express "There's too much going on here; I can't think!" One key to identifying the function of a child's behavior is to look at what happens after the behavior. If the child's tantrums are often followed by some kind of interaction with an adult (even if the interaction seems negative), the child may be communicating (in a maladaptive way) that he wants attention.

4. **Can I predict when the child will behave in a certain way?** The behaviors of children with autism are not always predictable. However, sometimes knowing what will happen next can allow a teacher to step in to prevent an outburst. If Candice starts biting herself every day after coming in from the playground, it is probably safe to assume that she enjoys being outside and does not want to come indoors. In this case, the teacher can try cuing Candice with a special signal right before it is time to come inside. This gives the child time to end the activity she is enjoying and transition to the next one.

Other Ways a Child with Autism Might Communicate

Approximately 40 percent of all children with ASD are nonverbal (Charlop & Haymes 1994). However, just because a child is nonverbal, it does not mean she cannot learn to communicate. Several alternative or augmentative forms of communication are used with children with autism. These include

Sign language. Some children with autism can use the same signs used by people who are deaf.

Communication devices. Computer-like tools can speak for the child when activated by the push of a button or selection of a picture.

Communication pictures. A child can point to specific pictures to tell what is happening, what he needs, or what he wants. Many children with autism respond better to real pictures than to line drawings (Willis 2009).

Among the many tools commercially developed for children with communication deficits is the Picture Exchange Communication System (PECS) (Frost & Bondy 1994). PECS is simple to use, relatively inexpensive, and helps children with autism develop a way to communicate with others (Charlop-Christy et al. 2002). Because of communication and behavior issues, many children with ASD do not initiate interactions with others. What makes the PECS system unique is that, unlike other systems of communication, it requires that the child initiate interaction by using a representative picture (Bondy 2001). In general, when used consistently, the PECS helps children with autism have more meaningful communication interactions. Communication with others is an important social skill that helps any child make friends.

What Do We Do When a Child Won't Interact with Others?

Because children with autism generally do not initiate interactions, social skills training, including how to respond in social situations, should begin as early as possible and continue throughout the child's education (Stichter & Conroy 2006). Some strategies can help a child learn how to greet people and introduce himself (for an example, see "Strategy 1: Making New Friends").

It is important to work with the child's family and other teachers and specialists to prioritize which social skills should be taught. Learning too many new skills without enough time for practice can be overwhelming, and the child may react with maladaptive behavior. To encourage positive social interactions, it is vital to structure the environment to help the child succeed.

How Do We Arrange a Preschool Environment for Success?

Children with autism function best when they have

- structure and a predictable routine,
- environments that do not distract,
- verbal reminders of what will happen next, and
- picture schedules.

Teachers should define the environment as much as possible for a child with autism. To reduce the child's anxiety, create and post in each center or learning area a picture schedule using photographs or other images to display the day's events. The child can look at the picture to get an idea of what is supposed to occur in that area. Children with autism like to know what they are supposed to do, so a picture schedule is reassuring.

In learning centers, teachers also can set up activities that encourage interaction, such as group art projects or activities

Strategy 1: Making New Friends

Objective: To help develop social interaction by showing the child how to introduce himself.

1. Make an introduction cue card with two cues, one for the child's name and one to remind him to wait for the other person to respond. If possible, laminate the card.
2. Explain to the child that the cue card will help him know what to do when he meets someone new.
3. Ask several children to help you and the child practice meeting people.
4. Sit in a circle and practice what to say and how to wait for the other person to respond.
5. Remind the children that when you are meeting someone for the first time, it is a good idea to look at him or her.
6. Look for opportunities for the child to practice using the cue card to introduce himself.

Helpful Hints

- When the child becomes familiar with this routine, add additional cues, such as one showing something that he likes to do or asking a new friend to play a game.
- Make a set of cue cards for the child to take home.
- Alert the family that the child is working on introducing himself and other social skills, so they can help him practice.

Adapted with permission from C. Willis, *Teaching Young Children with Autism Spectrum Disorder* (Beltsville, MD: Gryphon House, 2006).

that require two people to complete them. Remember, children with autism may not be particularly interested in an activity or specific center. Allowing use of a child's preferred object can greatly increase the probability that the child will take part in an activity (Schwartz, Billingsley, & McBride 1998).

Transitions are times when a child with autism is likely to have an outburst. Plan smooth transitions. Music makes an excellent transition tool. Use the same song for each transition so the child learns that the song is a cue that something new is about to happen.

Here are some other ideas to facilitate smooth transitions:

- Go with the child to the picture schedule and point to the next activity.
- Set a timer to indicate that in a few minutes it will be time to change activities. Hourglass timers are less distracting than timers with loud continuous bells.
- Tap the child gently on the shoulder as a cue that it is almost time to stop.
- Ring a service bell (with one quick ring) or soft chime, such as wind chimes, as a reminder that it is time to change activities.

Note that making loud noises or flashing lights on and off are not good ways to signal transitions for a child with autism. The sensory stimulation can be overwhelming.

It is critical to remember that most children with autism will, in some fashion, have difficulty with sensory stimuli. They require an environment that is sensitive to their unique needs.

Why Do Children with Autism Have Difficulty with Sensory Stimuli?

Most children with autism have some form of sensory integration disorder whereby they cannot filter or screen out sensory-related input (Kranowitz 2005). The common "feely box" that many preschool teachers use to introduce new textures can be very distressing for many children with autism. For them, the information they receive from their environment—such as through a feely box—becomes distorted and unreliable.

The quiet center is also a space where a child can go to complete especially stressful activities, such as counting, working a puzzle, or writing her name.

Children with autism need a special place in the classroom where they can go without distraction and without all the sensory input they receive elsewhere. Locate this place in the quietest part of the room and provide soft, indirect lighting, a comfortable chair or cushion, and some activities that the child likes. Teachers should always be able to observe the child in the special place. This quiet center is also a space where a child can go to complete especially stressful activities, such as counting, working a puzzle, or writing her name (Willis 2006).

After the child spends time in the quiet center, allow her to return and finish any activity she started before visiting the quiet center. Quiet centers should be used routinely to allow the child to be in a place where she feels safe and secure. They should *never* be used as a form of punishment.

How Can We Prepare for a Child with Autism?

The best way teachers can prepare themselves and the other children in the class for a child with autism is to get to know as much as possible about the child before enrollment. Encourage the family to come with their child to visit your classroom before the first day of school. This initial visit is an opportunity to meet the family and the child and let him become familiar with the classroom. This introductory visit should happen when other children are not present, and more than one visit may be necessary. One way to help a child learn more about his new classroom is to take the child on a classroom hunt (see "Strategy 2: Classroom Hunt—I Spy!").

Strategy 2: Classroom Hunt— I Spy!

Objective: To encourage the child with autism to explore areas of the classroom, interact with toys, or try new activities.

Materials: A basket with a handle and one item from each learning center.

1. Gather one representative item from each of the centers in the room—a block from the block area, a magnetic letter from the literacy center, a paint-brush from the art area, a book from the reading center, and so on.
2. Place the items in a basket or box. A basket works best because you can carry it on your arm. The child may even want to carry it for you.
3. Tell the child you need help putting the things in your basket back in the centers where they belong.
4. Start each hunt with the same phrase, "Here is a ____. I wonder where it goes."
5. Refocus a child who looks away or appears disinterested by holding the item in front of her.
6. Hold up an object and ask, "____ [the child's name], where do you think this goes?"
7. Prompt a child who does not reply or does not take the object by walking to a center and asking, "Do you think it goes here?"
8. When the child figures out where the object belongs, ask her to place the item in/on the correct bin or shelf. Continue with the other objects in the basket.

Helpful Hints

- Say the name of the object aloud.
- Vary the activity. For example, if you use picture cards, match the object to the correct picture card before returning it to its proper location.
- Put the object in the wrong location if the child appears uninterested or bored. Wait to see if she corrects you. Sometimes, even nonverbal children have an extraordinary sense of place and know in fine detail where items belong.

(Later, after the child has gotten used to being at school, it might be fun to do the activity with a second child so that the three of you look for the correct center.)

Adapted with permission from C. Willis, *Teaching Young Children with Autism Spectrum Disorder* (Beltsville, MD: Gryphon House, 2006).

Many preschools have a family information form, but you will need to find out much more about the child than is typically included on such forms. Here are some questions to ask the family before a child with ASD arrives at the program:

1. What does she like to eat? Are there foods that she will not eat or that cause her to react in a certain way?
2. What are her particular interests? Does she have an object that she is attached to?
3. Does she have a favorite activity or song?
4. How does she communicate with others?
5. What might cause her to become upset or frustrated?
6. What do you see as her strengths?
7. What do you consider her challenges?
8. What other services has she been receiving? Speech therapy? Occupational therapy? Who provides the services? How often and in what setting?
9. What do you do when/if she has an outburst at home?
10. How much experience has she had interacting with other children?
12. What is her daily routine?

How Do We Set up the Daily Routine for a Child with Autism?

Children with autism are less frustrated when they can follow predictable and organized routines. When setting up a daily routine for a child with autism, it is important for the child to understand what you are asking him to do. How the day begins often determines how the child will behave during the rest of the day. If there is any variation in the schedule, even a minor change, let the child know in advance.

When the child arrives, greet him and discuss the daily schedule. Use familiar picture cards to show each activity for the day. Make sure the schedule is on a level the child can understand. For some children, this may be an object schedule, and for others, a simple first then card. A first–then card is a series of picture pairs in which the first shows what happens first and the second shows what happens next (Small & Kontente 2003; Willis 2006). When possible, use the identical daily routines, such as saying the same morning greeting each day (see "Strategy 3: Morning Greeting").

Concluding Thoughts

Jim Sinclair puts it best: "Autism isn't something a person has, or a 'shell' that a person is trapped inside. There's no normal child hidden behind the autism. Autism is a way of being. It is pervasive; it colors every experience, every sensation, perception, thought, emotion, and encounter, every aspect of existence. It is not possible to separate the autism from the person—and if it were possible, the person you'd have left would not be the same person you started with" (1993, n.p.).

All children can learn, and children with autism spectrum disorder are no exception. To help them be as successful as possible in your classroom, remember that they function best when they have the following:

- structure and a predictable routine,
- environments that do not distract,
- verbal reminders of what will happen next,
- picture schedules to give them clues about what to do,
- a quiet place to go where they can be alone for a few minutes, and
- nothing to overwhelm their senses with too much light or noise.

Strategy 3: Morning Greeting

Objective: To establish a morning routine that starts the day on a positive note.

1. Use the same words and phrases each day, perhaps something as simple as "Good morning, *[child's name]*." Wait to see if the child responds, then say, "Let's check and see what we do first."
2. Bend down to eye level and use a picture schedule to show the child what you want him to do.
3. Try singing to a child who does not respond to a spoken welcome. You might sing the following to the tune of "Three Blind Mice" (first verse):

    [Child's name], welcome.
    [Child's name], welcome.
    I'm glad you're here.
    I'm glad you're here.

4. Direct the child to his cubby. If he hesitates, walk with him. A picture of the child above the cubby will help him identify it more easily. Show him the picture cards that relate to putting up his backpack, coat, and so on.
5. Tell him what to do next: "After you put up your backpack, go to the ____ center." Even if you start the day with independent center time, direct the child to a specific place each morning.
6. Say or sign thank you.
7. Guide the child to the center if he does not go on his own; walk with him.
8. Vary the welcome only after he is accustomed to the morning routine. For example, suggest two or more center choices. Expect that when you first tell him to choose where he wants to go, he will likely stand still or hide in his cubby.

Helpful Hints

- Stay focused on your primary objective, which is to start each day with a calm and predictable sequence.
- Keep in mind, regardless of your morning routine, that consistency will make the child with autism feel more secure.
- Accept that some children, even children without autism, are just not morning people and need a little more time to wake up. If the child is prone to rugged mornings, begin each day by allowing him to go to the quiet center until he has adjusted to the routine.
- Make sure that when you are absent, the substitute or teacher's assistant follows your morning welcome routine.

Adapted with permission from C. Willis, *Teaching Young Children with Autism Spectrum Disorder* (Beltsville, MD: Gryphon House, 2006).

References

Autism Society of America. 2006. *Autism facts.* www.autism-society .org/site/PageServer?pagename=about_whatis_factsstats

Bondy, A. 2001. PECS: Potential benefits and risks. *The Behavior Analyst Today 2* (2): 127–32.

Charlop, M.H., & L.K. Haymes. 1994. Speech and language acquisition and intervention: Behavioral approaches. In *Autism in children and adults: Etiology, assessment, and intervention,* ed. J.L. Matson. Pacific Grove, CA: Brooks/Cole.

Charlop-Christy, M.H., M. Carpenter, L. Loc, L. LeBlanc, & K. Kellet. 2002. Using the Picture Exchange Communication System (PECS) with children with autism: Assessment of the PECS acquisition, speech, social-communicative behavior, and problem behavior. *Journal of Applied Behavior Analysis* 35 (3): 213–31.

Edelson, S. 1995. Stereotypic (self-stimulatory) behavior. www.autism.org/stim.html

Frost, L.A., & A.S. Bondy. 1994. *The Picture Exchange Communication System training manual.* Cherry Hill, NJ: Pyramid Educational Consultants.

Kranowitz, C. 2005. *The out-of-sync child: Recognizing and coping with sensory processing disorder.* New York: Perigee.

Lee, S., S.L. Odom, & R. Loftin. 2007. Social engagement with peers and stereotypic behavior of children with autism. *Journal of Positive Behavior Interventions* 9 (2): 67–79.

Schwartz, I.S., F. Billingsley, & B. McBride. 1998. Including children with autism in inclusive preschools: Strategies that work. *Young Exceptional Children* 2 (1): 19–26.

Sicile-Kira, C. 2004. *Autism spectrum disorders.* New York: Penguin.

Sinclair, J. 1993. Don't mourn for us. *Our Voice: The Newsletter of the Autism Network International* 1 (3). http://ani.autistics .org/dont_mourn.html

Small, M., & L. Kontente. 2003. *Everyday solutions: A practical guide for families of children with autism spectrum disorder.* Shawnee Mission, KS: Autism Asperger Publishing.

Stichter, J.P., & M.A. Conroy. 2006. *How to teach social skills and plan for peer social interactions.* Series on autism spectrum disorders. Austin, TX: Pro-Ed.

Willis, C. 2006. *Teaching young children with autism spectrum disorder.* Beltsville, MD: Gryphon House.

Willis, C. 2009. *Creating inclusive learning environments for young children: What to do on Monday morning.* Thousand Oaks, CA: Corwin.

CLARISSA WILLIS, PhD, is a speaker and consultant based in Winston-Salem, North Carolina; author of *Teaching Young Children with Autism Spectrum Disorder* and *Creating Inclusive Learning Environments for Young Children;* and coauthor of *Inclusive Literacy Lessons for Early Childhood.* In addition to earning a doctorate in early childhood special education, Clarissa worked more than 20 years in schools and child development centers and as a speech pathologist. Clarissa@clarissawillis.com

From *Young Children,* January 2009, pp. 81–82, 84–89. Copyright © 2009 by National Association for the Education of Young Children. Reprinted by permission. [Boxed text on pp. 72, 74, 75, 76 from *Autism Spectrum Disorder,* by Clarissa Willis, (ISBN 978-0-87659-008-9), and reprinted with permission from Gryphon House, Inc., Silver Spring, MD, ph. 800-638-0928.]

Including Children with Disabilities in Early Childhood Education Programs
Individualizing Developmentally Appropriate Practices

JOHN FILLER AND YAOYING XU

Early childhood educators are facing the challenge of creating quality educational programs for young children from an increasingly diverse mix of racial and cultural backgrounds. Programs that, in the past, have largely ignored the diversity of their participants must now re-examine approaches that emphasize the universality of linear lists of developmental milestones; they must pursue practices that reflect a pluralistic approach to both content and methods of instruction. Too many educators assume that children reach developmental milestones at similar points, leading to rather simplistic attempts to justify singular content and approach. Yet a multicultural, multi-ethnic, and multi-ability student population demands a unique and nontraditional approach, characterized by individualization and sensitivity to unique expressions of group identity.

The realities of diversity do not mitigate the fact that all children do seem to exhibit a finite set of accomplishments (milestones) that build, one upon the other, and proceed in an age-related fashion. We recognize the relevance of a developmental approach that is based upon the work of such theorists as Rousseau, Locke, Pestalozzi, Froebel, Piaget, and Vygotsky, exemplified by Itard's techniques, the Montessori approach, and the Head Start movement in the 1960s, as well as numerous other, more recent, examples of successful early childhood education programs. However, some children acquire skills at an earlier age than their age-mates, while others acquire those same skills much later than their peers or not at all. For example, not all children begin walking up stairs by placing both feet on each step before they move to the next step. Some alternate, placing only one foot on each step—a skill that Brigance (2004) claims one should expect to see exhibited 6 to 12 months after the two-feet per step approach. Some children seem to skip steps in a developmental sequence while others do not. Such variations are viewed as part of the "normal" range of individual differences, defined as falling less than one to two standard deviations above or below the theoretical mean for a given developmental area (such as cognitive, gross and fine motor, or social or language skills). Most of our attempts to adapt curriculum and strategies to diversity have been based upon either sociocultural differences or ability differences that fall within the range of what might be termed "normal variation."

The realities of a multicultural, multi-ethnic, and multi-ability student population demand a unique and nontraditional approach, characterized by individualization and sensitivity to unique expressions of group identity.

Individually and Developmentally Appropriate Practices

Developmentally appropriate practice (DAP) is considered the foundation of early childhood education and serves as a guideline for curriculum development. The National Association of Education for Young Children (NAEYC) defined DAP in three dimensions (Bredekamp & Copple, 1997, p. 9):

- What is known about child development and learning—knowledge of age-related human characteristics that permits general predictions within an age range about what activities, materials, interactions, or experiences will be safe, healthy, interesting, achievable, and also challenging to children
- What is known about the strength, interests, and needs of each individual child in the group to be able to adapt for and be responsive to inevitable individual variations
- Knowledge of the social and cultural contexts in which children live to ensure that learning experiences are meaningful, relevant, and respectful for the participating children and their families.

On the one hand, this NAEYC statement views children as members of an overall group who follow similar predictable developmental patterns. Yet it also emphasizes the importance of valuing young children as individuals, with different personalities or temperaments and learning styles. Furthermore, children are considered part of a cultural group, members of the community in which children and their families live and by which they are influenced in every aspect of living. Additionally, the NAEYC statement encourages early childhood professionals to move from "either-or thinking" to "both-and thinking" (Gonzalez-Mena, 2000). As is often the case, what is developmentally appropriate is not always individually or culturally appropriate. Instead of having to make a falsely dichotomous choice, educators often need to combine all dimensions and know the child as a whole person with individual needs and cultural differences.

The nature of DAP encourages the placement of children, with and without disabilities, in the same setting. In fact, most professional organizations support the concept of inclusive programs for all children, regardless of the nature or severity of the disability. For example, the Division for Early Childhood of the Council for Exceptional Children issued its "Position Statement on Inclusion," which was endorsed that same year by NAEYC: "DEC supports and advocates that young children and their families have full and successful access to health, social, educational, and other support services that promote full participation in family and community life" (Sandall, McLean, & Smith, 2000, p. 150). The statement also proposed that young children participating in group settings (such as preschool, play groups, child care, or kindergarten) be guided by developmentally and individually appropriate curriculum. The Association for Childhood Education International published a brochure that discusses the benefits of inclusion for the children with disabilities, the children without disabilities, and the parents, school, and community (Kostell, 1997). The Association for Persons With Severe Handicaps (TASH) endorses the inclusion of children with severe disabilities in regular education settings and argues that inclusion implies more than just physical presence; it includes access to the curriculum that is taught in the regular education classroom (TASH, 2000).

Clearly, leading professional organizations endorse the concept of inclusive programming for children with disabilities; there also exists a strong legal basis for inclusion. The assumption of the universal relevance of the general education curriculum is readily apparent in the 2004 re-authorization of the Individuals With Disabilities Education Act (P.L. 108-446). This law requires that we reference the content of our curriculum for students with disabilities to that of their typically developing peers. For example, each student's individualized educational program (IEP), a written document that describes the needs of the child, must contain a statement of the child's present levels of educational performance, including how the child's disability affects his or her involvement and participation in appropriate activities. Furthermore, the IEP must include a statement of *measurable annual goals,* related to "meeting the child's needs that result from the child's disability to enable the child to be involved in and progress in the general curriculum" (Sec. 614; 20 USC 1414), and there must be a justification for non-participation in the regular class. Part C of P.L. 108-446 requires

that children from birth to 3 years of age receive early intervention services in environments that are *natural,* or normal for children the same age who have no disabilities (IDEA Rules and Regulations, 1998). This stipulation extends the requirements of the Americans With Disabilities Act (Public Law 101-336) by requiring each state to not only ensure reasonable access by infants with disabilities to child care/educare programs, but also deliver early intervention services in such settings.

Planning for Inclusion: Adapting Developmentally Appropriate Practices

While examples of curricula for young children can be found that do provide substantive suggestions for adapting to meet the needs of children with sensory, cognitive, motor, emotional, and/or learning disabilities (e.g., Bricker & Waddell, 2002a, 2002b; Hauser-Cram, Bronson, & Upshur, 1993), most do little by way of providing meaningful, practical suggestions to the early childhood teacher. This means that the task of planning to include these children will fall upon the shoulders of those whose formal training and experience may not have prepared them for such diversity (Gelfer, Filler, & Perkins, 1999; Heller, 1992). To be successful at what can, at first, appear to be a very daunting task, teachers will have to plan for modifications in both content and strategy. Numerous authors have recognized the importance of instructional flexibility and the need for an approach that includes the individual modifications that are often necessary in order to meet the needs of diverse groups of learners (Allen & Cowdery, 2004; Friend & Bursuck, 2002; Giangreco, Broer, & Edelman, 2002; Pretti-Frontczak & Bricker, 2004). Inclusion is not accomplished by simply placing a child with disabilities in a setting with his typically developing peers. It is realized only when we have succeeded in designing a set of activities that ensure the full participation of all children, including the child with disabilities. Participation and not mere geographical proximity is the necessary pre-condition for *achievement,* and so meaningful participation requires systematic planning.

Table 1 contains a description of the steps involved in planning for the inclusion of a child with disabilities in a typical early childhood program. The planning process begins with the selection of a team of knowledgeable individuals who will be responsible for developing the plan. Team planning is essential, because the success of efforts to include students with disabilities, especially those with severe disabilities, is not the sole responsibility of any single individual. This planning team should include the parents and/or any other family members who share in daily caregiving activities; the general education early childhood teacher and the early interventionist or early childhood special education teacher; and the program administrator and any related service personnel, such as speech or occupational therapists who may provide services to the child and family.

The second step in the planning process is to construct a simple schedule of the daily activities for the setting in which the target child with disabilities will be included from start to finish. When listing the activities, it is important to note the average length of time devoted to each activity and to include all activities in which the child will likely be included throughout the week, since activities may vary from day to day.

Step 3 involves a careful specification of the instructional goals for the target child, which are taken directly from the IEP or the Individualized Family Service Plan (IFSP). Since these documents contain goals and/or objectives that may cover six months to a year, only those that are currently being addressed are listed. Here, it is important to indicate the family's priorities for instruction. The family and the educators may feel differently about the relative importance of goals and objectives. For example, the family may not believe that the child learning a particular social behavior is as important as the child acquiring gross motor skills, while the teacher might think that more emphasis should be placed upon sharing and cooperative play than upon learning to throw and run. Such differences present opportunities to jointly discuss how both priorities can be addressed simultaneously in one or more activities. An important additional consideration is whether or not the child has a behavior support plan, the presence of which indicates the need to carefully and systematically pay attention to a recurring, potentially serious, form of inappropriate behavior.

Step 4 is, perhaps, the most important aspect of the planning process; it is the determination of exactly how many opportunities exist in the typical schedule to address the individual needs of the child with a disability and what program supports are needed to make an opportunity a successful reality. Each skill targeted in the IEP/IFSP must be referenced to the activities of the typical early childhood program. The team must ask (and answer) the question, "Does this activity provide an opportunity to address any of the skills in the IEP or IFSP?" and "If so, which ones?" In answering the questions, it becomes important to examine what the focus of the activity is for typically developing children. If it seems reasonable to the team that the activity may provide a context in which the needs of the child with disabilities can be addressed, *without completely altering the meaningfulness of the activity for typically developing children,* then the team can examine what adaptations may be needed. The effort to ensure that activities provide opportunities to address the needs of all children is central to what has been termed *activity-based instruction* (Pretti-Frontczak & Bricker, 2004).

As indicated in Table 1, adaptations may consist of two types. One involves individualizing the content of the activity by changing its focus or fundamental purpose for the target child. A modified content, or even a different content entirely, may be taught to the child with disabilities while the other children receive content appropriate for their needs. A second kind of adaptation involves changing the physical layout, modifying materials for the child, or even changing the way that staff conduct the activity. For example, while children with sensory disabilities, like blindness or low vision, may still function at age level and require no modification of content, they will require large print or Braille reading material. A child with cerebral palsy and an associated motor disability may require special equipment, such as a cut-out table and chairs with supports, wedges to facilitate upper body movement while in a prone play position, or a prone board to provide support in an upright

position (Campbell, 2006). In some situations, it may even be necessary to add staff during the activity to ensure adequate instructional support without sacrificing instructional time for the other children. This might be the case with a child who presents a significant challenging behavior that requires an involved support plan, the focus of which is to teach a positive incompatible replacement behavior (see Figure 2).

Step 5 involves determining what related services are required and how often and how long each related service session should be. Children with significant disabilities often require such services as occupational therapy and speech therapy, and may need to receive one-on-one instruction from an early childhood special educator. While the preference is to provide these services in the natural setting of the early childhood classroom, it may be necessary to remove the child to a different setting for the service. If that is the case, then the team must decide what classroom activity (or activities) is (are) least important and thus could be missed by the child. This is usually accomplished by viewing each activity in terms of the opportunities it provides for addressing skills from the IEP or IFSP, and then selecting times for the child to leave the classroom when activities are occurring that provide the fewest number of individually relevant instructional opportunities. Sometimes, however, the schedule of those professionals who are delivering the service may need to be taken into account when making the choice.

The final step, Step 6, is also an extremely important aspect of team planning. Parents and other family members have their own perspective on what, among all of the skills that may be included in the IEP or IFSP, is most important. It is critical that staff respect those priorities by making sure that, first, they are aware of parental priorities and, second, adequate opportunities exist to address high-priority skills during daily program activities. In addition, families may have concerns regarding skills or behaviors that are best addressed outside of the formal confines of the program setting. It is extremely important that the skills learned at the center also are taught and practiced in natural settings—those settings in which the skill or behavior is most likely to be demanded or exhibited. Natural settings are the environments where children with disabilities would participate or function if they did not have a disability. These environments may include the child's home, the neighborhood playground, community activity or child care centers, restaurants, Head Start programs, or other settings designed for children without disabilities (Cook, Klein, Tessier, & Daley, 2004). While it is unlikely that program staff will be able to provide continuous, direct instructional support at home or in the community, it still would be possible to make visits and provide occasional community-based instruction. Making suggestions to the family as to how to generalize procedures employed at the center is another important aspect of the child's program. These procedures need to be planned for as carefully as you would the daily activities.

The Activity Matrix

A good way to summarize and represent the results of this six-step planning process is to construct what has been referred to as an "Activity Matrix" (Fox & Williams, 1991). Figures 1 and 2

Table 1 Steps in Planning for Inclusion

STEP ONE: Form the inclusion planning team.	1.1 Invite the target child's parents and/or other significant caregivers to participate in planning for inclusion.
	1.2 Invite the EC program administrator to participate, along with the general early childhood education (EC) teacher and the special education (ECSE) teacher or early interventionist (EI).
	1.3 Determine if there are others who should be invited to participate on the planning team (e.g., speech or occupational or physical therapists who may be delivering related services).
STEP TWO: List each daily activity of the typical EC program	2.1 One member of the team (typically, the EC teacher) lists each activity from arrival to departure.
	2.2 If the daily activities vary from day to day, then care must be taken to include all activities.
	2.3 Note the typical length of time devoted to each daily activity.
STEP THREE: Determine the areas of instructional emphasis for the target child.	3.1 From the child's IEP or IFSP, list each <u>current</u> instructional target (these may be taken directly from the IEP objectives or child outcome statements that have not yet been met).
	3.2 Determine which of these objectives is a priority for the family.
	3.3 Note whether the child exhibits any particular behavior problems for which a support plan may have been developed.
	3.4 Inquire as to whether the family has any additional instructional concerns that may not have been noted in the IEP or IFSP. List these as well.
STEP FOUR: Determine what opportunities to address the needs of the target child may be provided by the daily EC program activities.	4.1 The team determines which of the activities in the typical program setting provide a reasonable opportunity to address the instructional needs of the target child.
	4.2 The team discusses and determines if an adaptation is required to address the instructional target.
	4.3 If an adaptation to the activity, as it is typically conducted, is needed to make a determination as to the nature of the adaptation; modification of content (changes in focus, rules, and/or materials); and/or modification in the way the activity is conducted (changes in physical setting, materials, and/or staffing).
STEP FIVE: Determine what modifications are necessary to meet the target child's possible need for related services.	5.1 From the IEP or IFSP, note the target child's need for a related service, the weekly schedule for each service, and the beginning date and length of time for each service visit.
	5.2 Discuss and determine whether the service can reasonably be delivered in the typical program setting by modifying an activity.
	5.3 If the service cannot reasonably be delivered in the natural setting of the classroom, then determine which activities the child will miss in order to receive the service in a different room or program setting.
STEP SIX: Determine what needs the family may see for addressing skills/ behavior at home or in the community.	6.1 Note any concerns of the family that are more appropriately addressed at home or in the community.
	6.2 Indicate which skills from the IEP/IFSP also can be addressed in these "other," more natural environments.

contain an example format for an activity matrix. Figure 1 is an Activity Matrix for Chu Chu, a Chinese American boy with moderate mental retardation. Figure 2 was developed for Nikki, an African American girl with autism spectrum disorder and moderate cognitive delay. Each of the daily activities of the typical early childhood program is written in one of the columns to the right of the box labeled "Activities" across the top of the form (planning Step 2). Directly below is a space for the "Length of Time," where the duration, in minutes, of each activity is entered. Since some children, particularly those with disabilities, may need to be involved in an alternative activity (e.g., speech therapy), space is provided to list those activities that could be substituted at an appropriate time for one of the regularly scheduled activities (planning Step 5). We have found it helpful to number each of these alternative activities directly above the activity

name and then refer to the activity by that number. Writing the number above one of the scheduled activities indicates that the alternative activity will occur instead of the scheduled activity. Down the left side of the matrix, room is provided for the individual instructional goals or objectives from the child's IEP or IFS (planning Step 3).

As suggested in Table 1, Step 4, the process continues by reading the first objective for the child and then looking at the first activity (arrival). You then ask yourself, "Does 'arrival' present an opportunity to address this objective?" Let's say, for the purpose of discussion, that the first objective for Chu Chu is from the "social skills/self-help" domain and it is "Chu Chu will greet his friends." Does "arrival" (i.e., coming into the room, hanging up his coat, putting his backpack away, and going to the table) present any opportunities for Chu Chu to

Child: Chu Chu Age: 4.2 years Setting: Rainbows Date: _____

Alternative Activities Listed by Number	1		2							Special Activities 1	2	Home/Family
TYPICAL DAILY ACTIVITIES	Arrival	Free Choice Time	Outdoor Play	Large Group Time	Learning Centers	Closing Group Time	Outdoor Play	Departure		Speech Therapy	Special Ed. Resource (1:1)	Eats at Restaurant
Length of Time for Activity	15 mins	30 mins	30 mins	15 mins	30 mins	15 mins	30 mins	15 mins		30 mins	30 mins	
Adaptation: Modified Content	X	X					X					
Adaptation: Modified arrangement / staffing	X	X					X	X				
TARGET CHILD SKILL AREAS FROM CURRENT IEP or IFSP (√ indicates skill is a family priority)												
Social Skill: Greets friends	√		√	√		√						√
Language: Expressive vocab.	X	X	X	X	X	X	X	X				X
Self Help: Washes hands					X							X
Fine Motor: Pincer grasp	X	X	X	X	X	X	X	X				X
Gross Motor: Kicks ball		X					X					
Self Help: Signals need for BR	√	√	√	√	√	√	√	√				√
BEHAVIOR SUPPORT PLAN?												

Figure 1 Early Childhood Activity Matrix.

Child: Nikki Age: 3.5 years Setting: Ladybugs Date: _____

Alternative Activities Listed by Number	1		2							Special Activities 1	2	Home/Family
TYPICAL DAILY ACTIVITIES	Arrival	Opening Group	Outdoor Play	Snack	Learning Centers	Closing Group Time	Outdoor Play	Departure		Speech Therapy	Special Ed. Resource (1:1)	Quietly occupies self during church service
Length of Time for Activity	15 mins	30 mins	30 mins	30 mins	30 mins	15 mins	30 mins	15 mins		30 mins	30 mins	
Adaptation: Modified Content	X		X				X					
Adaptation: Modified arrangement / staffing		X	X	X	X	X	X	X				X
TARGET CHILD SKILL AREAS FROM CURRENT IEP or IFSP (√ indicates skill is a family priority)												
Social Skill: Plays and/or works cooperatively		√	√	√		√						√
Language: Expressive vocab.	X	X	X	X	X	X	X	X				X
Language: Receptive vocab.					X							X
Fine Motor: Pincer grasp	X	X	X	X	X	X	X	X				X
Self Help: Uses utensils					X							
Self Help: Signals need for BR	X	X	X	X	X	X	X	X				√
BEHAVIOR SUPPORT PLAN?	yes	yes	yes	yes	yes	yes	yes	yes				yes

Figure 2 Early Childhood Activity Matrix.

acknowledge the presence of the other children by saying "hello"? Of course, that is a natural sub-activity involved in "arrival," so an "X" is placed in the box out from it and under "arrival" to indicate that a naturally occurring opportunity exists to practice the skills involved in "greeting friends" during this activity. What of the next activity? Does free choice time provide an opportunity to work on "greeting friends"? Probably not, so leave that box blank and look across the page, still on the row for the first objective, to the next activity, which is "outdoor play." Does it present any natural opportunities to practice greeting friends? Do the same thing for the next objective, and the next, until you have examined each activity in terms of its potential for each of Chu Chu's current IEP objectives. Those with high potential will have more Xs in the boxes under them; those with less potential will have fewer Xs. Skills that are of high priority to parents are indicated by a ✓ instead of an X. The last row in the matrix is left blank so that additions can be made if, upon reflection, the team feels a certain skill or behavior not included in the IEP or IFSP would benefit from focused attention.

It is important to remember that while an activity presents an opportunity to address the needs of a student with disabilities, it does not necessarily require *adaptations*. As indicated in Table 1, Step 4.3, an *adaptation* refers to the need to either change the content or substantive purpose of an activity, or change the way in which the activity is conducted by changing the setting arrangements, staffing patterns and responsibilities, or materials. Again, to use Chu Chu as the example, we have suggested in Figure 1 that arrival provides an opportunity to address his need to learn to greet his friends, a social skill goal taken from his IEP. Since this is not typically a skill that is the focus of instruction during arrival time, an adaptation of the first type (change in focus or content) is indicated by placement of an "X" to indicate Adaptation: Modified content/ focus. But in order to accomplish this goal, the teacher will have to change how she behaves during the arrival of all of her students by focusing her attention specifically upon Chu Chu, prompting him to say "hello" and acknowledge others' greetings. Since this focused structure is not a typical part of the teacher's behavior during arrival, it would constitute an *adaptation* of the second type (Adaptation: Modified arrangement/ staffing) and may require additional staff to help out with the other children while the teacher concentrates her attention on Chu Chu. Or, perhaps a "special friend" can be designated to help.

As is evident from Figure 1, arrival also provides an opportunity to address three other goals from Chu Chu's IEP: expressive vocabulary, pincer grasp, and signaling to use the bathroom should he need to do so. Because teaching these skills is not a part of the arrival activity for the other children, it needs further adaptation. Later, while outside, Chu Chu can practice greeting friends and using his expressive language and fine motor pincer grasp, but the signs indicating the need for an adaptation suggest that Chu Chu's caregivers will need to more carefully structure his activities so that he has sufficient opportunities to practice these skills each time he goes outside.

As required by his IEP, Chu Chu also will receive two types of related services, outside of the classroom (planning Step 5). Looking at Figure 1, it is evident that his team believed that the best time for him to miss a class activity to receive these services was during free choice time and part of the time devoted to learning centers. Additionally, Chu Chu's Activity Matrix indicates two family priority skills (planning Step 3.2): the social skill of greeting friends and the self-help skill of signaling his need to use the bathroom. The family also had indicated that they very much want Chu Chu to exhibit age-appropriate skills at restaurants, since they enjoy eating out as a family (planning Step 6). Staff plan to help identify non-obtrusive strategies that the family may use to reinforce Chu Chu's use of appropriate

social and communication skills in this community environment. Those that involve signaling his need to use the bathroom are of particular concern.

Figure 2 is similar to Figure 1. Activities of the early childhood (EC) program are listed in which Nikki, a 3-year-old with autism and moderate cognitive delay, is included. Skills that are the focus of instruction are taken directly from her IEP and are recorded down the left side of the matrix; an "X" is entered for each activity for each skill that may be addressed during that activity, and the need for adaptations is noted where necessary. As is the case with Chu Chu, Nikki's family's priorities are included. Attending church services is one of their top priorities. Therefore, their desire to have Nikki develop non-disruptive ways of occupying herself during the main service (so that they can all sit together as a family) is recorded in the matrix.

One major difference between Chu Chu's matrix and Nikki's is the indicated need for a behavior support plan for Nikki. She will often scream and hit when blocked from engaging in a behavior or if she is otherwise frustrated in an attempt to gain attention or access to a desired object. The support plan is the primary responsibility of those who are also responsible for the IEP, typically the ECSE teacher, behavior specialists with the public school district, and the family. However, since it will have to be implemented throughout the day in the regular early childhood setting, as well as in the community, it becomes essential that the EC program staff are involved in a determination of the adaptations that may be necessary to ensure success in the inclusive setting. Children with severe behavior problems often provide the greatest challenge to successful inclusion. We have found, however, that careful team planning with an eye toward modifications and supports, along with a willingness to try alternatives, will greatly reduce potential disruptions and go a long way toward creating an atmosphere of acceptance.

Conclusion

Developmentally appropriate practices in early childhood education programs must be implemented with a clear understanding of and appreciation for the extremes of individual variation that are likely to be encountered. Cultural, ethnic, and racial diversities are important and valued characteristics of the population of young children currently served by early childhood education programs. We now recognize the importance of curricula that celebrate different values and associated expressions of those values in both the content and strategy of instruction. As Noonan and McCormick (1993) noted, it is important to reference the early childhood curriculum to the child's social environment. However, recent social and legal imperatives have given additional meaning to "diversity." Children with a range of disabilities, including those with severe cognitive, motor, emotional, and behavioral disabilities, are a valuable aspect of the differences that we celebrate in our early childhood education programs. Their presence should cause us to pause and take a closer look at what we believe about how all children grow and learn and how we teach them.

If children are to benefit from the participation that inclusion brings, then educators, administrators, related service professionals, and parents must be ever-mindful that participation and achievement require that we emphasize the uniqueness of each child.

References

Allen, K. E., & Cowdery, G. E. (2004). *The exceptional child: Inclusion in early childhood education.* (5th ed.). Albany, NY: Thomson/Delmar Publishers.

Association for Persons with Severe Handicaps, The. (2000). *TASH Resolution on Quality Inclusive Education.* Baltimore: Author.

Bredekamp, S., & Copple, C. (Eds.). (1997). *Developmentally appropriate practice in early childhood programs* (Rev. ed.). Washington DC: National Association for the Education of Young Children.

Bricker, D., & Waddell, M. (2002a). *Assessment, evaluation and programming system (2nd ed.): Curriculum for birth to three years: Volume 3.* Baltimore: Paul H. Brookes.

Bricker, D., & Waddell, M. (2002b). *Assessment, evaluation and programming system (2nd ed.): Curriculum for three to six years: Volume 4.* Baltimore: Paul H. Brookes.

Brigance, A.H. (2004). *Brigance Diagnostic Inventory of Early Development* (2nd ed.). North Billerica, MA: Curriculum Associates.

Campbell, P. H. (2006). Addressing motor disabilities. In M. E. Snell & F. Brown (Eds.), *Instruction of students with severe disabilities* (6th ed., pp. 291–327). Upper Saddle River, NJ: Merrill.

Cook, R. E, Klein, M. D, Tessier, A., & Daley, S. (2004). *Adapting early childhood curricula for children in inclusive settings* (6th ed.). Upper Saddle River, NJ: Pearson Prentice Hall.

Fox, T. J., & Williams, W. (1991). *Implementing best practices for all students in their local school.* Burlington, VT: Center for Developmental Disabilities, The University of Vermont.

Friend, M., & Bursuck, W. D. (2002). *Including students with special needs: A practical guide for classroom teachers* (3rd ed.). Boston: Allyn and Bacon.

Gelfer, J., Filler, J., & Perkins, P. (1999). The development of a bachelor's degree in early childhood education: Preparation for teaching inclusive education. *Early Child Development and Care, 154,* 41–48.

Giangreco, M. F., Broer, S. M., & Edelman, W. (2002). "That was then, this is now!" Paraprofessional support for students with disabilities in general education classrooms. *Exceptionality, 10*(1), 47–64.

Gonzalez-Mena, J. (2000). *Foundations: Early childhood education in a diverse society.* Mountain View, CA: Mayfield.

Hauser-Cram, P., Bronson, M. B., & Upshur, C. C. (1993). The effects of the classroom environment on the social and mastery behavior of preschool children with disabilities. *Early Childhood Research Quarterly, 8,* 479–497.

Heller, H.W. (1992). A rationale for departmentalization of special education. In W. Stainback & S. Stainback (Eds.), *Controversial issues confronting special education* (pp. 271–281). Needham Heights, MA: Allyn and Bacon.

Individuals with Disabilities Education Act (IDEA), §303.18 of Rules and Regulations (1998).

Individuals with Disabilities Education Improvement Act. 20 U.S.C. 1414, §614 (2004).

Kostell, P. H. (1997). *Inclusion.* (*ACEI Speaks* brochure.) Olney, MD: Association for Childhood Education International.

Noonan, M. J., & McCormick, L. (1993). *Early intervention in natural environments: Methods and procedures.* Belmont, CA: Brookes/Cole Publishing.

Pretti-Frontczak, K., & Bricker, D. (2004). *An activity-based approach to early intervention* (3rd ed.). Baltimore: Paul H. Brookes.

Sandall, S., McLean, M. E., & Smith, B.J. (2000). *DEC recommended practices in early intervention/early childhood special education.* Longmont, CO: Sopris West.

JOHN FILLER is Professor, Department of Education, University of Nevada, Las Vegas. **YAOYING XU** is Assistant Professor, Department of Special Education and Disability Policy, Virginia Commonwealth University, Richmond.

UNIT 4

Supporting Young Children's Development

Unit Selections

18. **Play and Social Interaction in Middle Childhood,** Doris Bergen and Doris Pronin Fromberg
19. **Twelve Characteristics of Effective Early Childhood Teachers,** Laura J. Colker
20. **Health = Performance,** Ginny Ehrlich
21. **Which Hand?: Brains, Fine Motor Skills, and Holding a Pencil,** *Texas Child Care*
22. **Keeping Children Active: What You Can Do to Fight Childhood Obesity,** Rae Pica
23. **The Truth about ADHD,** Jeannette Moninger
24. **When Girls and Boys Play: What Research Tells Us,** Jeanetta G. Riley and Rose B. Jones

Key Points to Consider

- Why is it important for children to play throughout childhood?

- Describe some characteristics you remember in teachers who made an impact on your life.

- Why has childhood obesity become such an epidemic in our country today?

- Have you thought about the way children develop handedness? What can teachers do to support development in that area?

- How can the teacher assist children with ADHD in the classroom?

- How would the elimination of play and recess from the school setting affect children?

Student Website
www.mhhe.com/cls

Internet References

Action for Healthy Kids
www.actionforhealthykids.org
American Academy of Pediatrics
www.aap.org

Normally, as editor I wouldn't consider an article for *Annual Editions: Early Childhood Education* with the word middle in the title. There is an *Annual Editions: Education* that may be better suited for an article aimed at middle childhood, those years from age 8 through age 12. But upon a second and then third reading of the article "Play and Social Interaction in Middle Childhood" by two very well known early childhood educators, Doris Bergen and Doris Pronin Fromberg, I realized the message is vitally important for all early childhood educators to read as well. The middle years follow early childhood and build upon a child's initial encounters with his or her family, environment, and formal learning experience. Children in the middle years are now undergoing tremendous pressure to often act, dress, and perform like teenagers. Recognition of the importance and value of play and other experiences unique to the middle years are important for early childhood educators. The middle childhood years continue to build on the strong foundation laid during the early childhood years and, when supported by family members and educators, can serve to strengthen the experiences children will take into their teen and adult years. I do find it disheartening to read the first sentence in Bergen and Fromberg's summary, "Play has always been important in middle childhood, but its forms have changed with society and, in some cases, its very existence has been threatened." Unfortunately, that statement could also be applied to play during the early childhood years. Schools are eliminating recess and reducing the opportunities for free choice play materials in preschool and kindergartens all across the country. Both early and middle childhood educators must advocate for hands-on, experiential-based experiences for the children in our classrooms.

The unit continues with Laura J. Colker's article, "Twelve Characteristics of Effective Early Childhood Teachers." If the readers of this book think back about the effectiveness of the many teachers they have had over the years, a pattern will begin to emerge. Historically, researchers have found knowledge of child development, enthusiasm, a caring attitude, and a child-centered approach to learning to be the characteristics of successful teachers. You may recognize a favorite teacher from your past just by seeing this list of characteristics or remember some of your best teachers as having other qualities. Colker wanted to directly ask teachers what makes an effective teacher, so she conducted extensive interviews that required the participants to reflect on why they work in the field, skills they need, the challenges they face along with the rewards. She found that twelve consistent responses emerged, and expands on those in this article. How many of these twelve characteristics such as passion, patience, creativity, and high energy are a part of your repertoire of dispositions?

Issues related to the health of young children continued to emerge this year and two articles in this unit address that topic. "Health = Performance" and "Keeping Children Active: What You Can Do to Fight Childhood Obesity" address the importance of a healthy body for optimal educational performance. Ginny Ehrlich shares suggestions for adults who want to provide an environment to support a healthy lifestyle in "Health = Performance."

© Laurence Mouton/Photoalto/PictureQuest RF

She states that adults are powerful role models for young children and should participate in healthy lifestyle choices. Childhood obesity is noticeable every time one enters a fast-food restaurant and hears a child order a meal by its number on the menu because he is so familiar with the selection at that particular restaurant. It is also evident on a playground where children just sit on the sideline not wanting to participate with their peers due to negative body image. Teachers can apply the suggestions provided in the article on obesity that will help children develop appropriate eating habits and an active lifestyle. Parents and educators must work together to promote healthy living with one-third of children classified as overweight and one-fifth of children as obese. Teachers should also participate in healthy-living activities. Only then will our society begin to realize that a lifestyle that includes good nutrition and exercise is one of the best ways to lead a long and healthy life. Teachers can model an active healthy lifestyle for the children in their classroom. Teachers can walk around the playground when the children are outside instead of standing in a group and talking to the other teachers. They can also talk about the foods eaten for breakfast, lunch, and dinner and share healthy eating tips with the children.

Continuing with the theme of the importance of teachers carefully observing children to determine their preferences, strengths, and needs is the article, "Which Hand?: Brains, Fine Motor Skills, and Holding a Pencil." Parents and teachers worry about handedness of children and are confused about the best ways to help children feel confident with the hand that feels most comfortable to them. For every successful left-handed major league baseball pitcher with a multimillion dollar contract, there are thousands of left-handed children struggling to learn in a right-handed world. About ten to twelve percent of the population is left-handed. Strategies for helping all children strengthen motor skills that support learning are included.

The title of this unit, once again, must be stressed: "Supporting Young Children's Development." Teachers who see their job of working with young children as finding the approach that best supports each child's individual development will be most successful. We are not to change children to meet some idealistic model, but become an investigator whose job it is to ferret out the individual strengths and learning styles of each child in our care. Enjoy each day and the many different experiences awaiting you when you work with young children and their families.

Play and Social Interaction in Middle Childhood

Play is vital for a child's emotional and cognitive development. But social and technological forces threaten the kinds of play kids need most.

Doris Bergen and Doris Pronin Fromberg

Play is important to the optimum development of children during their middle childhood years. Unfortunately, though there is abundant research evidence showing that play supports young children's social, emotional, physical, and cognitive development, it has often been ignored or addressed only minimally (Fromberg and Bergen 2006). However, when young adults are asked to recall their most salient play experiences, they typically give elaborate and joyous accounts of their play during the ages of eight to 12 (Bergen and Williams 2008). Much of the play they report involves elaborate, pretense scripts conducted for a long duration at home, in their neighborhood, or in the school yard. The respondents report that they either personally played the roles or used small objects (action figures, cars, dolls) as the protagonists. They also report games with child-generated rules that they adapted during play. For example, they might have had bike-riding contests or played a baseball-like game that uses fence posts for bases and gives five-out turns to the youngest players. These young adults believed that their middle childhood play helped them learn "social skills," "hobbies," and often "career decisions" that influenced their later, adult experiences.

Many schools, especially those considered to be poor performers, have reduced or eliminated recess.

For many children, the opportunities for such freely chosen play are narrowing. Much of their play time at home has been lost to music, dance, or other lessons; participation on sport teams (using adult-defined rules); and after-school homework or test preparation sessions. At the same time, many schools, especially those considered to be poor performers, have reduced or eliminated recess (Pellegrini 2005). Often, the only outdoor time in the school day is the 10 to 15 minutes left from a lunch period, with rules such as "no running allowed." Thus, the importance of play during middle childhood must be reemphasized by educators who understand why it facilitates skilled social interaction, emotional regulation, higher cognitive processing, and creativity.

Defining Middle Childhood Play

At any age, for an activity to count as play, it must be voluntary and self-organized. Children identify an activity as play when they choose it, but they define the same activity as work when an adult chooses it for them (King 1992). Play differs from exploring an object because such exploration answers the question: "What can it do?" In contrast, play answers the question: "What can I do with it?" (Hutt 1976).

Play in middle childhood continues to include practice play (repeating and elaborating on the same activities, often in the service of increasing skill levels), pretense (using symbolic means to envision characters and scenarios, using literary and other media experiences, as well as real-life experience sources), games with rules (revising existing games or making up elaborate games that have negotiated rules), and construction play (building and designing structures or artistic works). All of these types of play show increasing abilities to deal with cognitive, social, and emotional issues, as well as increases in physical skills.

The rules of play become apparent as children oscillate between negotiating the play scenarios and seamlessly entering into the activities, whether in selecting teams and rules for game play or borrowing media characters to "become" the pretend characters. Script theory, a kind of grammar of play (Fromberg 2002), outlines this oscillating collaborative process. The play process develops throughout the middle childhood years with 1) props becoming more miniaturized, 2) play episodes more extended, 3) language more complex, 4) themes more coherent, and 5) physical prowess more refined.

The Value of Middle Childhood Play

As the memories of young adults testify, play continues to be very valuable during the middle childhood years. Social and emotional competence, imagination, and cognitive development are fostered by many types of play.

Social and emotional competence. Although adults may provide the space and objects with which their children play, during play children practice their power to self-direct, self-organize, exert self-control, and negotiate with others. Even when engaged in rough-and-tumble play, if it was a mutual decision, the children involved demonstrate self-control (Reed and Brown 2000). Such experiences build confidence in deferring immediate gratification, persevering, and collaborating. Even when the play deals with hurtful themes, the children's intrinsic motivation ensures that the play serves a pleasurable, meaningful purpose for the players. For example, role playing threat, aggression, or death can help children deal with the reality of such issues.

Affiliation. Children who negotiate their play together fulfill their need for affiliation. How to enter into play successfully is a negotiation skill, and it requires practice and the opportunity to be with peers. The loner child who stands on the outside of a group and observes may not have these skills; these children may meet their needs for affiliation by joining a gang or by resorting to bullying and violence.

Cognitive development. Middle childhood play fosters cognitive development. Children exercise their executive skills when planning pretense scripts, using symbols in games, designing constructions, and organizing games with rules. For example, in construction play with blocks, exploratory manipulation precedes the capacity to create new forms. These three-dimensional constructions help older children develop the visual-spatial imagery that supports learning in mathematics, chemistry, and physics. Outdoor seasonal games that require eye-hand coordination and aiming—such as hopscotch, jump rope, tag, and baseball—also build the imagery that supports such concepts. Fantasy play can involve scripts that go on for days and become extremely elaborate. Sociodramatic play is a form of collaborative oral playwriting and editing, which contributes to the writer's sense of audience (Fromberg 2002). Thus, scripts often are written to guide the play.

Most humor involves cognitive incongruity, which demonstrates what children know.

Humor is very evident in middle childhood play, and although some is "nonsense" humor, most involves cognitive incongruity, which demonstrates what children know. That is, by using puns, jokes, exaggerations, and other word play, they show their knowledge of the world and gain power and delight in transforming that knowledge in incongruous ways. Much of this joking is designed to shock adults, but it also demonstrates children's increasing knowledge of the world. Playful use of language also shows up in "Pig Latin" and other code languages, which both include the play group and exclude others. Learning and performing "magic" tricks is also a delight and requires understanding the laws of objects and thus how to appear to bypass those laws.

Imagination and creativity. Children dramatize roles and scenarios with miniature animals, toy soldiers, and media action figures, using themes from their experiences, including "playing school." Some urban children might dramatize cops and gangs. Children in both urban and rural areas engage in such pretense, trying on a sense of power and independence, by imagining "what if" there were no adult society. As they try roles and pretend possible careers, they seek privacy from adults during much of this play, preferring tree houses, vacant lots, basements, or other "private" spaces. Symbolic games, such as Monopoly (using a board or online forms), as well as other computer or board games, add to the development of social learning and competence as children increasingly become precise about following the rules of the game.

When children have had opportunities to practice pretense and use their imaginations, researchers have found that they're more able to be patient and perseverant, as well as to imagine the future (Singer and Singer 2006). Being able to imagine and role play a particular career, rent and furnish an apartment, and negotiate other aspects of daily living makes those actions seem less daunting later on.

Contemporary Middle Childhood Play

Play for children in this age group has changed. Today, there are virtual, technology-enhanced play materials, a constriction of play space from the neighborhood to one's own home and yard, and the actual loss of free time and school time to devote to active play.

Technology. For children in the middle childhood years, virtual reality technology now provides three-dimensional interactive games, such as Nintendo's Wii, which uses hand-held devices that can detect motion. These interactive games may be so engaging that children, mainly boys, abandon other activities that build negotiation skills and social competence with other children. Children also increasingly "instant message," creating abbreviation codes—a form of power—and demonstrate their deepening digital literacy. In addition, they listen to music on iPods, play virtual musical instruments, and make virtual friends with whom they interact. This period of childhood affords different opportunities for children in less affluent families, however, resulting in a widening gap in types of technology-enhanced play materials and experiences among children from different socioeconomic levels. For example, though children can initially access some websites without cost, devices and software require purchases that are seductive, with consoles and accessories rising in cost.

Gender roles also are affected by technology. Virtual reality computer games for girls, such as Mattel's Barbie Girls, reinforce stereotypes. Boys are especially interested in virtual action games.

Suburban parents may believe that homes are too far apart to allow children to walk to friends' houses.

Spaces for play. Many parents are reluctant to allow their children to range far in their neighborhoods for the kinds of social experiences that were common for earlier generations. This could be caused by frequent media reports of potential dangers (Louv 2008). Parents may see city environments as too dangerous, and suburban parents may believe that homes are too far apart to allow children to walk to friends' houses or gather in neighborhood outdoor areas.

Time for freely chosen play. Administrators and teachers pressured to increase academic performance often reduce recess to a short period or omit it altogether because they believe this time is "wasted" or that it just will be a time for children to engage in bullying or other unacceptable behaviors. They also may fear lawsuits because of perceived dangers in freely chosen play, as indicated by prohibitions against running. In spite of research indicating that attention to school tasks may be greater if periods of recess are interspersed (Opie and Opie 1976), some adults don't seem to realize the potential of play as a means of supporting academic learning. Thus, time for play has been reduced both in the home and school environments.

Adult Facilitation of Play

Because middle childhood play is so valuable for social, emotional, cognitive, and physical development and because some trends seem to prevent play's full elaboration and development during these years, adults must become advocates for play and facilitators of play in middle childhood. There are a number of ways they can do this.

Providing play resources. When adults provide indoor and outdoor space and materials, children can adapt and use them creatively. The best kinds of materials have more than a single use but can be modified by interaction with others and elaborated with imagination.

Engaging in play interaction. When adults provide real choices, children can build the trust they need to cope with solving physical problems and negotiating emerging interpersonal play. Adults should appreciate process and effort without judging outcomes. They might assist less play-competent children's interactions by offering relevant materials to help

their children be invited into pretense games that other children have started.

Assessing play competence. Educators, in particular, often find that most children comply with their suggestions about play activities, but there may be one or two who do not appear to be participating or, on closer observation, appear to comply, but in their own ways. Teachers, in particular, need to appreciate the multiple ways in which children may represent experiences and display a sense of playfulness. In addition, teachers' assessments should also include observations of children's play competence, especially as it relates to development of imaginative and creative idea generation.

Supporting gender equity. Gender equity and children's aspirations are affected by sanctions and warrants. For example, boys have traditionally dominated play involving 3-D constructions, though some girls are now participating in Lego Robotics teams. To make girls more likely to participate, teachers should place themselves near 3-D construction areas or planned "borderwork" (Thorne 1993). Teachers should be sure to provide materials and equipment that do not have gender-suggestive advertising (Goldstein 1994). In this way, all children can be encouraged to have greater expectations for themselves.

Summary

Play has always been important in middle childhood, but its forms have changed with society and, in some cases, its very existence has been threatened. Parents and educators can facilitate aspects of play that support emotional, social, cognitive, and creative growth. To understand the importance of play for these children, they only have to recall the salience of their own play during this age period.

References

Bergen, Doris, and Elizabeth Williams. "Differing Childhood Play Experiences of Young Adults Compared to Earlier Young Adult Cohorts Have Implications for Physical, Social, and Academic Development." Poster presentation at the annual meeting of the Association for Psychological Science, Chicago, 2008.

Fromberg, Doris P. *Play and Meaning in Early Childhood Education.* Boston: Allyn & Bacon, 2002.

Fromberg, Doris P., and Doris Bergen. *Play from Birth to 12.* New York: Routledge, 2006.

Goldstein, Jeffrey H., ed. *Toys, Play, and Child Development.* New York: Cambridge University Press, 1994.

Hutt, Corinne. "Exploration and Play in Children." In *Play: Its Role in Development and Evolution,* ed. Jerome S. Bruner, Alison Jolly, and Kathy Sylva, 202–215. New York: Basic Books, 1976.

King, Nancy. "The Impact of Context on the Play of Young Children." In *Reconceptualizing the Early Childhood Curriculum,* ed. Shirley A. Kessler and Beth Blue Swadener, 42–81. New York: Teachers College Press, 1992.

Louv, Richard. *Last Child in the Woods: Saving Our Children from Nature-Deficit Disorder.* Chapel Hill, N.C.: Algonquin Books, 2008.

Opie, Iona A., and Peter M. Opie. "Street Games: Counting-Out and Chasing." In *Play: Its Role in Development and Evolution,* ed. Jerome S. Bruner, Alison Jolly, and Kathy Sylva, 394–412. New York: Basic Books, 1976.

Pellegrini, Anthony D. *Recess: Its Role in Education and Development.* Mahwah, N.J.: Lawrence Erlbaum Associates, 2005.

Reed, Tom, and Mac Brown. "The Expression of Care in Rough and Tumble Play of Boys." *Journal of Research in Childhood Education* 15 (Fall-Winter 2000): 104–116.

Singer, Dorothy G., and Jerome L. Singer. "Fantasy and Imagination." In *Play from Birth to 12: Contexts, Perspectives, and Meanings,* ed. Doris P. Fromberg and Doris Bergen, 371–378. New York: Routledge, 2006.

Thorne, Barrie. *Gender Play: Girls and Boys in School.* New Brunswick, N.J.: Rutgers University Press, 1993.

DORIS BERGEN is distinguished professor of educational psychology at Miami University, Oxford, Ohio, and co-director of the Center for Human Development, Learning, and Technology. With Doris Pronin Fromberg, she co-edited the book, *Play from Birth to Twelve,* 2nd ed. (Routledge, 2006). **DORIS PRONIN FROMBERG** is a professor of education and past chairperson of the Department of Curriculum and Teaching at Hofstra University, Hempstead, New York.

From *Phi Delta Kappan,* by Doris Bergen and Doris Pronin Fromberg, February 2009, pp. 426–430. Reprinted with permission of Phi Delta Kappa International, www.pdkintl.org, 2009. All rights reserved.

Twelve Characteristics of Effective Early Childhood Teachers

Laura J. Colker

What does it take to be an effective early childhood teacher? This is a question that has long gnawed at reflective teacher educators, idealistic teachers (especially those just beginning their careers), and worried families who place their young children in the care of another adult. Many educators feel that effectiveness as a teacher stems from a combination of knowledge, skills, and personal characteristics (Katz 1993).

While aspiring teachers can increase their knowledge and develop their skills, their personal characteristics—which involve the socioemotional and spiritual realms in addition to the cognitive—are likely to be more fixed. As Cantor (1990) notes, one can have both knowledge and skills, but without a disposition to make use of them, very little will happen. *Having* is not the same as *doing.*

Because personal characteristics are rooted in feelings and beliefs, we can neither observe them directly nor assess them through traditional methods (Ostorga 2003), which makes them difficult to identify. Nevertheless, teacher educators and administrators would benefit greatly from knowing the characteristics of an effective early childhood teacher, as they strive to improve the quality of the field. New teachers and those at a crossroads in their career would also benefit if they could confirm that the interpersonal and intrapersonal beliefs they possess are those demanded by the field.

Reviewing the Literature

With these goals in mind, this article summarizes an attempt to identify some of the key characteristics early childhood teachers need to excel in their job. This is by no means a novel idea. The literature cites numerous examples of positive teacher dispositions (Ebro 1977; Smith 1980; Glenn 2001; Usher 2003; Adams & Pierce 2004). These examples often include characteristics such as enthusiasm and a good attitude.

Although they serve a definite need, the existing examples have limitations. Characteristics, or *dispositions,* as they are sometimes called, are frequently used interchangeably with traits and skills in the literature, when in fact they are not the same. DaRos-Voseles and Fowler-Hughey (2007) make the point that traits, unlike dispositions, are unconscious behavioral habits.

Skills such as "being organized," "having command of the classroom," and "asking probing questions" are teacher abilities but not characteristics.

A second problem with the current literature on teacher characteristics is that most of the lists of characteristics were developed with teachers of students in grades beyond the primary years in mind. Indeed, the most common focus is on teachers in higher education; none of the lists of desired teacher characteristics apply exclusively to early childhood teachers. Such a list would certainly benefit the field. Because early childhood teachers need unique knowledge and skills, it is also likely that they need to have characteristics that are unique to them as a group.

A final limitation of the existing literature is that in most instances, teacher educators are the ones attempting to define characteristics of effective teachers. While there is value in this approach, dispositions compiled by experts working with practitioners do not necessarily represent characteristics that practitioners themselves consider important. Because characteristics involve personal perceptions, consulting the beliefs of those doing the job is essential when drawing up a master list of characteristics common among effective early childhood teachers.

In the literature, there are two exceptions in which researchers solicited practitioner perceptions. A study at Ball State University (Johnson 1980) surveyed 227 Indiana public school teachers and 14 school principals to determine the characteristics correlated with teacher effectiveness.

Teachers reported four key characteristics. According to these respondents, effective teachers

- Have a sound knowledge of subject matter.
- Take a personal interest in each student.
- Establish a caring/loving/warm atmosphere.
- Show enthusiasm with students.

Principals offered a slightly different list of characteristics they consider most important. They said effective teachers

- Conduct thorough instructional planning/organizing.
- Are child oriented.
- Show enthusiasm with students.

A more recent study (Taylor & Wash 2003) at Lander University surveyed 3,000 K–12 teachers and administrators in seven school districts. Participants completed a modified Delphi survey, ranking the priority of dispositions indispensable to K–12 teachers. Survey participants identified the following as the top 10 characteristics (in descending rank order) of an effective teacher: enthusiastic, an effective communicator, adaptable to change, a lifelong learner, competent, accepting of others, patient, organized, hardworking, and caring.

A New Survey

To begin to address the gaps in the literature, I interviewed 43 early childhood practitioners to obtain their perceptions about the personal characteristics of effective early childhood teachers. These participants represent a wide range of backgrounds in terms of ethnicity, gender, geographic location, and experience. Although some respondents are no longer classroom teachers (they are mentor teachers, supervisors, trainers, and the like), all were early childhood teachers for a number of years.

Because personal characteristics involve feelings and spirit as well as thought, I did not ask survey participants to simply compose a list of characteristics. Instead, I posed questions about what attracted them to the field of early childhood education, the skills they needed to do their jobs, the challenges they faced, and the rewards they reaped. By reflecting on their practice in this way, respondents described the characteristics of effective teachers.

While this is by no means a perfect approach, it provides insight into a construct that is difficult to define and describe. What follows is a qualitative analysis of the responses provided by the 43 participants. I have organized their responses into 12 themes. The content is entirely the respondents'; the analysis is mine.

What Draws Teachers to the Field of Early Childhood Education?

The reasons people choose a profession offer insight into the characteristics they need to do their job well. Common threads link the practitioners interviewed for this article. People do not enter the early childhood education field for monetary reward or occupational glamour.

I had a need to make a difference in children's lives and ensure they got all the opportunities and nurturing they needed and deserved.

The majority of respondents realized at a young age that they wanted to be early childhood teachers. Many, including Renee Hamilton-Jones, who taught preschool for 13 years, reported feeling that "destiny" led them to their career choice.

Donna Kirsch, a supervisor of early childhood teachers, termed teaching a *calling:* "I had a need to make a difference in children's lives and ensure they got all the opportunities and nurturing they needed and deserved. It was mostly a calling, much like the ministry—but I don't say that out loud to too many people."

The need to make a difference in children's lives was echoed by nearly every respondent, including longtime kindergarten teacher Joanna Phinney: "I entered the field of early childhood education because I wanted to make a difference in the world. I felt that the place to start was with young children because you can make the biggest difference when children are young."

If you ask early childhood educators who entered the field for idealistic reasons whether they made the right career choice, you'll find few regrets. In the group of 43 surveyed here, no one expressed regret. Here's what two prominent early childhood educators who were once classroom teachers said:

> At a certain point in my career I was offered a position that would have been a promotion, but it was not in early childhood. I debated the decision carefully because I was a single parent of two young children at the time and could have used the additional money that came with the promotion. I chose to stay in early childhood education primarily because I knew my heart was with children's programs. In the end, staying with children's programs was the best decision. Even at the time I did not regret the decision because knowing myself as I do, it was more important for me to believe in the cause than to make money.

—Linda Smith, Executive Director, National Association of Child Care Resource and Referral Agencies

> I can honestly say that I have never, not once, reconsidered my decision to be an early childhood educator. Quite the contrary, I have often marveled at my luck. This profession has never disappointed me. Sometimes it is hard and I am not always successful, but I have an abiding belief in the value of my contributions. Early childhood education has definitely been my "calling," and because of the good match, I have been able to apply my talents and skills in an arena that both needed and valued my insights.

—Linda Espinosa, Professor of Early Childhood Education, University of Missouri–Columbia

What Characteristics Make Early Childhood Teachers Effective?

All the survey participants felt strongly that the early childhood profession has been a good match for their personalities and life goals. What then are the personal characteristics that contributed to making early childhood education a good career match?

1. Passion. Probably more than anything else, teachers report that it's important to have a passion for what you do. In many of the studies referenced in the literature, participants singled out "enthusiasm for children" as a key attribute. For the teachers in this study, however, something stronger than enthusiasm makes a truly effective teacher; it is closer to *drive*.

Being an early childhood educator is not always easy. There may be physical and financial challenges, for example. But if you feel that what you are doing makes a difference, that sense of accomplishment can sustain and motivate you. John Varga, a Head Start site supervisor, counsels those who do not have a passion for early childhood to find a different career. "This is not a career for someone just looking for a job working with kids because they are cute and it looks like fun. This is a career that must ignite your passion."

2. Perseverance. This is another characteristic frequently cited. Some respondents referred to perseverance as "dedication;" others felt it was "tenacity." Whatever term they used, what participants described is the willingness to fight for one's beliefs, whether related to children's needs or education issues. Teachers have to be willing to be long-term advocates for improving the lives of children and their families. Respondents in this study believe children need and deserve teachers who can overcome bureaucracy and handle red tape.

3. Willingness to take risks. A third related characteristic is the willingness to take risks. Successful educators are willing to shake up the status quo to achieve their goals for children. Great teachers are willing to go against the norm. Taking a risk means not settling for a no answer if a yes will improve the quality of a child's education.

For example, one teacher reports wanting to team teach her preschool class with a self-contained special education program adjacent to her room. Integration of programs had never been done before at her school, and faculty and administration alike looked at the idea with skepticism. To secure administration approval, the teachers had to conduct research, do a parent survey, and bring in outside experts. They held parent meetings to convince both the families of children with disabilities and those of children without disabilities that their children would benefit. After much energy and effort, the program was initiated on a trial basis. Five years later, it is one of the most successful and popular programs at the school (Villa & Colker 2006).

4. Pragmatism. Pragmatism is the flip side of perseverance and willingness to take risks. Pragmatists are willing to compromise. They know which battles are winnable and when to apply their resources in support of children. The important point, respondents felt, is that effective teachers understand that by temporarily settling for small wins, they are still making progress toward their goals.

5. Patience. In line with pragmatism is the characteristic of patience. Respondents cite the need to have patience both when dealing with "the system" and when working with children and families. Not every child learns quickly. Some behaviors can challenge even the most effective teacher. Children need reminder after reminder. Good teachers have a long fuse for exasperation, frustration, and anger. They regard all such challenges as exactly that—challenges. Effective teaching requires patience.

6. Flexibility. This is the sixth characteristic linked by study participants to successful teaching. Indeed, any job in early childhood education demands that you be able to deal well with change and unexpected turns. Whether it's raining outside and you have to cancel outdoor play, or your funding agency has drastically reduced your operating budget, you need to be able to switch gears at a moment's notice and find an alternative that works.

Indeed, any job in early childhood education demands that you be able to deal well with change and unexpected turns.

Sometimes the challenges are both drastic and sudden. Fresh out of college, Ashley Freiberg—one of the study respondents—had been a kindergarten teacher for only a few weeks when she found herself welcoming evacuees from Hurricane Katrina into her Baton Rouge, Louisiana, classroom: "I have 28 kindergarten children in my classroom, and it is my job to work with each of my students and present them with information that will help them to become readers, to master basic math facts, to know about the world around them, and to follow the classroom and school rules. I must do this leaving no child behind, teaching each individual student in the classroom, *without* a classroom aide!" Despite the pressures, Ashley adapted, doing what she had to for each child. Her flexibility exemplifies a vital character trait that respondents felt effective teachers must have.

7. Respect. Surveyed teachers strongly believed that respect for children and families is basic to being a good early childhood teacher. Some identified this characteristic as an "appreciation of diversity." They described it as not only respecting children and families of all backgrounds, but also as maintaining the belief that everyone's life is enhanced by exposure to people of different backgrounds who speak a variety of languages. We know that children's self-concepts flourish in an environment of respect. Good teachers create this environment naturally.

8. Creativity. An eighth characteristic respondents cited was creativity. It takes creativity to teach in a physical environment that is less than ideal or when resources are limited. It takes creativity to teach children from diverse backgrounds who might not approach education in the same way. It takes creativity to teach children with differing learning styles who think and learn in different ways. And most of all, it takes creativity to make learning fun. Creativity is a hallmark of an effective early childhood teacher.

9. Authenticity. This is another frequently cited characteristic of effective teaching. Some respondents referred to this attribute as "self-awareness." Being authentic means knowing who you are and what you stand for. It is what gives you integrity and conviction.

Young children are shrewd judges of character; they know whether a teacher is authentic, and they respond accordingly.

Young children are shrewd judges of character; they know whether a teacher is authentic, and they respond accordingly.

---

10. Love of learning. Respondents also singled out love of learning. To inspire children with a love of learning, they said, teachers themselves ought to exhibit this characteristic. Teachers who are lifelong learners send children the message that learning is an important part of life. Several participants felt that being an effective teacher involves seeking out knowledge about recent research on teaching. Respondents in this study regard both teaching and learning as dynamic processes.

11. High energy. Though it may have more to do with temperament than disposition, many teachers felt it important that teachers display high energy. Most children respond positively to teachers with high energy levels, valuing their enthusiasm. As Linda Espinosa observed, "The energy it takes to get up every day and work on behalf of young children and families is enormous."

12. Sense of humor. A final vital characteristic of effective teaching pinpointed by respondents in the study was having a sense of humor. Learning should be fun; nothing conveys this message more than a room that is filled with spontaneous laughter. John Varga summarizes the importance of this characteristic in teaching: "All children ask is that we love them and respect them and be willing to laugh when it's funny . . . even when the joke's on us."

Conclusion

Reflecting on their practice, 43 early childhood educators identified characteristics they believe are integral to effective teaching. The resulting 12 characteristics include: (1) passion about children and teaching, (2) perseverance, (3) risk taking, (4) pragmatism, (5) patience, (6) flexibility, (7) respect, (8) creativity, (9) authenticity, (10) love of learning, (11) high energy, and (12) sense of humor.

Interestingly—and not surprisingly—some of the identified characteristics parallel those already identified in the literature (patience, authenticity, and a love of learning, for example.) In other instances, practitioners identified characteristics not typically seen in the literature (perseverance, risk taking, and pragmatism, for example). A future research study could compare the findings; perhaps practitioners have identified trends not yet picked up on by teacher educators.

As acknowledged, data reported in this article were not scientifically collected nor are they meant to represent the view of the entire field. The article does, however, report what selected early childhood educators themselves believe are important characteristics for doing their work effectively. It is the difference between an expert telling a parent how to be a good parent and a parent giving his perspective on parenting. Thus, it is not a question of which is better. Rather, it is an attempt to honor the practitioner's own views about this hard to define but important component of teaching.

References

Adams, C.M., & R.L. Pierce. 2004. Characteristics of effective teaching. In *Traditions and innovations: Teaching at Ball State University.* Muncie, IN: Ball State University. www.bsu.edu/gradschool/media/pdf/chapter12.pdf

Cantor, N. 1990. From thought to behavior: "Having" and "doing" in the study of personality and cognition. *American Psychologist* 45 (6): 735–50.

Da Ros-Voseles, D., & S. Fowler-Haughey. 2007. The role of dispositions in the education of future teachers. *Young Children* 62 (5): 90–98.

Ebro, L.L. 1977. Instructional behavior patterns of distinguished university teachers. Doctoral dissertation, Ohio State University.

Glenn, R.E. 2001. Admirable teaching traits. *Teaching for excellence.* Spartansburg, SC: Author. www.education-world.com/a_curr/curr387.shtml

Johnson, M. 1980. Effective teaching as perceived by teachers and principals in selected Indiana school corporations. *Ball State University doctoral dissertations.* Abstract. Muncie, IN: Ball State University. www.bsu.edu/libraries/virtualpress/student/dissertations/author_list.asp

Katz, L.G. 1993. *Dispositions: Definitions and implications for early childhood practices.* Champaign-Urbana, IL: ERIC Clearinghouse on Elementary and Early Childhood Education. http://ceep.crc.uiuc.edu/eecearchive/books/disposit.html

Ostorga, A.N. 2003. The role of values in the development of dispositions. Paper presented at the Second Annual Symposium on Educator Dispositions, November 20–21, in Richmond, Kentucky.

Smith, R. 1980. A checklist for good teaching. Montreal, Quebec, Canada: Teaching and Learning Centre, Concordia University.

Taylor, B., & P. Wash. 2003. 3,000 educators respond to preferred dispositions. Paper presented at the Second Annual Symposium on Educator Dispositions, November 20–21, in Richmond, Kentucky.

Usher, D. 2003. Arthur Combs' five dimensions of helper belief reformulated as five dispositions of teacher effectiveness. Paper presented at the Second Annual Symposium on Educator Dispositions, November 20–21, in Richmond, Kentucky.

Villa, K., with L.J. Colker. 2006. A personal story: Making inclusion work. *Young Children* 61 (1): 96–100.

LAURA J. COLKER, EdD, is a curriculum developer and teacher trainer in Washington, D.C. She is a contributing editor to NAEYC's new publication, *Teaching Young Children.* The information in this article was collected for a project Laura collaborated on with NAEYC's Carol Copple and Sue Bredekamp of the Council for Professional Recognition. ljcolker@aol.com

---

Health = Performance

Efforts to increase student achievement also should address physical activity and a good diet.

GINNY EHRLICH

Looking to improve student achievement? Consider this: How healthy are your students?

Healthy children learn better—few statements in education are as unequivocal. We know this on a common-sense level, and the data backs it up. Research suggests that students' health and learning are inextricably linked. Studies also have shown that school health programs can boost students' academic performance and improve behavior and attendance.

So, efforts to increase student achievement should include a focus on health. School health programs and board policies can address physical activity and healthy eating—two areas that are particularly important in light of the obesity epidemic in the U.S. One in three children and adolescents is already overweight or obese, the Centers for Disease Control and Prevention (CDC) reports. Extra weight can cause a host of health problems in children, including asthma and Type 2 diabetes.

Perhaps the most established relationship of health and achievement is between eating breakfast at school and academic performance, no matter what the student's socioeconomic status. Studies have linked eating breakfast at school with improved performance on standardized tests and better math grades, as well as with improved student attendance.

Though research suggests that school breakfast has a positive impact on all students' performance, impact is greatest for students from food-insecure households.

Qualitative studies also cited the relationship between healthy eating and better student behavior. In a longitudinal child health study, teachers consistently cited the link between students' eating habits and their behaviors.

Some teachers said that students who participated in the school meals programs or who had consumed less sugar were less likely to display aggressive behavior and less likely to be referred out of the classroom. Both factors increase learning time for students who arguably need it the most.

Studies also show that there are correlations between students' physical activity and academic performance. A statewide study of students in California found a positive relationship between students' physical fitness levels and their standardized math and reading scores.

Further, students who were physically active every day were more likely to report getting mostly As and Bs in school than their more sedentary peers, according to a 2003 CDC study.

One obvious way to increase students' physical fitness is to offer quality physical education programs. Though several districts around the country have cut physical education programs to make room for more reading, math, and science instruction, the evidence suggests that spending more time in physical education class did not have a negative effect on students' standardized test scores, even though less time was available for other academic subjects.

Taking the Leap

Most school leaders and educators acknowledge the importance of these links between health and achievement, but given the stakes of meeting No Child Left Behind measures, there is little action taken. However, some districts have taken the leap to address the whole child, and they have reaped the benefits.

Most school leaders and educators acknowledge the importance of these links between health and achievement.

In McComb, Miss., former Superintendent Pat Cooper made a commitment to concentrate on the health needs of students. McComb is a small district that serves a vulnerable student population, most of whom live in poverty. Cooper implemented a coordinated school health approach to address the physical, social, and emotional barriers to learning.

McComb's program includes the eight components of the coordinated school health approach: school employee wellness, physical education, health education, nutrition services, parent and family involvement, school health services, mental health counseling, and environmental health.

The district has seen improvement in its students' academic achievement. Between 1996 and 2005, dropout rates decreased from 31 percent to 11 percent, and graduation rates increased to 95 percent. The district's ranking rose from 59th to 14th in the state.

Not only did students stay in school, but they also performed better. Standardized test scores improved in reading, writing, language arts, and math in every grade (except eighth, which remained the same). These scores now exceed state averages in several areas and all McComb schools qualify as "successful" (Level 3), as measured by the Mississippi state standards.

Tennessee has made a statewide commitment to addressing physical, social, and emotional barriers to learning that also has yielded positive returns. In 2002, Tennessee implemented a coordinated school health pilot program in 11 school districts throughout the state.

An independent evaluation conducted between 2002 and 2006 found that this initiative helped raise student achievement along with improving their health. Specifically, there is a substantial difference in dropout rates and graduation rates between the pilot districts and the state norm. Dropout rates in pilot districts were lower than the state norm in 2006 in nine of 11 systems and the high school graduation rates were higher than the state norm in 2006 in nine of 11 systems.

Additionally, competency rates in reading, writing, and language in kindergarten through eighth grade revealed that the majority of pilot sites exceeded the state norm for 2006. All of the school systems saw steady improvement from the baseline of 2003. Competency in mathematics and reading in kindergarten through eighth grade improved in all 11 school systems from 2003 to 2006, and all systems had higher mean scores on writing assessments in 2006 than in 2002.

What You Can Do

The Alliance for a Healthier Generation's Healthy Schools Program supports districts and schools in the implementation of a coordinated school health approach to promoting physical activity and healthy eating among students and school staff.

The Healthy Schools Program provides no-cost support to any school in the country through training, online tools, and phone consultation focused on district-wide promotion of physical activity and healthy eating for students and staff. Within the Healthy Schools Program Best Practice Framework, there are specific policy recommendations for supporting a healthier school environment. They include:

- Offering a healthy breakfast for every student every day. Consider extending a common practice, providing breakfast for all students during testing periods, to an everyday practice. The learning benefits can only increase gains in test scores. It is also important to ensure that the breakfast includes a healthy balance of lean proteins, whole fruits, and whole grains to fuel students for learning.

- Allocating adequate time for quality physical education. Given that evidence suggests that physical education time does not detract from student performance, it makes sense to maintain it within the curriculum. Quality physical education, based on state and national standards, offers many other benefits, such as keeping students active and building their skills to maintain lifelong physical activity.

- Providing access to healthier foods and beverages before, during, and after the school day. A consistent message about, and access to, healthier options across the school, in hallways, classrooms, cafeterias, and canteens, helps students to see these options as the norm and to establish their healthy eating patterns. Studies have shown a 1 percent increase in students' body mass index for every 10 percent increase in less healthy foods available at school.

- Dedicating time to quality health education. Health education not only contributes to building the knowledge and skills students need to build healthy habits, it also has been linked to improved reading scores in elementary-age students.

- Supporting school staff to be healthy role models. Parents are the primary role models for their kids, but given that the vast majority of school-age youth spend at least six hours a day in school, it is important that school staff communicate consistent messages. School employee wellness programs can help motivate staff to be more active and make healthier food choices. Their enhanced awareness of the benefits of wellness often results in them modeling and promoting healthier behaviors.

- It is important to consider the program and policy implications for establishing school environments that promote healthy eating and physical activity for all students as a critical part of education reform. The evidence clearly suggests a link between students' health behaviors and their educational performance.

- Healthy school environments support a better future for all of us by ensuring that students who are academically prepared are also healthy and live long enough to contribute their talents to the nation's future.

GINNY EHRLICH is the executive director of the Alliance for a Healthier Generation in New York, N.Y.

Which Hand?

Brains, Fine Motor Skills, and Holding a Pencil

LOUISE PARKS

- Right hand, left hand, or ambidextrous?
- What is handedness?
- How does handedness happen?
- Do left handed people think any differently than right-handed ones?
- When should children begin to show a hand preference?
- How does handedness affect how we use tools—spoons, toothbrushes, and pencils?

At birth, parents and physicians make a quick check: 10 fingers, 10 toes—a symmetrical body. Both sides are the same. As babies grow, we expect reflexes, muscles, and movements to be fairly balanced on the two sides.

But it's not uncommon for infants to hold one hand more fisted than the other, to wave one arm more vigorously, or to turn the head to one side more often. Still, we can't say that a baby has a preference for the left or the right.

Though not an exact science, handedness can often be predicted by these early infantile movements. Why?

Handedness: Does It Start with the Brain?

Theorists speculate that handedness has to do with brain specialization. Different brain functions take place in different parts of the brain.

During prenatal development, while the brain and spinal cord are forming, nerves cross from one hemisphere or side of the brain, across the midline of the body, and connect to muscles on the opposite side of the body. The right hemisphere of the brain controls the muscles on the left side of the body, and the left hemisphere controls the right.

For right-handed people, the left side of the brain has a better developed nerve network that supports motor development and skills. For left-handed people, the opposite is true.

How We Develop Fine Motor Skills

Motor skills involve the movement of muscles throughout the body. Gross motor skills involve larger movements—swimming, walking, and dancing, for example. Fine motor skills describe the smaller actions of the hands, wrists, fingers, feet, toes, lips, and tongue. Fine and gross motor skills develop in tandem. Many activities depend on their coordination.

Infants. Newborns have little control over their hands. Typically the fist is closed. Hand movement results from reflex and not deliberate control. For example, if you place a rattle in an infant's hand, the infant may grasp it momentarily and then drop it as hand muscles relax. The infant has no awareness of the object or its absence. Typically, babies swipe at objects when they are 1 month old and discover and play with their hands at 2 months.

Between 2 and 4 months, babies begin to coordinate their eye and hand muscles. Babies see an object and try to grasp it—often unsuccessfully.

By 5 months, most infants can grasp an object within reach—without looking at their hands. This important milestone in fine motor development allows more prolonged but clumsy grasps. Eager to discover and learn, infants not only grasp objects but also taste them. Hand-to-mouth exploration is a standard and expected developmental leap.

By 9 months, most babies begin to show a preference for reaching with their right hand—even if the toy is placed on their left side. They will, however, continue to use the non-preferred hand much of the time.

By the end of the first year, babies will usually be able to grasp an object with the entire hand, swipe surfaces, and poke at an object with one finger. Significantly, the pincer grip—the ability to hold an object between the thumb and index finger—typically appears at about 12 months. The pincer grasp gives infants the ability to manipulate and grasp an object and to deliberately drop it. At 12 months, babies can usually hold an object in each hand, drop an object into a bucket, and perform stacking and nesting tasks.

Toddlers. Toddlers continue to strengthen hand and finger muscles. They develop the ability to use their fingers independently—twisting, pulling, poking, pushing—and with greater control. They are typically able to turn the page in a board book. They are also able to hold a fat crayon in a palmer grasp (all fingers wrapped around the crayon).

By 15 months, most toddlers can eat independently, first with fingers and then with a spoon. Toddlers can reach for objects smoothly and with minimal effort. They can hold two objects in one hand, fit objects together (puzzles and snap toys, for example), and stack a few blocks into a tower.

By 30 months, most toddlers can draw using a finger grasp (holding a crayon with four fingers pushing in opposition to the thumb). They can pour liquids from one container to another, take off socks and shoes independently, and turn the faucet on and off when hand washing.

It's during this period that children start to display a preference for one side—that is, they use the preferred side more consistently than the non-preferred. This is clear not only when they grasp objects with the hand, hold a spoon, and turn pages in a book but also when they kick a ball, roll play clay into a snake, and push a wheel toy along a path.

Preschoolers. The preschool child's central nervous system is still developing and maturing, a process that enables the brain to send complex messages to the fingers.

By age 3 or 4, most children are able to complete complex fine motor tasks. These include drawing deliberate shapes, stringing beads, cutting with scissors, spreading paint and paste with the index finger, dressing and undressing dolls, opening and placing a clothespin to hang artwork, and folding paper in halves and quarters. Each of these tasks reinforces a child's hand preference.

As these preferences become evident, you can accommodate them to maximize a child's hand strength. For example, for a child who shows a left hand preference, you can provide left-handed scissors.

Because preschoolers are still developing small muscle strength and hand-eye coordination, it is inappropriate to expect handwriting skills. Children this age are generally not ready for precise handwriting instruction.

Instead, introduce writing activities slowly and gently, recognizing that each child will have a different skill set and a unique developmental level. For example, a 4-year-old who does not show a hand preference is likely to have less overall muscle control and coordination.

Some tools for writing are easier to use than others. Some teachers like to start with markers because they require little pressure and minimal muscle strength. Other teachers start with crayons because they require more focus and muscle strength. Make sure you provide many tool choices and encourage children to use the tools to draw and paint before you expect them to write.

As children indicate their interest in writing letters and words—and you have observed and documented readiness—make writing tools available for exploration. Generally, markers and felt-tipped pens are easiest for inexperienced fingers to control.

School age. By the age of 5, children will show better fine motor development and consistent hand preference for most tasks. Children can typically draw a complete human figure; cut out shapes with scissors; trace forms; manipulate buttons, zippers, and snaps; and copy letters. Some can play piano; build models; knit, crochet, and sew; use a computer keyboard and mouse; and help with basic household chores like sweeping, dusting, and washing dishes.

School-age children (as well as adolescents and adults) experiment with using the non-preferred side. And researchers hold that such experimentation can be useful in maintaining brain function and dexterity.

How Do We Develop Handedness?

From the developmental review, it's clear that handedness is not just about hands. Consider:

- Which foot do you kick with?
- Which eye do you use to peer through a magnifying glass?
- Which hand do you use to unscrew a jar, hold your toothbrush, or sign your name?

Many people are consistent—all left-sided functions or all right-sided. Some have a combination of left and right dominance, sometimes determined by the task. For example, a right-handed knitter may be able to make stitches more quickly using the left hand. Sometimes handedness is determined by efficiency. For example, a person may complete a jigsaw puzzle or cut flowers with the preferred hand because it's less frustrating.

Consider these historical facts and current investigations.

- The percentage of left-hand dominant people has remained consistent (10 to 12 percent) in the population for generations.
- In colonial America, left-handed people were considered witches and were executed. More recently, well-meaning teachers used harsh methods—slapping wrists or tying the left hand behind the child's back—to "cure" left-handedness.
- Some research suggests that left-handed children are more likely to be creative, with high verbal and math ability. Other research finds no difference between left- and right-handed children.
- Children with autism and other developmental disabilities, as shown by some research, have a higher percentage of left-handedness than the general population.
- Dorothy Bishop (1990) concluded there is no consistent link between IQ and handedness.
- Can openers, spiral notebooks, telephone keypads, and automobile consoles are built for the convenience of right-handed users.
- Left-handed people are more likely to have a left-handed relative, but researchers have not identified a left-handed gene.
- Most researchers believe that handedness preference is on a scale. Few people are strictly right- or left-handed. Most link a hand to a specific task: throw a ball with the left hand but stir a pot with the right, for example.
- Truly ambidextrous people—those indifferent to hand preference—are rare.
- In India and Indonesia, eating with the left hand is considered impolite.
- When necessary, such as after injury to the dominant hand or under cultural pressure, humans can learn to use the non-preferred hand.

About 1 person in 10 is left-hand dominant—a challenge in a right-hand dominant classroom and world. Some neurologists seek to explain the causes of handedness (likely a combination of genetics and environmental factors). Others explore whether left-handed people think differently. And teachers and parents strive to make left-handed children comfortable and successful in a right-handed world.

Hand to the Task

When children are ready to write, make sure tools and materials support the intense effort. Handwriting is more than forming symbols on a page. Writing effectively—and efficiently—includes the selection of writing tools, gripping the tool, positioning the tool on paper, and having fine muscle strength, coordination, and control in the hand doing the writing.

Use these tips for helping all children—left- and right-handed—develop fine motor control and fluid writing skills.

- Observe children's pencil grips. The pencil should be loosely held with the fingers above the shaved tip—about an inch up from the point—in a tripod grip. The index finger is on top of the pencil, the thumb and middle finger holding two sides. There should be equal pressure between the thumb, the side of the middle finger, and the tip of the index finger. The ring and pinky fingers are relaxed and in line with the middle finger. See diagram at right.

  Watch for excessive pressure on the index finger and all fingers pulled into a fist with knuckles flexed. When a child holds a pencil too tightly, fatigue and frustration will interfere with writing efficiency.
- Observe children's posture and body mechanics. When a child holds a pencil, the eraser end should point to the shoulder. The wrist should rest on the table surface. The arm from thumb to elbow should be in a straight line—the hand doesn't hook back toward the body.

  Position paper so that the sheet is angled—the right corner higher for right-handed writers, and the left corner higher for left-handed writers. The non-dominant hand should hold the paper in place.
- Provide child-sized chairs and writing table. Make sure the chair's height enables the child's feet to rest comfortably on the floor with hips and knees at a 90-degree angle. The table should be just above elbow height and support the arms without tensing and lifting or shrugging the shoulders.
- Help left-handed children discover that the best place at a table is not next to a right-handed friend. Bumping elbows while writing—or eating soup—is messy and frustrating.
- Help children relax. When a child has clenched teeth and a tense neck and makes deep indentations on paper from pressing too hard, it's wise to end the writing session and encourage general relaxation. Check the position of the pencil and the wrist.
- Schedule whole-body writing time with non-traditional materials. Invite children to write letters in the air with their hands or feet. Offer finger paint, shaving cream, and sand trays for finger writing. Invite children to write with water on the sidewalk or a brick wall.
- Explore print with tactile tools like Wikki-stix® and clay. Fill zipper-top bags with hair gel and invite children to form letters and shapes with one finger.
- Provide colored markers—felt-tipped and of varying thicknesses. Often children refine their grip—and relax muscles—when they are absorbed in color on unlined paper.

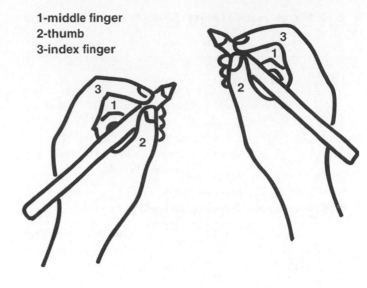

1-middle finger
2-thumb
3-index finger

- Offer a variety of writing implements—pencils, fat pencils, colored pencils, and markers—that have a triangular and not round shape.
- Explore pencil grips. Mechanical pencils and gel pens often have built-in grips. Encourage children with awkward to tight pencil grips to use them.
- Provide stencils, alphabet charts, and tracing grids for fun writing practice. Crossword puzzles give children practice in precise letter spacing.

Activities for Left and Right

Eric Chudler, University of Washington, has a website called "Neuroscience for Kids." It includes games, quizzes, and links to brain development and function. The following activities are adapted from his work.

Each activity offers school-agers opportunities for charting and graphing, surveying, and evaluating evidence. Have plenty of chart paper and markers on hand. Encourage children to make notes of their observations. If your classroom has Internet access, children can upload their data and exploration results.

Left Hand or Right Hand?

Rather than ask children which hand they use, set up observation experiments that rely on more than self-reporting. Prepare observation charts with three columns: Left Hand, Right Hand, Either Hand. Have observers chart peers in tasks such as using a fork, painting at an easel, turning a door knob, and throwing a ball.

Left Foot or Right Foot?

Set up the same observation system as in the previous activity. Have observers chart their peers in tasks such as kicking a ball, walking up stairs (Which foot steps first?), time spent balanced on each foot, and stepping on a picture of a cockroach.

Left Eye or Right Eye?

Check for eyedness. Chart these tasks: looking through a paper tube, looking through a magnifying glass, and winking (Which eye winks more easily?).

You can chart eye dominance too. Cut a coin-sized hole in a sheet of construction paper. Ask the subject to hold the paper and look through the hole at a distant object using both eyes. Ask the subject to bring the paper closer and closer to the face while still looking at the object. As the paper comes close to the face, only one eye will be looking through the hole. Which one?

Left Ear or Right Ear?

Chart which ear is preferred in different tests. Which ear does the subject cup to help make a whisper louder? Which ear does the subject hold against a small box when trying to determine what's inside? Which ear does the subject hold against a door to hear what's going on outside?

References

Chudler, Eric. *Neuroscience for Kids.* http://faculty.washington.edu/chudler/experi.html

Encyclopedia of Children's Health. 2006. "Fine motor skills." www.answers.com/topic/fine-motor-skills

Liddle, Tara Losquadro and Laura Yorke. 2003. *Why Motor Skills Matter: Improving Your Child's Physical Development to Enhance Learning and Self-Esteem.* New York: McGraw-Hill.

LiveScience. 2006. "What Makes a Lefty? Myths and Mysteries Persist." www.livescience.com/humanbiology/060321_left_hand.html

Needlman, Robert. 2001. "What is 'Handedness'?" www.drspock.com/article/0,1510,5812,00.html

Smith, Jodene Lynn. 2003. *Activities for Fine Motor Skills Development.* Westminster, Calif.: Teacher Created Materials.

Keeping Children Active
What You Can Do to Fight Childhood Obesity

RAE PICA

Just when you think that no more can be said about the childhood obesity crisis, along comes another frightening piece of information. We already know that today's children are fatter than they should be; approximately one-third of American children are overweight and one-fifth are obese. We know that overweight and obesity contribute to all manner of diseases, including heart disease, stroke, diabetes, and even several types of cancer. We've been told that overweight and obesity track from childhood to adulthood (the "baby fat" does not simply go away), meaning that children who start life overweight and obese already have a major strike against their health.

Now new studies, reported this past fall at an American Heart Association conference, have determined that obese children as young as 10 years old have the arteries of 45-year-olds, as well as other heart abnormalities that increase their risk for heart disease (Marcione, 2008).

Clearly, this trend must be reversed. And early childhood is the place to start.

Energy In/Energy Out

The formula for a balanced weight is pretty straightforward: energy in/energy out. This is the term nutritionists use to describe the intended balance between calories consumed and calories burned. If the level of physical activity is not great enough to burn the amount of calories taken in, weight increases. If this imbalance continues, overweight and possibly obesity result.

Given our fondness for fast food (an ever-growing fondness, due to ever-busier lives) and our tendency to "supersize," it's easy to imagine that caloric intake is the crux of the obesity problem. And certainly it is part of the problem, especially considering the quality of the calories consumed. (Evidence indicates that children get a full quarter of their vegetable servings in the form of potato chips and French fries! [Schlosser, 2005].) But studies both here and abroad have indicated that the greater problem may lie with the second half of the equation: energy out. Children are simply not moving enough!

The Need for Physical Activity

The trend toward greater accountability has not helped. Even at the preschool level children are expected to do more and more seatwork. And at the elementary-school level, physical education and recess are being eliminated in favor of more "academic" time. Since school is where children spend the majority of their waking hours, it's clear that under such conditions children are not meeting even the minimum requirements for physical activity.

The National Association for Sport and Physical Education (NASPE, 2002) recommends that:

- Young children should not be sedentary for more than 60 minutes at a time, except when sleeping.
- Toddlers should accumulate at least 30 minutes a day of structured physical activity and at least 60 minutes a day of unstructured physical activity.
- Preschoolers are encouraged to accumulate at least 60 minutes a day of both structured and unstructured physical activity.

While 60 minutes a day is the suggested minimum, it is further recommended that children accumulate "up to several hours" of physical activity daily.

For the early childhood professional, the concept of "accumulation" is comforting. It means you don't have to worry about setting aside huge blocks of time exclusively devoted to physical activity. Although it's developmentally appropriate for children to be engaged in active play most of the time (and that would certainly make the children happy), today's educational culture does not allow for that possibility. It's good to know, therefore, that you can fit in "bouts" of physical activity throughout the day and still meet the national guidelines and contribute to the fight against obesity.

Encouraging Unstructured Physical Activity

Unstructured physical activity, which involves free choice on the part of the children, is typically best experienced outdoors, where the children can run and jump and expend energy. While time spent outdoors has traditionally been considered "break" time—an opportunity for children to play without interference from adults and for teachers and caregivers to relax a bit—more and more early childhood professionals are realizing the potential of the outdoors as an extension of the indoor setting, with that time viewed as yet another opportunity to enhance children's development. Certainly, the outdoor setting provides the perfect opportunity to enhance the children's physical development and physical fitness.

If this is to happen, teachers and caregivers must become involved in children's outdoor play. This is not to say that they must go to the extreme of preparing structured lesson plans for every outdoor session, but many activities begun indoors can be continued and extended outdoors, including movement activities. (Batteries in the CD player mean even music can be a part of outdoor movement experiences.) Also, during playtime, adults can and should interact naturally and informally with the children, offering guidance and suggestions to extend the children's play.

Frost (1996) tells us the role of the teacher supporting outdoor play is that of a play leader, whom he defines as someone who interacts with the child by asking leading questions and providing guidance for certain skills. A play leader also "helps children plan where they will go to play, helps them deal with problems that come up, and talks with them about their play" (p. 27). Of course, teachers can also play with children in order to encourage more moderate to vigorous physical activity. For example, blowing bubbles for the children to catch encourages them to run and jump, contributing to both cardiovascular endurance and muscular strength and endurance.

Fitting Structured Physical Activity into the Day

Structured physical activity is organized and planned. It involves children in specific activities in which they're expected to achieve certain results. Naturally, that makes structured physical activity more challenging to incorporate into the curriculum than unstructured movement.

Early childhood professionals are charged with caring for the development of the whole child; therefore it is not unreasonable to expect that they will set aside a minimum of 30 minutes a day to focus on the acquisition and refinement of motor skills. Motor skills do not develop automatically from an immature to a mature level, so they must be taught and practiced just like any other skill in early childhood. While the prevailing belief may be that instruction in motor skills is less important than instruction in literacy and numeracy skills, children who are comfortable and confident with their motor skills are more likely to be physically active throughout their lives, helping to ensure a lifetime of physical fitness!

Of course, finding time for such instruction is a critical factor. Here are some simple solutions:

- Utilize substantial chunks of what is set aside for circle time.
- Take movement breaks throughout the day. These can incorporate moderate- to vigorous-intensity physical

activity (like walking briskly or running in place, pretending to be in a track meet), thereby contributing to cardiovascular endurance.
- Include gentle stretching that promotes both relaxation and flexibility, an important component of health-related fitness.

Transitions and Movement

Perhaps the simplest way to incorporate structured physical activity into your program is to utilize transition times. Because transitions usually require moving from one place to another, movement is the perfect tool for transition times. Children naturally enjoy movement, so transitions can become pleasurable experiences—even something to be looked forward to. And although you may be reluctant to make them more "active," the truth is that the more active they are, the more engaged children will be. As long as transitions are planned, as are other daily components of your program, the fewer discipline problems you'll have. Here are some activities to use for transitions.

Stand up/sit down. Upon arrival, once the children have removed outerwear and gathered in the center of the room, an activity called Stand Up/Sit Down can get both the brain and the body warmed up, while also working on the concepts of up and down. Doing this quickly will get the heart pumping, and because the children think it's funny, it's a great way to start the day.

Sit with the children, who are either in a circle or scattered throughout the space. Invite the children to alternately stand up or sit down if:

- they're glad to be there
- they're feeling good that day
- they're happy to see their friends
- they're happy to see their teacher
- they're looking forward to learning something new
- they're wearing something blue (green, yellow, etc.)
- if they're a boy (girl)
- if they have a cat (dog) at home

If the children are going to transition to another area of the room, end with a standing challenge. If you are going to do another activity with them for which they need to be seated, end with a sitting challenge.

Quick clean-up. Put on a piece of music with a fast tempo and challenge the children to clean up before the song ends!

Get ready, spaghetti. When it's time for lunch or snack, using a food-related transition makes the most sense. This activity encourages the children to consider the "before" and "after" of pasta. It also serves as a relaxation exercise (contracting and releasing the muscles) as the children wait for snack or lunch.

Talk to the children about the differences between uncooked and cooked spaghetti, letting them come up with ideas on their own. If they need prompting, you can ask them to tell you which is straighter and harder, and which is limp and squiggly. Then invite them to demonstrate uncooked and cooked spaghetti with their bodies. Alternate between the two, ending with the cooked version so the children's muscles are relaxed.

Here we go. Use this activity when it is time to move from where the children have gathered to another part of the classroom. This activity offers an opportunity for the children to experience a variety of locomotor (traveling) skills.

Challenge the children to move to their next destination in one of the following ways, making sure to ask them only to perform skills within their capabilities:

- jumping (two feet)
- hopping (one foot)
- marching
- walking (lightly; stomping)
- jogging
- galloping
- skipping

An alternate activity is to play Follow the Leader, using brisk and/or forceful movements (e.g., stomping) to transition.

Moving like animals. Moving like an animal stimulates the imagination, allows an opportunity to practice a variety of movements, and helps create empathy for the world's creatures. You can either designate the animal the children are to portray or allow them to choose the animal they would each like to be.

Conclusion

Use these examples as a starting point, creating and collecting other ideas as you work with children. If you plan for transitions, using movement to add personality, learning opportunities, physical activity, and fun to parts of the day that might otherwise be routine and dull, you will know that you and the children are making the most of every day. If you additionally encourage

unstructured physical activity, set aside time for instruction in motor skills, and make movement breaks part of your curriculum, you will know that you are making the most of every day and contributing to the fight against childhood obesity.

Because the children spend so much of their time with you, and because teachers of preschoolers can be more realistic than parents in assessing children's physical activity levels (Noland et al., 1990), your role as an early childhood professional is essential in combating obesity and promoting healthy lifestyles from an early age.

What are your thoughts? What activities do you use to get children moving to positively impact childhood obesity? *Exchange* invites you to share them in their online survey. Visit www.ChildCareExchange.com/ comments to submit your ideas!

References

Frost, J. L. (1996). Joe Frost on playing outdoors. *Scholastic Early Childhood Today, 10,* 26–28.

Marcione, M. (2008). Fat kids found to have arteries of 45-year-olds. http://news.yahoo.com/s/ap/20081112/ap_on_he_me/med_obese_kids_arteries

NASPE. (2002). *Active start: physical activity for children birth to 5 years.* Reston, VA: National Association for Sport and Physical Education.

Noland, M., Danner, F., & Dewalt, K. (1990). The measurement of physical activity in young children. *Research Quarterly for Exercise and Sport, 61*(2): 146–53.

Schlosser, E. (2005). *Fast food nation.* New York: Harper Perennial.

RAE PICA is a children's physical activity specialist and the author of 17 books, including the award-winning *Great Games for Young Children* and *Jump into Literacy*. Rae is known for her lively and informative workshop and keynote presentations and as host of the radio program "Body, Mind and Child" (www.bodymindandchild.com), in which she interviews experts in education, child development, the neurosciences, and more.

From *Exchange,* May/June 2009, pp. 30–33. Copyright © 2009 by Child Care Information Exchange. Reprinted by permission.

The Truth about ADHD

It's tougher than you think to tell which kids have this disorder. We set the record straight about diagnosis, drug dangers, and more.

JEANNETTE MONINGER

Attention-deficit/hyperactivity disorder (ADHD) may seem like a trendy diagnosis—the psychiatric condition is thought to affect about 4 million kids nationwide—but the truth is that ADHD may be both overdiagnosed and underdiagnosed. "Lots of high-energy, rambunctious kids don't have ADHD," says *Parents* advisor David Fassler, MD, clinical professor of psychiatry at the University of Vermont College of Medicine, in Burlington. "However, many kids with ADHD don't get diagnosed, particularly if their symptoms don't include the constant physical activity often associated with the disorder." Of course, all kids are hyper or distracted sometimes, but experts say that a child who truly has ADHD will have symptoms in a variety of situations (at home, at school, and with friends) for at least six continuous months starting before age 7. Update yourself on the latest info, based on recent landmark research, about potential causes, the best treatments, and other discoveries about ADHD.

1 Not All Kids with ADHD Are Constantly on the Go

We tend to think of them as being hyperactive and impulsive—they're the ones squirming in their seat, tapping their pencil, grabbing things that don't belong to them, and causing trouble. And they seem to know only one speed: overdrive. Although these behaviors are indeed classic signs of ADHD, some kids with the disorder are relatively calm. Girls, in particular, are more likely to have a type of ADHD that primarily makes it difficult for them to pay attention. They often daydream and have a difficult time following directions and focusing on schoolwork. But because these children aren't disruptive, their ADHD often goes undiagnosed and untreated, says Dr. Fassler.

2 It Can Be Diagnosed as Early as Age 3

Preschoolers naturally have a short attention span, so doctors may be hesitant to label them with ADHD. Kids are typically diagnosed around age 6—when they're expected to sit quietly in school, follow directions, and not interrupt—but the disorder doesn't suddenly appear then. "ADHD is a chronic condition that can start early," says *Parents* advisor Harold Koplewicz, MD, director of the New York University Child Study Center, in New York City. Signs include aggressiveness (which often gets children kicked out of child care or preschool), trouble focusing on activities like bedtime stories, and uncontrollable behaviors such as bolting into a busy parking lot. "By the time they're diagnosed with ADHD, most kids have had a long history of problem behaviors that can affect their self-esteem," says Dr. Koplewicz. In fact, a large study from the National Institute of Mental Health (NIMH) showed that children ages 3 to 5 can benefit greatly from treatment. Researchers found that low doses of medication are safe and effective, but since preschoolers are more sensitive to side effects than older kids are, they need to be closely monitored.

3 Something Else May Cause a Child's Symptoms

Other conditions—including sleep apnea, vision problems, and hearing impairments—could make it hard for him to focus or cause him to be disruptive. Traumatic events, such as the death of a grandparent or a divorce, also can trigger ADHD-like behaviors. If your child's pediatrician suspects ADHD, she'll probably refer you to a mental-health specialist, such as a child psychiatrist, psychologist, or behavioral neurologist. This clinician will gather information about your child's behavior from you, his teachers, and other caregivers, as well as perform a physical exam and review your child's medical history. She'll also interview and observe your child and rule out potential learning disabilities before she makes a diagnosis.

4 Many Kids Who Could Benefit from Medication Don't Take It

Another large NIMH study has proven that stimulant medication is the most effective treatment for school-age kids with ADHD—and yet almost half of kids diagnosed with the

Life with ADHD

Finding the right treatment has made a huge difference for these kids.

Jadyn Koss, Age 9

Treatment: Stimulant medication

Since she was diagnosed at 6½, Jadyn has tried five different stimulants because some of them caused side effects like irritability and sleep problems. Still, her mother, Melinda, says the medications have been a blessing. "Jadyn used to twirl around, run in circles, and tap her feet incessantly. Her eyes darted so much that she couldn't focus or learn to read." Now, with the help of the Daytrana skin patch, Jadyn is reading above grade level, and she's made friends with many kids in her class. "Parents shouldn't worry about ADHD medications turning their kids into zombies," says Melinda, of New City, New York. "Jadyn is still a high-energy kid. She's simply better able to direct her energy in positive ways that make her a delight to be around."

Andrew Owens, Age 7

Treatment: Combined therapy

Andrew wasn't diagnosed with ADHD until age 6, but his mother, Shelby, started using behavior-modification techniques with him when he was 3. That's because he was acting a lot like his older sister, Macey, who'd already been diagnosed with the condition. Shelby created sticker charts and began giving him small rewards to encourage him to follow through on tasks like getting ready for bed without too much fuss. She took away privileges like going to the library when he didn't listen or if he threw things when he became upset. "Even if it turned out that ADHD wasn't the cause of Andrew's uncontrollable energy, I thought these techniques would help improve his behavior," says Shelby, of Longwood, Florida. Like his sister, he now takes ADHD medication, but the Owens family continues to use behavioral methods. "We've found that our positive reinforcement gives him the little extra push he needs to try his best," Shelby says.

Will Kirby, Age 11

Treatment: Physical activity

Will is always on the move, and that's exactly how his mom, Stacia, likes it. "I make sure he does something physically active every day to burn off his excess energy," she says. Will's symptoms improved with medication after he was diagnosed at age 9, but he was extremely sensitive to the side effects. "One medication made him throw up for a week, and another sent him into a deep funk every evening," says Stacia, of Seattle. Will eventually bogged his parents to let him stop the drugs. Now, instead of swallowing pills, Will plays lacrosse, soccer, and basketball. Even gardening has become part of his therapy. So far, he's doing well in school. "He isn't disruptive in class, and he has lots of friends," says Stacia. "As long as Will's busy, he seems to do just fine."

disorder have never tried it. Although it might not make sense to give something called a stimulant to a child who already seems overly stimulated, these medications get their name because they "turn on" neurotransmitters in the brain that control attention and impulsiveness. Some parents worry that their child will have side effects like weight loss, headaches, irritability, or sleep problems, but doctors can usually reduce them by adjusting the dose, switching to another medication (there are now about 20 different ones), or changing the time a child takes it. Despite reports you may have heard, the American Academy of Pediatrics says that there's no link between stimulants and heart attacks in kids and that most kids don't need to have an electrocardiogram (ECG) before starting on medication. A doctor will order an ECG if a child has a history of heart problems or if something worrisome shows up on a physical exam.

5 But Medication Isn't the Only Answer

Adding behavioral strategies to drug therapy is helpful for kids of all ages. Parents can learn specific ways to praise and reward their child for good behavior, such as completing chores or doing his homework, and to take away privileges when he jumps on the furniture or refuses to sit quietly at the table. "Even if they take medication, children with ADHD still need help with key life skills like organization and time management,"

says Ann Abramowitz, PhD, chair of the professional advisory board for the nonprofit Children and Adults with Attention-Deficit/Hyperactivity Disorder. In fact, some kids improve so much with combined treatment that they're able to reduce their dose of medication. Although many kids with ADHD have tried some form of alternative treatment, such as vitamins, dietary changes, or biofeedback, there hasn't been enough research to prove that these offer any benefits. A recent study in the *Journal of the American Medical Association*, for example, found that the herb St. John's wort was no more effective than a placebo for kids with ADHD.

6 ADHD Usually Isn't a Child's Only Diagnosis

Many kids with ADHD also have a language or learning problem, and more than half have at least one other mental-health disorder—which can make medication treatment more complicated. Children with ADHD are most likely to have oppositional defiant disorder; they can be very hostile to adults and intentionally bother other people. Although an increasing number of kids are now being diagnosed with both ADHD and bipolar disorder—which share many symptoms—experts believe that most kids actually have only one or the other. The key distinction is that a child with bipolar disorder has a distorted sense of reality. "A child with ADHD might like to race around the house in his Superman cape, but a bipolar child might truly believe he has superpowers that can make him fly," says Dr. Koplewicz. However, more research still needs to be done to help doctors make the most accurate diagnoses.

7 Kids with ADHD Are Accident-Prone

They get injured more often than other kids because they don't always think twice before trying daredevil moves like skateboard stunts, and they tend to dash into the street without checking for cars. They're also more likely to be hospitalized for accidental poisonings. As a result, medical bills for ADHD kids are about twice as high as those for children without the disorder, according to the CDC. If your child has ADHD, make sure that he always wears a helmet and protective pads when he bikes or skates, and also keep harmful household products locked up and out of reach.

8 A Child's Behavior May Improve as She Gets Older

New research suggests that ADHD may be related to developmental delays in the frontal cortex areas of the brain that are responsible for attention, planning, and thinking. In kids with ADHD, this region doesn't fully mature until three years later than in children without ADHD. Although more than half of children with ADHD will continue to grapple with problems like focusing and planning through adulthood, this lag time may explain why some kids outgrow their hyperactive and impulsive tendencies once they're teenagers, says Dr. Fassler.

From *Parents*, November 2008, pp. 58, 60, 62–63. Copyright © 2008 by Jeannette Moninger. Reprinted by permission of the author.

When Girls and Boys Play: What Research Tells Us

JEANETTA G. RILEY AND ROSE B. JONES

Research on play suggests that children of all ages benefit from engaging in play activities (Bergen, 2004). With the recent emphasis on standards and testing, however, many teachers have felt the increased pressure to spend time on structured learning events, leaving few moments of relaxation in a child's day (Chenfeld, 2006). Many elementary schools have even reduced or eliminated recess times in an effort to give children more time to work on academics (Clements, 2000). That is unfortunate, as findings from studies of play indicate that play helps children to develop social, language, and physical skills.

While beneficial for both, play often differs for girls and boys (see Gallas, 1998; Gurian & Stevens, 2005). This article reviews research related to the differences found between the genders as they play and the benefits that elementary children can gain from play. In addition, the authors include suggestions for educators regarding children's play at school.

Social Development
Girls and Boys Sharing Social Interactions during Play

Researchers have found differences in the way the genders socialize during play. In an early study examining gender and play, Lever (1978) found several differences in how 5th-grade girls and boys play. For example, boys played more competitive, rule-oriented, group games than did girls; girls interacted in smaller groups, had conversations, and walked and talked with friends more often than did boys. Lever concluded that the nature of boys' team games and their experiences with rule-dictated play: 1) allowed for the development of cooperation skills between peers with differing ideas, 2) afforded them opportunities to work independently to accomplish a common task, and 3) provided motivation to abide by established rules.

Other recent studies have found results similar to those of Lever (1978). A study of elementary students at recess conducted by Butcher (1999) indicated that boys more often

participated in competitive games, and girls chose activities that allowed them to have conversations. Likewise, Lewis and Phillipsen (1998) found that elementary-age boys at recess played physically active group games with rules more often than did girls. However, in contrast to Lever's (1978) findings on groupings during recess, Lewis and Phillipsen (1998) noted that while girls tended to play in small groups, boys tended to play in groups of various sizes, from dyads to more than five children.

Also consistent with Lever's (1978) findings, a study of 4th-graders by Goodwin (2001) indicated that boys tended to form social structures, wherein the boys who were more skilled at the activity took the lead and directed the players. Boys with less skill were allowed to play but were not allowed a leadership role. In contrast, girls' leadership roles during games of jump rope did not depend on their ability to carry out the physical tasks of the game. Instead of one girl taking the lead, several girls directed the games; however, Goodwin (2001) found that the girls were more likely to exclude others from their play than were the boys.

Even very young children tend to be socially influenced by playing with same-sex peers. For example, Martin and Fabes' (2001) investigation of preschool and kindergarten children at play indicated that playing with same-gender peers affects play behaviors. Their research findings added to the evidence (e.g., Boyatzis, Mallis, & Leon, 1999; Thorne, 1993) that children often choose to play with same-sex peers. Additionally, Martin and Fabes found gender-typical behaviors for children who more often played with same-sex peers. For instance, the girls who most often played with other girls were generally less active during play and chose to play in areas close to adults. Boys who played with other boys more often engaged in play that was more aggressive and farther from adult supervision. This stereotypical play was found less often in children who tended to play with the opposite sex.

Not all students have positive social experiences during play activities. Some students may have difficulty developing the appropriate skills necessary for positive peer interactions. Children with inadequate social skills may tend to behave inappropriately during times of free play, such as recess (Blatchford, 1998). Rather than limit free play due to inappropriate behavior, however, these times can provide opportunities for conflict resolution interventions. In one study by Butcher (1999), the researchers trained college students to use conflict resolution strategies when interacting with 1st- through 6th-graders during recess times. The volunteers provided positive feedback, modeled appropriate social skills, and implemented strategies to increase cooperation among the children. As a result, when the numbers were analyzed, combining all grade levels, the means for the number of incidents of inappropriate targeted behaviors (i.e., violent behavior, verbal abuse, and inappropriate equipment use) declined during interventions. However, it is important to note that when the results were analyzed according to gender, significant differences were found in the reduction of targeted behaviors for boys only. No significant differences were found for girls' behavior. The researchers suggested that this lack of difference for the girls was due to the limited number of negative behaviors the girls initially exhibited (Butcher, 1999).

Overall Play and the Social Development of Children

By the time children reach school age, play typically becomes a social activity (Jarrett & Maxwell, 2000). As children play with others, they begin to learn what behaviors are expected and acceptable in their society. Playing with peers permits children to adjust to the expected norms (Fromberg, 1998).

Opportunities for free play with limited adult intervention provide time for children to explore which behaviors are accepted among their peers (Wortham, 2002). As younger children associate in play situations, they begin to realize that play ends if they do not negotiate behaviors and cooperate; therefore, play helps children learn to regulate their behaviors in order to continue playing together (Heidemann & Hewitt, 1992; Poole, Miller, & Church, 2004).

For older children, recess can be a time for learning about and adjusting to peer expectations. Pellegrini and Blatchford's (2002) findings suggest that recess play provides children with time to enter into social relationships early in the school year, which, in turn, helps them in social situations throughout the year. Pellegrini, Blatchford, Kato, and Baines (2004) also found that recess allowed opportunities for children to increase positive social experiences. For the 7- and 8-year-old participants in their study, basic games played at the beginning of the school year permitted the children time to get acquainted with peers, leading to more advanced play once the children became more familiar with each other. Additionally, Jarrett et al. (1998) speculated that children who move from one school to another find recess times helpful in adjusting and making new friends.

Language Development
Girls and Boys Expressing Language during Play

Research indicates that the types of games in which girls often engage may support language development differently than the types of games boys typically play. Blatchford, Baines, and

Pellegrini (2003) studied playground activities of children in England during the year the children turned 8 years old. The researchers found that girls held significantly more conversations and played significantly more verbal games than did boys. Goodwin (2002) also found that 4th- through 6th-grade girls spent most of their playtime talking with one another. Their games tended to require close proximity to one another, thus allowing for extended conversations. Conversely, some studies found that the games boys tended to choose often involved language usage that was more instruction-oriented, with boys verbally directing the play actions of one another (Boyle, Marshall, & Robeson, 2003; Goodwin, 2001).

Overall Play and Language Skill Development of Children

Play is a natural environment for children's language development (Perlmutter & Burrell, 1995). Children use language during their solitary play as well as in social play encounters (Piaget, 1962). Both expressive and receptive language skills are needed to plan, explain, and execute play activities. Language skills give children the ability to cooperate in creating and prolonging their play episodes (Van Hoorn, Monighan-Nourot, Scales, & Alward, 2003).

Developing language skills facilitates peer relationships. Piaget (1962) theorized that the talk of preschool-age children is egocentric (i.e., talk that is not for the sake of communicating with others). Very young children verbalize without a need for others to enter into the conversation; however, as older children begin to interact more often with adults and peers, the need to communicate arises. Egocentric speech gradually subsides and social speech takes over as children practice using language (Ginsburg & Opper, 1979).

Language in the context of play provides children with the ability to develop strategies for cooperation, engage in varied and complex play themes, and share perspectives about their world.

Language is a major factor in social play scenarios, such as sociodramatic play in which children create pretend play episodes and take on the roles of others. Language in the context of play provides children with the ability to develop strategies for cooperation, engage in varied and complex play themes, and share perspectives about their world (Van Hoorn et al., 2003). Children's language guides their play and provides the communication needed for the continuation of the play (Guddemi, 2000; Heidemann & Hewitt, 1992).

Language usage during play allows children to develop and test their verbal skills. Children experiment with language by telling jokes and riddles, reciting chants and poems, and making up words. As children use language during play, they create meaning for themselves concerning the nature of language and communication (Frost, 1992). Additionally, playing with language develops children's phonological awareness by allowing for experimentation with the sounds of words. Children learn that sounds can be manipulated as they rhyme words and create nonsense words (Johnson, Christie, & Wardle, 2005).

A more complicated form of play, games with rules, also requires children to expand their language skills. Once the egocentrism of earlier childhood diminishes, children can become more proficient at working together to negotiate the rules of games (Van Hoorn et al., 2003). Games with rules provide practice in cooperation, as well as opportunities to build language skills, as children create new games or discuss rules of known games.

Physical Development
Girls and Boys Engaging in Physical Activity during Play

Research indicates gender differences in physical activity during play. Studies have noted that boys, from infancy through adolescence, tend to participate in more physically active play than do girls (Campbell & Eaton, 1999; Frost, 1992; Lindsey & Colwell, 2003). For example, Lindsey and Colwell (2003) observed young children and found that boys playing with one other child engage in more physical play than girls playing with one other child. Additionally, a study by Sarkin, McKenzie, and Sallis (1997) compared gender differences in play levels of 5th-graders during physical education classes and recess. They found no significant differences between the boys' and the girls' activity levels during physical education classes. However, during recess times, boys more often played games requiring higher levels of physical activity than did girls. Girls played less strenuous games or held conversations as they walked around the playground. These results suggested that during times of unstructured activity, such as recess, boys tend to choose more active play than girls do.

Likewise, other researchers also concluded that the physical play of girls and boys often differs. Boys and girls tend to divide into gendered groups during outdoor play, and they often choose different types of activities (Thorne, 1993). Studies suggest that boys engage in play that involves more physical activity (Boyle, Marshall, & Robeson, 2003), more competition (Lever, 1978), and more space (Martin & Fabes, 2001) than do girls. Pellegrini and Smith (1993) suggested that boys tend to prefer playing outdoors, due to the need for open space to participate in their active games. One type of active play in which boys tend to engage in more frequently than girls is rough and tumble play (Martin & Fabes, 2001; Pellegrini, 1989; Thorne, 1993). Rough and tumble play involves such activities as grabbing and wrestling and may be a socially acceptable way for boys to physically demonstrate their feelings of friendship (Reed, 2000).

Overall Active Play and Physical Development in Children

The human body needs movement to stay healthy and well. Findings by the Centers for Disease Control and Prevention (2005) indicate that the incidence of childhood obesity is increasing. In today's world, many children spend most of their time in sedentary activities that do not enhance physical fitness. Active play encourages movement, thereby helping children's fitness. According to Huettig, Sanborn, DiMarco, Popejoy, and Rich (2004), young children need at least "thirty to sixty minutes of physical activity a day" (p. 54). Physical advantages that children gain from active play are increased motor control and flexibility (Brewer, 2001). Furthermore, with the added body control that develops as they play, children often become more competent in their skills and gain the self-confidence to play games with peers (Wortham, 2002).

Physical movement is necessary for the growth and development of the mind as well as the body. The brain needs movement in order to function properly.

Physical movement is necessary for the growth and development of the mind as well as the body. The brain needs movement in order to function properly (Gurian, 2001). Although indoor play encourages creativity and socialization, it provides only a limited amount of space for the type of physical movement children need each day. Time in outdoor play encourages physical activity, which, in turn, increases children's physical fitness. Consequently, outdoor recess periods provide the time and space for children to engage in the physically vigorous active play that is limited indoors (Sutterby & Frost, 2002).

Further Research Needs

Understanding more about how play benefits the social, language, and physical development of children can help teachers as they create learning environments; however, more research is needed to gain a clearer picture of how play enhances children's learning. For example, studies examining the influence of recess on classroom behaviors, such as concentration and amount of work produced, have yielded conflicting results (Jarrett et al, 1998; Pellegrini & Davis, 1993). Therefore, more work is necessary to determine how unstructured play correlates with behavior as well as academic achievement. Additionally, more research needs to be conducted about social interventions during play. Children who have been targeted as requiring assistance in developing positive social behaviors may have more difficulty during times of unstructured activity (Blatchford, 1998). Research to determine how to best assist these children, particularly during recess periods, is needed.

Finally, some researchers have included such variables as race and gender within the framework of their study of play; however, less often has the researcher's main purpose been to examine the educational implications based on the different ways girls and boys play. This aspect of play needs further examination if educators are to gain a better understanding of how to best structure learning environments for both genders.

Implications for Educators

Knowing the research about how children play and what they learn as they play can help educators and parents make sound decisions about how to provide appropriate play opportunities. To create learning environments in which children can thrive, adults must observe children's needs and try to accommodate those needs. The following are some suggestions for educators and parents.

- **Importance of Observations of Play Experiences:** Teachers can use playtimes to observe and assess children's social, emotional, physical, and cognitive development. Observing children's play can provide teachers with information about how to create appropriate learning environments. In some settings, recess may be a prime time to do this.

- **Girls' Play:** Girls have been found to engage in more sedentary, language-oriented activities during recess play than boys. Although this type of activity is important, girls also need to be encouraged to be physically active. While many boys may participate in physical movement through rough and tumble play, educators may need to help girls create activities in which they become more active. Providing areas and equipment for active play is the first step; additionally, ensuring that girls have the opportunity to engage in this type of physical play is necessary.

- **Boys' Play:** Rough and tumble play may provide an outlet for boys' physical, social, emotional, and verbal expression. Schools where all physical contact during play has been banned may need to consider how to reduce aggressive behaviors while allowing for this type of physical contact between boys. Recess monitors may need to be trained to recognize differences between acts of aggression and rough and tumble play. Additionally, the exploration of language that girls enjoy during play may need to be encouraged for boys by creating play environments that support language development. For example, teachers can lead boys in discussing their play activities.

- **Accommodations for Differences:** Children have various interests and styles of play; therefore, schools can provide a variety of play materials and equipment to accommodate the differences. Additionally, an assortment of resources can encourage children to expand and extend their play. Children with special needs should be considered in this process.

- **Parental Awareness:** Parents may be concerned that their young children are "only playing" at school. During Open House, at PTA meetings, and through newsletters, educators can make parents aware of growth and development that takes place as children play, both in classrooms and at recess. It is necessary to make adults aware that natural outdoor play environments are important for girls and boys and that these areas do not always require equipment. Rustic, wooded settings can provide children with many opportunities for creative movement, imaginative growth, and cognitive learning as they participate in such activities as nature walks with adult supervision.

- **Cooperative Activities:** Although research indicates that girls tend to enjoy cooperative activities while boys pursue competitive games, children need to learn about both cooperation and competition. Teachers can incorporate each type of activity into classroom lessons.

Conclusion

While some adults dismiss play as mere fun, much growth and development occurs during playtimes. As children play, they gain knowledge of the world and an understanding of their place in it. Although play may differ generally for girls and boys, it offers both genders opportunities to test and refine their developing social, language, and physical skills, which leads not only to academic achievement but also to a lifetime of success. Thus, play does benefit children.

References

Bergen, D. (2004). *ACEI speaks: Play's role in brain development* [Brochure]. Olney, MD: Association for Childhood Education International.

Blatchford, P. (1998). The state of play in schools. *Child Psychology and Psychiatry Review,* 3(2), 58–67.

Blatchford, P., Baines, E., & Pellegrini, A. (2003). The social context of school playground games: Sex and ethnic differences, and changes over time after entry to junior high school. *British Journal of Developmental Psychology,* 21(4), 481–505.

Boyatzis, C. J., Mallis, M., & Leon, I. (1999). Effects of game type on children's gender-based peer preferences: A naturalistic observational study. *Sex Roles: A Journal of Research,* 40(1–2), 93–105.

Boyle, D. E., Marshall, N. L., & Robeson, W. W. (2003). Gender at play: Fourth-grade girls and boys on the playground. *American Behavioral Scientist,* 46(10), 1326–1345.

Brewer, J. A. (2001). *Introduction to early childhood education: Preschool through primary grades* (4th ed.). Boston: Allyn and Bacon.

Butcher, D. A. (1999). Enhancing social skills through school social work interventions during recess: Gender differences. *Social Work in Education,* 21(4), 249–262.

Campbell, D. W., & Eaton, W. O. (1999). Sex differences in the activity level of infants. *Infant and Child Development,* 8(1), 1–17.

Centers for Disease Control and Prevention. (2005). *Preventing chronic diseases through good nutrition and physical activity.* Retrieved July 18, 2006, from www.cdc.gov/nccdphp/ publications/factsheets/Prevention/obesity.htm

Chenfeld, M. B. (2006). Handcuff me, too! *Phi Delta Kappan,* 87(10), 745–747.

Clements, R. L. (Ed.). (2000). *Elementary school recess: Selected readings, games, and activities for teachers and parents.* Boston: American Press.

Fromberg, D. P. (1998). Play issues in early childhood education. In C. Seefeldt & A. Galper (Eds.), *Continuing issues in early childhood education* (2nd ed.)(pp. 190–212). Upper Saddle River, NJ: Merrill Prentice-Hall.

Frost, J. L. (1992). *Play and playscapes.* Albany, NY: Delmar.

Gallas, K. (1998). *Sometimes I can be anything: Power, gender, and identity in a primary classroom.* New York: Teachers College Press.

Ginsburg, H., & Opper, S. (1979). *Piaget's theory of intellectual development* (2nd ed.). Englewood Cliffs, NJ: Prentice-Hall.

Goodwin, M. H. (2001). Organizing participation in cross-sex jump rope: Situating gender differences within longitudinal studies of activities. *Research on Language & Social Interaction,* 34(1), 75–106.

Goodwin, M. H. (2002). Exclusion in girls' peer groups: Ethnographic analysis of language practices on the playground. *Human Development,* 45(6), 392–415.

Guddemi, M. P. (2000). Recess: A time to learn, a time to grow. In R. L. Clements (Ed.), *Elementary school recess: Selected readings, games, and activities for teachers and parents* (pp. 2–8). Boston: American Press.

Gurian, M. (2001). *Boys and girls learn differently! A guide for teachers and parents.* San Francisco: Jossey-Bass.

Gurian, M., & Stevens, K. (2005). *The minds of boys: Saving our sons from falling behind in school and life.* San Francisco: Jossey-Bass.

Heidemann, S., & Hewitt, D. (1992). *Pathways to play: Developing play skills in young children.* St. Paul, MN: Redleaf Press.

Huettig, C. I., Sanborn, C. R, DiMarco, N., Popejoy, A., & Rich, S. (2004). The O generation: Our youngest children are at risk for obesity. *Young Children,* 59(2), 50–55.

Jarrett, O. S., & Maxwell, D. M. (2000). What research says about the need for recess. In R. L. Clements (Ed.), *Elementary school recess: Selected readings, games, and activities for teachers and parents* (pp. 12–20). Boston: American Press.

Jarrett, O. S., Maxwell, D. M., Dickerson, C., Hoge, P., Davies, G., & Yetley, A. (1998). Impact of recess on classroom behavior: Group effects and individual differences. *The Journal of Educational Research,* 92(2), 121–126.

Johnson, J. E., Christie, J. R, & Wardle, F. (2005). *Play, development, and early education.* Boston: Pearson Education.

Lever, J. (1978). Sex differences in the complexity of children's play and games. *American Sociological Review,* 43(4), 471–483.

Lewis, T. E., & Phillipsen, L. C. (1998). Interactions on an elementary school playground: Variations by age, gender, race, group size, and playground area. *Child Study Journal,* 2S(4), 309–320.

Lindsey, E. W., & Colwell, M. J. (2003). Preschoolers' emotional competence links to pretend and physical play. *Child Study Journal,* 33(1), 39–52.

Martin, C. L., & Fabes, R. A. (2001). The stability and consequences of young children's same-sex peer interactions. *Developmental Psychology,* 37(3), 431–446.

Pellegrini, A. D. (1989). Elementary school children's rough-and-tumble play. *Early Childhood Research Quarterly,* 4(2), 245–260.

Pellegrini, A. D., & Blatchford, P. (2002). The developmental and educational significance of recess in schools. *Early Report,* 29(1). Retrieved March 16, 2004, from www.education.umn.edu/ceed/publications/earlyreport/spring02.htm.

Pellegrini, A. D., Blatchford, P., Kato, K., & Baines, E. (2004). A short-term longitudinal study of children's playground games in primary school: Implications for adjustment to school and social adjustment in the USA and the UK. *Social/ Development,* 13(1), 107–123.

Pellegrini, A. D., & Davis, P. (1993). Relations between children's playground and classroom behaviour. *British Journal of Educational Psychology,* 63(1), 88–95.

Pellegrini, A. D., & Smith, P. K. (1993). School recess: Implications for education and development. *Review of Educational Research,* 63(1), 51–67.

Perlmutter, J. C, & Burrell, L. (1995). Learning through 'play' as well as 'work' in the primary grades. *Young Children,* 50(5), 14–21.

Piaget, J. (1962). *Play, dreams, and imitation in childhood* (G. Gattegno & F. M. Hodgson, Trans.). New York: W.W. Norton & Company.

Poole, C., Miller, S., & Church, E. B. (2004). Working through that "It's Mine" feeling. *Early Childhood Today,* 18(5), 28–32.

Reed, T. (2000). Rough and tumble play during recess: Pathways to successful social development. In R. L. Clements (Ed.), *Elementary school recess: Selected readings, games, and activities for teachers and parents* (pp. 45–48). Boston: American Press.

Sarkin, J. S., McKenzie, T. L., & Sallis, J. F. (1997). Gender differences in physical activity during fifth-grade physical education and recess periods. *Journal of Teaching in Physical Education,* 17(1), 99–106.

Sutterby, J. S., & Frost, J. L. (2002). Making playgrounds fit for children and children fit on playgrounds. *Young Children,* 57(3), 36–41.

Thorne, B. (1993). *Gender play: Girls and boys in school.* New Brunswick, NJ: Rutgers University Press.

Van Hoorn, J., Monighan-Nourot, P., Scales, B., & Alward, K. R. (2003). *Play at the center of the curriculum* (3rd ed.). Upper Saddle River, NJ: Merrill Prentice-Hall.

Wortham, S. C. (2002). *Early childhood curriculum: Developmental bases for learning and teaching* (3rd ed.). Upper Saddle River, NJ: Merrill PrenticeHall.

JEANETTA G. RILEY is Assistant Professor, Department of Early Childhood and Elementary Education, Murray State University. **ROSE B. JONES** is Assistant Professor of Early Childhood Education/ Literacy, The University of Southern Mississippi.

UNIT 5
Educational Practices

Unit Selections

25. **Enhancing Development and Learning through Teacher-Child Relationships,** Kathleen Cranley Gallagher and Kelley Mayer
26. **Developmentally Appropriate Practice in the Age of Testing,** David McKay Wilson
27. **What Research Says about . . . Grade Retention,** Jane L. David
28. **Back to Basics: Play in Early Childhood,** Jill Englebright Fox
29. **Scripted Curriculum: Is It a Prescription for Success?,** Anita Ede
30. **Using Brain-Based Teaching Strategies to Create Supportive Early Childhood Environments That Address Learning Standards,** Pam Schiller and Clarissa A. Willis
31. **Successful Transition to Kindergarten: The Role of Teachers and Parents,** Pam Deyell-Gingold
32. **The Looping Classroom: Benefits for Children, Families, and Teachers,** Mary M. Hitz, Mary Catherine Somers, and Christee L. Jenlink
33. **Beyond *The Lorax*?: The Greening of the American Curriculum,** Clare Lowell

Key Points to Consider

- Describe strategies teachers could use to develop positive working relationships with children.

- What is causing the pressure to push the curriculum down from the primary grades into preschool? How can teachers of young children resist that pressure?

- How can teachers use the research when making decisions about grade retention?

- Can you think of a few brain-based activities that teachers could incorporate into their daily plans?

- What caused the large increase in scripted curriculum programs on the market?

- Make a brief list of the components of developmentally appropriate practice that you believe are vital.

- How can teachers and parents assist young children as they move from preschool to kindergarten?

- What are some of the best design features of a preschool classroom where you have worked or observed?

- Why is the ability to make choices a crucial skill to learn in the early years?

- What will be the consequences for this generation of children who do not have adequate experiences playing outside? How can teachers work to overcome this deficit?

Student Website
www.mhhe.com/cls

Internet References

Association for Childhood Education International (ACEI)
   http://www.acei.org
Early Childhood Education Online
   http://www.umaine.edu/eceol
Reggio Emilia
   http://www.ericdigests.org/2001-3/reggio.htm

When talking to a group of educators about what constitutes good teaching practices in early childhood education, many thoughts were shared, but the conversation always returned to one word: action.

Good early childhood teaching is distinguished by action, good practice is children in action: children busy constructing, creating with materials, enjoying books, exploring, working in small groups, experimenting, inventing, finding out, building and composing throughout the day. Good practice is teachers in action: teachers busy holding conversations, guiding activities, questioning children, fostering the environment, challenging children's thinking, observing, drawing conclusions, planning and monitoring activities and documenting the learning occurring throughout the day.

Make sure there is action in your classrooms, both children in action as they ask questions and work to find the answers to their questions as well as teachers in action supporting the investigations in their classrooms.

Each spring, the issue of grade retention creeps into the vocabulary of teachers and parents. Educators struggle to best address the needs of students who did not meet the standards or content expectations for that particular year. It is a challenge for teachers, parents, and the children who face another year in the same grade, which, research has consistently found, is not the best approach. Many countries do not retain students at all, while the United States retains over two million children each year. Is spending another year in the same grade the solution, or are there other ways educators can support struggling learners? Support for families, differentiated instruction, and outside services are successful strategies for children who do not achieve at the same level as their peers. Jane L. David's "What Research Says about . . . Grade Retention" will help answer some questions about this often misused educational practice.

I am distressed with the increasing push to have young children do things at an earlier and earlier age as the life expectancy keeps increasing. Children born today have an excellent chance of living into their 90s and beyond. There is no great need to rush and acquire skills that can easily be learned when the child is a little older at the expense of valuable lifelong lessons that are best learned when they are young. How to get along with others, make choices, negotiate, develop a sense of compassion, and communicating needs are all skills that require introduction and practice during the preschool years. "Back to Basics: Play in Early Childhood" by Jill Englebright Fox focuses on the importance of developmentally appropriate play experiences for young children, and not on the basics of core academic skills as many would think. The basics to which Fox refers are a solid foundation in understanding how things work, many opportunities to explore and manipulate materials, and opportunities for creative expression. How all this can be accomplished in the new world of standards is the balancing act that many teachers now do.

© Ablestock/Alamy RF

The passage of the No Child Left Behind legislation has many implications for early childhood care and educational practices. As academic assessment and accountability measures are implemented, many publishers have rushed to develop scripted curriculum for teachers to use. Most of these programs are centered on teaching reading. In "Scripted Curriculum: Is It a Prescription for Success?," Anita Ede examines the politics behind the development of scripted curriculum and both positive and negative research findings.

Teachers knowledgeable about best practices for brain-based learning can help their students succeed. In "Using Brain-Based Teaching Strategies to Create Supportive Early Childhood Environments That Address Learning Standards," Pam Schiller and Clarissa A. Willis share strategies for teachers to infuse inquiry-based learning experiences.

We now know teaching IS rocket science and does require committed individuals who are well prepared to deal with a variety of development levels and needs, as appropriate, intentional learning experiences are planned for all children. Good teaching does make a difference and children deserve no less than adults who truly are passionate about being with young children on a daily basis. Teaching cannot be viewed as a great profession for people who want their summers off. Teachers well prepared to provide exemplary learning experiences for their children can make a real difference in the lives of their students.

In "Successful Transition to Kindergarten: The Role of Teachers and Parents," the author provides ways in which teachers and parents can help young children make the major transition to kindergarten. For some children, kindergarten is their first experience with formal schooling. For many others, it means a different school, classroom, and teacher than they had during their preschool years. With this new experience come many different expectations.

This unit ends with a focus on the importance of getting children outside to play. Clare Lowell wrote "Beyond *The Lorax?*

The Greening of the American Curriculum" as another way of reaching educators and parents about the importance of getting children out of doors. Richard Louv's popular book, *Last Child in the Woods: Saving Our Children from Nature-Deficit Disorder* first explored the concept of children growing up nature deficient and not familiar with the great outdoors. Children today spend hours inside playing video games when their parents spent hours outside playing games and riding bikes. The article has significance for educators who work in school settings without playgrounds and limited if any recess opportunities.

Enhancing Development and Learning through Teacher-Child Relationships

KATHLEEN CRANLEY GALLAGHER, PhD AND KELLEY MAYER, PhD

From across the room, Miss Jilane notices that Maria has lost her toy to another toddler and is leaning toward the other child. She has seen Maria in these frustrating situations before and recognizes she may be about to bite her classmate. Calling her name gently, Jilane distracts her: "Maria, please help me with snack; I need a great snack helper. When we're done, you can play with that toy."

Tamara, the teacher, sits on a beanbag chair with Nick, a prekindergartner, reading a book about cars. They stop the story to talk about their own cars, with Tamara sharing what she likes about her truck and Nick explaining how his minivan has lots of room. They talk about what car Nick might get when he's "big" and what features it will have. They agree it will have to be a car that "is safe and goes fast."

Adam, the first-grade teacher, bends over a set of connecting blocks with Kwame. Tears are welling in Kwame's eyes, reflecting the frustration he feels trying to solve a math problem. Adam reassures Kwame that math can be hard work and proceeds to "think out loud" with him about how to solve the problem, regrouping the connecting blocks. "You don't have to do math alone, Kwame," Adam tells him. "It often helps to do it with another person. We can figure this out together."

How to be in a relationship may be the most important "skill" children ever learn.

Some researchers believe that children form ideas about relationships from their early experiences with their parents and apply these ideas to other relationships (Sroufe 2000). Others believe that children learn from teachers' modeling and imitate their social behavior (Baumrind 1973). It is likely that children use both of these strategies and more to learn about relationships. How to be in a relationship may be the most important "skill" children ever learn. While many teachers acknowledge their importance in helping children learn early academic and social skills, they sometimes underestimate the value of their personal relationships with children as supports

for children's healthy development and learning. As the opening vignettes illustrate, teachers use their attunement to and knowledge of children to effectively scaffold children's development and learning.

This article reviews research on relationships between young children (birth to age 8) and their teachers, with the goal of offering research-proven strategies teachers can use to develop and sustain high-quality relationships with children at each stage of early childhood. This article considers the unique qualities and influences of teacher-child relationships for infants and toddlers, preschoolers, and primary-age children and provides ideas for how teachers can reflect on and enhance relationships in their daily classroom routines.

When teachers develop high-quality relationships with young children, they support problem solving, allowing the children to experience success without too much or too little assistance.

Early Relationships and Development

High-quality relationships in early childhood support the development of social, emotional, and cognitive skills (Goosens & van IJzendoorn 1990; Howes, Galinsky, & Kontos 1998). When children have secure relationships with their primary caregivers, they have better language skills (Sroufe 2000), more harmonious peer relationships (Howes, Hamilton, & Matheson 1994; Howes, Matheson, & Hamilton 1994), and fewer behavior problems (Rimm-Kaufman et al. 2002). In high-quality teacher-child relationships, teachers respond to children's needs appropriately and in a timely manner. Teachers are gentle and take frequent opportunities to interact face-to-face with children. When teachers develop high-quality relationships with young children, they support children's problem solving, allowing the children to experience success without too much or too little assistance (Bredekamp & Copple 1997).

Teachers in high-quality relationships with young children also support learning by assessing the children's instructional needs and offering support at each child's level. For example, when helping a young child comprehend a difficult story, the teacher may introduce key vocabulary words *before* the reading, helping to scaffold the child's understanding of the story while preventing the child from becoming too overwhelmed by the complexity of the language in the text. The teachers in the vignettes provide this kind of childspecific support—a delicate dance in which learning emerges in the context of the teacher-child relationship.

Relationships between teachers and children do not develop in isolation, however. They develop ecologically, influenced by many factors such as child and teacher characteristics, interactive processes, and contextual factors over time (Bronfenbrenner & Morris 1998). Teachers certainly set the tone for their relationships with children, but some children have a behavior style, or temperament, that challenges caregivers (Sturm 2004) and may make relationship building more difficult. Research suggests that children who respond to the environment with intense negative emotion, who are highly fearful, or who are very resistant to outside guidance are more likely to have relationships with teachers that are less close and higher in conflict (Birch & Ladd 1998). Children with disabilities, especially language-based disabilities that make communicating their needs more difficult, sometimes have difficulty building relationships (Mahoney & Perales 2003).

Culture and ethnicity are associated with differences in aspects of children's relationships with teachers. For example, some studies report that teachers feel closer to White and Hispanic children than to African American children (Saft & Pianta 2001; Hughes & Kwok 2007). Researchers speculate that ethnic match between teachers and students may be more important for relationships than ethnicity of the student (Saft & Pianta 2001), although few studies have included diverse samples of teachers to examine this issue (Saft & Pianta 2001). Based on the results of a recent study, in which both White and African American teachers reported more conflict in their relationships with children who were African American (Gallagher et al. 2006), more research is needed to understand how ethnicity is associated with relationships among children and teachers.

To enhance development and learning, it is important to know individual children and their families well and to "establish positive, personal relationships with children to foster the child's development and keep informed about the child's needs and potentials. Teachers listen to children and adapt their responses to children's differing needs, interests, styles, and abilities" (Bredekamp & Copple 1997, 17). Children have different needs, and their needs change as they develop. As their needs change, their relationships with teachers change as well. For example, in a study examining the stability of teacher-child relationships over the early childhood years from 10 to 56 months, most children established secure attachment relationships with their child

care teacher (Howes & Hamilton 1992). When children were younger (18–24 months old), their relationships with teachers suffered when teacher turnover was frequent, but older toddlers (30-plus months) were less affected by turnover.

It is important to consider teacher-child relationships across development and schooling, paying particular attention to how such relationships function to sustain and enhance development at each age. Knowledge of individual children's needs at each developmental stage helps teachers understand how to best support children in their development and learning. The following sections highlight features of teacher-child relationships at different developmental periods and ways teachers and programs can enhance these relationships.

Teachers' Relationships with Infants and Toddlers

In infancy, social interaction forms the basis for the developing brain, supporting development of emotion regulation and attention (Shonkoff & Phillips 2000). Social relationships also teach infants and toddlers what they can expect from interacting with people. By crying, cooing, and smiling, infants express their needs and draw adult attention. Adults anticipate, sense, and interpret the infants' behaviors and then respond in a timely and appropriate manner. Through their positive affect, body language, and tone of voice, adults communicate warmth, positive regard, and safety. Infants, sensing comfort, safety, and security in the adult's presence, explore their environment and attempt new challenges.

John Bowlby ([1969] 1983) believed that children form cognitive schemas of their interactions with adults and use them to form ideas about self and relationships. For example, infants whose caregivers respond sensitively to their needs learn to expect that their needs will be met and their future interactions with adults will be positive. In these positive interactions, infants come to feel that they are "worthy" of these interactions and relationships. In contrast, infants whose needs are not met responsively, or are met inconsistently, learn that they cannot rely on others to care for them. These infants may become detached or aggressive in their relationships (Sroufe 2000).

The secure infant stays close to a trusted caregiver, watching newcomers with a healthy suspicion.

Before children are 6 months old, it may be difficult to tell the quality of teacher-child relationships by observing the child. But soon after a child begins to crawl, evidence of his relationship with a caregiver is reflected in several behaviors. The secure infant stays close to a trusted caregiver, watching newcomers with a healthy suspicion. Observation methods of examining teacher-infant relationships have been important in describing teacher behaviors that foster healthy relationships and influence children's development (Goosens & van IJzendoorn 1990; Howes & Smith 1995; Howes, Galinsky, & Kontos 1998). Sensitive teachers respond to children's cues and comfort distressed children (Howes & Smith 1995; Howes, Galinsky, & Kontos 1998). They provide multiple opportunities for creative play, engage toddlers in prolonged conversations, and frequently join in their play to encourage children's successful cognitive development. When children misbehave, sensitive teachers redirect and gently remind children of expectations; they assert their expectations for children's respectful social behavior while affirming their affection toward the child (Howes & Smith 1995; Howes, Galinsky, & Kontos 1998).

When teachers behave in a sensitive, responsive manner, children seek closeness and contact with them, share with them excitement and discovery in their play, and respond to teachers' suggestions and directions readily (Goosens & van IJzendoorn 1990; Howes & Smith 1995; Howes, Galinsky, & Kontos 1998). Children with close relationships with teachers have better relationships with other children (Howes, Matheson, & Hamilton 1994; Howes & Phillipsen 1998). In one study, toddlers who demonstrated a secure relationships with their teacher were, at 4 years of age, less aggressive with peers and more sociable and skilled in imaginative peer play (Howes, Hamilton, & Matheson 1994).

Implications for Infant/Toddler Teachers and Programs

Because secure attachment is so important to an infant's development, programs serving infants and toddlers must make supporting the development of relationships a priority (Bredekamp & Copple 1997). To that end, programs serving infants and toddlers must take care to maintain the lowest child-to-teacher ratios possible. However, low ratios alone are not sufficient for creating an environment that supports intimacy between teachers and young children (Lally, Torres, & Phelps 1994). Program environments should be touchable and comfortable. Spaces for infants and toddlers should be inviting and should contain interesting objects and textures to explore as well as interesting and attractive visual stimuli. The lighting should be soft, and there should be plenty of soft, comfortable seating or floor space where caregivers and children can interact with one another comfortably (Lally, Torres, & Phelps 1994). To provide for infants' and toddlers' need for continuity of care, each child should have the same primary caregiver for as long as possible.

Low child-to-teacher ratios help teachers provide one-on-one attention, and sufficient preparation time helps teachers plan for individual children's needs.

As in all teaching, but particularly with infants and toddlers, teachers need to attend to the individual needs of children in the context of a group (Lally, Torres, & Phelps 1994). In order to respond to infants' and toddlers' individual needs, teachers must be attuned to children's cues and be keen observers of child behavior. Likewise, programs must do what they can to ensure that teachers have the time to observe and interpret children's behavior. For example, low child-to-teacher ratios help teachers provide one-on-one attention, and sufficient preparation time helps teachers plan for individual children's needs.

Finally, each child lives in a unique family culture that a teacher must understand in order to develop a quality relationship with the child. Therefore, programs should support teachers' relationships with children's families by setting aside time for communication, conferencing, and home visits.

Teachers' Relationships with Preschoolers

As children enter preschool, they are typically ready for more complex relationships. Their language, motor, and cognitive abilities allow them to more easily initiate interactions and respond to other people. Preschoolers' readiness for new and more complex relationships is apparent in the classroom's stimulating environment and in their interests in the people and world around them.

Interactions between teachers and children are essential to the quality of the teacher-child relationship and to children's learning and development (Kontos & Wilcox-Herzog 1997a). When exploring interactions between teachers and children, researchers have observed key teacher behaviors that enhance relationships with children (Rimm-Kaufman et al. 2002) and support social and academic competence (Kontos & Wilcox-Herzog 1997a). Teachers who have high-quality relationships with children help children to focus their attention and interpret their emotions (Howes & Hamilton 1992). Sensitive and responsive teachers assess children's learning styles and use that knowledge to meet children's instructional and social needs (Hamre & Pianta 2005). The highest quality relationships between teachers and children are characterized by closeness (warmth and open communication) and low conflict (hostility and opposition) (Pianta, Hamre, & Stuhlman 2003).

Research emphasizes the importance of intentional, responsive teaching for children's learning in the context of play (Kontos & Wilcox-Herzog 1997b; Lobman 2006). Reflecting a complex set of practices, responsive teaching involves assessing children's individual needs, contextual needs, and cognitive and social competencies and responding in a timely and appropriate manner. Because different children require varying levels and qualities of teacher involvement, responsive teaching is a delicate, but not impossible, dance. Lobman (2006) elaborates on the complex processes of responsive teaching through the lens of theatrical improvisation. Using this lens in a case study, one teacher participated in preschool children's play, leading and responding to innovation and eventually leading to more complex, collaborative play. Lobman demonstrates that even subtle language differences within the realm of responsive teaching modifies the trajectory of children's engagement with the teacher, peers, objects, and ideas. Collectively, this evidence suggests that what teachers do and say matters highly in children's development and learning.

Close relationships with teachers have remarkable benefits for children. Children who develop close relationships with their teacher tend to explore the classroom environment (Coplan & Prakash 2003) and demonstrate more complex play than their peers who are not as close to their teacher. They are also sought out more by their playmates (Howes, Matheson, & Hamilton 1994). Finally, preschoolers with close teacher relationships have better school achievement, better social skills, and fewer behavior problems in first grade and throughout elementary school (Hamre & Pianta 2001; Pianta & Stuhlman 2004).

Implications for Preschool Teachers and Programs

Developmentally appropriate practice optimizes opportunities and strategies for developing teacher-child relationships (Bredekamp & Copple 1997). Children should begin the school day with a feeling of warmth and comfort as they transition from their family's care to their teacher's. Teachers who focus on their relationships with children take time to recognize children individually, personally greeting them and their families each morning and again at their departure. Acknowledging children's presence and welcoming them involves modeling very basic principles of respect and commitment to relationships.

> **Children enjoy knowing about their teachers' lives outside of school and develop empathy as they understand the different roles in people's lives.**

Teachers can build positive relationships with children by spending time with them in individual and small group settings. To improve their relationships with children, teachers may engage in one-on-one activities such as shared story reading (Gallagher et al. 2006; Gallagher et al. under review). Story reading with individual children can stimulate meaningful conversations about topics such as the children's families, after-school experiences, and pets. The teacher should also feel comfortable sharing things that are important to her. Children enjoy knowing about their teachers' lives outside of school and develop empathy as they understand the different roles in people's lives. Becoming familiar with children's interests helps teachers meet their needs while also modeling for children how to care for another person.

When children experience conflict in relationships, teachers can encourage them to express their feelings through conversation or through writing and drawing. Having paper and

writing materials in the quiet corner gives children a healthy outlet to express their anger or sadness (Mayer 2007). When a child uses negative behavior, the teacher should discuss the incident with the child in private and in the context of expectations based on respect. When teachers value relationships, they recognize that learning how to be in relationships is challenging and that children will learn acceptable social behavior over time.

Teachers' Relationships with Primary School Children

In the primary classroom, teachers usually are responsible for a larger group of children than in younger classrooms while at the same time focusing on academics and state standards (Barnett et al. 2005). Despite the greater responsibility to provide effective instruction in all content areas, teachers must continue to provide caring, supportive environments in which children feel emotionally supported and valued if children are going to benefit academically and socially from schooling (Hamre & Pianta 2001; Davis 2003; Pianta, Hamre, & Stuhlman 2003; Klem & Connell 2004; Koomen, van Leeuwen, & van der Leij 2004; La Paro, Rimm-Kaufman, & Pianta 2006).

Furthermore, emerging evidence suggests that teachers' support is even more important for children who are vulnerable to school failure (Henricsson & Rydell 2004; Hamre & Pianta 2005; Hughes, Gleason, & Zhang 2005; Picklo 2005; Hughes & Kwok 2007). Highstakes standards, larger class sizes, and decreased time for informal, relaxed engagement in primary grades mean teachers must work harder to build strong relationships with children.

Research demonstrates that classroom climate, specifically teachers' emotional and instructional support, is associated with teachers' relationships with children in the primary grades (Hamre & Pianta 2005). Teachers providing high levels of emotional support tend to be aware of the children's needs and interests, engage in conversations, and show positive affect toward children while also maintaining high yet attainable expectations for appropriate behavior. Teachers high in instructional support spend considerable time and effort on literacy instruction, give children evaluative feedback, encourage child responsibility, and offer conversational (not just didactic) instruction (Hamre & Pianta 2005).

In addition to teacher support in the classroom, relationships between teachers and individual children are associated with academic growth, social competence, and engagement in the primary grades. When kindergarten teachers' relationships with children were high in conflict, first grade teachers reported more behavioral problems and poorer social competence (Pianta & Stuhlman 2004). Subsequently, these children's relationships with their first grade teachers were associated with their social skills *and* academic achievement in first grade. Throughout research, children in close teacher-child relationships participated more in classroom activities (Ladd, Birch, & Buhs 1999), exhibited better work habits (Hamre & Pianta 2001; Baker 2006), and liked school more, while children with high conflict teacher-child relationships reported liking school less (Birch & Ladd 1998) and had poorer academic achievement (Hughes, Gleason, & Zhang 2005; Hughes & Kwok 2007). The quality of the teacher-child relationship also influences children's relationships with peers in the primary grades. When teachers reported less closeness and more conflict in their relationships with second-graders, these children showed more aggression with their classroom peers. When teachers reported closer, lower conflict relationships with second-graders, the children were more prosocial with classroom peers (Howes 2000).

Implications for Primary Teachers and Programs

The instructional methods teachers use are important for determining children's success in learning as well as their comfort and security when interacting with the teacher. Primary grade teachers need time for individual instruction with children (Ostrosky & Jung 2003). During this time, the teacher can observe and interact with the child while engaged in a learning activity. This helps teachers better assess children's needs. It also gives children opportunities to ask questions and express ideas in a safe space.

As with preschoolers, teachers can also build positive relationships with primary-age children through interactive storybook reading (Gallagher et al. 2006). Teachers can read aloud to children and encourage children's involvement in the story by engaging children in extended conversations about the text and making personal connections (Neuman, Copple, & Bredekamp 2000). These proven comprehension strategies help children process story information and allow teachers opportunities to become familiar with children's personal experiences.

Children can participate in family conferences as well, assessing achievements and setting goals.

Individual conferences between teachers and children provide opportunities for children to receive both emotional and instructional feedback from teachers. Involving the child's family in the conference can help the teacher build a relationship with the family as well as with the child. Children can participate in their conferences as well, assessing achievements and setting goals. This enables the children to feel care and support from the multiple adults responsible for their education and to own their own progress. Teachers can find opportunities to get to know children by having lunch with them or taking time to talk with them on the playground. Primary grade teachers can also get to know children better through participation in after-school activities and events. Attending such events allows teachers to see children immersed in their interactions with family members and peers, helping teachers to learn more about what is important to these children.

Summary

Research confirms that "children's development in all areas is influenced by their ability to establish and maintain a limited number of positive, consistent primary relationships with adults and other children. These primary relationships begin in the family but extend over time to include children's teachers and members of the community" (Bredekamp & Copple 1997, 15). To appropriately address children's needs, teachers and programs must put children's relationships at the forefront of planning and implementation of interactions and activities.

Putting relationships at the forefront involves recognizing the child, becoming familiar with the child and family, respecting the child's individuality, and committing to the ongoing process of being in the relationship (Gallagher & Mayer 2006). The beauty of working with young children is that while we, as teachers, practice building relationships, we also model relationship-building practices for them.

The privileges of caring for and educating children are not separate. We do both every day, building relationships with children and supporting their development and learning. Prospective parents would often ask, "Is your program child *care* or a pre*school*?" The response has always been, "We are both. We cannot care for children without educating them, and we cannot educate children without caring for them." We do both by building relationships.

References

Baker, J. 2006. Contributions of teacher-child relationships to positive school adjustment during elementary school. *Journal of School Psychology* 44 (3): 211–29.

Barnett, W. S., J. T. Hustedt, K. B. Robin, & K. L. Schulman. 2005. *2005 State preschool yearbook*. Third volume in the series The State of Preschool. New Brunswick, NJ: National Institute for Early Education Research (NIEER).

Baumrind, D. 1973. The development of instrumental competence through socialization. In *Minnesota symposia on child psychology: Volume 7*, ed. A. D. Pick, 3–46. Minneapolis: University of Minnesota Press.

Birch, S. H., & G. W. Ladd. 1998. Children's interpersonal behaviors and the teacher-child relationship. *Developmental Psychology* 34 (5): 934–46.

Bowlby, J. [1969] 1983. *Attachment*. Vol. 1 of *Attachment and loss*. New York: Basic Books.

Bredekamp, S., & C. Copple, eds. 1997. *Developmentally appropriate practice in early childhood programs*. Rev. ed. Washington, DC: NAEYC.

Bronfenbrenner, U., & P. Morris. 1998. The ecology of developmental processes. In *Theoretical models of human development*, ed. R. M. Lerner. New York: Wiley.

Coplan, R. J., & K. Prakash. 2003. Spending time with teacher: Characteristics of preschoolers who frequently elicit versus initiate interactions with teachers. *Early Childhood Research Quarterly* 18 (1): 143–58.

Davis, H. A. 2003. Conceptualizing the role and influence of student-teacher relationships on children's social and cognitive development. *Educational Psychologist* 38 (4): 207–34.

Gallagher, K. C., & K. L. Mayer. 2006. Teacher-child relationships at the forefront of effective practice. *Young Children* 61 (6): 44–49.

Gallagher, K. C., K. L. Mayer, P. Sylvester, M. P. Bundy, & P. Fedora. 2006. Teacher-child relationships and developing literacy and social-emotional skills in pre-kindergarten. Poster paper presented at the Annual Meeting of the American Educational Research Association, in San Francisco.

Gallagher, K. C., P. R. Sylvester, K. L. Mayer, & M. P. Bundy. Under review. Storytime in prekindergarten: Teacher-child story reading and associations with temperament, development, and teacher-child relationship. *Early Education and Development.*

Goosens, F. A., & M. H. van IJzendoorn. 1990. Quality of infants' attachments to professional caregivers: Relation to infant-parent attachment and day-care characteristics. *Child Development* 61: 832–37.

Hamre, B. K., & R. C. Pianta. 2001. Early teacher-child relationships and the trajectory of children's school outcomes through eighth grade. *Child Development* 72 (2): 625–38.

Hamre, B. K., & R. C. Pianta. 2005. Can instructional and emotional support in the firstgrade classroom make a difference for children at risk for school failure? *Child Development* 76 (5): 949–67.

Henricsson, L., & A.-M. Rydell. 2004. Elementary school children with behavior problems: Teacher-child relations and self-perception. A prospective study. *Merrill-Palmer Quarterly* 50 (2): 111–38.

Howes, C. 2000. Social-emotional classroom climate in child care, child-teacher relationships, and children's second grade peer relations. *Social Development* 9 (2): 191–204.

Howes, C., E. Galinsky, & S. Kontos. 1998. Child care caregiver sensitivity and attachment. *Social Development* 7 (1): 25–36.

Howes, C., & C. E. Hamilton. 1992. Children's relationships with child care teachers: Stability and concordance with parental attachments. *Child Development* 63: 867–78.

Howes, C., C. E. Hamilton, & C. C. Matheson. 1994. Children's relationships with peers: Differential associations with aspects of the teacher-child relationship. *Child Development* 65: 253–63.

Howes, C., C. C. Matheson, & C. E. Hamilton. 1994. Maternal, teacher, and child care history correlates of children's relationships with peers. *Child Development* 65: 264–73.

Howes, C., & L. Phillipsen. 1998. Continuity in children's relations with peers. *Social Development* 7 (3): 340–49.

Howes, C., & E. W. Smith. 1995. Relations among child care quality, teacher behavior, children's play activities, emotional security, and cognitive activity in child care. *Early Childhood Research Quarterly* 10 (4): 381–404.

Hughes, J., K. A. Gleason, & D. Zhang. 2005. Relationship influences on teachers' perceptions of academic competence in academically at-risk minority and majority first grade students. *Journal of School Psychology* 43 (4): 303–20.

Hughes, J., & O. Kwok. 2007. Influence of student-teacher and parent-teacher relationships on lower achieving readers' engagement and achievement in the primary grades. *Journal of Educational Psychology* 99 (1): 39–51.

Klem, A. M., & J. P. Connell. 2004. Relationships matter: Linking teacher support to student engagement and achievement. *Journal of School Health* 74 (7): 262–73.

Kontos, S., & A. Wilcox-Herzog. 1997a. Influences on children's competence in early childhood classrooms. *Early Childhood Research Quarterly* 12 (3): 247–62.

Kontos, S., & A. Wilcox-Herzog. 1997b. Teachers interactions with children: Why are they so important? *Young Children* 52 (2): 4–12.

Koomen, H., M. van Leeuwen, & A. van der Leij. 2004. Does well-being contribute to performance? Emotional security, teacher support and learning behaviour in kindergarten. *Infant and Child Development* 13: 253–75.

Ladd, G. W., S. H. Birch, & E. S. Buhs. 1999. Children's social and scholastic lives in kindergarten: Related spheres of influence? *Child Development* 70 (6): 1373–1400.

Lally, J. R., Y. L. Torres, & P. C. Phelps. 1994. Caring for infants and toddlers in groups: Necessary considerations for emotional, social, and cognitive development. *Zero to Three* 14 (5): 1–8.

La Paro, K. M., S. E. Rimm-Kaufman, & R. C. Pianta. 2006. Kindergarten to first grade: Classroom characteristics and the stability and change of children's classroom experiences. *Journal of Research in Childhood Education* 21 (2): 189–202.

Lobman, C. L. 2006. Improvisation: An analytic tool for examining teacher-child interactions in the early childhood classroom. *Early Childhood Research Quarterly* 21 (4): 455–70.

Mahoney, G., & F. Perales. 2003. Using relationship-focused intervention to enhance the social-emotional functioning of young children with autism spectrum disorders. *Topics in Early Childhood Special Education* 23 (2): 77–89.

Mayer, K. L. 2007. Emerging knowledge about emergent writing. *Young Children* 62 (1): 34–41.

Neuman, S. B., C. Copple, & S. Bredekamp. 2000. *Learning to read and write: Developmentally appropriate practices for young children.* Washington, DC: NAEYC.

Ostrosky, M. M., & E. Y. Jung. 2003. Building positive teacher-child relationships. In What Works Briefs. Champaign, IL: Center on the Social and Emotional Foundations for Early Learning. www.vanderbilt.edu/csefel/briefs/wwb12.html

Pianta, R. C., B. Hamre, & M. Stuhlman. 2003. Relationships between teachers and children. In *Educational psychology,* eds. W. M. Reynolds & G. E. Miller, 199–234. Vol. 7 of *Handbook of psychology,* ed. I. B. Weiner. Hoboken, NJ: Wiley.

Pianta, R. C., & M. W. Stuhlman. 2004. Teacher-child relationships and children's success in the first years of school. *School Psychology Review* 33 (3): 444–58.

Picklo, D. M. 2005. Behaviorally at-risk African American students: The importance of student-teacher relationships for school outcomes. Dissertation Abstracts International, Section A: Humanities and Social Sciences, ProQuest Information & Learning.

Rimm-Kaufman, S. E., D. M. Early, M. J. Cox, G. Saluja, R. C. Pianta, & C. Payne. 2002. Early behavioral attributes and teachers' sensitivity as predictors of competent behavior in the kindergarten classroom. *Applied Developmental Psychology* 23: 451–70.

Saft, E. W., & R. C. Pianta. 2001. Teachers' perceptions of their relationships with students: Effects of child age, gender, and ethnicity of teachers and children. *School Psychology Quarterly* 16 (2): 125–41.

Shonkoff, J. P., & D. A. Phillips, eds. 2000. *From neurons to neighborhoods: The science of early childhood development.* Report of the National Research Council. Washington DC: National Academies Press.

Sroufe, A. L. 2000. Early relationships and the development of children. *Infant Mental Health Journal* 21 (1-2): 67–74.

Sturm, L. 2004. Temperament in early childhood: A primer for the perplexed. *Zero to Three* 24 (4): 4–11.

KATHLEEN CRANLEY GALLAGHER, PhD, is an assistant professor in the School of Education at the University of North Carolina at Chapel Hill. Having worked with children and families in early education programs for 15 years, Kate's research and teaching now focus on children's social relationships with families, peers, and teachers. kcgallag@email .unc.edu KELLEY MAYER, PhD, is an assistant professor at the College of Charleston, in South Carolina. Her research addresses associations between teacher-child relationships and children's early literacy development. Kelley was previously a literacy consultant and taught kindergarten in a public school. mayerk@cofc.edu. This Research in Review article was edited by journal research editor Sharon K. Ryan, EdD, associate professor of early childhood education, Graduate School of Education, Rutgers—The State University of New Jersey.

From *Young Children*, November 2008, pp. 80–87. Copyright © 2008 by National Association for the Education of Young Children. Reprinted by permission.

Developmentally Appropriate Practice in the Age of Testing

New reports outline key principles for preK–3rd grade.

DAVID MCKAY WILSON

As the push to teach literacy and math skills reaches farther into preschool and kindergarten, educators are warning that teachers need to address young students' social, emotional, and physical needs as well as their cognitive development. Among their concerns:

- Teachers in preK–3rd grade increasingly focus on a narrow range of literacy and math skills, with studies showing some kindergarteners spend up to six times as much time on those topics and on testing and test prep than they do in free play or "choice time."
- Many schools have eliminated recess or physical education, depriving children of their need to move and develop their bodies.
- Instruction is often focused on "scripted" curricula, giving teachers little opportunity to create lessons in response to students' interests.
- Some state standards for literacy are too stiff, such as one state's standard that all students be able to read by the beginning of first grade.

In light of these concerns, several prominent early childhood organizations have issued reports on the importance of incorporating developmentally appropriate practice into elementary school classrooms, based on what research has confirmed about early learning.

The National Association for the Education of Young Children (NAEYC) is so concerned about the pressure to prepare students for third-grade standardized tests that it adopted a position statement in early 2009 on developmentally appropriate practice for educators in preK through third grade. In their report, "Developmentally Appropriate Practice in Early Childhood Programs: Serving Children from Birth Through Age 8," NAEYC researchers outlined 12 principles of child development that can be incorporated into classroom teaching (see "NAEYC's 12 Principles of Child Development").

The report urges educators to incorporate play into daily instruction, devise classroom tasks that are challenging yet attainable, and become attuned to the needs of each student so that materials can be adapted to a child's individual needs. It also urges educators in preK through third grade to learn from each other: While preschool educators can benefit from understanding the standards children are expected to meet by third grade, NAEYC believes primary-grade teachers can improve the quality of their instruction by learning more about children's developmental needs from early childhood educators.

The Alliance for Childhood's report, "Crisis in Kindergarten: Why Children Need to Play in School," cites nine new studies that focus on the role of play, child-initiated learning, highly structured curricula, and standardized testing. One study found that the preponderance of time in 254 New York City and Los Angeles kindergartens was spent on literacy and math. Teachers reported that the curricula didn't have room for dramatic play, blocks, or artistic activities, and that school administrators didn't value such activities. A report from the American Academy of Pediatrics, however, concluded that play was essential for healthy brain development. And a cross-national study of 1,500 young children in 10 countries found that children's language at age seven improved when teachers let them choose their activities rather than teaching them in didactic lessons.

"The studies showed that teachers were spending two to three hours a day hammering in their lessons, with little time for play," says Joan Almon, executive director of the Alliance for Childhood. "The brain is eager to learn at this age, but the kids are more eager to learn from things they can touch and feel."

Charging that "developmental psychology and education have grown apart," the FPG Child Development Institute in Chapel Hill, N.C., is also advocating for more professional development and coursework for teachers in the science of child development. The institute's researchers emphasize the importance of four foundations of learning: self-regulation, representation, memory, and attachment (see "Four Foundations of Learning").

"The ability to focus, pay attention, and work with others is very predictive of long-term success in school," says Carol

NAEYC's 12 Principles of Child Development

- All domains of development and learning—physical, social and emotional, and cognitive—are related.
- Children follow well-documented sequences to build knowledge.
- Children develop and learn at varying rates.
- Learning develops from the dynamic interaction of biological maturation and experience.
- Early childhood experiences can have profound effects, and optimal periods exist for certain types of development and learning.
- Development proceeds toward greater complexity and self-regulation.
- Children thrive with secure, consistent relationships with responsive adults.
- Multiple social and cultural contexts influence learning and development.
- Children learn in a variety of ways, so teachers need a range of strategies.
- Play helps develop self-regulation, language, cognition, and social competence.
- Children advance when challenged just beyond their current level of mastery.
- Children's experiences shape their motivation, which in turn affects their learning.

Copple, coeditor of the NAEYC report. "Those things are typically emphasized in preschool, but they are important for older children as well."

Responsiveness and Engagement

Developmentally appropriate practice is based on the recognition that child development generally occurs in a predictable sequence of stages. While children may develop at different rates, each stage of development lays the groundwork for the acquisition of new skills and abilities in the next phase. Research has long indicated that children do best when they are supported to achieve goals just beyond their current level of mastery.

In crafting their report, NAEYC researchers reviewed recent educational research, interviewed scores of experts, and observed classrooms. They note the crucial connection between children's social and emotional life and their academic competence. Children make the biggest strides, the authors found, when they are able to cement secure, consistent relationships with responsive adults.

For classroom teachers, they say, being responsive means being able to adapt the curriculum to address their students' needs and interests and to allow children to discuss their experiences, feelings, and ideas. That can be difficult when teachers are following the highly regimented lesson plans now mandated in many classrooms.

Four Foundations of Learning

Teachers of children from preK to age eight should focus as much on self-regulation, representational thought, memory, and attachment as they do on basic skills, say researchers at the University of North Carolina's School of Education.

These four issues serve as the foundation for young children's development, according to Sharon Ritchie, a senior scientist at FPG Child Development Institute and coauthor of the report, "Using Developmental Science to Transform Children's Early School Experiences." She offers the following examples:

- *Self-regulation* is often developed through play. For example, when kindergartners play "restaurant," they must regulate their behavior to stay in the role of customer, waiter, cashier, or store manager. As children grow older, their play follows more complex rules, as when third-graders act out a story they have read.
- Secure *attachment* relationships help young children feel comfortable exploring the world to learn. Teachers can nurture good relationships by helping students express their feelings and resolve conflicts.
- *Representational thought* is the ability to use an expression—be it a word, gesture, or drawing—to depict an idea. Teachers need to help children find ways to express their own ideas before guiding them to new understanding.
- *Memory* is a crucial part of learning. Strategies to help strengthen students' memory include encouraging students to talk about what they have just learned or, as they grow older, reflecting on what they do when they need to remember something. Teachers can also structure their classes to help children remember the most important items taught that day.

Developing an enthusiasm for learning is especially important in the primary grades. Even students who have excelled in preK or kindergarten can find first or second grade so trying that they turn off to learning. Such disengagement has become so widespread that Sharon Ritchie, a senior scientist at FPG Child Development Institute, has worked with educators on a dropout-prevention project that focuses on children in preK through third grade.

"You can walk into a classroom and see kids who by third grade are done with school," she says. "They are angry and feel school is not a fair place or a place that sees them as the individual that they are."

Some of that disengagement, Ritchie says, is rooted in the way students in second or third grade are taught. She found that students in preK classes spent 136 minutes a day involved in hands-on projects. That dropped to 16 minutes by kindergarten and 12 minutes a day by second and third grade.

She encourages teachers to use hands-on activities in kindergarten and the early primary grades to allow students to experience learning through inquiry. In a first-grade lesson on evaporation, for instance, Ritchie suggests that the teacher ask the children to describe where they think rain comes from and have them draw pictures depicting their theories. Based on that information, the children can discuss their hypotheses and begin to investigate what actually happens. For example, they might observe an ice cube at room temperature as it melts and then evaporates. Older children could deepen their inquiry through library research or designing and performing their own experiments.

Teachers also need to listen to what interests their young students. Patricia Lambert, principal of the Barnard Early Childhood Center in New Rochelle, N.Y., says listening to students can spark engaging lessons. At her school, which serves children from preK through second grade, teachers are encouraged to weave district-mandated outcomes into lessons that teach but do not drill. "Our goal by the end of kindergarten is to have children count from zero to 20," she says. If the children are learning about sharks, she adds, "we may use a model of a shark, and count the shark's teeth."

"I'm all for exposing preschool children to numbers and letters," Lambert says, "but we introduce by listening to what the children are interested in and then gently imposing these concepts on their interests."

Learning through Play

Young children do much of their learning through play, says Robert Pianta, dean of the Curry School of Education at the University of Virginia, but adults need to guide their play to help them learn. "It's a misinterpretation to think that letting students loose for extended periods of time is going to automatically yield learning gains," he says. "This is particularly true for students struggling to self-regulate and communicate."

Teachers must intentionally engage with their students, shaping play in a way that's enjoyable, while providing the child with the information and skills to allow playful exploration to produce learning. With blocks, for example, a teacher can talk about shapes, sizes, and colors to help the student bring those concepts to life.

That intentional engagement, says Sharon Kagan, the Marx Professor of Early Childhood and Family Policy at Columbia's Teachers College, should be subtle and keyed to a child's particular needs. If a boy is having trouble using scissors, then scissors, paste, and other art supplies should be set up for him at a table. "The teacher shouldn't push the child to the table, but needs to provide encouragement," she says. "Then the teacher can watch and monitor and guide."

Other advocates, however, note that some of the richest learning for children comes through child-initiated or child-directed play. The Alliance for Childhood report recommends at least three daily play periods of an hour or longer in a full-day, six-hour kindergarten program, with at least one hour spent playing outdoors.

Let's Get Physical

At a time when some schools are cutting recess and physical education classes in favor of academic instruction, researchers say these districts are depriving children of essential school-based activities that prepare them for learning. The NAEYC report, for example, recommends that children play outside every day, have regular physical education classes, and have ample opportunities to use their large muscles for balancing, running, jumping, and other vigorous activities.

A recent study in *Pediatrics* detailed the benefits of recess for third-graders. Dr. Romina Barros, pediatrician at Albert Einstein College of Medicine in New York City, surveyed about 11,000 eight-year-olds and found that 30 percent had little or no recess. Those who had at least 15 minutes of recess exhibited better classroom behavior than those who didn't have a break.

The study shows that giving children a break from their studies helps them with self-regulation, a key predictor of long-term success in school. On the playground, children learn how to resolve conflicts, control their actions in a game, and take turns. They also get to use some of that natural energy that spills out of some children in the classroom and can be seen as disruptive.

"You can't move forward with another half-hour of math if you see the kids are bouncing out of their skins," says Alice Keane, a first-grade teacher at Lake Bluff Elementary School in Shorewood, Wis. "We might take what we call a 'wiggle walk' around the school because the kids in the class have too many wiggles. It's amazing how more receptive the children are after they've moved around."

DAVID MCKAY WILSON is a freelance education journalist who lives in New York State.

What Research Says about . . . Grade Retention

In this new column, Jane L. David shares with readers what research says about the effectiveness of current education reforms.

In the coming months, David will examine the research behind such approaches as incentives to attract teachers to high-poverty schools and small learning communities. In framing the issues and drawing conclusions, she will draw on articles from peer-reviewed journals and reports from research institutions as well as her own 35 years of experience studying schools and districts.

We welcome readers' comments at edleadership@ascd.org.

JANE L. DAVID

Today's expectation that all students will meet high standards has contributed to a backlash against "social promotion." In this environment, grade retention has been making a comeback.

What's the Idea?

Educators and policymakers have debated for decades whether struggling students benefit more from repeating a grade or from moving ahead with their same-age peers. The argument for retention is that students who have not met grade-level criteria will fall further and further behind as they move through the grades. A failing 2nd grader, retention advocates argue, would be better served by repeating 2nd grade than by moving on to 3rd grade. Surely a student who could not succeed in 2nd grade will have an even harder time succeeding in 3rd grade.

What's the Reality?

School systems cannot hold back every student who falls behind; too many would pile up in the lower grades. Moreover, it is expensive to add a year of schooling for a substantial number of students. Therefore, in practice, schools set passing criteria at a level that ensures that most students proceed through the grades at the expected rate.

Although solid statistics are hard to come by, estimates of the number of students retained at least once in their school career range from 10 to 20 percent. Black students are more than twice as likely to be held back as white students, and boys twice as likely as girls (National Center for Education Statistics, 2006).

> **Estimates of the number of students retained at least once in their school career range from 10 to 20 percent.**

In the past, teacher judgment played a larger role in decisions about individual students. More recently, in the context of high-stakes testing, states and urban districts have begun formalizing and tightening requirements for promotion, often using a single test score. Drawing such a line in the sand aims to limit teacher discretion to promote students who are struggling academically; it also aims to motivate students to work harder to avoid retention. Policymakers believe that stricter requirements for promotion will increase the proportion of students likely to meet standards at higher grade levels.

What's the Research?

Published research on retention is vast. Hundreds of studies have been carried out during the last century, most focused on the elementary grades. As with any large body of research, the studies ask different questions, look at different consequences, and are fraught with methodological problems. It's tricky in most cases to determine whether the students in the study would have fared better if they had been promoted instead of retained.

Jackson (1975) reviewed 44 studies that met a minimal set of methodological criteria. Finding few with significant results or even compelling patterns, he concluded that the evidence was insufficient to support the claim that grade retention is more beneficial than grade promotion. About 10 years later, Holmes and Matthews (1984) reviewed an additional 44 studies that all included some type of comparison group of students. These researchers concluded that promoted students had higher academic achievement, better personal adjustment, and more positive attitudes toward school than retained students did.

Moving ahead another 17 years, Jimerson (2001) summarized the historical research and added a carefully culled set of studies conducted between 1990 and 1999, all of which included comparison groups of promoted students. Most of the comparisons showed no significant differences between promoted and retained students on measures of achievement or personal and social adjustment. In those studies that did show a difference, the results favored the promoted students, especially on measures of achievement.

Recent studies have investigated retention in the context of state and district policies to require students to achieve a certain score for promotion. For example, Roderick and Nagaoka (2005) studied the effects of the Chicago Public Schools policy that bases promotion in grades 3, 6, and 8 on standardized test scores. Using comparison groups of students who just missed the promotion cutoff, these researchers found that 3rd graders struggled during the repeated year, had higher rates of special education placement, and two years later showed no advantage over those who had been promoted. Retained 6th graders had lower achievement growth than similar students who were not retained.

Retention can increase the likelihood that a student will drop out of school. Students who drop out are five times more likely to have been retained than those who graduate (National Center for Education Statistics, 2006). Using data from Chicago, Jacob and Lefgren (2007) concluded that students retained in 8th grade were more likely to drop out than their peers, a finding that was not true for retained 6th graders. They speculated that the 6th graders had more opportunities to catch up.

Studies with the strongest research methods compare students who were retained with similar students who were not retained. They ask whether repeating a grade makes a difference in achievement as well as personal and social adjustment over the short run and the long run. Although individual studies can be cited to support any conclusion, overall the preponderance of evidence argues that students who repeat a grade are no better off, and are sometimes worse off, than if they had been promoted with their classmates.

A major weakness in the research on retention is documenting the educational experiences of students who are retained. Roderick & Nagaoka (2005) argue that retention under high-stakes testing presumes the problem lies with the student, not with the school. If the goal of retention is to provide an opportunity for students to catch up, the quality and appropriateness of their academic experiences is likely to be the determining factor. After all, why should repeating the same experience produce a different result?

What's One to Do?

For most students struggling to keep up, retention is not a satisfactory solution. Nor is promotion. Juxtaposing the two as if these are the only options casts the debate in the wrong terms.

The challenge is figuring out what it takes to help failing students catch up. Understanding why a particular student has fallen behind points to the best course of action.

Juxtaposing retention and promotion as if these are the only options casts the debate in the wrong terms.

For many students, especially those who start school far behind their peers, intensive intervention, even prior to kindergarten, may be the best path to success. For students who are frequently absent, understanding and addressing the reasons for their absences might be the solution.

Retention usually duplicates an entire year of schooling. Other options—such as summer school, before-school and after-school programs, or extra help during the school day—could provide equivalent extra time in more instructionally effective ways. Without early diagnosis and targeted intervention, struggling students are unlikely to catch up whether they are promoted or retained.

References

Holmes, C. T., & Matthews, K. M. (1984). The effects of nonpromotion on elementary and junior high school pupils: A meta-analysis. *Review of Educational Research, 54*(2), 225–236.

Jackson, G. B. (1975). The research evidence on the effects of grade retention. *Review of Educational Research, 45*(4), 613–635.

Jacob, B., & Lefgren, L. (2007). *The effect of grade retention on high school completion* (Working Paper No. 13514). Cambridge, MA: National Bureau of Economic Research. Available: www.nber.org/papers/w13514.

Jimerson, S. R. (2001). Meta-analysis of grade retention research: Implications for practice in the 21st century. *School Psychology Review, 30*(3), 420–437.

National Center for Education Statistics. (2006). *The condition of education: Grade retention* [Online article]. Washington, DC: Author. Available: http://nces.ed.gov/programs/coe/2006/section3/indicator25.asp.

Roderick, M., & Nagaoka, J. (2005). Retention under Chicago's high-stakes testing program: Helpful, harmful, or harmless? *Educational Evaluation and Policy Analysis, 27*(4), 309–340.

JANE L. DAVID is Director of the Bay Area Research Group, Palo Alto, California; jld@bayarearesearch.org. She is the author, with Larry Cuban, of *Cutting Through the Hype: A Taxpayer's Guide to School Reform* (Education Week Press, 2006).

From *Educational Leadership,* March 2008, pp. 83–84. Copyright © 2008 by ASCD. Reprinted by permission. The Association for Supervision and Curriculum Development is a worldwide community of educators advocating sound policies and sharing best practices to achieve the success of each learner. To learn more, visit ASCD at www.ascd.org

Back to Basics
Play in Early Childhood

JILL ENGLEBRIGHT FOX, PHD

Kyle plays with blocks and builds a castle. Tony and Victoria play fire station and pretend to be firefighters. Kenzo and Carl play catch with a ball. Children playact with playmates in the playhouse. Playgroups on the playground choose players to play ball. As an early childhood professional, you probably use the word "play" a hundred times per day.

Research indicates that children learn best in an environment which allows them to explore, discover, and play. Play is an important part of a developmentally appropriate child care program. It is also closely tied to the development of cognitive, socio-emotional, and physical behaviors. But what exactly does it mean to play and why is play so important for young children?

What Is Play?

Although it is simple to compile a list of play activities, it is much more difficult to define play. Scales, et al., (1991) called play "that absorbing activity in which healthy young children participate with enthusiasm and abandon" (p. 15). Csikszentmihalyi (1981) described play as "a subset of life . . . an arrangement in which one can practice behavior without dreading its consequences" (p. 14). Garvey (1977) gave a useful description of play for teachers when she defined play as an activity which is: 1) positively valued by the player; 2) self-motivated; 3) freely chosen; 4) engaging; and 5) which "has certain systematic relations to what is not play" (p. 5). These characteristics are important for teachers to remember because imposing adult values, requirements, or motivations on children's activities may change the very nature of play.

According to *Webster's Desk Dictionary of the English Language,* the word play has 34 different meanings. In terms of young children and play, the following definitions from Webster's are useful:

- light, brisk, or changing movement (e.g., to pretend you're a butterfly)
- to act or imitate the part of a person or character (e.g., to play house)
- to employ a piece of equipment (e.g., to play blocks)
- exercise for amusement or recreation (e.g., to play tag)
- fun or jest, as opposed to seriousness (e.g., to play peek-a-boo or sing a silly song)
- the action of a game (e.g., to play duck-duck-goose)

Why Is Play Important?

According to Fromberg and Gullo (1992), play enhances language development, social competence, creativity, imagination, and thinking skills. Frost (1992) concurred, stating that "play is the chief vehicle for the development of imagination and intelligence, language, social skills, and perceptual-motor abilities in infants and young children" (p. 48).

Garvey (1977) states that play is most common during childhood when children's knowledge of self, comprehension of verbal and non-verbal communication, and understanding of the physical and social worlds are expanding dramatically.

Fromberg (1990) claims that play is the "ultimate integrator of human experience" (p. 223). This means that when children play, they draw upon their past experiences—things they have done, seen others do, read about, or seen on television—and they use these experiences to build games, play scenarios, and engage in activities.

Children use fine and gross motor skills in their play. They react to each other socially. They think about what they are doing or going to do. They use language to talk to each other or to themselves and they very often respond emotionally to the play activity. The integration of these different types of behaviors is key to the cognitive development of young children. According to Rogers and Sawyer (1988), "until at least the age of nine, children's cognitive structures function best in this unified mode" (p. 58). Because children's play draws upon all of these behaviors, it is a very effective vehicle for learning.

Play and Cognitive Development

The relationship between play and cognitive development is described differently in the two theories of cognitive development which dominate early childhood education—Piaget's and Vygotsky's.

Piaget (1962) defined play as assimilation, or the child's efforts to make environmental stimuli match his or her own concepts. Piagetian theory holds that play, in and of itself, does not necessarily result in the formation of new cognitive structures. Piaget claimed that play was just for pleasure, and while it allowed children to practice things they had previously learned, it did not necessarily result in the learning of new things. In other words, play reflects what the child has already learned but does not necessarily teach the child anything new. In this view, play is seen as a "process reflective of emerging symbolic development, but contributing little to it" (Johnsen & Christie, 1986, p. 51).

In contrast, Vygotskian theory states that play actually facilitates cognitive development. Children not only practice what they already know, they also learn new things. In discussing Vygotsky's theory, Vandenberg (1986) remarks that "play not so much reflects thought (as Piaget suggests) as it creates thought" (p. 21).

Observations of children at play yield examples to support both Piagetian and Vygotskian theories of play. A child who puts on a raincoat and a firefighter's hat and rushes to rescue his teddy bear from the pretend flames in his playhouse is practicing what he has previously learned about firefighters. This supports Piaget's theory. On the other hand, a child in the block center who announces to his teacher, "Look! When I put these two square blocks together, I get a rectangle!" has constructed new knowledge through her play. This supports Vygotsky's theory.

Whether children are practicing what they have learned in other settings or are constructing new knowledge, it is clear that play has a valuable role in the early childhood classroom.

Play—Indoors and Out

Early childhood teachers have long recognized the value of play in programs for young children. Unfortunately, teachers often fail to take advantage of the opportunities play provides for observing children's development and learning. Through such observations teachers can learn about children's social interactions, cognitive and language abilities, motor skills, and emotional development.

Frost (1992) recommends that observing children at play be a daily responsibility for early childhood professionals. Regular observations provide teachers with assessment information for identifying children with special needs, planning future play experiences, evaluating play materials, determining areas of strength and weakness for individual children, planning curriculum for individual children, reporting to parents, and checking on a child's on-going progress. The increased use of authentic assessment strategies is making observations of children's play more commonplace in early childhood classrooms.

Hymes (1981) recommends that children have two classrooms—one indoors and one outdoors. The outdoor play environment should be used as an extension of the indoor classroom. It should be a learning environment as carefully planned as the indoor activity centers and should encourage motor and social skills as well as help children refine existing cognitive structures and construct new ones. Used in this way, the outdoor play environment provides a basis for observational assessment in all areas of development.

Fox (1993) researched the practicality of observing young children's cognitive development during outdoor play. Her observations of four- and five-year-old children during outdoor play found examples of addition and subtraction, shape identification, patterning, one-to-one correspondence, number sense, sequencing of events, use of ordinal numbers, knowledge of prepositions, and identification of final and initial consonants. Fox's outdoor observations also found multiple examples of problem-solving, creative thinking, social competence, language use, and gross and fine motor skills. Although outdoor observations do not replace classroom assessment, they can provide valuable information for teachers of young children. As Fox stated, "These observations can be performed unobtrusively, without intruding upon the children's activities and without placing children in a stressful testing situation" (p. 131).

Parten's Five Types of Play

Play for young children assumes many different forms. Mildred Parten (1932) was one of the early researchers studying children at play. She focused on the social interactions between children during play activities. Parten's categories of play are not hierarchical. Depending on the circumstances, children may engage in any of the different types of play. Parten does note, however, that in her research with two- to five-year-olds, "participation in the most social types of groups occurs most frequently among the older children" (p. 259).

Extra playtime allows children to become involved in more complex and productive play activities.

- **Onlooker behavior**—Playing passively by watching or conversing with other children engaged in play activities.
- **Solitary independent**—Playing by oneself.
- **Parallel**—Playing, even in the middle of a group, while remaining engrossed in one's own activity. Children playing parallel to each other sometimes use each other's toys, but always maintain their independence.
- **Associative**—When children share materials and talk to each other, but do not coordinate play objectives or interests.
- **Cooperative**—When children organize themselves into roles with specific goals in mind (e.g., to assign the roles of doctor, nurse, and patient and play hospital).

How Much Should Children Play?

Indoors and outdoors, children need large blocks of time for play. According to Christie and Wardle (1992), short play periods may require children to abandon their group dramatizations or constructive play just when they begin to get involved. When this happens a number of times, children may give up on more sophisticated forms of play and settle for less advanced forms that can be completed in short periods of time. Shorter play periods reduce both the amount and the maturity of children's play, and many important benefits of play, such as persistence, negotiation, problem solving, planning, and cooperation are lost. Large blocks of time (30 to 60 minutes, or longer) should be scheduled for indoor and outdoor play periods. Christie and Wardle remind teachers that extra playtime does not result in children becoming bored. Instead, it prompts children to become involved in more complex, more productive play activities.

The Teacher's Role

The early childhood teacher is the facilitator of play in the classroom. The teacher facilitates play by providing appropriate indoor and outdoor play environments. Safety is, of course, the primary concern. Age and developmental levels must be carefully considered in the design and selection of materials. Guidelines for selecting safe and appropriate equipment for outdoor play environments are available through the U.S. Consumer Product Safety Commission's Handbook for Public Playground Safety and the Playground Safety Manual by Jambor and Palmer (1991). Similar guidelines are also available for indoor settings (Torelli & Durrett, 1996; Caples, 1996; Ard & Pitts, 1990). Once appropriate environments and materials are in place, regular safety checks and maintenance are needed to ensure that the equipment is sound and safe for continued play.

Teachers also facilitate play by working with children to develop rules for safe indoor and outdoor play. Discussion about the appropriate use of materials, the safe number of participants on each piece of equipment, taking turns, sharing, and cleaning up provides the children with information to begin their play activities. These discussions need to be ongoing because some children may need frequent reminders about rules and because new situations may arise (e.g., new equipment).

By providing play materials related to thematic instruction, early childhood teachers can establish links between the children's indoor and outdoor play and their program's curriculum. Thematic props for dramatic play can be placed in the dramatic play center or stored in prop boxes and taken outside to extend the dramatic play to a new setting. An art center in the outdoor play environment may encourage children to explore the possibilities of using leaves, twigs, pebbles, and sand in their three-dimensional art productions. Painting easels and water tables may also be moved outside periodically for children's use during outdoor play periods. Finally, a collection of books stored in a wagon to be taken outside during play time may offer some children a needed alternative to more active play.

As facilitators of children's play, teachers should closely observe children during play periods not only for assessment purposes, as stated earlier, but also to facilitate appropriate social interactions and motor behaviors. It is important that children be the decision-makers during play, choosing what and where to play, choosing roles for each player, and choosing how play will proceed. Occasionally, however, some children will need adult assistance in joining a play group, modifying behavior, or negotiating a disagreement. Careful observation will help the teacher to decide when to offer assistance and what form that assistance should take.

Conclusion

Although play is a difficult concept to define, it is very easy to recognize. Children actively involved in play may be engaged in a variety of activities, independently, with a partner, or in a group. Because play is closely tied to the cognitive, socioemotional, and motor development of young children, it is an important part of developmentally appropriate early childhood programs.

JILL ENGLEBRIGHT FOX, PhD, is an assistant professor of early childhood education at Virginia Commonwealth University. She taught kindergarten and first grade in the Texas public schools for eight years, and is currently an active member of the International Play Association-USA. Her research interests focus on play and aesthetic development in young children, and professional development schools.

From *Earlychildhood NEWS*, March/April 2006, pp. 12–15. Copyright © 2006 by Excelligence Learning Corporation. Reprinted by permission.

Scripted Curriculum
Is It a Prescription for Success?

ANITA EDE

Imagine walking down the halls of your school and hearing the same sentences read, the same questions asked, and the same teacher comments coming from each classroom. "Impossible," you say to yourself. "This could not possibly be happening." But it is. This scenario is becoming more and more commonplace throughout schools in the United States as scripted curriculum materials are implemented more widely. In 2001, one in every eight schools in California used Open Court, a scripted reading program (Posnick-Goodwin, 2002). Nationwide, 1,551 elementary schools in 48 states use Success for All, another scripted reading program (Dudley-Marling & Murphy, 2001). Scripted curriculum materials are instructional materials that have been commercially prepared and require the teacher to read from a script while delivering the lesson (Moustafa & Land, 2002). Scripted materials reflect a focus on explicit, direct, systematic skills instruction and are touted as a method to boost sagging standardized test scores and narrow the achievement gap between children growing up in poverty and those who are more affluent (Coles, 2002).

Politics and the Scripted Curriculum

The goal of the education system in the United States has long been to provide an effective public education for all children in order that they may realize their full potential. Precisely how this is to be achieved, however, is the subject of a great deal of debate.

In April 1999, the National Reading Panel (NRP), based on its review of 100,000 studies of how children learn to read, provided a guide for scientifically based reading instruction (cited in Coles, 2002). Those numbers are a little misleading, however. The NRP began by looking at 100,000 studies on reading that had been conducted since 1966. It then established criteria that limited the studies to those relating to instructional material that the panel decided, ahead of time, represented key areas of good reading instruction. The field was further narrowed to studies that had been conducted "scientifically"; that is, using only quantitative data. When all was said and done,

the 100,000 studies had been pruned to 52 studies of phonemic awareness, 38 studies of phonics, 14 studies of reading fluency, and 203 studies related to comprehension instruction (Coles, 2002). After examination of the aforementioned 307 studies, the NRP concluded that the most effective course of reading instruction included explicit and systematic instruction in phonemic awareness and phonics (Metcalf, 2002)—that is, the scripted curriculum.

It is important for teachers to understand the politics of the scripted curriculum, as well as who profits, its basic structure, current research as to its effectiveness, and concerns about its effect on students as well as teachers.

One week after becoming president, George W. Bush sent Congress an education reform bill that referred to the NRP's research findings; he promised to eliminate reading inequalities and ensure that all children would read at grade level by the time they reached the 3rd grade. This would be achieved through the use of scientifically based reading instruction. These education reforms became law when the No Child Left Behind Act (NCLB) was passed in 2002.

The Reading First initiative, the portion of NCLB that applies to reading instruction, provides funding to schools on the condition that they adopt "scientifically based" reading programs. The "scientifically based" (quantitative) research by the NRP that resulted in the funding for "scientifically based" reading programs by Reading First is the basis for the scripted reading curriculum. Programs qualifying as scientifically based are those that incorporate explicit and systematic instruction in phonemic awareness, phonics, fluency, vocabulary, and comprehension. Two such highly scripted and very profitable curriculum programs are Open Court and Success for All (SFA).

Profits and the Scripted Curriculum

The Reading First initiative provides an enormous amount of taxpayer dollars to states in the form of grants. States then dispense the money to individual school districts in the form of sub-grants. For example, Oklahoma received a multi-year Reading First grant in 2003 that provided $12.5 million to schools implementing scientifically based reading programs (The National Right to Read Foundation, 2003) in its first year. Over the next six years, Oklahoma will receive a total of $82 million to further implement these programs. Taking into account that 49 other states will also receive federal funds to implement scientifically based reading programs, it stands to reason that the companies publishing these programs will make a resounding profit. In the third quarter of 2003, SRA/McGraw-Hill, which publishes Open Court, one of the most frequently used scripted reading programs, posted an increased net income of $14.1 million (5.1 percent) over the same period in the previous year (McGraw-Hill Newswire, 2003). Success for All (SFA), another highly scripted reading curriculum, published by a nonprofit foundation, has flourished into a $45 million-a-year business (Mathews, 2000).

Scripted curriculum materials are a costly solution for school districts that are having difficulty raising their students' academic achievement.

Socioeconomics and the Scripted Curriculum

Students in high poverty areas have a much higher likelihood of being taught in schools using a scripted curriculum than those living in more affluent school districts. Schools in which more than 50 percent of all students are on free or reduced-price lunches qualify for Title I funds from the federal government. Currently, Title I regulations specify that "all participating schools must use program funds to implement a comprehensive school reform program that employs proven methods and strategies based on scientifically based research" (Comprehensive School Reform Program, n.d., p. 2). In essence, these regulations prescribe the use of scripted curriculum materials because these are the only ones that qualify as being scientifically based. Schools that do not receive Title I funds (i.e., those located, in general, in more affluent areas) are free to spend their district's funds on the curriculum of their choice.

The Scripted Curriculum

As noted, two of the most widely used scripted reading curriculum programs are Open Court and Success for All. Both deliver explicit, systematic instruction by way of a script the teacher is required to follow in the areas of phonemic awareness, phonics, fluency, vocabulary, and comprehension. Open Court and SFA share certain characteristics. Both publishers advocate grouping students by reading level during the reading portion of the lesson. Both programs are available in English as well as Spanish and are available for a wide range of age and grade levels. Open Court is available for students ranging from Pre-K to 6th grade and SFA is available for students ranging from Pre-K to 8th grade.

Depending on the teacher's familiarity with either the Open Court or SFA material and the students' abilities, up to three hours of class time every day may be needed to cover the lesson script, thus leading to a significant narrowing of the curriculum. In a survey conducted in the fall of 2003 by the Council for Basic Education, principals reported that their schools currently spent 37 percent less time teaching civics and 35 percent less time teaching geography than they had previously (Perkins-Gough, 2004). Other principals surveyed for this study reported that their schools spent 29 percent less time teaching languages and 36 percent less time teaching the arts than they had in the past (Perkins-Gough, 2004). Given that many schools have already curtailed children's exposure to geography, civics, languages, and art, one must question if these subjects would be completely eliminated following the implementation of a scripted curriculum.

The diverse ethnic and cultural makeup of today's classrooms makes it unlikely that one single curriculum will meet the needs and interests of all students.

Reading Achievement and the Scripted Curriculum
Positive Research Findings

One study in an urban Title I school (no geographic information was given) compared the word recognition, reading comprehension, vocabulary growth, and spelling achievement of three groups of 1st- and 2nd-grade students. They were taught using one of three methods: Open Court, the district's standard curriculum, and less direct instruction embedded in a connected text (Foorman, Fletcher, Francis, Schatschneider, & Mehta, 1998). The latter approach emphasized the teacher-as-facilitator, children's active construction of meaning using learning centers, and portfolio assessment. Achievement test scores at the end of the year indicated that the children who had used Open Court approached the national average in their decoding skills (43rd percentile) and passage comprehension (45th percentile). The group using the district's standard curriculum scored in the 27th percentile for decoding skills and the 33rd percentile for passage comprehension. The group using less direct instruction embedded in the text scored in the 29th percentile for word decoding and the 35th percentile for passage comprehension. Spelling skills were not significantly different for any of the groups.

On first impression, it appears that the performance of students taught using Open Court clearly exceeded that of students taught using different methods. However, even though the

285 students in this study were randomly grouped by age, gender, and ethnicity, no mention is made of the students' ability levels prior to their assignment to a group. Without knowing the ability levels of the participants and ensuring that they were evenly distributed among all three groups, it would be difficult to attribute performance increases to a particular instructional method.

In a study conducted in Memphis, Tennessee, students from eight SFA schools were matched with students in statistically similar non-SFA schools. After two years of SFA instruction, the students in the SFA schools performed significantly better than their comparison groups on measurements of reading, language, science, and social studies (Slavin & Madden, 2001). In Baltimore, where SFA actually began, a longitudinal study conducted from 1987–93 comparing Comprehensive Test of Basic Skills (CTBS) scores of students in the five original SFA schools to students in five control schools indicated that SFA students' scores exceeded those of students in the control group at each grade level (Slavin & Madden, 2001).

It must be noted that subsequent researchers disagreed with these findings. Pogrow (2002) notes that only students who had been in the same school for five years were included in this study and that almost no special education students were included. In other words, the group of students that reflected the greatest gain from SFA was not representative of the population as a whole. He further notes that when the same data were reevaluated, this time including all students who were assessed, students' reading levels ranked, on average, three years below grade level by the time they got to 6th grade. SFA has since been dropped by the Baltimore city school district.

Negative Research Findings

A study of 2nd- through 5th-grade students in California comparing the Stanford Achievement Test, Ninth Edition (SAT 9) scores of children in urban schools using Open Court to students in comparable schools using non-scripted materials found no evidence that Open Court fosters higher reading achievement (Moustafa & Land, 2002). In an all-grade comparison study of SAT 9 scores, 28 percent of the students in non-scripted programs were in the bottom quartile, compared to 57 percent of the students using Open Court. The researchers found that 72 percent of the students from non-scripted programs scored above the bottom quartile, compared to only 43 percent of the students taught using Open Court.

A study comparing the standardized test scores of Title I elementary school students using SFA to the scores of students in comparable Title I schools using a different reading program found that, over a three-year period, students in non-SFA schools experienced an average gain of 17 percent in the reading proficiency section, compared to an average gain of 8.5 percent in the reading proficiency of students in schools using the SFA reading curriculum (Greenlee & Bruner, 2001).

English Language Learners

Both Open Court and SRA offer program adaptations in Spanish that may be used in Spanish-only, Spanish-English, and English-only classrooms. Literature compiled by Open Court states that the English scores of 2nd-grade students rose in all but four of Sacramento's 60 elementary schools in 1998 (Open Court, 2002). Slavin and Madden (2001), the founders of SFA, cite studies in California and Arizona in which English language learners using SFA scored higher on English reading measures than did comparable students who were using a different curriculum. In contrast, a three-year study of Miami-Dade County schools in Florida found that English language learners who attended SFA schools actually made smaller gains in English language proficiency than did comparable students at schools not using SFA (Pogrow, 2002).

Concerns

As scripted curriculum materials become more and more commonplace, certain concerns must be addressed. The diverse ethnic and cultural makeup of today's classrooms makes it unlikely that one single curriculum will meet the needs and interests of all students. Curriculum must be flexible so that teachers are able to construct lessons that will be of high interest to their unique group of students, and actively engage them in creating knowledge. Reading aloud scripted lessons that have been created for a generic group is unlikely to accomplish this goal.

Another concern is whether scripted curriculum challenges gifted learners as well as supports those who are struggling. A typical classroom consists of students with a wide spectrum of learning strengths and needs. Classroom teachers are in the best position to identify individual strengths and needs and adjust a curriculum to address them. Again, reading aloud scripted lessons that have been created for a generic group is unlikely to accomplish this goal.

What about the long-term success of students who are read aloud scripted lessons? If the focus of curriculum is on test-driven instruction and rote memorization, will critical-thinking skills and comprehension be overlooked? Students learn when curriculum is relevant to their lives, when it is of personal interest to them, and when they are actively engaged in the pursuit of knowledge.

What about time? If it takes between two to three hours to deliver a script, will science, social studies, art, music, and physical education be eliminated? All of these subject areas contribute to children's overall learning, and their elimination would result in a watered-down educational experience.

What about the teacher? Will teachers be willing to spend their days reading from a script, rather than planning and facilitating lessons that further their students' construction of knowledge? Perhaps teachers with the most experience and education would transfer to school districts that do not use a scripted curriculum, leaving the least experienced teachers to read the script to students with the greatest needs.

These concerns must be addressed in order to determine whether or not the use of a scripted curriculum is truly a prescription for success or a one-size-fits-all approach that does not reflect sound pedagogical practice.

References

Coles, G. (2002). Learning to read scientifically. *Rethinking Schools Online.* Retrieved February 2, 2005, from www .rethinkingschools.org/special_reports/bushplan/Read154.shtml

Comprehensive School Reform Program. (n.d.) Guide to U.S. Department of Education Programs. Retrieved April 3, 2005, http://wdcrobcolp01.ed.gov/CFAPPS/GTEP_PUBLIC/index

Dudley-Marling, C., & Murphy, S. (2001). Changing the way we think about language arts. *Language Arts, 78*(6), 574–578.

Foorman, B. R., Fletcher, J. M., Francis, D. J., Schatschneider, C., & Mehta, P. (1998). The role of instruction in learning to read: Preventing reading failure in at-risk children. *Journal of Educational Psychology, 90*(1), 37–55.

Greenlee, B. J. & Bruner, D. Y. (2001). Effects of Success for All reading programs on reading achievement in Title I schools. *Education, 122*(1), 177–188.

Mathews, J. (2000, January). Prepackaged school reform. *The School Administrator.* Retrieved April 2, 2005, from www.aasa.org/publications/sa/2000_/mathews.htm

McGraw-Hill Companies. (2003, October). *Investors: News releases.* Retrieved April 2, 2005, from http://investor.mcgraw-hill.com

Metcalf, R. (2002, January). Reading between the lines. *The Nation.* Retrieved April 2, 2005, from www.thenation.com/docprint .mhtml?i=20020128&s–metcalf

Moustafa, M., & Land, R. E. (2002). The reading achievement of economically disadvantaged children in urban schools using Open Court vs. comparably disadvantaged children using non-scripted reading programs. 2002 Yearbook of the *Urban Learning, Teaching, and Research Special Interest Group of the American Educational Research Association,* 44–53.

National Right to Read Foundation, The. (2003, February). Paige announces $12.5 million Reading First grant for Oklahoma children. Retrieved February 6, 2005, from www.nrrf.org/pr_OK-RF_2-6-03.htm

Open Court. (2002). *Programs & Practices.* Retrieved on April 3, 2005, from www.sra4kids.com

Perkins-Gough, D. (2004). The eroding curriculum. *Educational Leadership, 62*(1), 84–85.

Pogrow, S. (2002, February). Success for All is a failure. *Phi Delta Kappan, 83*(6), 463–468.

Posnick-Goodwin, (2002). Scripted learning: A slap in the face? *California Educator, 6*(7), 6–16.

Slavin, R. E., & Madden, N. (2001). Research on achievement outcomes of Success for All. *Phi Delta Kappan, 82*(1), 38–66.

ANITA EDE is a doctoral student, College of Education, Oklahoma State University, Stillwater.

From *Childhood Education,* Fall 2006, pp. 29–32. Copyright © 2006 by the Association for Childhood Education International. Reprinted by permission of Anita Ede and the Association for Childhood Education International, 17904 Georgia Avenue, Suite 215, Olney, MD 20832.

Using Brain-Based Teaching Strategies to Create Supportive Early Childhood Environments That Address Learning Standards

PAM SCHILLER AND CLARISSA A. WILLIS

Learning (or content) standards are intended to set the bar for student achievement. They can help create equity among learners by ensuring that all children are prepared to meet the challenges of an increasingly complex, demanding world. Although standards vary state by state, they generally have similar broad goals for children in the primary grades (National Institute for Early Education Research 2008). As they mature and develop from ages 5 to 8, young children are expected to achieve the following:

1. develop as effective readers;
2. expand their abilities to use complex mathematical applications;
3. deepen their understandings of science concepts; and
4. broaden their social studies skills and learn the concepts necessary to be responsible citizens.

Many learning standards also address a wider range of skills children can master in technology, art, music, theater, health education, and physical education. The Early Childhood Education Assessment Consortium of the Council of Chief State School Officers defines early learning standards as

> Statements that describe expectations for the learning and development of young children across the domains of: health and physical well-being; social and emotional well-being; approaches to learning; language development and symbol systems; and general knowledge about the world around them. (CCSSO 2008)

This definition is broad in nature, specific to domains, yet consistent with nurturing the whole child. It is also compatible with brain research timetables for neurological wiring.

It's important to understand that standards are *not* intended to fence in creative teachers or to become obstacles for learners with special needs. Instead, they can guide, support, and encourage enterprising and knowledgeable primary teachers to create intriguing and motivating educational environments and experiences that are developmentally appropriate for each child and optimize learning for all (NAEYC & NAECS/SDE 2002).

Creating Conditions for Success

Enormous potential exists in applying early brain development research findings to the implementation of learning standards. Here are three research findings that can be used with learning standards to optimize learning.

Experiences impact the architecture of the brain. At birth the human brain is in an amazingly unfinished state. The hardware is present but the connections are yet to be made. The child's experiences in the larger world result in connections that are reinforced as the experiences are repeated. This becomes the neural circuitry that lays the foundation for the child's lifelong learning (Shonkoff & Phillips 2000).

A predictable process assists the brain in channeling stimuli into long-term learning. When teachers present information in a sequence that supports this process, it is much

> The National Association of Early Childhood Specialists in State Departments of Education (NAECS/SDE) works to improve instruction, curriculum, and administration in education programs for young children and their families. Of Primary Interest is written by members of NAECS/SDE for kindergarten and primary teachers. The column appears in March, July, and November issues of *Young Children* and Beyond the Journal (online at www.journal.naeyc.org/btj).

easier for children to learn (Sousa 2006). To help children focus on a lesson, begin by asking them a relevant question or showing them intriguing photos. When presenting the actual content (learning standard) of the lesson, show children how the new information is similar to other information familiar to them. Point out any patterns that occur in the new information. Allow children to practice using new information, through hands-on activities when possible. Finally, encourage children to think about how they will use the new information and to ask themselves, How is this information relevant to my life?

Environmental influences—such as safety, emotions, novelty, humor, music, choices, physical movement, and hands-on activities—**can contribute to increased alertness and memory** (Jensen 2001). Keeping these influences in mind when implementing learning standards sets the stage for success.

Applying Brain Research in Implementing Learning Standards

Standards guidelines and brain research findings are the tools needed to implement standards. Then the following brain-based strategies become a means to optimize learning for all children.

1. Safe Environments Matter

Safety and well-being come before anything else. The brain attends to these needs first. A child who comes to school hungry, ill, or frightened by something that happened on the way will find it difficult, if not impossible, to focus on what is going on in the classroom. Children will struggle with learning if they feel afraid because a classroom setting is too restrictive, a home environment is very demanding, or a classmate's behavior is aggressive. To evaluate what changes are needed, take these steps:

- **Make sure the physical classroom is free of anything that could scare a child.** For example, some kindergarten children (ages 5 and 6) may be afraid of certain classroom pets or science specimens, such as snakes or spiders. What have you included in your science center? Are children spending the day checking on the snake in the aquarium to make sure it has not escaped?
- **Start the children's day with a safety ritual.** For example, try a greeting such as, "We are safe when we are at school" or "We are a community of learners who take care of one another." Positive affirmations help to reduce fears. For children with special needs, such as autism or anxiety disorders, create a symbolic representation of a safe haven. Have the child place his name or photo in a classroom box with a lid, then close it to represent his being safe inside.
- **Remind children they are in your safekeeping.** Reassure children who have emotional challenges or who have difficulty separating from a parent. Explain that your job is to keep them safe while they are at school. Listen to a timid child and acknowledge her

fears. Then redirect her attention to an engaging activity or invite another child to be her peer buddy. Encourage the buddies to do an activity together. Never dismiss a child's fear, even if it seems irrational to you.

2. Emotions Are Effective Tools

Emotions affect memory and brain function. When a person feels content, the brain releases endorphins that enhance memory skills (Jensen 2005).

- **Start the day with humor.** Tell a funny story or share a silly picture. Laughing makes children feel secure and content.
- **Sing a few songs together.** Incorporate dance and movement with singing whenever possible. Children can draw, paint, or do other creative projects while listening to various types of music.
- **Sequence and pace daily activities.** Children can feel overwhelmed by too much new information and unfamiliar materials. After presenting new information, give children time to practice and reflect on what they are learning.
- **Help learners feel in control of their learning.** Researchers tell us that keeping lessons short and relative to the topic is more compatible with the brain's processing ability (Sousa 2006). You can use several strategies to help children master large amounts of information over time. For example, break down activities or routines into steps. Display pictures of each step to teach and remind children of what to do next. This works particularly well for children with special needs, such as a child with cognitive delays, autism, or a language delay.
- **Be proactive.** Use guidance strategies that reflect the natural or logical consequences for inappropriate behavior rather than threats and punishment. Negative emotions can impede learning. For example, if you know that a child has difficulty transitioning from indoor to outdoor play, alert him before the transition so he knows what is going to happen next.
- **Nurture social and emotional intelligence.** Children must learn to follow directions, work with others, stay on task, finish their work, and take initiative to master new information. They also must learn to control their verbal and behavioral impulses, solve problems, and take responsibility for their own actions (Bilmes 2008). Nurture these skills by providing time for cooperative learning, collaboration, and teamwork.

3. Multisensory Practices Make Sense

The more senses involved during learning, the more likely the brain will receive and process information. By using multiple senses to learn, children find it easier to match new information to their existing knowledge (Schiller 1999; Willis in press).

- **Use real materials.** Familiar and tangible objects demonstrating concepts can help make ideas concrete. For example, rather than talking about birds with 5- and

6-year-olds, go outside to observe them, then make a graph of all the different birds the children see and hear. Seven- and 8-year-olds might begin classifying birds by common characteristics or migration patterns.

- **Use chants and rhymes.** Rhythmic patterns stick in the brain. For kindergarten, use *Chicka Chicka Boom Boom*, by Bill Martin Jr. and John Archambault, to teach the alphabet. For first and second grade, use a chant like the one below to practice spelling words.

It's time to spell!
Let's show what we know.
It's time to spell!
Ready, set, go!

Shhh, shhh, shhh, shhh, shhh, shhh
Spell bear.
Bear. B-e-a-r.

Shhh, shhh, shhh, shhh, shhh, shhh
Spell chair.
Chair. C-h-a-i-r. [*Continue the chant with more words.*]

(Schiller unpublished; for other chants and rhymes, see Schiller & Willis [2008], pp. 262–65)

- **Make it fun!** Sing, dance, play games, and laugh. These activities use multiple senses and at the same time increase memory (Jensen 2005).
- **Provide natural environments.** Use places where an activity would ordinarily occur—home, school, outdoors, the zoo, or anyplace where learning is more meaningful than sitting at a desk. For example, when studying nature, go outdoors for a nature hunt rather than show children pictures of trees. Teach a child with special needs, such as Down syndrome, how to brush his teeth in the bathroom instead of the classroom.

4. Differentiated Teaching Practice Is Supportive

The term *differentiated* once meant that teachers planned ways to address children's differences in age, development, and learning styles. Now, this term encompasses everything that makes a child unique, such as culture, family, temperament, multiple intelligences profile, personality style, and special needs or developmental delays. These differences are even greater in the primary years because young children develop on individual timetables that often vary greatly. Primary teachers may wonder if it is even possible to teach every child as an individual. They can begin by first looking at how learning is consistent.

- **Provide a focus to hold children's attention.** This might be a photograph, a finger play, a song, or a provocative question. For example, in the primary grades, play a song in French before starting a discussion about France.
- **Break teaching into small parts.** Children are better able to focus on important information when they

receive less, rather than more, information. When first-graders are learning about animals, focus on one species at a time. Teach the two critical attributes of mammals: they nurse their young and they have hair. Have the children sort animals into mammals and nonmammals. When they are successful, use the same process to add reptiles and eventually amphibians and birds.

- **Provide hands-on practice.** Hands-on manipulation increases the chance by 75 percent that new information will be stored in long-term memory (Hannaford 1995; Sousa 2006). Hands-on investigation increases sensory input, which helps learners focus. It allows for experimentation by letting children use trial and error, which increases the chance that learners will make sense of and establish relevancy for what they are learning (Sousa 2006).
- **Use an integrated approach.** Combine math, reading, spelling, and writing to teach children about plants. To extend learning, have the class plant a butterfly garden together. Offer the children feedback on their progress, and build in time for their reflection.

Application of these strategies and commitment to the concept that all children learn based on their development and experience level make differentiated teaching possible in every classroom.

5. Special Needs Are Met through Planning

In today's blended or fully inclusive classrooms, children with special needs (visual or hearing impairments, cognitive challenges, motor or speech/language delays, or emotional/behavioral issues) learn in the same environment along with their peers (see Schiller & Willis 2008). This can be a positive experience for all children when teachers shape their practices to do the following:

- **Present concepts in simple steps.** Provide materials that enable a child who cannot fully participate in an activity to be engaged with his peers and to participate in his own way. For example, a child with language delays might work with a peer to write a journal entry together.
- **Look for ways to modify tools and materials.** Provide pencil or crayon grips for a child with motor challenges or picture schedules for a child with communication issues.
- **Recognize signs of developmental delay.** Be alert to a child whose development appears to be delayed, and provide extra opportunities for the child to practice using new information. Try several methods to introduce learning concepts.
- **Set appropriate goals.** Goals for learning should fit a child's age and stage of development. For example, most of the class may work on identifying letters, while a child with special needs, such as a cognitive or general developmental delay, learns the first letter of her name.

6. Sense and Meaning Are Essential

The brain processes new information by making sense and meaning of it (Sousa 2006). The process of sense making requires finding the patterns. One way to do this is by having children ask themselves questions, such as, How is this new information like the information I already have? How is it different? What parts of this information do I understand? Which parts are confusing?

For information to have meaning children must find its relevance. Teachers can help children when they

- **Tap into prior knowledge.** Review what the children already know before introducing new information. Point out any patterns in children's prior knowledge that overlap with new information. For example, "Remember last week, when we talked about the days of the week and we found them on a calendar? Today we are going to talk about the months of the year, which are also found on a calendar."
- **Use organizers.** Graphic organizers help children to see relationships between several pieces of information. Story maps, word wheels, and K-W-L (a chart or graphic representation that reflects "What I know, What I want to know, and What I just learned") work well with kindergarten children and first-graders.
- **Provide hands-on practice.** Offer Wikki Sticks and magnetic, sandpaper, and three-dimensional letters to help children learn alphabet letters.
- **Give the children time to reflect.** After a group activity or discussion, teachers can ask questions such as, How will you use this new information? How would what we learned today be different if ———? How do you feel about ———?

Conclusion

With careful planning, knowledge of brain research findings, and a little creativity, primary teachers can offer engaging, brain-based activities that encourage exploration and learning and support learning standards. Teachers and children can build a strong community of learners who see learning as an opportunity to be successful problem solvers while anticipating each new challenge as another exciting adventure.

References

Bilmes, J. 2008. Beyond behavior management. St. Paul, MN: Redleaf. CCSSO (Council of Chief State School Officers), Early Childhood Education Assessment Consortium. 2008. Glossary. Washington, DC: Author. www.ccsso.org/projects/SCASS/projects/early_childhood_education_assessment_consortium/publications_and_products/2892.cfm

Hannaford, C. 1995. *Smart moves: Why learning is not all in your head.* Arlington, Va: Great Ocean Publishers.

Jensen, E. 2001. Fragile brains—Damage to the brain and environmental influences can account for certain learning problems. *Educational Leadership* 59 (3): 32.

Jensen, E. 2005. *Teaching with the brain in mind.* 2nd ed. Alexandria, VA: Association for Supervision and Curriculum Development.

NAEYC & NAECS/SDE (National Association of Early Childhood Specialists in State Departments of Education). 2002. Early learning standards: Creating the conditions for success. Joint position statement. www.naeyc.org/about/positions/pdf/position_statement.pdf

National Institute for Early Education Research (NIEER). 2008. State standards database. http://nieer.org/standards/statelist.php

Schiller, P. 1999. *Start smart: Building brain power in the early years.* Beltsville, MD. Gryphon House.

Schiller, P., & C. Willis. 2008. *Inclusive literacy lessons for early childhood.* Beltsville, MD: Gryphon House.

Shonkoff, J.P., & D.A. Phillips, eds. 2000. *From neurons to neighborhoods: The science of early childhood development.* Report of the National Research Council and Institute of Medicine. Washington, DC: National Academies Press.

Sousa, D. 2006. *How the brain learns.* 3rd ed. Thousand Oaks, CA: Corwin.

Willis, C. In press. *Creating inclusive learning environments for young children.* Thousand Oaks, CA: Corwin Press.

PAM SCHILLER, PhD, is a curriculum specialist and freelance author and speaker. She has worked as a child care administrator and taught in public schools. Pam served as head of the Early Childhood Department at the University of Houston and directed its Lab School. She is the author of five early childhood curriculums and more than 30 teacher resource books. **CLARISSA A. WILLIS**, PhD, is a full-time author, speaker, and consultant, and former associate director of the Center of Excellence in Early Childhood Learning and Development at East Tennessee State University. As a consultant, she has provided workshops and keynote addresses for schools and organizations across the country and abroad. Clarissa@clarissawillis.com

Successful Transition to Kindergarten
The Role of Teachers and Parents

PAM DEYELL-GINGOLD

While new kindergartners are worrying about whether or not anyone will be their friend and if they'll be able to find the bathroom, their preschool teachers are wondering if they've succeeded at preparing their small students for this big transition. In recent years the role of kindergarten has changed from an extension of preschool to a much more academic environment because of new standards in the public schools that "push back" academic skills to earlier grades.

How can we ensure that our students make a smooth transition? Are our students mature enough? What can we do to make them "more" ready? This article will explore the skills that constitute kindergarten "readiness," how preschool teachers can collaborate with parents and kindergarten teachers to make the process more rewarding for all, and activities to help prepare children for what will be expected of them in kindergarten.

The Transition Process

Children go through many transitions throughout their lives, but one of the most important transitions is the one from a preschool program to kindergarten. "During this period behavior is shaped and attitudes are formed that will influence children throughout their education" (PTA and Head Start, 1999). Children's transitions are most strongly influenced by their home environment, the preschool program they attend, and the continuity between preschool and kindergarten (Riedinger, 1997).

In 1995, Head Start and the Parent Teacher Association (PTA) began a plan to create a partnership between the two organizations in order to create effective transition practices and to promote continuity in parent and family involvement in the schools. Three pilot programs were studied to determine "best practice" in kindergarten transition, and to foster the continued strong involvement of families in their children's education. They worked with elementary schools to create parent-friendly environments and to develop strategies that lessen the barriers to involvement (Head Start & PTA, 1999). Even Start, a federal program for low-income families implemented to improve educational opportunities for children and adults, also helps parents to work with the school system to help their children

succeed. Their research found that parents felt that the way in which Even Start focuses on the family strengths rather than weaknesses and allows the families to identify their own needs, empowered them more than anything else to help them to support their children in school (Riedinger, 1997).

Kindergarten Readiness

A 1998 study by the National Center for Early Development & Learning of nearly 3,600 kindergarten teachers nationwide indicated that 48 percent of children have moderate to serious problems transitioning to kindergarten. Teachers are most often concerned about children's skills in following directions, academics, and working independently. There seems to be a discrepancy between the expectations of teachers and the actual skills of kindergarten children. Therefore, a need for kindergarten teachers to collaborate with both parents and preschool teachers exists (Pianta & Cox, 1998). School readiness is more than a matter of academics, though. As reported in a National Education Goals Panel in 1998; "The prevailing view today, however, is that readiness reflects a range of dimensions, such as a child's health and physical development, social and emotional development, approaches to learning, language and communication skills, and cognitive and general knowledge" (California Department of Education, 2000).

Historically, kindergarten was a "children's garden": a place to interact for the first time with a group of agemates, and to learn basic skills through play. Today, because of increasing numbers of working mothers, single-parent families, and strict welfare regulations, many children begin having group experiences in a child care program or family child care home at a much earlier age. Together with the concern that America's children are not getting adequate education to compete in a global market, our schools began to make the transition from the children's garden to "curriculum escalation" (Shepard & Smith, 1988) and "academic trickle-down" (Cunningham, 1988). While the trend towards focusing on academic skills continues at a fast pace, early childhood professionals argue for a more integrated curriculum that addresses the developmental needs of each child.

Social Adjustment

Although academics may be becoming increasingly more important, research shows that social skills are what most affect school adjustment (Ladd & Price, 1987; Ladd, 1990). Preschool teachers should not feel pressured into teaching academics beyond what is developmentally "best practice" (Bredekamp & Copple, 1997) but should continue to focus on social and emotional development. Children who have been rejected by their peers in kindergarten tend to have poor school performance, more absences, and negative attitudes towards school that last throughout their school years. "Three particular social skills that are known to influence children's peer acceptance: play behavior, ability to enter play groups, and communication skills" (Maxwell & Eller, 1994).

Play Behavior and Communication Skills

Specific behaviors that cause rejection by fellow students include things like rough play, arguing, upsetting things in class, trying to get their own way, and not sharing. Children who exhibit these behaviors also tend to be less independent and less cooperative than their peers. Most children prefer playing with others who are polite, caring, and attentive. Preschool teachers and parents need to teach young children social skills, especially how to enter social groups. For example, children who say, "Looks like that's a fun game, can I play?" are more likely to be accepted than those who shove others aside and whine, "I want a turn!"

Another important social skill is the ability to participate in complicated fantasy games and take part in making up and extending the story. Children who lack sufficient experience playing with agemates may feel frustrated at not being able to keep up with the capabilities of their classmates. "A generous amount of guided social experience with peers prior to kindergarten helps children do well in this new world" (Maxwell & Eller, 1994). Some children need assistance to learn how to play make-believe. A teacher can help model this by giving verbal cues like, "You be the mommy, and I'll be your little girl. Can I help you make dinner, Mommy?" Some children need reminders to keep them focused on their roles. Others may need help to read the emotions on people's faces. "Look at Nick's face. He is sad because you pulled the hat away from him." Because young children do not have a large enough vocabulary to express themselves, teachers can help them find words to express their feelings such as, "You're feeling frustrated. Let's go find a puzzle with fewer pieces."

Communication skills, such as being able to take part in a conversation, listen to others, and negotiate are also important. For example, children who speak directly to peers, are attentive to others in the group, and respond to the initiations of others tend to be liked by the other children. Disliked children are more likely to make irrelevant comments, reject the initiations of other children without reasons or explanations, and often make comments without directing them to anyone (Maxwell & Eller, 1994). Part of a teacher's task is to quietly remind children to look at the person they're talking to, and listen to what another child is saying.

Immaturity and Redshirting

A common practice when dealing with children who are not socially mature is to keep them out of school for a year, in the hope that "readiness will emerge." In academic circles this is referred to as "redshirting," a term borrowed from college athletics. However, "Research shows that redshirts are not gaining an academic advantage, and the extra year does not solve the social development problems that caused initial concern" (Graue, 2001). Parents who are told that their children need to stay home for a year should ask for the reasons.

"Developmentally appropriate practice is less common in kindergarten, and primary teachers face many constraints and pressures that teachers of younger children are not yet experiencing in the same intensity [although preschool appears to be next in line for "push-down" curriculum]." (Jones, Evans, & Rencken, 2001). "If we think inclusively we have to problem-solve in ways to accommodate the incredible diversity presented by the characteristics of kindergartners. . . . Redshirting and retention are outmoded tools that should be replaced by more appropriate practices. One step in the right direction is collaboration between preschool and elementary school educators" (Graue, 2001). A second step is to have parents understand what experiences can help their child have a successful transition.

Learning about Classroom Styles

In collaborating with kindergarten teachers, preschool teachers and parents need to visit the school and pay close attention to details that may affect their students in kindergarten. "When teachers and parents agree on a philosophy of education, children usually adjust more easily" (Maxwell & Eller, 1994). Children feel more secure in their new environment if they feel that their parents support the teacher and the school.

The first step may be either a meeting with the kindergarten teacher or a class field trip to the elementary school. "Observe kindergarten classrooms to identify teaching styles, classroom management techniques, and routines. Also try to identify skills that are needed to be successful in participating in the kindergarten classroom" (Karr-Jelinek, 1994).

In her research, Karr-Jelinek used a checklist of what parents (and teachers) should look for in a kindergarten classroom, to see if their children—both normally developing and with special needs— are ready for the classroom they visit (Karr-Jelinek, 1994):

- How many steps are given at a time in directions?
- What types of words are children expected to understand?
- How does each individual child compare to the other children?
- How long are children expected to sit still in a group?
- How often do children speak out of turn or move around when they should be sitting?
- How much independence is expected?
- What type of work is being done? (small groups, seatwork, etc.)
- Where might my special needs students need extra help?
- What kind of special information can I pass along to the teacher about each child?

Although expectations vary by teacher and school district, by the time children reach kindergarten they should be able to listen to a story in a group, follow two or three oral directions, take turns and share, follow rules, respect the property of others, and work within time and space constraints. They need to learn the difference between work and play, knowing when and where each is appropriate. "Most five-year-olds can express themselves fluently with a variety of words and can understand an even larger variety of words used in conversations and stories" (Nurss, 1987).

Many kindergartens make use of learning centers, small group instruction, and whole group language activities. However, others use "structured, whole group paper-and-pencil activities oriented to academic subjects, such as reading and mathematics. The curriculum in these kindergartens often constitutes a downward extension of the primary grade curriculum and may call for the use of workbooks, which are part of a primary level textbook series. Many early childhood professionals have spoken out on the inappropriateness of such a curriculum" (Nurss, 1987).

Preparing Parents for the Transition

High-quality preschool programs encourage parent involvement in the home and in the classroom. Volunteering to read during story time, to share cultural traditions, or to be a lunch guest are all ways for parents to feel that they are a part of their child's school life. According to the National PTA, parent and family involvement increases student achievement and success. If preschool teachers can make parents feel welcome helping in the classroom, they will be more likely to remain involved in their child's future education.

Many parents worry about their children entering elementary school because of their own negative school experiences. They may feel intimidated by teachers and uncomfortable showing up at school events—even for orientation and enrolling their children in school (Reidinger, 1997). Parents' expectations of how well children will do in school influence children's performance. It appears that parents who expect success may provide more support, encouragement and praise, which may give their children more self-esteem and confidence. The most important thing is that children who believe in their own abilities have been found to be more successful in school (Dweck, 1991).

To assist parents, preschool teachers can arrange visits to the school and take parents along on the kindergarten field trip. They can ask for children to be paired with a kindergarten "buddy" who can take them around, while parents meet with the teacher or go to the office to register their child. A study done by Rathbun and Hauskin (2001) showed that the more low-income students that were enrolled in a school, the less parental involvement there was. Involving low-income families in the schools may help to break the cycle of poverty of future generations.

One way to really help the family with transition is to empower the parents to act as advocates for their children. Parent

Kindergarten Readiness Is . . .

A Child Who Listens

To directions without interrupting
To stories and poems for five or ten minutes without restlessness

A Child Who Hears

Words that rhyme
Words that begin with the same sound or different sounds

A Child Who Sees

Likenesses and differences in pictures and designs
Letters and words that match

A Child Who Understands

The relationship inherent in such words as up and down, top and bottom, little and big
The classifications of words that represent people, places and things

A Child Who Speaks and Can

Stay on the topic in class discussions
Retell a story or poem in correct sequence
Tell a story or relate an experience of her own

A Child Who Thinks and Can

Give the main idea of a story
Give unique ideas and important details
Give reasons for his opinions

A Child Who Adjusts

To changes in routine and to new situations without becoming fearful
To opposition or defeat without crying or sulking
To necessity of asking for help when needed

A Child Who Plays

Cooperatively with other children
And shares, takes turns and assumes his share of group responsibility
And can run, jump, skip, and bounce a ball with comparative dexterity

A Child Who Works

Without being easily distracted
And follows directions
And completes each task
And takes pride in her work

*Adapted from Howlett, M.P. (1970, February 18). Teacher's edition: *My Weekly Reader Surprise*, Vol. 12, Issue 20.

meetings and newsletters can help parents learn how to work with school staff, learn about volunteer opportunities at school, as well as how to prepare their child at home for kindergarten. They may need some advice on how to help their children and themselves cope with anxieties related to transitions from preschool to kindergarten.

Preparing Children for Transition

In the last few weeks of summer, children start getting excited about going to kindergarten, and are apprehensive at the same time. It is important for parents to treat the child's entrance into kindergarten as a normal occurrence and not build up the event in children's minds. An important way to provide continuity for the child is to find preschool classmates or other children who will be in their kindergarten class. According to research, children who have a familiar peer in a new group setting have fewer problems adjusting to new environments (Howes, 1988).

Transition Activities for Parents and Children

The more you discuss this transition in a matter-of-fact way, the more comfortable children will become. Encourage parents to prepare their child for kindergarten with the following:

- Visit the school so the children can meet the kindergarten teacher and see what kindergarten is really like. Try to arrange for them to see more than one type of classroom activity, such as seatwork time and free choice time.
- Show them where the bathroom and cubbies are located.
- Find out what lunchtime will be like. If the children are going to be getting a school lunch, they may have to learn how to open new kinds of containers.
- Read books about kindergarten.
- Answer children's questions in a straight forward way about what they will do in kindergarten. Tell them they will listen to stories, do counting activities, have group time, and play outside.
- Explore how long the kindergarten day is and what the daily routine will be like. They will want to know what will be the same as preschool and what will be different.
- If the children are going to a school that presents more diversity than they are familiar with, talk honestly with them about racial and ethnic differences and disabilities.
- If children are going to be taking the schoolbus for the first time, you will need to discuss schoolbus safety rules.
- Reassure children that they will be picked up from school every day just as they are in preschool.
- Check to make sure your pre-kindergarten children are capable of basic kindergarten "readiness" skills. (See sidebar.)

Conclusion

The transition from preschool to kindergarten can be a stressful time for both children and parents. However, if preschool teachers can facilitate collaboration between parents and kindergarten and familiarize children with the workings of kindergarten, it will be a smoother process. Parents need to try to find a developmentally appropriate class for their child by observing different classrooms and talking to teachers about educational philosophies. Preschool teachers, with their knowledge of different learning styles and the temperaments of their students, can help everyone with this important transition.

References

Bredekamp, S. & Copple, C. (1997). *Developmentally appropriate practice for early childhood programs*. Revised edition. Washington, DC: NAEYC.

California Dept of Ed., (2000). *Prekindergarten learning and development guidelines*. Sacramento, CA.

Cunningham, A. 1988. Eeny, meeny, miny, moe: Testing policy and practice in early childhood. Berkeley, CA: National Commission on Testing and Public Policy In Graue, E (2001, May) What's going on in the children's garden today? *Young Children*.

Dweck, C.S. (1991). Self-theories and goals: their role in motivation, personality and development. In *Nebraska symposia on motivation*, Vol. 36, ed. by R. Dienstbier, 199–235, Lincoln: University of Nebraska Press. [In Maxwell, Eller, 1994]

Graue, E. (2001, May) What's going on in the children's garden today? *Young Children*, pp. 67–73.

Howes, C. (1988). Peer interaction of young children. Monographs of the Society for Research in Child Development 53 (2. Serial No. 217). In Maxwell, K. and Eller, C. (1994, September) Children's Transition to Kindergarten, *Young Children*.

Howlett, M.P. (1970, February 18). Teacher's edition: *My Weekly Reader Surprise*, Vol. 12, Issue 20.

Jones, E., Evans, K., & Rencken, K. (2001) *The Lively Kindergarten*, NAEYC publications.

Karr-Jelinek, C. (1994). *Transition to kindergarten: Parents and teachers working together*. Educational Resources Information Center.

Ladd, G.W., 1990. Having friends, keeping friends, making friends and being liked by peers in the classroom: Predictors of children's early school adjustment? *Child Development* (61) 1081–100.

Ladd, G.W., & J.M. Price. 1987. Predicting children's social and school adjustment following the transition from preschool to kindergarten. *Child Development*, (58) 1168–89.

Maxwell, K. & Eller, S. (1994, September). Children's transition to kindergarten. *Young Children*, pp. 56–63.

National PTA & National Head Start Association. (1999). *Continuity for success: Transition planning guide*. National PTA, Chicago, IL. National Head Start Association, Alexandria, VA.

Nurss, J. 1987, *Readiness for Kindergarten*, ERIC Clearinghouse on Elementary and Early Childhood Education, Urbana, IL; BBB16656.

Pianta, R. & Cox, M. (1998). Kindergarten Transitions. Teachers 48% of Children Have Transition Problems. *NCEDL Spotlights Series*, No. 1, National Center for Early Development & Learning: Chapel Hill, NC.

Rathbun, A. & Hauskin, E. (2001). How are transition-to-kindergarten activities associated with parent involvement during kindergarten? Paper presented at the Annual meeting of the American Educational Research Foundation: Seattle, WA.

Reidinger, S. (1997), *Even Start: Facilitating transitions to kindergarten*. Dept. of Education: Washington, DC: Planning and Evaluation Service.

Shepard, I.A. & M.I. Smith. (1988) Escalating academic demand in kindergarten: counterproductive policies. *The Elementary School Journal*, (89) 135–45. In Maxwell, K. and Eller, C. (1994, September) Children's Transition to Kindergarten, *Young Children*.

Pam Deyell-Gingold is a graduate student in Human Development at Pacific Oaks College. She works as master teacher at Head Start, teaches child development classes for Merced Community College, and is a freelance writer and anti-bias curriculum enthusiast. Her home is in the Sierra foothills near Yosemite National Park, California.

From *Earlychildhood NEWS*, May/June 2006, pp. 14–19. Copyright © 2006 by Excelligence Learning Corporation. Reprinted by permission.

The Looping Classroom
Benefits for Children, Families, and Teachers

Mary M. Hitz, Mary Catherine Somers, and Christee L. Jenlink

The second week of school, the second-graders work intently in small groups or individually. They require little direct teacher instruction and clearly understand their responsibilities and the teacher's expectations. How did this independence develop so early? What did the teacher do?

Welcome to a looping classroom! "Looping—which is sometimes called multiyear teaching or multiyear placement—occurs when a teacher is promoted with her students to the next grade level and stays with the same group of children for two or three years" (Rasmussen 1998, 1). What results is a continuity of relationship with their teacher that enables children to flourish (Wynne & Walberg 1994).

America's one room schoolhouse was a looping classroom, with the teacher teaching the same children over a period of several years.

Looping Origins

The practice of looping is not a new concept in education. America's one room schoolhouse was a looping classroom, with the teacher teaching the same children over a period of several years. In Germany in 1919 Rudolf Steiner developed the Waldorf School model. Oppenheimer suggests that one unusual aspect of education in the Waldorf School "Is a system called looping, whereby a homeroom teacher stays with a class for more than a year . . . from first through eighth grade" (1999, 82). Also in the early 1900s, Italian pediatrician Maria Montessori introduced the Montessori Method, characterized by relationship development over several years on the part of the teacher, child, and parents (Seldin n.d.).

The Multiage Classroom

Two or more grade levels are intentionally placed in a single classroom. Children are taught as a class and regrouped as necessary for different activities based on interests and/or abilities rather than on chronological age or grade level. At the end of each year, the older students move to a new class, and a group of younger students joins the class. In a multiage grouping, children can experience being both younger and older among the students in their class.

Generally, in modern Germany, student groups formed in first grade remain together over the next four years (Zahorik & Dichanz 1994). In China, grouping is by grade level, with a homeroom teacher who stays with students two to three years in elementary school and for three years in both junior and senior high schools. Many subject area teachers also choose to teach the same students for two to three years (Liu 1997).

In 1974 Deborah Meier founded the Central Park East Elementary School in New York City. Because she believed it takes time to build relationships, in this school the children and teachers stayed together for two years (Meier 1995).

In other instances, U.S. schools developed looping classrooms to solve scheduling problems or manage the significant population shifts in enrollment numbers per grade. This led to teachers being assigned to different or combined grades especially in small rural schools where school populations fluctuate each year. The multiage model is another popular form of looping (see "The Multiage Classroom").

Introducing Looping Today

It is not expensive or difficult to begin a school looping program. Two teachers volunteer for the assignment on any two contiguous grade levels. For example, teacher A teaches first grade and teacher B teaches second grade. The next year, teacher A moves with her class to teach second grade, and teacher B cycles back to begin with a group of new first-graders. Prior to looping, the two teachers and their administrator thoughtfully plan for this structural change (see "Starting a Looping Program").

Benefits of Looping for Children

In today's rapidly altering world, many children's lives are filled with change: of residence, in family structure, in economic status. Numerous children come from single parent homes or have two parents both working full-time away from home. Children can benefit from the looping classroom's stability and teacher continuity (Nichols & Nichols 2002).

Children in typical settings. Because children typically attend school six or more hours a day, five days a week, the teacher is a significant adult in their lives. Staying together two years or longer enhances the bonding and trust established between children and teacher (Grant, Johnson, & Richardson 1996). Pianta and LaParo, in discussing how to improve early school success, conclude that "relationships that children have with adults and other children in families, child care, and school programs provide the foundation for their success in school" (2003, 27). When children form secure relationships with teachers and other caregivers, both social and cognitive competence show improvement (Kontos & Wilcox-Herzog 1997; Gallagher & Mayer 2006).

In the looping classroom children build relationships over time with an adult confidant. Grant and Johnson suggest, "For a lot of children today, their teacher is often the most stable, predictable adult in their life" (1995, 34). Several examples of benefits follow from two coauthors' (Hitz and Somers) primary grades looping classrooms.

Makayla, an eight-year-old, was one of four children, including a sister who was very bright and two brothers with cognitive disabilities. She brought a great deal of pent-up anger to school. During the first year in the looping class, her many angry outbursts involved lashing out at anyone nearby. By her second year in the looping class, she trusted us enough to tell us what was happening. When necessary, Makayla could choose to move to a more isolated area to work alone or, with teacher permission, could go to the office to talk with the assistant principal. Makayla's aggressive expressions lessened, and she gained a sense of control over her emotions.

With additional time together, teachers can become more familiar with each child's learning style, interests, strengths, and needs and respond with individualized learning experiences (Seldin n.d.). In a looping classroom children are not apprehensive about their second or next years; they already know their teacher and classmates (Lacina-Gifford 2001). The familiar environment also allows a shy child to blossom. For example,

At the beginning of his first looping year, Eric cried when called upon during any kind of discussion. Later in the year he would raise his hand to volunteer, only to shrink inside himself at being recognized. Once in a while he worked with another child.

Starting a Looping Program

- Form a proposal study group
- Read about looping programs
- Enlist and build support from administrators and other teachers
- Involve parents in the planning
- Design the program to allow for change
- Provide time for staff development
- Visit other looping programs
- Invite teachers to volunteer for looping classrooms
- Work with administrators on the careful selection of the teachers for looping

---

Knowing we would have Eric for two years, we did not feel the pressure to force participation in the first year. We offered support and encouragement when he attempted to participate but also allowed him needed time to mature.

Although Eric struggled in reading all that first year, during the second year he volunteered more often and answered questions. Eric was on grade level at the end of the year. His mother was glad he was in a looping classroom. He was still quiet, but he knew he could do well in a new third grade classroom.

In a looping classroom, the teacher and the children experience a sense of community. The bonds between children grow strong; they share achievements and disappointments, resolve problems, and learn to trust each other. Teachers personalize their teaching and talk about their individual interests and their families.

One of the most positive elements of looping is that it allows a child to grow at his or her own pace, not at an arbitrary fixed-grade rate. John Goodlad reminds us that children "don't fit into a nice, neat age-grade package, either collectively or individually. Each individual child differs in regard to the various areas of accomplishment" (Stone 1999, 265). An example from our classroom follows:

Austin, a young first-grader, worked hard in class and at home with his parents. By the end of the year, however, he was barely able to read at the preprimary level. His mother asked if we should retain Austin in first grade. We suggested waiting, since as a looping class we could monitor Austin's progress in the coming year.

Austin bloomed that second year. Reading became his favorite activity, and by the end of the year he was reading above grade level. In third grade he moved into the gifted program. Had Austin been in a nonlooping classroom, he might have been retained.

English-language learners. The looping classroom supports children and their families for whom English is a second language. As English-language learners (ELLs) adjust to a new school and become comfortable with their teacher, they develop confidence in practicing their new language. Eventually they may help others who are new to the class or have little knowledge of U.S. culture. When children who are ELLs are members of a class, the other children can learn firsthand from a peer about another culture and country. The experience results in respect and understanding among all the students (Haslinger, Kelly, & O'Lare 1996).

Maritza uses both English and Spanish. One day, in her second year, she and three other Spanish-speaking friends chose a book to read to the class and designed follow-up activities. They read the story aloud—in Spanish. The other children gained an idea of what ELL students experience when learning a second language. Because Maritza and her friends felt safe and secure in their classroom, they could make this presentation to their peers.

Looping Pluses for Others

Looping provides time for teachers to get to know each child and family in a personal way, and it fosters stronger bonds between teachers and families.

Teachers. In nonlooping classrooms, each year teachers spend the first four to six weeks determining each child's skills, abilities, and interests. In contrast, in the second year of a looping classroom cycle, the teacher already knows the students and is able to immediately support their learning, thus making better use of instructional time (Little & Dacus 1999). Effective teaching and learning can begin on the first day of the second year after a brief review of rules and procedures (Burke 1996).

Many teachers provide summer learning packets to help children bridge from one year to the next. In looping classrooms the children are returning to the same classroom and teacher, and it is easy to design packets and follow up with them the second year. Children are excited to share journals kept over the summer, stories they wrote, or special books they read. The looping teacher can build on children's previous year's experiences and use the summer packets to lead into the second year's curriculum.

One of the most positive elements of looping is that it allows a child to grow at his or her own pace, not at an arbitrary fixed-grade rate.

Usually teachers choose to loop because they believe in developmentally appropriate practices, including the importance of encouraging emotional development (Dunn & Kontos 1997). Such teachers understand young children's need for stability and how the looping classroom addresses that need.

In looping classrooms, collaborating teachers learn new skills and curriculum (Albrecht et al. 2000) by sharing materials and ideas. They have a chance to know more about the children— where they live, who needs extra motivation, who works best

with whom (Burke 2000). Units of study can extend into the next year. Looping gives teachers an extra year to consider high-stakes decisions regarding retention or referral for testing for special services (Jacobson 1997; Liu 1997; Bracey 1999).

Families. Looping classrooms foster stronger bonds between families and teachers. "Because parents are the most significant people in a child's life, the relationship between the teacher and the parents is paramount" (Albrecht et al. 2000, 24). Parents tend to place more trust in a teacher the second year, with the development of a relaxed relationship conducive to a positive attitude toward the teacher (Nichols & Nichols 2002). Conversely, the teacher values input from the home, a direct result of the collaborative relationship that has been forged in this type of classroom setting.

Parents get to know the teacher's philosophy of education and how it relates to their child. Because a trusting relationship builds over the long span of a looping classroom, families may be more willing to accept a teacher's constructive suggestions (Chirichello & Chirichello 2001) and tend to be comfortable sharing the challenges they face with their child at home. Our looping classroom provides this example:

Zach had difficulty completing classroom assignments on time. At home, his family reported he was never ready on time and every morning was a fight to get dressed for school. Zach's mother called one morning to say he would be at school on time, but in his pajamas. We were proud of the other children for not making fun of Zach or teasing him. But ever after, Zach was always ready for school.

For the families of children who are English-language learners, the stability of having the same teacher for a span of two years helps them gain confidence in talking with the teacher about their children's progress. The teacher can also smooth this transition by having materials translated as frequently as possible into the family's home language and arranging for translators to attend conferences.

A looping classroom favors both the child and the teacher and adds stability to children's lives.

What Concerns Might Arise in Looping?

While the advantages of a looping classroom are many, some concerns do arise. One issue parents express is a fear of their child being locked in for two years with a possibly ineffective teacher. Other potential problems include a teacher-child personality conflict, a child who simply does not get along with the other children, or a parent who does not get along with the teacher. Although looping teachers report that these occurrences are rare; each school needs to have procedures for reviewing class placements. The school principal plays an important role in identifying teacher-child personality conflicts as well as ensuring that teachers have the skills and work ethic necessary to create a successful looping classroom.

In our looping classroom two sets of parents came to us with concerns about their children. In both instances the issues reflected differences about teaching philosophy. After discussions, with both sets of parents, we jointly decided to place each child in a traditional classroom. Involvement of the school principal is essential in such situations to ensure making the best decision for the child.

Another challenge involves a new child entering the program, especially in the second year when children are already familiar with each other and the classroom. The looping teacher must prepare and encourage the children to welcome and accept the new student and help the child become part of the community.

Conclusion

At the end of the school year, it is always difficult to say good-bye, but when a teacher and children have been together for two years, it is doubly difficult. The class is a learning community that has shared joys as well as the sadness of departure. Some teachers plan special events to highlight their two years together. The children outline their advice to the incoming group of younger students and write letters to their future teachers to introduce themselves. Receiving teachers visit the looping class to be introduced to their new students when possible.

Good-bye is a bittersweet time. Sometimes it's harder for parents. Not only do looping teachers have to reassure the children that they will succeed, but also they have to reassure the families.

The concept of a looping classroom is being revisited by many teachers today. It favors both the child and the teacher and adds stability to children's lives. It provides time—time for children to grow and develop at their own rates and time for teachers to get to know each child and family in a personal way.

Looping may not be a good fit for everyone nor solve all the problems in education. But teacher proponents express it this way: Looping provides the most rewarding opportunity for helping children succeed (Rasmussen 1998).

References

Albrecht, K., M. Banks, G. Calhoun, L. Dziadul, C. Gwinn, B. Harrington, B. Kerr, M. Mizukami, A. Morris, C. Peterson, & R.R. Summers. 2000. The good, the bad and the wonderful! Keeping children and teachers together. *Child Care Information Exchange* (136): 24–28.

Bracey, G.W. 1999. Going loopy for looping. *Phi Delta Kappan* 81 (2): 169–70.

Burke, D.L. 1996. Multi-year teacher/student relationships are a long-overdue arrangement. *Phi Delta Kappan* 77 (5): 360–61.

Burke, D.L. 2000. Learning to loop and loving it. *The School Administrator Web Edition*. Online: www.aasa.org. publications/content.cfm?ItemNumber=3831

Chirichello, M., & C. Chirichello. 2001. A standing ovation for looping: The critics respond. *Childhood Education* 78 (1): 2–10.

Dunn, L., & S. Kontos. 1997. What have we learned about developmentally appropriate practice? *Young Children* 52 (5): 4–13.

Gallagher, K.C., & K. Mayer. 2006. Teacher-child relationships at the forefront of effective practice. *Young Children* 61 (6): 44–49.

Grant, J., & B. Johnson. 1995. *A common sense guide to multiage practices, primary level*. Columbus, OH: Teachers' Publishing Group.

Grant, J., B. Johnson, & I. Richardson. 1996. *Our best advice: The multiage problem solving handbook*. Petersborough, NH: Crystal Springs Books.

Haslinger, J., P. Kelley, & L. O'Lare. 1996. Countering absenteeism, anonymity, and apathy. *Educational Leadership* 54 (1): 47–49.

Jacobson, L. 1997. 'Looping' catches on as way to build strong ties. *Education Week* 17 (7): 1–3.

Kontos, S., & A. Wilcox Herzog. 1997. Teachers' interactions with children: Why are they so important? *Young Children* 52 (2): 4–12.

Lacina-Gifford, L.J. 2001. The squeaky wheel gets the oil, but what about the shy student? *Education* 122 (2): 320–21.

Little, T.S., & N.B. Dacus. 1999. Looping: Moving up with the class. *Educational Leadership* 57 (1): 42–45.

Liu, J. 1997. The emotional bond between teachers and students: Multi-year relationships. *Phi Delta Kappan* 78 (2): 156–57.

Meier, D. 1995. *The power of their ideas: Lessons for America from a small school in Harlem*. Boston, MA: Beacon.

Nichols, J.D., & G.W. Nichols. 2002. The impact of looping classroom environments on parental attitudes. *Preventing School Failure* 47 (1): 18–25.

Oppenheimer, T. 1999. Schooling the imagination. *The Atlantic Monthly* 284 (2): 71–83.

Pianta, R.C., & K. LaParo. 2003. Improving early school success. *Educational Leadership* 60 (7): 24–29.

Rasmussen, K. 1998. Looping: Discovering the benefits of multiyear teaching. *Education Update* 40 (2): 41–44.

Selden, T. N.d. Montessori 101: Some basic information that every Montessori parent should know. Online: www.montessori.org/sitefiles/Montessori_101_nonprintable.pdf.

Stone, S.J. 1999. A conversation with John Goodlad. *Childhood Education* 75 (5): 264–68.

Wynne, E.A., & H.J. Walberg. 1994. Persisting groups: An overlooked force for learning. *Phi Delta Kappan* 75 (7): 527–30.

Zahorik, J.A., & H. Dichanz. 1994. Teaching for understanding in German schools. *Educational Leadership* 51 (5): 75–77.

Beyond *The Lorax?*

The Greening of the American Curriculum

Getting children outside to play and stay in touch with nature is important for their health and for developing environmental awareness.

CLARE LOWELL

There is a classic *Peanuts* cartoon that features little yellow-haired Sally, ensconced in a bean-bag chair, watching TV, telling big brother Charlie Brown that he should check out the enthralling program she's watching on the tube. "You should watch this," she urges. "They're showing pictures of huge snowflakes falling gently on this beautiful snow covered meadow . . ."

Charlie Brown looks at the TV and tells her, "You can see the same thing right now if you go outside," pointing out the window. The final frame shows Sally—clearly appalled and momentarily distracted from her TV viewing—exclaiming in horror, "OUTSIDE?!"

It might be funnier if it weren't so scarily true: Our children are growing up without nature—clearly preferring their electronic diversions to the real thing.

What Sally didn't know at the time is that, not only is there a name for her affliction, it's a syndrome that is virtually dominating the younger generation. "Videophilia," defined as the new human tendency to focus on sedentary activities involving electronic media,[1] has virtually supplanted the need for "biophilia," or the urge to affiliate with other forms of life. This particular theory is bolstered by research that supports the positive reaction of people to natural landscapes. The quality of this exposure affects human health and child development at an almost cellular level.[2]

As recently as a generation ago, playtime usually meant outdoor play and activity that put children in touch with nature and encouraged direct involvement with their physical environment. Now chat rooms, video games, and indoor playdates occupy much of their playtime. Playrooms as opposed to playgrounds; virtual nature as opposed to the real thing.

Caring about Nature

It's not too much of a stretch to say that, if children don't care about nature today, they won't care about conserving it tomorrow when they're adults. And, if one doesn't care about something, there will be no investment in protecting it. In addition, with most of the populace living in urban areas, people will be even more disconnected from the natural world. Considering the looming environmental issues that await this generation (climate change, population/human consumption, carbon footprints, etc.), this creates a downright depressing, if not apocalyptic, view of the future.

It's not too much of a stretch to say that, if children don't care about nature today, they won't care about conserving it tomorrow when they're adults.

Richard Louv's recent bestseller, *Last Child in the Woods: Saving Our Children from Nature-Deficit Disorder,* discusses the "criminalization of natural play," in which communities, more concerned with property values and lawsuits, have outlawed unstructured outdoor nature play.[3] From public government to community associations, rules govern and restrict children in everything from building tree houses to erecting basketball hoops. When climbing a tree on public land can be actionable as an illegal activity designed to "injure" the landscape, children move indoors to recreate, electronically, what they are missing in real life. As recently as this past summer, teenagers who turned public land in Greenwich, Connecticut, into a Wiffle® ball field were threatened with litigation and unending complaints by locals who wanted them out. In the words of one Wiffle®-ball athlete, "People think we should be home playing 'Grand Theft Auto'."[4]

Whether this can be attributed to a shrinkage of open space (thereby encouraging overuse of the accessible natural areas) or the overstructuring of childhood, a generation of American children is being raised indoors. From 1977 to 2003, the proportion of 9- to 12-year-olds who engage in outside activities such as hiking, walking, fishing, beach play, and gardening has declined by 50%. In addition, children's free play time in a typical week has declined by a total of nine hours over a 25-year period.[5]

While this physical restriction of childhood may be an unintended outgrowth of an urban society, there may be correspondingly unintended consequences as a result. As nature deficit grows, so does the increase of childhood disorders such as Attention Deficit Hyperactivity Disorder (ADHD) and obesity.[6] In a series of studies designed to explore potential new treatments for ADHD, the inclusion of after-school and weekend activities centered on natural outdoor environments may be widely effective in reducing symptoms of the disorder. The advantages of these relatively simplistic approaches are many: They are widely accessible, inexpensive, non-stigmatizing, and free of side effects.[7]

And, lest one think that children in rural areas are immune from the urban blight of constricted space and diminished play, studies demonstrate otherwise. While adults may delight in idyllic country life images of open fields, green pastures, and limitless opportunity for play, nothing could be further from the reality of today's youth. Images of *Lassie* aside, most rural children are in the same sedentary boat as their urban counterparts: inside, in front of a screen. Statistics reflect this, with 16.5% of rural kids qualifying as obese, compared with 14.4% of urban kids (according to a 2003 National Survey of Children's Health). In many ways, they are more disadvantaged than their suburban counterparts because their homes may not be near areas suitable for play and often lack a support system for activity. According to David Hartley, director of the Maine Rural Health Center, children living in isolated communities tend to have fewer places to walk and play. In addition, they also suffer from decreased opportunities to buy healthy foods (a situation often referred to as "nutritional isolation"), an ironic twist on the fresh-air-and-good-food misconception most Americans have of country life.[8]

In addition to a high-fat, high-calorie daily menu, other factors contribute to this situation. American homes have become high-def, Web-enabled, TiVo-driven entertainment meccas that offer 24-hour-a-day diversion from anything that would get a kid out of his or her rocker lounge chair. After a full day at a school desk, the American child comes home to spend, on average, three or more sedentary hours in front of some kind of screen. What's worse, school budgets have slashed physical education programs in cost-cutting moves that have resulted in plummeting participation in daily physical education—down to 25% from 42% 17 years ago.[9]

Vision for Environmental Education

So what's a school board/principal/teacher to do? Throw away our old classroom science kits and take the kids out to play? Close.

Recent proposals, such as the Vision for Environmental Education in Ontario, Canada, promote innovative programs and partnerships with community-based environmental organizations as well as outdoor education centers. In doing so, the Canadian Ministry of Education is offering a vision for environmental education that provides a context for applying knowledge and skills to real-world situations through an integrated approach. Their science curriculum embraces education for sustainability as well as outdoor education. Consequently, students are afforded opportunities for experiential learning that foster connections to local places, develop a greater understanding of ecosystems, and supply a unique context for learning.[10]

Closer to home, the Open Spaces program of the Urban Resources Initiative (under the aegis of Yale University) is on the same track. Open Spaces balances classroom learning on key ecological concepts with outdoor experiences that bring these ideas to life. Whether students are identifying trees and habitats in a schoolyard or connecting human history to the environment, this program opens kids' eyes to nature in the city and teaches them how to protect urban resources.[11]

Regardless of the worldwide location—be it New Haven or New South Wales—the objectives of enlightened environmental education policies are predictably consistent: to create eco-schools in coordination with a holistic, participatory approach through a combination of learning and action. Raising awareness through inspiring and motivating students is integral to comprehensive program design.

The Lorax

Which brings us to *The Lorax*. Theodore Seuss Geisel, a.k.a. "Dr. Seuss," created this celebrated story almost 40 years ago, but its prescient message is as timely today as though it were written during the last election cycle. In it, Dr. Seuss introduces the "Once-ler," who cuts down the beautiful truffula trees so that he can use their bright-colored, silky tufts to knit "thneeds." The blissful world of happy "Brown Barba-loots," who play in the shade of the trees and eat their fruits, is destroyed by the factory built by the Once-ler and the Super Axe Hacker, who cuts down four trees at a time. Enter the Lorax, who speaks up in defense of the trees, animals, air, and water that the Once-ler is destroying in pursuit of bigger and bigger profits. Finally, when the last truffula tree is cut down, production of the thneeds ends. Closed factories, polluted air, polluted water, and an uninhabitable wasteland are all that remains. The Lorax can no longer live there, but he leaves a small pile of rocks on which the word "UNLESS" is inscribed.

What's left, ultimately, is one last truffula seed and the hope that the forest will come back, bringing with it the Lorax and all of his friends.

The basic message of *The Lorax* deals with ecosystems and the interrelatedness of all parts—living and non-living—as a viable, functioning unit. Environmental impact is told from a simplistic yet environmentally accurate viewpoint, demonstrating the conflict between natural resources and man-made production.

This fable of reckless deforestation and its dire ecological consequence was an outgrowth of the environmental reform movement of the 1960s, which peaked with the nation's first Earth Day on April 22, 1970. Issues of the day were presented in a means that allowed children to equate the ideas in the story with real, present-day situations.[12]

For years, teachers have used *The Lorax* to help students understand the need for conservation as well as the effects of lifestyle changes that will result from the thoughtless devastation of the natural world.

And yet, there is an environmental movement that goes beyond the obvious message. The interrelatedness of environmental education and the reconnection of children with nature are at the heart of both. Perhaps the message should be, "Heal the globe, and you heal yourself."

Conservation will fail unless it is better connected to people, and people start out as children who need to revere their connection to nature from a personal, rather than intellectual, viewpoint. And so we must bridge the rhetoric/reality gap between conservation for its own sake and conservation for the sake of the health and well-being of our children.

Dr. Seuss rhymes aside, how do we cast as wide a net as possible in capturing the imagination of children in inspiring them to become an active part of their ecological environment? Is it something that can be legislated, or is it an intangible passion that can only be appreciated through firsthand experience? Actually, research suggests both.

No Child Left Inside

To address the problems voiced here, the No Child Left Inside Coalition—a broad-based organization of more than 200 member groups throughout the U.S.—has focused its efforts on legislation that would authorize hew funding for states to provide high-quality, environmental instruction. The No Child Left Inside Act (NCLI) would provide subsidies to support outdoor learning activities both at school and in non-formal environmental education centers, teacher training, and the creation of state environmental literacy plans.[13]

The intersection between healthy people and a healthy environment is critical to the future of youngsters everywhere, yet the movement to reconnect children with nature is still in its infancy. The retreat indoors is not only limiting to the next generation, it's downright dangerous. Public health workers already see the effects in fatter, sicker children whose life expectancy is alarmingly shorter than that of their parents. As the American Public Health Association notes in its publication, *The Nation's Health,* "The future . . . is in the hands of today's children, many of whom are more likely to view nature through the screen of a television rather than the netted screen of a camping tent."[14]

"Which brings us back to little Sally Brown, still in her bean-bag chair, still watching nature on TV. Take note, little yellow-haired girl: Get up, put on your mittens, and go out and play in the snow. Your future depends on it.

Notes

1. Patricia A. Zaradic and Oliver R.W. Pergams, "Videophilia: Implications for Childhood Development and Conservation," *Journal of Developmental Processes,* Spring 2007, pp. 130–47.
2. Edward O. Wilson, *Biophilia* (Cambridge, Mass.: Harvard University Press, 1984).
3. Richard Louv, *Last Child in the Woods* (New York: Workman, 2008).
4. Peter Applebome. "Build a Wiffle Ball Field in Greenwich, and Lawyers Will Come," *New York Times,* 10 July 2008, pp. A1, A15.
5. Sandra L. Hofferth and John F. Sandberg, "How Children Spend Their Time," *Journal of Marriage and Family,* May 2001, pp. 295–308.
6. Frederick J. Zimmerman, Dimitri A. Christakis, and Andrew N. Meltzoff, "Television and DVD/Video Viewing in Children Younger than 2 Years," *Archives of Pediatrics and Adolescent Medicine,* May 2007, pp. 473–79.
7. Frances E. Kuo and Andrea F. Taylor, "A Potential Natural Treatment for Attention-Deficit/Hyperactivity Disorder: Evidence from a National Study," *American Journal of Public Health,* September 2004, pp. 1580–86, www.pubmedcentral.nih.gov.
8. Bryan Walsh, "It's Not Just Genetics," *Time,* 23 June 2008, pp. 70–80.

9. Jeffrey Kluger, "How America's Children Packed on the Pounds," *Time*, 23 June 2008, pp. 66–69.

10. Roberta Bondar, *Shaping Our Schools, Shaping Our Future: Environmental Education in Ontario Schools* (Toronto: Working Group on Environmental Education, 2007), www.edu.gov.on.ca/curriculum-council/shapingSchools.pdf.

11. Pegnataro, Justin, "Open Spaces as Learning Places," Urban Resources Initiative, 2005, www.yale.edu/uri/programs/osalp.html.

12. Christine Moseley, "The Continuing Adventures of the Truffula Tree Company," *Science Scope*, May 1995, pp. 22–25.

13. Chesapeake Bay Foundation, "No Child Left Inside," 2008, www.cbf.org, search on title.

14. Kim Krisberg, "Movement to Reconnect Kids with Nature Growing Nationwide: Working to Improve Children's Health," *The Nation's Health*, October 2007.

CLARE LOWELL is an assistant professor of education at Marymount Manhattan College in New York City.

UNIT 6

Helping Children to Thrive in School

Unit Selections

34. **Play: Ten Power Boosts for Children's Early Learning,** Alice Sterling Honig
35. **Ready or Not, Here We Come: What It Means to Be a Ready School,** Paula M. Dowker, with Larry Schweinhart and Marijata Daniel-Echols
36. **"Stop Picking on Me!": What You Need to Know about Bullying,** *Texas Child Care*
37. **Developmentally Appropriate Child Guidance: Helping Children Gain Self-Control,** Will Mosier
38. **Fostering Positive Transitions for School Success,** Jayma Ferguson McGann and Patricia Clark
39. **A Multinational Study Supports Child-Initiated Learning: Using the Findings in Your Classroom,** Jeanne E. Montie, Jill Claxton, and Shannon D. Lockhart
40. **The Power of Documentation in the Early Childhood Classroom,** Hilary Seitz

Key Points to Consider

- What does it mean to be a ready school?

- How can children be involved in establishing the learning environment and an attitude of caring?

- Why is emotional stability so important to develop during the preschool years?

- Is it possible to prevent disruptive behavior before it occurs?

- How can a teacher build positive relationships with children?

Student Website

www.mhhe.com/cls

Internet References

Busy Teacher's Cafe
 http://www.busyteacherscafe.com
Future of Children
 http://www.futureofchildren.org
You Can Handle Them All
 http://www.disciplinehelp.com

Early childhood teaching is all about being proactive and establishing policies that support young children's development and learning. Good teachers are problem solvers just as children work to solve problems. Every day, teachers make decisions about how to guide children socially and emotionally. In attempting to determine what could be causing a child's emotional distress, teachers must take into account a myriad of factors. They should consider the physical, social, environmental, and emotional factors, in addition to the surface behavior of a child. Whether it is an individual child's behavior or interpersonal relationships, the pressing problem involves complex issues that require careful reflection and analysis. Even the most mature teachers spend many hours thinking and talking about the best ways to guide and support young children's behavior: What should I do about the child who is out of bounds? What do I do to best prepare the learning environment to meet the needs of all children? How can I develop effective relationships with children and their families? These are some of the questions teachers ask as they interact with young children on a day-to-day basis.

Alice Sterling Honig shares ten strategies for supporting young children's learning in her article, "Play: Ten Power Boosts for Children's Early Learning." Dr. Honig has consistently been a reassuring voice for teachers struggling to meet the needs of all children.

When those outside of the education profession talk about getting children ready to learn, many early childhood professionals instinctively say to themselves, "Children come to us already learning. Our job is to make our schools and classrooms ready to accept all children." That is the theme of "Ready or Not, Here We Come: What It Means to Be a Ready School" by Dowker, Schweinhart, and Daniel-Echols. It is our responsibility to accommodate the learning environment and provide the support for children and their families to successfully transfer to the next phase in their learning.

This unit addresses teachers who establish positive relationships with children. "Developmentally Appropriate Child Guidance: Helping Children Gain Self-Control" supports the need for positive relationships as the cornerstone for building rapport. The other theme that is woven throughout the articles in this unit is the importance of social and emotional development on all areas of development. Teachers who rush to teach academic skills at the expense of fostering the children's social and emotion development will find there are many unexpected hurdles to jump. Children who are not secure or confident in their surroundings or comfortable with the adults in their life will not be strong learners. "Fostering Positive Transitions for School Success" highlights the importance of socioemotional development and sets a proactive tone by providing teachers with an overview of the importance of children feeling secure about themselves and their place in life.

When my husband and I sent our two sons off to college, I thought about the many ways their universities prepared them, and their parents, for this major transition. First-year orientation programs, welcome week activities, and parents' weekend were all carefully planned to assist the new students adjusting to

© Digital Vision/Getty Images RF

college. Most companies have new employee orientation programs to help employees adjust to their new environment. However, we do little to help five-year-olds who are also making a significant transition in their life. It is time preschool teachers, kindergarten teachers, administrators, and families collaborate to ensure a smooth progression to the next learning experience. For some children it will be another out-of-the-home formal learning experience, but for other children it will be their first encounter with a teacher and a group of peers that could number 25 or more. If we are cognizant of the emotions and questions children may have as they make the transition to a new school level, we can provide the support needed to help ensure a successful experience.

As educators across the country work to implement an antibullying environment, it is important for teachers to work diligently to establish an environment that is supportive of all children and discourages and stops any attempt at bullying. "'Stop Picking on Me!': What You Need to Know about Bullying" provides suggestions for teachers to establish a positive climate in their classrooms. Children who believe they are accepted and respected in the classroom feel confident and are able to develop genuine relationships with their peers and with their teacher. Teachers who have a limited number of disruptive children in their class are those teachers who take precautionary steps to establish firm rules, establish a supportive environment, and help children learn about the consequences of their behavior.

Determining strategies for guidance and discipline is an important work for an early childhood teacher. Because the teacher-child relationship is the foundation for emotional well-being and social competence, guidance is more than applying a single set of guidance techniques. Instead of one solitary model of classroom discipline strictly enforced, a broad range of techniques is more appropriate. It is only through careful analysis and reflection that teachers can look at children individually, assessing not only the child but the impact of family cultures as well, and determine appropriate and effective guidance. Recently, one of my graduate students shared that the teachers at her school decided to stop using the traffic light system of management they had used for the past few years. The traffic light system allows children to talk quietly when the light in the classroom or cafeteria is green, whisper when the light is moved to yellow, and not talk at all when it is red. Some lights are noise sensitive so the noise level of the children determines the color of the light displayed, not the adult in the room. My student said the teachers recognized the program was not working and had many negative consequences. I am always pleased to hear when teachers and administrators alter programs based on observation and the gathering of data. Some educators stay with one practice that does not prove to be effective, yet they don't know what else to do so they stick with a poor plan. I applaud teachers who are constantly searching for ways to reach their children and will modify practice when needed.

Children crave fair and consistent guidelines from caring adults in their world. They want to know the consequences of their behavior and how to meet the expectations of others. When the expectations are clear and the students see a direct relation between their behavior and the consequences, they begin to develop the self-control that will be so important as they move through life.

This unit ends with Hilary Seitz's "The Power of Documentation in the Early Childhood Classroom." Seitz describes the benefits of documentation and shares suggested ways to document learning. Teachers who take responsibility to educate others about the learning in their classroom will have successful partnerships with others, including family members and administrators.

Play: Ten Power Boosts for Children's Early Learning

ALICE STERLING HONIG

Many adults think of play and learning as separate domains. Indeed, some people believe that academic school work is learning but that play is just what young children do to get rid of lots of energy. The truth learned from research is that rich, varied play experiences strongly boost children's early learning (Kaplan 1978; Bergen 1998; Johnson, Christie, & Yawkey 1999).

Children gain powerful knowledge and useful social skills through play.

Children gain powerful knowledge and useful social skills through play. This article offers 10 ideas about what children learn through play.

Play Enhances Dexterity and Grace

Preschoolers learn eye-hand coordination and skillful toy manipulation through play. They spin a top, stack blocks, wind up a jack-in-the-box, and try out ways to solve the chain bolt or buttoning activity on a busy board. The variety of hand motions required to latch, lace, or twirl a top enhances hand dexterity. As they eat with a spoon, infants and toddlers are learning wrist coordination. Teachers support this control learning when they provide interesting activities, such as tossing a beanbag or throwing a soft yarn ball into baskets placed nearer or farther away. Babies adore filling and dumping games and will try to work a windup toy over and over again.

Place babies on their tummies on safe, warm surfaces. This gives them opportunities to stretch and reach for favorite chew toys. As they push up on their arms, infants practice coordination of their shoulder and chest muscles. Such body games are particularly important today because infants are habitually placed on their backs for safe sleeping in cribs.

Learning how to ride a tricycle or scooter enhances the coordination of muscles in legs and feet for toddlers and preschoolers.

Older children learn to play sports. They kick and throw basketballs, baseballs, and soccer balls. These games help children coordinate use of both sides of the body. Sports help children develop confidence and pride in their control over body movement in space.

"Hold-operate" skills in play are important for later learning. For example, a preschooler holds an eggbeater with one hand and turns the handle vigorously to make lots of bubbles during water play. A school-age child holds a book page open with one hand and writes notes with the other. Making a pop-it bead necklace is a challenging activity allowing toddlers to push and pull with their fingers. To promote whole body gracefulness, play soft, slow music, such as the "Skater's Waltz," and invite children to move their bodies.

Peer Play Promotes Social Skills

With admirable patience, teachers help children gradually learn how to take turns riding a tricycle, to share materials, and to work and build together. Soon they learn the pleasures of playing with peers (Smilansky & Shefatya 1990). As buddies, older infants giggle and take turns crawling or running into the cardboard house in the play area and popping their heads through the play-house window to shout "Hi" to a grinning peer peeking in. Toddlers might help put a train track together on the floor and play at being engineers. Preschoolers collaborate on lugging a wagon full of blocks or filling it with a heap of scooped up snow for building a snowman together.

Some children need a teacher's encouraging words to ask a peer for permission to join in a game (Honig & Thompson 1994). Henry pulls his wagon, and Jerry wants his pet cat to go for a ride too. Giving words to such longings boosts a child's ability to learn a variety of ways to get to play with a peer, instead of standing on the sidelines. In a warmly encouraging voice, the adult suggests, "Tell Jerry, 'I want to put my cat in the wagon.'"

Children sometimes need an adult's unobtrusive arrangement of props to encourage more advanced sociodramatic play. Others need innovative, adult suggestions to encourage more *inclusive* play. Overhearing some preschoolers tell Kao he cannot play house with them because they already have a mommy, a daddy, and children in their play scenario, the teacher comments, "Suppose there is going to be a birthday party. Kao can be the mail carrier delivering birthday presents to your home." The children take over from there.

In a tussle over a toy, an adult may need to model prosocial solutions for children who struggle to come up with social problem-solving ideas on their own. Shure's (1994) ICPS (I Can Problem Solve) techniques can be helpful. "Julio wants to play blocks, and you want him to play Batman dress-up. Can the two of you find a way to play what you want some of the time and what Julio wants the rest of the time? If you each get a turn choosing an activity, both of you can get your wish and have fun together." Getting children to think through the consequences of interactions is a daily challenge. Teachers can help boost children's ability to figure out how to make and keep a play pal by role-playing helpful scenarios: "Howie, if you go on the seesaw with me awhile, then we can play in the sandbox together." Children learn social skills combined with body coordination in games such as Hokey Pokey and London Bridge Is Falling Down.

Teaching social skills in play is crucially important for children with neurological or developmental disabilities.

Not excluding other children from play is a noble task for which Vivian Paley has instituted a classroom rule: You can't say you can't play. Her book (1992) by this name describes the day-to-day struggles of children to gain empathy and lessen the hurt others feel when they are excluded from peer play. Teaching social skills in play is crucially important for children with neurological or developmental disabilities such as autism spectrum disorders, who may need help decoding the emotions of others and responding in socially effective ways.

Children's Play Sharpens Cognitive and Language Skills

Teachers who carefully prepare materials for sensory motor activities are helping children learn tasks that involve what Piaget ([1951] 1962) calls "means-ends separations" and "causal relationships." When a baby pulls a toy on a string to move it closer or shakes a bell to hear it ring, she is delightedly learning that from certain actions, she gets a specific effect. The toddler banging a stick on a xylophone and miraculously producing musical notes also learns that those specific actions cause interesting results. Scientists use these same early life lessons in their laboratories every day.

Singing with young children creates a pleasurable form of play that enhances brain development and learning.

Infants who play with syllables in their cribs are practicing coordination of lips, tongue, palate, and vocal chords. Singing with young children creates a pleasurable form of play that enhances brain development and learning. Some young toddlers stretch their language abilities amazingly as they try to sing along with the words (Honig 1995). This learning counters theories that play is purely for sensory, personal, or social pleasure. Musical play involves lots of word learning; listen as an enthusiastic group of toddlers tries hard to copy the teacher's words as she sings "Frère Jacques."

Teachers can play rhyming games with toddlers and preschoolers. Start out with easy syllables: "I have a little gray mouse, and he lives in a little gray _____!" If children have trouble at first hearing the sounds, give them the answers and start the rhyming couplet game again. The ability to enjoy and participate in rhyming games is one predictor of success in learning to read.

Play promotes language mastery. Children talk together as they build houses with blocks, piece puzzles together, or construct a space tower using Legos. They talk excitedly as they pretend to get "hurt people" from a car crash scene into ambulances. Social play strengthens language interactions, and teachers may provide a word here and there as catalysts for language interchanges (Honig 1982). Housekeeping corners with dress-up clothes and workbenches and tables with safety goggles and woodworking tools promote feelings of efficacy and self-esteem as well as purposeful, harmonious peer interactions and accomplishments.

Preschoolers Acquire Number and Time Concepts

The Piagetian concept of *conservation of number* is difficult learning during the preschool years (Piaget [1951] 1962). By playing with toys with large, separate parts (that cannot be swallowed!), a preschooler begins to find out that whether he stacks the pieces, lays them out in a circle, or sets them out in one long row, he will still count the same number if he puts his finger carefully on each item while counting. Learning that the sum total does not depend on configuration may be easier if children feel encouraged to experiment with different arrangements of small animals, cars, or blocks.

Concepts such as *soon* or *later* and *before* or *after* are hard for young children to understand. To make the child's construction work, inserting one special piece *before* adding another piece may be the secret. Lego blocks that fit together into three-dimensional space require learning which parts to put together first and which ones to add on later to make the structure stable.

Using a digital camera helps children become more aware of different spatial aspects and directions and viewpoints in space. Will Giana's picture of a small ball rolling really fast (or even slowly) down a chute into a basin capture the ball's action? Preschoolers will enjoy taking real pictures of favorite activity areas. A child might take a photograph while peering down from a raised reading loft or one at eye level while lying on her tummy.

Cooking activities offer rich possibilities for math learning. Children learn varieties of colors and textures of foods and first-before-next scientific procedures, such as measuring just one-half teaspoon of oil for each muffin pan before filling it with three tablespoons of batter.

When music play is embedded in the daily curriculum, children learn "sequences of time" as rhymes and rhythms of chants and songs vary in their patterns and progressions. Even eight-month-old babies can bounce to the musical syllables you emphasize as you chant or sing songs, such as "Hickory dickory dock! The mouse ran up the clock!" Offer play experiences with wrist bells, maracas, tambourines, and keyboards, and sing the same songs over and over. As children move their bodies to musical syllables, especially if they clap out rhythms, they learn one-to-one correspondence between a syllable and a clap of the hands.

Play Areas Promote Children's Spatial Understanding

Learning space concepts occurs gradually through the early years. Toddlers gain understanding of spatial extents, boundaries, and pathways as they develop the surety to run, twirl, jump, career around corners, or stop to bend down and pick up something with ease while galloping past an interesting toy. Preschoolers hop, jump, slide, swing from hanging bars, and climb up rope ladders—exploring spatial dimensions ever more bravely.

Some items, like a cardboard box tunnel, allow infants to crawl through and learn about *forward* and *backward*. Such toys as a car or truck with a front and back or a set of wooden toy trains connected by magnets at each end help babies and toddlers learn *front* and *back, longer* and *shorter, first* and *last.* As a toddler steers herself forward, cheerfully mindful of the wonderfully satisfying noise of the Corn Popper toy she pulls behind her, she is maneuvering and navigating through space, sometimes solving the problem of how to continue forward under the legs of a play table.

After three years of age, many children still have not learned to consider bounded space over their heads while getting out from under a table where they have crept to retrieve a toy. To promote spatial learning, a toy barn, house, or fire station is a fine prop. Children learn that the height of the door makes it easy or difficult to bring in a toy horse, stroller, or fire engine.

Play Prompts Children's Reasoning of Cause and Effect

From early infancy, play with various materials supports children's learning of *if-then* reasoning required for early experimentation and scientific thinking. Play with materials can introduce basic concepts in physics and in chemistry. Children learn how liquids mixed together form solutions with different properties, such as a change in color. A spinning gyroscope overcomes gravity, a lever lifts or moves something

heavy, balances measure weights, and an eyedropper sucks in a liquid. As the preschoolers enjoy seesaw (spring-loaded for safety) rides with friends, they learn how important weight and balance are in keeping the seesaw going.

Teachers' preparation of materials for science play arouses intense curiosity and leads to creative play experiments.

Water play is a particularly wondrous activity for experimenting. As children play with wooden and plastic cups, sifters and strainers, and eggbeaters at the water table, they learn that objects float or sink, pour or sprinkle. Teachers' preparation of materials for science play arouses intense curiosity and leads to creative play experiments. Block building is particularly fine for learning causal and space concepts. Smaller blocks seem to balance on bigger ones but not vice versa, no matter how many times a toddler determinedly tries. Toddlers often walk their toy animals down a slide and are not aware of how gravity could help. A preschooler easily depends on the awesome power of gravity as he launches himself down the playground slide. At play, children learn that things can roll if they have rounded sides but not if they have square sides or bumpy sides, like a not-quite-round potato!

Other science concepts learned in play are how to group objects together because of color, shape, size, or pattern design. Children learn too that things exist within larger groups: knives and forks are silverware, sofas and chairs are furniture.

Sociodramatic Play Clarifies the World of *Pretend* versus *Real*

Young children are not too certain what is *real.* For years, some children fervently believe in the tooth fairy and monsters under the bed. Remember the shepherd boy in Menotti's opera, *Amahl and the Night Visitors,* and the three kings on their way to Bethlehem? Amahl comes into the hut and exclaims excitedly to his mother that he has seen a "star with a tail as long as the sky!" A child may not be telling a lie; but imagination does fuel fantasy.

TV programs also encourage belief in fantasy and propel imaginative flights of pretense. After the Mars landing of an exploring robot, one preschooler gave his teacher a toy car, saying, "We are going to Mars, and we can drive our cars on Mars." His teacher nodded agreeably but was quiet. The child added reassuringly, "We just pretending!"

Imagination and pretend play are important giant steps forward in learning how to create dramatic scenarios in complex play with peers. Three-year-olds stirring pop-it beads in a pot pretend to make popcorn to eat. Play promotes the use of a rich imagination. An adult may be nonplussed when a preschooler objects to her sitting down on the couch, explaining that his imaginary playmate is already sitting there. When Talya proclaims she is a superhero and grabs Terry's toy, Terry's firm "My toy!" helps Talya learn the difference between the seemingly unlimited power of a TV fantasy character and the real needs and preferences of a playmate.

Play Enriches Children's Sensory and Aesthetic Appreciation

Listening to music of various genres or exploring color combinations with finger paints can arouse different feelings in children and their appreciation of beauty. Watch the glow on their faces as children carefully add drops of color to a small pan of water and then rejoice in the subtle color-patterned swirls they have created.

Teachers support aesthetic appreciation when they hang up colorful Kente cloth, tape large posters of Monet's *Water Lilies* on the wall, and play fast-paced salsa tunes for dancing. Providing squares of rainbow-colored nylon gauze adds aesthetic pleasure as well as bodily grace to children's dancing. Toddlers blowing and chasing bubbles to catch them in cupped hands is a game that combines aesthetic pleasure with increasing hand dexterity. It also enhances toddlers' abilities to estimate how far and how fast to run to catch a bubble before it pops.

Children delight in watching the unfolding of a fern's graceful fronds or the production of giant flowers by a big, brown amaryllis bulb they have planted. Their eyes widen in awe at the goldfish's graceful flick of its tail while swimming across the aquarium. Children seem primed early on to become lovers of beauty.

Play Extends Children's Attention Span, Persistence, and Sense of Mastery

Some children are cautious and slow in temperament, while others tend to be more impulsive. When children become absorbed in play, even children with shorter attention spans often stretch out their playtimes. Skillful, adult play partners can help children with short attention spans to extend their play. By providing intriguing toys and experiences and encouragement geared to the unique interests of each child, teachers help strengthen children's abilities to prolong play. This ability to focus attention and to persist at challenging learning tasks is a crucial component for later academic success in school.

When play is child initiated, children control the play themes and feel empowered. They come to realize their capabilities of mastering the roles, scenarios, and logistical problems that may arise in the course of sociodramatic play. No kennel for the stuffed puppy? OK, what can we use as a substitute kennel? As playmates arrange props and environments, teachers are superb helpers in facilitating child mastery of play themes.

Play Helps Children Release Emotions and Relieves Separation Anxiety

Learning to express and regulate emotions appropriately is a major challenge for young children. Somctimes they repetitively play out the central emotional concerns in their lives (Honig 1998).

Some children suffer anxious feelings from repeated separations and tearful parting from playmates who have become good friends. Children in military families may have already moved quite a few times, and if parents are deployed, the children may move again to stay with relatives they do not know. Hearing scary talk on the radio and TV may increase children's fears and lead to sadness and distress, bed-wetting, nail-biting, or fighting with peers instead of playing harmoniously. Caring teachers may notice a child's compulsive war play with toys and wisely give the child space, time, and acceptance to act out separation anxieties and fantasies in play, along with extra hugs, lap time, and soothing supportive actions.

Pretend play, even scary war play, provides a deep release for emotions. A toddler may soothingly feed a bottle to a baby doll or put a baby bear to bed in a toy crib. Teachers can build on this tender play to reassure the child how much an absent parent loves the child. Toddlers love telephone talk and gain opportunities to practice social interaction skills. Pretend telephone talk also comforts young children experiencing separation anxieties and lets them feel connected to their families, especially with ones far away.

Teachers need to be attuned to the sometimes worrisome messages that children's play can reveal. By observing how children express troubled feelings in play, teachers may better figure out ways to help young children feel nurtured and safe. After the events of 9/11, many preschoolers built block towers and crashed toy airplanes into them. Children's play provides a valuable window for tuning in to the worries, fears, angers, and happiness in their emotional lives.

Play deepens a child's sense of serenity and joy.

In closing, play deepens a child's sense of serenity and joy. Children digging in the sand at a neighborhood pocket park resemble scruffy cherubs, their faces and arms covered with sand or dirt. Their bodies look so relaxed. One rarely hears them crying.

Tuned-in teachers can shape almost any play experience into an opportunity for children to learn more about the world and how it works. Water play, sand play, block play, ball play, searching for signs with different shapes and colors on a neighborhood walk—all become grist for early learning as well as early pleasure in play.

As teachers promote and encourage play, they enhance children's feelings of security, of being deeply acceptable, of being a welcomed friend. In carving out safe, leisurely, and generous times for children's play, teachers provide the cognitive and social groundwork for children's future learning.

References

Bergen, D., ed. 1998. *Play as a medium for learning and development: A handbook of theory and practice.* Portsmouth, NH: Heinemann.

Honig, A.S. 1982. *Playtime learning games for young children.* Syracuse, NY: Syracuse University Press.

Honig, A.S. 1995. Singing with infants and toddlers. *Young Children* 50(5): 72–78.

Honig, A.S. 1998. Sociocultural influences on sexual meanings embedded in playful experiences. In *Play from birth to twelve and beyond: Contents, perspectives, and meanings,* eds. P.Fromberg & D. Bergen, 338–47. New York: Garland Press.

Honig, A.S., & A. Thompson 1994. Helping toddlers with peer group entry skills. *Zero to Three* 14(5): 15–19.

Johnson, J.E., J.F. Christie, & T.D. Yawkey. 1999. *Play and early childhood development.* 2nd ed. Upper Saddle River, NJ: Allyn & Bacon/Longman/Pearson Education.

Kaplan, L. 1978. *Oneness and separateness.* New York: Simon & Schuster.

Paley, V. 1992. *You can't say you can't play.* Cambridge, MA: Harvard University Press.

Piaget, J. [1951] 1962. *Play, dreams, and imitation in childhood.* New York: Norton.

Shure, M. 1994. *Raising a thinking child: Help your young child to resolve everyday conflicts and get along with others.* New York: Henry Holt.

Smilansky, S., & L. Shefatya. 1990. *Facilitating play: A medium for promoting cognitive, socio-emotional and academic development in young children.* Gaithersburg, MD: Psychosocial and Educational Publications.

ALICE STERLING HONIG, PhD, professor emerita of child development, Syracuse University, New York, has authored more than 450 chapters and articles and more than a dozen books. She teaches annually the National Quality Infant/Toddler Workshop and lectures widely on prosocial and language development and gender patterns in play.

Ready or Not, Here We Come
What It Means to Be a Ready School

PAULA M. DOWKER, WITH LARRY SCHWEINHART, PHD, AND MARIJATA DANIEL-ECHOLS, PHD

In the game hide-and-seek, one player counts to 10 while the others run and hide. Now, depending on how fast the one who is "it" counts, some players may find they are not ready and hiding when that person comes looking for them. The problem of not being ready could stem from many causes: perhaps the player did not have the proper shoes, which made running difficult; maybe the player did not understand the rules and was not sure what to do; or perhaps the player had never played the game before. We educators of young children, prekindergarten through grade 3, encounter many of the same readiness issues when it comes to the children in our classrooms, because each child enters school with a completely different set of experiences and abilities.

Planning effectively for children with diverse backgrounds, learning styles, and school-readiness levels can be daunting. To better understand and respond to such challenges, early elementary educators need to become familiar with what it means to be a ready school, so they can assess and implement strategies to ensure success for all students. Those of us working with young children who will soon be entering school need to provide quality early childhood education and care that extends beyond preschool settings. When children move from high-quality early childhood experiences into ready schools, they benefit from having a strong foundation and access to superior tools with which to continue building upon that foundation.

We all have a stake in seeing that our children's schools are ready schools. A ready school is a comprehensive vision of what a school can do to ensure that all children who enter its doors will fulfill their potential as learners:

The idea of a ready school broadens the definition of school readiness. Instead of only focusing on whether or not children arrive at school ready to learn, a more inclusive definition of readiness also considers whether or not school policies and practices support a commitment to the success of every child. The concept of school readiness must align the best of early childhood practices and elementary education in ways that build upon the strengths of each and locus equally on child outcomes, adult behaviors, and institutional characteristics. It is expected that children should come to school ready to learn and schools should

open their doors able to serve all children. (High/Scope Educational Research Foundation 2006, 1)

Is your school, or the school that the young children you serve, a ready school? Are its classrooms ready classrooms? Consider your answers to the following assessment, which will give you some idea of how to evaluate a school in terms of readiness:

- Does the principal communicate a clear vision for the school—a vision that is committed to the success of every child?
- Are parents of incoming children contacted about registration and school entry three or more months before school starts?
- Do kindergarten teachers communicate with preschool/child care staff about children and curriculum on an ongoing basis?
- Do classrooms have a variety of manipulative materials and supplies for art, building, and hands-on learning?
- Are procedures in place for monitoring the fidelity of implementation of all instructional materials/methods?
- Does the school promote community linkages by making and following up on appropriate referrals of children and families to social service and health agencies?
- Do classroom activities provide accurate, practical, and respectful information regarding peoples' cultural backgrounds and experiences?
- Does the school employ improvement strategies that are based on an assessment of the quality of the classroom as well as children's progress? (High/Scope Educational Research Foundation 2006)

Between 2003 and 2006 the High/Scope Educational Research Foundation, funded by a grant from the W.K. Kellogg Foundation, researched, designed, and developed the Ready School Assessment. The assessment focuses on eight key dimensions that teachers and schools should evaluate when asking, "Are we a ready school?" The work of the National Education Goals Panel (Shore 1998) was an important source in identifying these dimensions. The dimensions were developed after researchers conducted intensive research and reality testing with practitioners throughout the nation. Assessment using the dimensions, listed here, can assist educators in evaluating their individual school's state of readiness:

1. **Leaders and leadership.** The principal, with the assistance of the teachers, advocates for and leads the ready school. For example, the principal encourages teachers to take responsibility for and implement ready school strategies. The principal provides professional development and resources on these strategies.

2. **Transitions.** Teachers, staff, and parent groups work with families, children, and the preschool teachers and caregivers before kindergarten and with families and children during kindergarten to smooth the transition from home to school. For example, teachers and staff at feeder early childhood programs are informed about registration before school starts so they can pass on to families information about kindergarten roundup dates, orientation dates, and any other planned transition activities.

3. **Teacher supports.** Classrooms, schedules, teams, and activities are organized to maximize the support for all adults to work effectively with children during the school day. For example, teachers from feeder early childhood programs (including those not part of the school) are invited to participate in professional development programs along with K–3 staff. This allows *all* adults to work effectively with children in both teaching venues and it allows teachers to share curriculum goals and benchmarks with each other.

4. **Engaging environments.** The school's learning environments employ elements that make them warm and inviting and actively engage children in a variety of learning activities. For example, classrooms have a variety of manipulative materials and supplies for art, building, and hands-on learning.

5. **Effective curricula.** The teachers and school diligently employ educational materials and methods shown to be effective in helping children achieve objectives required for grade-level proficiency. For example, teachers and staff are well informed about and well trained in developmentally appropriate methods and strategies for early childhood learners.

6. **Family, school, and community partnerships.** The teachers and school take specific steps to enhance parents' capacities to foster their children's readiness and to support children's learning in and outside of school. For example, teachers use an open-door policy that allows for, welcomes, and involves families' participation in classroom activities at all times of the day.

7. **Respecting diversity.** The teachers and school help all children succeed by interacting with children and families in ways that are compatible with individual needs, family backgrounds, and life experiences. For example, classrooms include many materials that reflect a variety of cultural backgrounds and experiences. Teachers plan classroom activities that provide accurate, practical, and respectful information regarding peoples' cultural backgrounds, traditions, languages, and experiences.

8. **Assessing progress.** Teachers and staff engage in ongoing improvement based on information that rigorously and systematically assesses classroom experiences, school practices that influence them, and children's progress toward curricular goals. For example, teachers address clearly defined and clearly stated curricular goals for each group/subgroup of children. In addition, the quality of the classroom experiences is assessed using a standardized, systematic approach. This results in teachers taking a focused look at what they are doing and making changes to the classroom experience so all students can achieve success (High/Scope Educational Research Foundation 2006).

A ready school is many things. It is a place where instruction is gauged to meet the learning level of each student, where diversity is welcome, where teachers have the support they need to do their best work for every learner. In this place partnerships between school, families, and community reinforce the education process. Most important, a ready school is a place that builds on its strengths and addresses challenges through the process of focused, ongoing school improvement.

Is your school, or the school that the young children you serve will attend, a ready school? For more information about becoming a ready school or about the Ready School Assessment, please contact Paula Dowker (pdowker@highscope.org) at the High/Scope Educational Research Foundation.

References

High/Scope Educational Research Foundation. 2006. *Ready School Assessment.* Ypsilanti, MI: High/Scope Press. Online: www.readyschool assessment.org.

Shore R. 1998. *Ready Schools.* A report of the Goal 1 Ready Schools Resource Group. Washington, DC: National Education Goals Panel. Online:http://govinfo.library.unt.edu/negp/Reports/readysch.pdf.

Paula Dowker is education specialist at High/Scope Educational Research Foundation in Ypsilanti, Michigan. Paula has been involved in Michigan's public education system for 16 years. She has been a teacher, administrator, and curriculum director. Paula is responsible for the dissemination of information regarding the Ready School Assessment nationwide and also is the designer and facilitator of the Ready School Training modules. **Lawrence J. Schweinhart,** PhD, is president of High/Scope Educational Research Foundation. A former member of the NAEYC Governing Board, Larry served as chair of the NAEYC Program Panel on Quality, Compensation, and Affordability. **Marijata C. Daniel-Echols,** PhD, is chair of the research division at the High/Scope Educational Research Foundation. She has served as the project director for High/Scope's W.K. Kellogg Foundation-funded Ready School Assessment instrument development project.

From *Young Children*, March 2007, pp. 68–70. Copyright © 2007 by National Association for the Education of Young Children. Reprinted by permission.

"Stop Picking On Me!"

What You Need to Know about Bullying

Barbara A. Langham

"Hi, guys," says Robert, the after-school program specialist, greeting his first graders. "Anybody hungry?"

The children take off their backpacks and help themselves to granola bars, apples, and milk. Willie, the smallest boy, gets pushed aside by bigger boys but manages to grab a granola bar before they're all gone.

"Willie is a weenie. Willie is a weenie," chants Jake, a large blond youngster with red cheeks. Two boys behind him chuckle, and most of the other children settle down into eating their snack.

Willie, his chin quivering, turns to Robert in a silent plea for help. Jake sees the gesture and smirks, "Willie is a tattle tale."

If you were Robert, what would you do in this situation?

1. Ignore the teasing. After all, "Kids will be kids."
2. Say to Jake: "Cut it out. Words can hurt, and we don't allow teasing."
3. Take Willie aside. "Hey, if someone is bothering you, you need to learn to stand up for yourself." Brainstorm ways to respond to future taunts.
4. Plan a learning activity on how to stop hurtful behavior. As a group, read and discuss books on teasing and bullying. Empower all children to speak out against hurtful behavior when they see it happen.

Many of us can remember being in situations like the one above when we were children. Or perhaps we ourselves were the target of such behavior. Experts say teasing and bullying are commonplace in schools, not just in the United States but around the world.

Bullying in particular has gained increased attention in recent years. Hundreds of books and research articles have been published on the subject, and at least 30 states have passed anti-bullying legislation (National Conference of School Legislatures 2008).

Why the attention? Research in the aftermath of school shootings, including Columbine High School in Colorado, has found that the shooters had been severely bullied by classmates. A study of school violence by the U.S. Secret Service and U.S. Department of Education found that "almost three-quarters of the attackers felt persecuted, bullied, threatened, attacked or injured by others prior to the incident" (2002).

Among girls, bullying is more likely to take the form of emotional hurt.

Research indicates that boys do most of the bullying, and they target girls as well as other boys. Among girls, bullying is more likely to take the form of emotional hurt, such as spreading hurtful rumors about another girl or excluding her from a group.

Most bullying takes place at school, typically in places with little or no adult supervision, such as the playground, cafeteria, and restroom. According to research, when teachers and other adults see or hear about bullying, they generally do nothing to stop it.

Teasing and bullying begin in the early grades and peak in middle school. The timing is linked to development. By fourth grade, children are comparing themselves to each other and become self-conscious, especially about appearance and ability. Consequently, a perceived difference is sometimes—not always—a trigger for teasing and bullying behavior.

Research findings like these have spurred the call for improved disciplinary policies and prevention efforts in schools as well as after-school programs, youth clubs, and summer camps. The fact that teasing and bullying can show up in the primary grades suggests that the precursors of this behavior may be found in early childhood and that parents and child care professionals also play a role in prevention.

A Continuum of Hurtful Behavior

According to Barri Rosenbluth, director of school-based services at SafePlace, a domestic violence and sexual assault center in Austin, teasing and bullying can be viewed as part of a continuum of intentionally hurtful behavior. At one end of the continuum is hurtful teasing, which can include making fun of someone, name-calling, put-downs, insults, and negative gestures. At the other end is abuse and assault, which can include the use of weapons. Teasing becomes bullying when it is repeated over time. Like teasing, bullying can take many forms—name-calling, threats, hitting—but it usually involves an imbalance of power. The bully is often bigger, older, smarter, or more popular than the targeted child.

Sexual harassment may seem out of place in a discussion of preschool and primary school behavior, but all educators need to be aware of it. According to a study by the American Association of University Women Educational Foundation, one-third of students who experienced sexual harassment said it first occurred in sixth grade or earlier (2001).

Sexual harassment is teasing or bullying of a sexual nature using words, gestures, pictures, or actions. Boys as well as girls can be the targets, and the harassment can be about the body, boy-girl friendships, or speculation about homosexuality. Sexual harassment may occur once or many times.

In the public schools, sexual harassment is serious because it's a form of sex discrimination prohibited by Title IX of the Education Amendments of 1972. Under this law, school officials must take reasonable steps to prevent and eliminate sexual harassment because it "can interfere with a student's academic performance and emotional and physical well being" (Office for Civil Rights 2001).

Tune in to Teasing

Because intent plays a part in defining whether a behavior is hurtful, child development experts might argue that teasing and bullying don't occur until children can understand the feelings of others.

"Preschoolers say funny and absurd things that are not necessarily targeted at anyone," says Judy Freedman, an elementary school social worker, in her book *Easing the Teasing* (2002). "They are often experimenting with words they have recently learned."

Teasing becomes sharper as children expand their vocabulary and improve their verbal skills. "They think it's funny to rhyme a word with someone's name, as in the case of a second-grader who was called 'Fartin' Martin,'" says Freedman. But as children develop empathy, they are less likely to ridicule someone for a name or other qualities beyond a person's control.

Experienced teachers also recognize that much teasing is good-natured and friendly.

Experienced teachers also recognize that much teasing is good-natured and friendly. Best friends may josh each other for fun, and children might tease another child as a sign of welcome into a group.

What's harder to discern is teasing that's iffy, as though the teaser is testing for a reaction. If the targeted child cringes or punches back, the teaser may continue, delighted at finding a hot button. But if the targeted child tosses it off, the two may continue joking around, or the teaser may look for another target.

Experts say teasing becomes hurtful if the teaser intends to be cruel or if the targeted child feels upset, angry, or afraid as a result, regardless of the intent.

How's a teacher to know? "Talk to the targeted child privately," advises Rosenbluth. "Don't just assume the child will come to you." Ask: "What did you feel after Marianne's comment about your freckles?" or "How did you feel when Aaron shoved you?"

Why It Matters

For children targeted by teasers and bullies, school is miserable and frightening. They may experience headaches, stomachaches, bedwetting, and restless sleep. They can feel depressed, inadequate, and lonely. Other children may avoid them, fearing they may also become targets, leaving the targeted child with no friends.

Targeted children may resist going to school out of fear for their safety. They may develop a dislike for school and fall behind their peers in learning. In extreme cases, if the bullying continues into the teen years, students can react by harming themselves or seeking revenge.

Children who do the teasing and bullying are usually popular and confident. But experts say they lack empathy and believe that such behavior is OK, even desirable. They need positive role models and help in learning social skills. Without that, they become at risk for other problem behaviors.

Bullying also affects bystanders. Non-targeted children can feel afraid and vulnerable at school. Their learning may falter as well.

Why It Happens

Many authorities say teasing and bullying are part of the larger issue of aggressive behavior in much of modern life. Studies attribute aggression to media violence, poverty, poor child-rearing practices, abusive home environments, and other factors.

Researchers Pamela Orpinas and Arthur Horne (2006) say the roots of hurtful behavior are better described as *risk factors,* not *causes.* Risk factors refer to personal or environmental characteristics that indicate a greater likelihood of behaving a certain way. For example, harsh parental punishment by itself does not make a child tease and bully others. But several risk factors taken together may indicate a greater tendency to hurt other children.

Orpinas and Horne argue that in addition to risk factors, educators must also consider protective factors—that is, characteristics that help diminish the likelihood of teasing and bullying.

Teachers and caregivers can do a great deal to prevent hurtful behavior, but no one can do it alone. The most effective prevention, says Rosenbluth, is a "caring community."

Assess the Environment

Survey teachers and parents about their perceptions of the climate in your program. Do children enjoy being there? Have they bonded with staff? Do they have friends? Are teasing and bullying an issue? Invite an expert on the subject to speak at a parents meeting and distribute handouts to provide more information. (For free, downloadable tip sheets, see http://stop bullyingnow.hrsa.gov/index.asp)

Talk with officials in public and private schools in your neighborhood. What are they doing about bullying prevention? Consult with leaders of nearby libraries, parks, and youth clubs about the programs they offer. Look for ways to collaborate in prevention efforts.

Examine your policies that deal with child guidance and supervision, particularly in your after-school program. According to the authors of *Quit it!* (1998), a teacher's guide for teasing and bullying prevention, a clearly stated, consistent school-wide policy is "an effective tool in combating teasing and bullying."

Rosenbluth, who has trained public school administrators and teachers in bullying prevention, says the ideal school policy specifically prohibits hurtful teasing and bullying. The policy also provides a way to document students' and parents' complaints, outlines an investigation process, and provides a stay-away agreement to separate the bully and the targeted child.

As you review policies, inform everyone in your school community—board members, teachers, staff, volunteers, and parents. Provide training so teachers and staff recognize and respond appropriately to hurtful behavior. Offer a workshop for parents to help them talk with their children about the subject.

Set Clear Rules and Consequences

As children learn social skills, they are influenced by many factors. Perhaps the most powerful is the behavior they see in adults and other children. If they see adults and playmates acting with kindness and respect, children are likely to develop kind and respectful behavior.

Another powerful influence is culture. Children learn how they are expected to behave from home life, their racial or ethnic group, church, and community life. They get messages from stories, television, toys, games, sports, clothing, advertising, and store displays. Research has shown that boys are often encouraged to take risks, seek adventure, and be aggressive. Girls, on the other hand, are encouraged to be nurturing, show their emotions, and seek protection.

When boys ridicule or shove someone and get away with it, children learn that boys are behaving in a normal and accepted way. The same is true when girls whisper hurtful things about another girl and exclude her from their play.

Counteract these influences by modeling desired behavior and challenging gender stereotypes. Address gender put-downs just as you would address racial or ethnic slurs. Encourage boys to express their feelings and be nurturing, and urge girls to take reasonable risks and stand up for themselves.

Rethink areas or times when supervision may be lacking, such as nap time and outdoor play. Train staff to improve the way they monitor areas, and consider involving other staff or volunteers as extra eyes and ears.

Review with children the rules for appropriate behavior and the consequences for breaking rules. Younger children often need reminders. About age 4 or 5, you can engage children in discussing the reasons behind rules and get their input on setting rules for the classroom.

An emphasis on rules may bring an increase in tattling. Experienced teachers know that some children use tattling to get attention or get another child in trouble. They handle it by having children write their complaints and drop them in a tattle box, which the teacher later reads. It may also help to consider the tattle-versus-tell guideline: Is the child trying to get someone in trouble (tattling) or get someone out of trouble (telling)?

Tattling may also be a way for children to test what a rule is and how you will enforce it. You can confirm (or deny) the rule and assure the child that you will handle it. If the information indicates a child is at risk of physical or emotional harm, you need to deal with the situation immediately.

Teach Positive Social Skills

Review your curriculum unit on friends. Help children learn effective ways of joining a play group, making conversation, and sharing interests. When children squabble, teach problem-solving techniques.

Offer cooperative games and learning opportunities. Call attention to children's positive behaviors such as sharing, listening, and helping when you see them happening.

Encourage teachers and after-school caregivers to learn about each child in the group as an individual.

Encourage teachers and after-school caregivers to learn about each child in the group as an individual. Knowing every child's personality, friendships, and behavior patterns will help you distinguish between friendly and hurtful teasing, and between rough play and bullying.

In group time, read books on teasing and bullying. Engage children in discussion: How did the targeted child feel? How did the bully feel? How did the bystanders feel? What happened to stop the hurtful behavior? What might you do if you saw the same thing happen to a classmate?

Brainstorm with children about what they might do to help someone being teased or bullied. If they feel safe, they might tell the bully to stop or invite the targeted child to play with them. If they don't feel safe, they might tell an adult.

Emphasize that they should not just stand and watch. Explain that speaking up takes courage and that telling an adult about hurtful behavior is not tattling. Children can ask a friend to help befriend the targeted child or go with them to tell an adult. Explain that the adult will listen and do something.

Intervene in Hurtful Behavior

When hurtful teasing and bullying occur, adults have a responsibility to stop it. Ignoring hurtful behavior can inadvertently promote it and all its negative effects. Some tips:

- Stand between the teasers or bullies and the targeted child. Do not send any participants or bystanders away. Using a moderate tone of voice, state what you heard or saw happening. State that teasing and bullying are against school rules.
- Reassure the targeted child. Don't force the child to answer questions in front of the other children. If the child is upset, talk in private. Increase supervision of the child to make sure bullying does not happen again. Give the child time to express anger or sadness. Help the child find classmates who can offer support.
- Speak to the bystanders. If they did nothing, say, "Maybe you didn't know what to do." Explain that teasing and bullying are "not cool." Suggest that next time they could tell the bully to stop, involve the targeted child in play, or go to an adult for help. If they acted appropriately, acknowledge the behavior without lavish, public praise.
- Impose consequences on the teasers or bullies, as outlined in your policy. Make sure the consequences are reasonable and related to the behavior.
 Be prepared to hear defenses such as, "I didn't mean to hurt him," or "I just called him a name." Respond by restating what happened: "It did hurt" or "Name-calling is hurtful."
- Allow children time to cool off. Don't force an apology. Watch the children closely for possible future hurtful behavior. Help them learn to take responsibility for their actions and offer activities to help them develop empathy.
- If appropriate, notify parents of children who are involved. Set up a parent-teacher conference and discuss social skills. For the targeted child: "How can we help Willie make friends and develop more self-confidence?" For the teaser: "How can we help Jake understand that name-calling is hurtful?"

It's Not a One-Shot Solution

It should be clear that in the opening example about Willie and Jake, ignoring hurtful behavior is not the answer. It should also be clear that stopping hurtful behavior is not a one-person, one-time fix.

Reducing aggressive behavior in school is everyone's problem and requires a long-term solution.

Reducing aggressive behavior in school is everyone's problem and requires a long-term solution. After-school caregivers

What NOT to Do

- Many people believe the solution to bullying is to urge the targeted child to fight back. It's not uncommon to hear stories about this method's success: "I hit Joey in the mouth, and he never bothered me again."
 While fighting back may work on occasion, it has drawbacks. The targeted child may suffer injury, or the incident may set in motion a cycle of revenge attacks. Most important, urging children to fight back reinforces the message that some problems can best be solved with violence.
- Well-meaning adults may suggest having the bully and targeted child sit down together and work out their "conflict." This suggestion is misguided for three reasons.
 First, having the bully sit face-to-face with the targeted child may put the child at further risk of humiliation and harm.
 Second, the behavior is not about conflict any more than child abuse is about disagreement. The teaser or bully intends to inflict harm. Calling it a conflict sends the message that both children are partly responsible.
 Third, there is no evidence that conflict resolution or peer mediation is effective in stopping bullying.

U.S. Department of Health and Human Services, Health Resources and Services Administration. Stop Bullying Now campaign. "Misdirections in Bullying Prevention and Intervention," http://stopbullyingnow.hrsa.gov/index.asp

can help children learn positive social skills and intervene in hurtful behaviors. Early childhood educators can work with parents to create a caring environment at home and at school that builds a foundation for learning.

Everyone agrees children should feel safe in school. They need to feel at ease and free to play and learn. They cannot learn if they feel threatened or afraid of their peers.

Books for Children

Ludwig, Trudy. 2003. *My Secret Bully.* Ashland, Ore.:
 Riverbend Books.
 Monica is having headaches and stomachaches. Under questioning from her mother, Monica starts crying and reveals that a longtime friend has been saying bad things about her to other girls. Mom teaches Monica how to stand up for herself.
McCain, Becky Ray. 2001. *Nobody Knew What To Do:*
 A Story About Bullying. Morton Grove, Ill.: Albert
 Whitman & Co.
 Children observe bullying at recess. The next day when the targeted child doesn't come to school, one boy reports the incident to his teacher. Both the teacher and the principal take action.

Romain, Trevor. 1997. *Bullies Are a Pain in the Brain.* Minneapolis, Minn.: Free Spirit Publishing.

This popular children's book author explains in simple words and black-and-white cartoons what bullying is and how to avoid it. He addresses most of the book to targeted children but devotes a few pages to bullies and ends with a message to teachers and parents.

Thomas, Pat. 2000. *Stop Picking on Me: A First Look at Bullying.* Hauppauge, N.Y.: Barron's Educational Series, Inc.

Using compassionate words and aided by vivid watercolor illustrations, author Pat Thomas explains what bullying is and how to stop it.

Books for Teachers and Parents

Bott, C.J. 2004. *The Bully in the Book and in the Classroom.* Lanham, Md.: Scarecrow Press.

This book contains annotated bibliographies in four sections: grades K-3, 4-6, 7-8 and 9-12. In addition, the author spotlights 8-10 books in each section with a brief summary and cover photo as well as discussion questions to use with children.

Froscshl, Merle; Barbara Sprung, and Nancy Mullin-Rindler. 1998. *Quit it! A Teacher's Guide on Teasing and Bullying for Use with Students in Grades K-3.* A joint publication of Educational Equity Concepts Inc., New York; Wellesley College Center for Research on Women, Wellesley, Mass.; and the National Education Association, Washington, D.C.

Lee, Chris. 2004. *Preventing Bullying in Schools: A Guide for Teachers and Other Professionals.* Thousand Oaks, Calif.: SAGE Publications, Inc.

Mullin, Nancy. 2003. *Selected Bibliography About Teasing and Bullying for Grades K-8: Revised and Expanded Edition.* Wellesley, Mass.: Wellesley College Center for Research on Women.

For more than three decades, the Wellesley Centers for Research on Women have studied issues such as gender equity in education, sexual harassment, and child care, resulting in changes in practices and policies. This bibliography can be ordered for $15 at http://www.wcwonline.org.

References

American Association of University Women Education Foundation. 2001. *Hostile Hallways: Bullying, Teasing, and Sexual Harassment in School* (p.25). http://www.aauw.org/research/upload/hostilehallways.pdf.

Freedman, Judy S. 2002. *Easing the Teasing: Helping Your Child Cope with Name-Calling, Ridicule, and Verbal Bullying.* New York: Contemporary Books.

National Conference of State Legislatures. 2008. *School Bullying.* http://www.ncsl.org/programs/educ/bullyingoverview.htm.

Office for Civil Rights, U.S. Department of Education. 2001. "Revised Sexual Harassment Guidance," http://www.ed.gov/about/offices/list/ocr/docs/shguide.html.

Orpinas, Pamela, and Arthur Horne. 2006. *Bullying Prevention: Creating a Positive School Climate and Developing Social Competence.* Washington, D.C.: American Psychological Association.

U.S. Department of Health and Human Services, Health Resources and Services Administration. Stop Bullying Now campaign. http://stopbullyingnow.hrsa.gov/index.asp.

Developmentally Appropriate Child Guidance: Helping Children Gain Self-Control

WILL MOSIER, EdD

Dealing with disruptive behavior in the classroom is one of the most difficult issues an early childhood educator faces. In trying to redirect or extinguish disruptive behavior, teachers need to use developmentally appropriate practices as laid out by the National Association for the Education of Young Children (NAEYC).

According to these practices, the purpose of child guidance, or discipline, is not to control young children but to help them learn to be cooperative. The most effective techniques help children learn how to accept responsibility for their actions and empower them to exercise self-control.

Discipline should not be punishing. Instead, it should provide children with learning experiences that nurture an understanding of social consciousness. Those learning experiences include participating in generating class rules, receiving positive reinforcement for pro-social behavior, experiencing the natural and logical consequences of their behavior, and observing adults in pro-social, person-to-person interactions. Ultimately, any child guidance technique must nurture each child's social, emotional, and cognitive development.

Discipline should not be punishing.

Involve Children in Creating Classroom Rules

An important initial step in ensuring a developmentally appropriate pro-social environment is to create a set of classroom rules in cooperation with all the children in your room on the first day of the school year. A cooperative approach is the key.

With 3-year-olds, you may need to propose two or three simple rules, explain the reasons behind them, and invite their cooperation. By the time they turn 4, most children will be able to propose rules and discuss them. Ideally, classroom rules are not teacher-dictated. They must evolve from ideas discussed with and agreed upon by the children.

By encouraging children to participate in setting rules, you are laying the foundation for a community of learners who follow rules, not because they will be punished by the teacher if they don't, but because they feel a part of that which they help to create. Using a democratic group process helps children to develop moral reasoning.

Creating rules helps clarify behavior expectations. If children are to know what behavior is expected, the guidelines must be stated as positive actions. Help children with wording that says what they are expected to do, not what they can't do.

For example, instead of a rule that says "No running," the rule would read "Running is an outside activity. I walk inside." Other examples:

"I touch people gently."

"I talk in a quiet tone of voice."

"When I finish with an activity, I put it back where I found it."

"I place trash in the wastebasket."

Once the rules have been established, create opportunities to practice them. During the first few weeks of the year, reinforce the class rules through role playing, singing songs, and reading children's books about the rules.

In addition, you must model the rules and socially competent behavior in general. Children best learn rules by seeing them practiced by the adults in their lives. Modeling pro-social behavior demonstrates how human beings should interact with one another. It reinforces behaviors that are respectful of others.

Use Positive Reinforcement

Make a commitment to verbally reinforcing the socially competent behavior you expect in young children. Use positive feedback to reinforce prosocial, productive behavior, and to minimize disruptive behavior.

To reinforce pro-social behavior, simply look for it. When it happens, use a three-part "I" message, as explained below, to reinforce it. When disruptive behavior occurs, use positive feedback to draw attention to classroom behavior that you would like to see. Avoid focusing on the disruptive behavior.

Reinforcing pro-social behavior should not be confused with praise. Praise can damage a child's self-esteem by making a child feel pressured into attaining arbitrary standards. Praise implies an objective value judgment. For example: "Josh, your painting is beautiful." If praise does not continue, Josh may perceive that his value, as a person, is diminishing. A young child may start to assume that a person's value is directly tied to an ability to produce a specific product.

A better alternative is recognition and encouragement. Encouragement is specific and focuses on the process the child used to produce the artwork or how the child is feeling at the moment. For example: "I like the effort you put into your picture" or "I see that you're happy with the red lines and green circles." In these examples, neither the child nor the product is labeled good or bad. The focus is on the process or behavior. When stated as positive affirmations, words of encouragement can help nurture self-esteem.

An encouragement system can also use tokens as positive feedback. For example, children could be offered tokens when displaying behavior you want to reinforce. The tokens are not used as rewards, and they are not redeemed for some tangible prize. Additionally, the tokens would never be taken away once given to a child.

This system encourages a child to repeat desired behavior and will tend to stimulate intrinsic motivation. When a child sees or hears a classmate being reinforced for a particular behavior, the attention given to the targeted behavior increases the odds that the disruptive child will be motivated to try the same behavior.

Examples of developmentally appropriate tokens are construction paper leaves that can be placed on a personalized paper tree, and paper ice cream scoops that can be stacked on a paper ice cream cone. Every child would have a tree trunk or ice cream cone on a designated bulletin board. Early in the year the children would cut out leaves or ice cream scoops and place them in a large container near the board. When a teacher observes a desired behavior, she states the behavior, how she feels about it, and invites the child to get a token. "Tyron, when I see you picking up those blocks, I feel so excited, I invite you to put a leaf on your tree!" Phrasing a message in this manner tends to encourage intrinsic motivation.

Use Natural and Logical Consequences, Not Punishment

Natural and logical consequences can effectively motivate self-control without inflicting the cognitive, social, and emotional damage caused by punishment. When appropriate, allow natural and logical consequences to redirect inappropriate or disruptive behavior. This will encourage self-direction and intrinsic motivation.

Assume, for example, that Melissa leaves her painting on the floor instead of putting it on the drying rack, and a minute later another child accidentally steps on the artwork and ruins it. Melissa ends up with a torn painting as a natural consequence.

Use logical consequences when natural consequences are not practical. If a child is throwing blocks, for example, a logical consequence would be to lose the privilege of playing in the block area for a set time. Children need the opportunity to connect their behavior and its consequences. Using logical consequences allows children to learn from their experience.

By contrast, punishment relies on arbitrary consequences. It imposes a penalty for wrongdoing. For example, "Steven, because you hit Johnny, you don't get to sit in my lap for story time." Loss of lap time here is an arbitrary consequence, unrelated to the hitting behavior.

Being punished for unacceptable behavior conditions young children to limit behavior out of fear and leads to lowered self-esteem. Experiencing logical consequences, on the other hand, allows children to see how to achieve desired goals and avoid undesired consequences.

Wanting attention is not a bad thing.

Inappropriate, disruptive behavior is typically motivated by the need to gain attention. Wanting attention is not a bad thing. The issue is how to gain it. Children need to learn that they can choose to satisfy needs in socially acceptable ways. Logical consequences help young children become self-correcting and self-directed.

Model Clear, Supportive Communication

Supporting a child's cognitive, emotional, and social development requires well-honed communication skills. When talking to young children about behavior, differentiate between the child and the behavior. It's the behavior that's "good" or "bad," not the child.

"I" Messages

Speaking in three-part "I" messages is an effective tool for keeping your focus on the child's behavior. This is a three-part, non-blaming statement that helps a young child hear which behaviors are not acceptable without damaging the child's social, emotional, or cognitive development. "I" messages can be used to address inappropriate or disruptive behavior as well as to reinforce socially competent and positive behavior.

Use this template for constructing "I" messages that encourage pro-social behavior: "When I see you —— (identify acceptable behavior), it makes me feel —— (identify your feelings about the behavior) that I want to —— (identify what you want to do). For example: "Wow, Tara, when I see you turning the pages carefully as you read your book, I feel so happy I want to give you a high five."

To extinguish disruptive behavior, adapt the template as follows: "Tara, when I see you hit Mary, I get so sad that I am going to keep you with me until I think you understand about touching people gently."

Empathic Understanding

Empathy is the ability to identify with someone else's feelings. As early childhood educators, we are responsible for nurturing the development of emotional intelligence in young children. We need to reinforce behavior that is sensitive to the emotional needs of others.

An example of when to use this skill is when children are tattling. Children tattle as a passive-aggressive way to solicit adult attention. Assume, for example, that Takesha complains, "Johnny hit me." A developmentally appropriate response would be "You didn't like that, did you?"

This type of response does three things: 1) The focus remains on the child's feelings, rather than on the actions of another child. 2) It models words that help a child express what she is feeling. 3) It encourages the child to talk about how she feels, which helps her develop enhanced awareness of her feelings and pro-social ways to express them.

Attentive Listening

Children need to feel they are being listened to. To communicate that you are paying attention to a child, maintain eye contact, smile attentively, and use appropriate, gentle touch to convey that you have unconditional positive regard for the child. Use the same communication skills with children that you want others to use with you.

Common listening errors that adults make when interacting with young children are analyzing the child's words rather than focusing on the child's feelings, rushing the child through the expression of feelings, and interrupting the child's expressing of feelings. A teacher displaying impatience, for example, can stifle language development and discourage a child from sharing feelings. But a teacher who listens attentively helps children develop emotional intelligence.

Be Consistent

A critical factor for successfully implementing developmentally appropriate child guidance is consistency. You need to enforce rules consistently, even when it may be easier to look the other way.

Children need to know what is expected of them. They have difficulty adjusting to unexpected change. When they display disruptive behavior, keep in mind that it may have been conditioned into them since toddlerhood. It's unrealistic to assume that it will be extinguished in just one day. Behavior reinforced prior to the child's being exposed to your classroom will take time to reshape. Don't expect an overnight change.

You can change disruptive behavior by using a consistent, systematic process, such as the 12 levels of intervention.

Developing self-control is a process. Throughout the process early childhood educators must demonstrate considerable patience and be consistent in reinforcing productive, socially competent behavior.

References

Adams, S. K. 2005. *Promoting Positive Behavior: Guidance Strategies for Early Childhood Settings.* Columbus, Ohio: Pearson/Merrill/Prentice Hall.

American Academy of Pediatrics. 2007. Discipline for Young Children. Retrieved April 23, 2007, from American Academy of Pediatrics website, www.aap.org.

Bredekamp, S. and C. Copple (Eds.). 2009. *Developmentally Appropriate Practice in Early Childhood Programs, 3rd Edition.* Washington, D.C.: National Association for the Education of Young Children (NAEYC).

Cangelosi, J. S. 2000. *Classroom Management Strategies: Gaining and Maintaining Students' Cooperation,* 4th Edition. New York: John Wiley & Sons, Inc.

DiGiulio, R. 2000. *Positive Classroom Management,* 2nd Edition. Thousand Oaks, Calif.: Corwin Press, Inc.

Essa, E. 1999. *A Practical Guide to Solving Preschool Behavior Problems,* 4th Edition. New York: Delmar Publishers.

Feeney, S. and N. K. Freeman. 1999. *Ethics and the Early Childhood Educator: Using the NAEYC Code.* Washington, D.C.: NAEYC.

Ferris-Miller, Darla. 2007. *Positive Child Guidance,* 5th Edition. Clifton Park, N. Y.: Thomson Delmar Learning.

Gartrell, D. 2004. *The Power of Guidance: Teaching Social-Emotional Skills in Early Childhood Classrooms.* Washington, D.C.: NAEYC.

Menke-Paciorek, K. 2002. *Taking Sides: Clashing Views on Controversial Issues in Early Childhood Education.* Guilford, Conn.: McGraw-Hill.

NAEYC, Division of Early Childhood of the Council for Exceptional Children, and National Board for Professional Teaching Standards. 1996. *Guidelines for Preparation of Early Childhood Professionals.* Washington, D.C.: NAEYC.

Mosier, W. (Ed.). 2005. *Exploring Emotional Intelligence with Young Children: An Annotated Bibliography of Books About Feelings.* Dayton, Ohio: Dayton Association for Young Children.

NAEYC. 1999. *NAEYC Position Statements.* Washington, D.C.: NAEYC.

NAEYC. 1998. *Accreditation Criteria and Procedures.* Washington, D.C.: NAEYC.

NAEYC. 1998. *Early Childhood Teacher Education Guidelines.* Washington, D.C.: NAEYC.

NAEYC. 1999. *The NAEYC Code of Ethical Conduct.* Washington, D.C.: NAEYC.

Rand, M. K. 2000. *Giving It Some Thought: Cases for Early Childhood Practice.* Washington, D.C.: NAEYC.

WILL MOSIER, EdD, is an associate professor in teacher education at Wright State University in Dayton, Ohio. He is a licensed independent marriage and family therapist in Dayton.

From *Texas Child Care Quarterly,* Spring 2009, pp. 2–5. Copyright © 2009 by Texas Child Care Quarterly. Reprinted by permission.

Fostering Positive Transitions for School Success

JAYMA FERGUSON MCGANN AND PATRICIA CLARK, PHD

It is the week before school starts, and Ridgeview Elementary is holding a Popsicle Night for children entering kindergarten and their families. As families arrive in the school cafeteria, the principal and a kindergarten teacher welcome each kindergarten child with a T-shirt bearing the school name and logo.

The children excitedly greet their former preschool teachers, who also attend. With their families, the children choose from the variety of activities prepared by the preschool and kindergarten teachers. At an appointed time, the principal gathers the children and reads to them a story about going to kindergarten. Afterward, the families follow the kindergarten teachers to the children's new classrooms for a visit and short talk about kindergarten. The evening ends with Popsicles for everyone.

W hy is it that fewer than 20 percent of U.S. schools have transition practices in place to support children entering kindergarten and welcome their families (Love et al. 1992)? This is an important transition for young children, and its success has a lasting effect on children's school success in later years (Alexander & Entwisle 1988; Ensminer & Slusarcick 1992; Early, Pianta, & Cox 1999; Ramey et al. 2000).

Clearly, educators, schools, and communities must work together to ensure that young children's entry into kindergarten and elementary school is a smooth passage rather than a rocky road. It seems well worth the effort to find ways to support children and families during this crucial transition.

Indiana Steps up to the Challenge

The Indiana Department of Education, through the Ready Schools Initiative, works with 12 communities across the state to help local elementary schools support children's transitions to kindergarten. The communities range from large cities with dozens of elementary schools to small towns and rural areas with one school serving an entire county.

The guiding question has been, "What can we do—in early childhood programs, in elementary schools, with families, and in the community—to facilitate children's successful transition into kindergarten and the elementary grades?" While each community addresses the issue differently based on its resources and needs, in Indiana we have pinpointed some common concerns and found a number of ways to address the transition process.

Encouraging Successful Transitions

Activities for improving children's transitions to school fall into two broad categories: (1) improving connections between early childhood programs and elementary schools, and (2) reaching out to children and families before children enter kindergarten.

Connections between Early Childhood Programs and Schools

Preschool programs and elementary schools need to find ways to communicate. Kindergarten teachers need to know about the early childhood programs their new kindergartners attended, and preschool teachers need to know about kindergarten teachers' expectations for the children. Here are some of the ways the Indiana Ready Schools communities encourage connections:

- Kindergarten teachers visit early childhood programs to get a better idea about the programs, their curricula, and the children.
- Preschool teachers visit kindergarten classrooms, often with the children who will be going to the kindergarten.
- Kindergarten and preschool teachers share dinner and conversation to discuss issues important to both.
- Elementary school districts incorporate procedures for obtaining records from the variety of programs children attend. Schools prepare and distribute to early childhood programs parent permission forms to allow the programs to transfer children's records to the school.
- Communities provide families with a pamphlet that they can read and complete to communicate personal information about their child. These pamphlets are distributed at community fairs, through prekindergarten programs, and

A Read-Aloud for Families

A number of principals read *The Kissing Hand,* by Audrey Penn, at family-welcoming events in Indiana. Parents with tears in their eyes have attested to the power of this story about a young raccoon preparing to go to kindergarten.

Remember, a child going off to kindergarten can be as big a step for the family as it is for the child.

at kindergarten registration, and then are returned to the kindergarten teacher.

- School districts involve early childhood teachers who work in programs outside the schools, as well as those within the schools, and kindergarten teachers in joint professional development experiences.

Connections between Schools and Families

The extent to which families are involved in their children's education is a strong predictor of children's academic success (Henderson & Berla 1994). To facilitate family-school communication and linkages, ready schools reach out to families, establish links *before* the first day of school, and make personal contacts (Pianta & Walsh 1996). However, typical elementary school transition practices often involve experiences taking place *after* the start of school and/or making contact through flyers, brochures, and group open houses.

Here are some of the things that the Indiana Ready Schools communities do to reach out to families before kindergarten:

- Special events held before the school year begins welcome incoming kindergarten children and families. The events often happen in the evening and include a light supper, activities for children and families together, an opportunity to meet the kindergarten teachers and visit the classrooms, and the principal reading a story aloud (see "A Read-Aloud for Families")
- Elementary schools invite preschoolers and their families to Family Night during the school year before the children's kindergarten entry.
- Teachers make home visits before school begins to the families whose children will be starting kindergarten in the fall.
- Communities distribute brochures, videos, and home activity calendars to children and families at community events, through pediatricians and libraries, and with the help of community agencies that work with families (housing authority, social service agencies, etc.). The resources emphasize the importance of the early years and encourage families to contact their local elementary school before their child enters kindergarten.

Conclusion

Nearly half of all kindergarten teachers nationally report that 50 percent of children experience some degree of difficulty in the transition to formal schooling and 16 percent face serious adjustment

problems (Rimm-Kaufman, Pianta, & Cox 2000). Strategies to prepare children for change and address the challenges of adjustment can help ensure that children's transitions to school are positive.

The transition to kindergarten is a process among partners rather than an event happening to a child. According to Pianta and Kraft-Sayre, "most important for the transition process are the relationships—those between children and teachers, parents and teachers, children and their peers, and children and their parents" (1999, 52). Effective practices are planned locally, taking into consideration children's cultural backgrounds and the multiple characteristics of the community, including family income levels, cultures, physical location and resources. Using what we know about young children and transitions, teachers, schools, and communities can adapt strategies to local needs and resources to promote children's successful transition to kindergarten and school success in the years after.

References

Alexander, K., & D. Entwisle. 1988. Achievement in the first two years of school: Patterns and processes. *Monographs of the Society for Research in Child Development* 53 (1): 157.

Early, D., R. Pianta, & M. Cox. 1999. Kindergarten teachers and classrooms: A transition context. *Early Education and Development* 10 (1): 25–46.

Ensminer, M., & A. Slusarcick. 1992. Paths to high school graduation or dropout: A longitudinal study of a first-grade cohort. *Sociological Education* 65: 95–113.

Henderson, A., & N. Berla. 1994. *A new generation of evidence: The family is critical to student achievement.* Columbia, MD: National Committee for Citizens in Education.

Love, J., M.E. Logue, J.V. Trudeau, & K. Thayer. 1992. *Transitions to kindergarten in American schools.* U.S. Department of Education report. ED 344693. Hampton, NH: RMC Research Corporation.

Pianta, R., & M. Kraft-Sayre. 1999. Parents' observations about their children's transitions to kindergarten. *Young Children* 54 (3): 47–52.

Pianta, R., & D. Walsh. 1996. *High-risk children in schools: Constructing sustaining relationships.* New York: Routledge.

Ramey, C., S. Ramey, M. Phillips, R. Lanzi, C. Brezausek, C. Katholi, & S. Snyder. 2000. *Head Start children's entry into public school: A report on the National Head Start/Public School Early Childhood Transition Demonstration Study.* Washington, DC: Head Start Bureau.

Rimm-Kaufman, S., R. Pianta, & M. Cox. 2000. Teachers' judgments of problems in the transition to kindergarten. *Early Childhood Research Quarterly* 15 (2): 147–66.

JAYMA FERGUSON MCGANN is director of the Division of Prime Time in the Indiana Department of Education, where she has worked for 10 years. She is responsible for the state's early childhood pre-K to grade 3 initiatives, including Foundations for Young Children and Ready Schools, and issues related to kindergarten and early intervention. E-mail: jferguso@ doe.state.in.us. **PATRICIA CLARK,** PhD, is an associate professor in the Department of Elementary Education at Ball State University in Muncie, Indiana. She has worked for the past four years with the Indiana Department of Education on the Ready Schools Initiative and is currently researching its impact. E-mail: pclark@bsu.edu.

A Multinational Study Supports Child-Initiated Learning

Using the Findings in Your Classroom

JEANNE E. MONTIE, JILL CLAXTON, AND SHANNON D. LOCKHART

Scenarios like these are found in preschool classrooms all over the world. In a new longitudinal study, researchers observed and followed five thousand four-year-olds and their teachers in preschools and child care centers in 15 countries and diverse cultures. Across all countries, they identified certain classroom practices that related to better language and cognitive skills at age seven, as well as other practices associated later with poorer language and cognitive skills.

Sponsored by the International Association for the Evaluation of Educational Achievement (IEA), the IEA Preprimary Project (Olmsted & Montie 2001; Weikart, Olmsted, & Montie 2003; Montie, Xiang, & Schweinhart 2007) is a multinational study of unprecedented size and scope (see "The IEA Preprimary Project"). At age seven, in primary school, more than eighteen hundred children from 10 of the participating countries had follow-up assessments.

The study affirms that preschool teachers' educational backgrounds and classroom practices matter, that how teachers organize their classrooms and learning activities makes a difference. Four findings, consistent across countries, emerged. At age seven, the children

- whose preprimary teachers or caregivers had had more years of education had higher language scores;
- who had more opportunities in preschool to choose their own activities, rather than spending their time in personal care (such as hand washing, eating, or dressing) and group social activities (like show-and-tell), had higher language scores;
- who spent less time in whole group activities at age four had higher cognitive scores;
- who were in preschool classrooms with a greater number and variety of materials had higher cognitive scores.

The seven-year-olds did better on language assessments if their preschool settings had emphasized free-choice activities and if their teachers had had more years of education.

In other words, the seven-year-olds did better on language assessments if their preschool settings had emphasized free-choice activities and if their teachers had had more years of education. They did better on cognitive assessments if they had spent more preschool time in small group activities, by themselves, or with one or two other children and if they had

The IEA Preprimary Project

The International Association for the Evaluation of Educational Achievement (IEA), a nongovernmental, nonprofit organization of research institutions in more than 50 countries, is well known for its sponsorship of cross-national research in education. The IEA Preprimary Project is its first cross-national study of preschool education. Fifteen countries took part in a preprimary observational study. Ten of those countries (including Finland, Greece, Hong Kong [SAR], Indonesia, Ireland, Italy, Poland, Spain [Catalonia], Thailand, and the United States) participated in the longitudinal study reported here.

The High/Scope Educational Research Foundation served as the international coordinating center for the study. More information about the study is online at www.highscope.org/Content.asp?ContentID=256.

As the teacher, Maria, scans the room during free-choice time, she notes the high level of activity and chatter. Three of the four-year-olds are in the block area, building a garbage truck. Each child offers an idea and all eventually agree to use blocks for the truck body and materials from the art area for "garbage." Now, they hunt for items to serve as the steering wheel and control knobs.

In the house area, a few children pretend to cook dinner using acorns and pinecones, while others make playdough cookies.

A small group gathers to watch the computer screen as two children manipulate the controls. Much discussion ensues as the children consider how to sequence pictures so the volcano will erupt.

The sound of banging diverts Maria's attention to the woodworking table, where a boy and a girl are splitting nuts with hammers and a vise grip. They count the number of nuts they are going to feed the squirrels during outside time.

Maria turns her attention to the art area, where two friends are writing letters to their parents and decorating them with glue, felt, sequins, and foil. They ask Maria how to spell *love, blue,* and *thank you.*

In another preschool, Barbara announces to her class, "Time for show-and-tell!" Seventeen four-year-olds rush to their backpacks to retrieve the items they brought from home and then gather in a circle on the rug.

Barbara asks Paul, "What did you bring today?" Paul stands, holds out a spotted horse, and says that his grandma got it for him. Barbara asks if anyone has a question for Paul. No one responds.

She asks Kim, seated next to Paul, "What did you bring with you today?" Without speaking, Kim holds out her hand, showing a square plastic container. Barbara asks, "What's inside?" Kim doesn't answer. Before Barbara can ask Kim another question, José says, "I didn't see!" and two other children begin talking about why they need a blanket from the house area to cover up the figurines they've brought from home.

For about 30 minutes Barbara continues around the circle, asking each child in turn to present her or his item. Meanwhile, many of the children stare out the window, play with the toys they brought, or talk to a neighbor. Barbara finds herself stopping frequently to ask for their attention.

access to a greater number and variety of materials (Montie, Xiang, & Schweinhart 2006).

It is striking that these relationships between classroom practices and children's skills are found in countries with very different cultures (Ireland and Indonesia, for example). As might be expected, other findings from the study are more complex and vary from one country to another, but the cross-cultural consistency of these four findings is significant. Within the world's diversity, there are common threads that guide development and offer clues as to how to best support children's learning.

Interpreting the Findings for Your Classroom

The fact that teachers' education is positively linked to children's language skills makes intuitive sense and is supported by other research in both home and preschool settings. Children learn language by hearing it and using it. Research (Hart & Risley 1995) shows that parents with higher levels of education use more words and more complex language with their children, and the same is likely to be true for teachers. Teachers with higher levels of education are more likely to introduce rare words—words that children don't encounter every day—and to engage in analytical conversations with children (Dickinson 2001b).

In this study, teachers and care-givers' average years of education ranged from 10 to 16 across the countries. In some countries, there were caregivers who had had as few as three or four years of education.

> The informal nature of free play allows teachers to engage children in conversation specific to their play and to introduce new vocabulary relevant to the children's interests.

Concerning the other two findings of this study, what is it about the nature of free-choice and small group and individual activities that leads to better language skills? Children tend to choose activities that are interesting and engaging and of a suitable difficulty level. The first scenario in the article's opening depicts a classroom in which each child can choose from a variety of activities and materials and engage directly in an activity that interests him or her. Free-choice activities provide the opportunity and, often, the necessity for children to talk with other children in one-on-one or small group play—as they assign roles for pretend play, establish rules for games, make plans for block building, and so forth. The informal nature of free play allows teachers to engage children in conversation specific to their play and to introduce new vocabulary relevant to the children's interests.

The authors of a major study exploring the long-term effects of preschool education in England note that "freely chosen play activities often provided the best opportunities for adults to extend children's thinking," and they suggest that child-initiated play is one of the best ways for children to learn (Siraj-Blatchford et al. 2002, 3). Dickinson puts it this way: "Free play is the time when children flex their linguistic and conceptual muscles and contribute to each other's development" (2001a, 253). His research shows positive links between children's performance on literacy measures and child-child interaction and pretend play during free play in preschool.

On the other hand, when teachers like Barbara (in the second scenario) propose a specific activity for the entire class, such as a number lesson or show-and-tell, some children may find the activity too easy or too difficult or simply not interesting. These children may participate, but they are not likely to learn much. As the second scenario illustrates, children who are not directly engaged in showing their treasures tend to get bored and restless if the activity goes on too long. In activities like show-and-tell, preschoolers may learn to express themselves in front of the group, but because they have short attention spans, they soon disengage from the activity. Show-and-tell modifications such as bringing in special items or stories to share are much more engaging.

Learning and creativity grow when situations pique children's interest and stretch their imaginations. By definition, activities for the whole group—with the exception of free play—are not tailored to an individual child's interest or learning ability. To build cognitive skills, young children need to solve problems and explore materials on their own. In settings with an inadequate number or variety of materials, children do not have as many opportunities to experiment and solve problems at their own pace. With enough materials, teachers can promote small group and individual activities that invite all the children to participate (see "Low-Cost Materials for Your Classroom").

Learning and creativity grow when situations pique children's interest and stretch their imaginations.

Making the Most of Whole Group Activities

Whole group activities involve all of the children participating in the same classroom activity at the same time. They occur when the teacher plans and leads a special activity (such as a game, song, or story), or they occur naturally as part of the daily routine (for example, during snack time and cleanup). The challenge for teachers is to plan so that each child is engaged and there is little waiting or down time. The following suggestions may help.

- Have music cued and materials ready for distribution ahead of time.
- Have enough materials for a music and movement activity so that each child has an instrument, ball, scarf, or streamer.

Low-Cost Materials for Your Classroom

A classroom chock-full of varied materials invites children to expand their thinking. Materials need not cost a lot. What we adults might consider junk, young children see as treasures. As they manipulate scraps of wood, plastic bottle caps, or corks, for example, children may sort them by color, stack them on top of each other, or make something by putting the objects together.

Ask families and friends to donate

- fabric, ribbon, leather; and yarn scraps
- bottle caps and small containers
- cardboard boxes of all sizes
- buttons, beads, and costume jewelry
- covers of greeting cards and outdated calendars
- twigs, nuts, pinecones, and shells
- leftover home improvement items, such as plastic plumbing pieces, wood scraps, or nuts and bolts.

For more ideas and sources for reusable resources, visit www.reusableresources.org.

- Act out stories with each child playing a part.
- Ask children to bring in special objects or stories to share on different days, instead of having traditional show-and-tell for all children on the same day.
- Divide the group in half, with one classroom staff member leading the group while the other interacts with the rest of the children.
- Invite children to make up their own variations on familiar songs, games, and stories.
- Find positive ways to use waiting time, such as singing songs or doing finger plays, while most of the class waits for a few children to go to the bathroom or put away their materials.
- Offer self-serve snacks to eliminate waiting during distribution.
- Give several children responsibility for passing out snacks and supplies rather than assigning the task to one child.
- Plan for more than one thing at the same time—for example, some children can wipe off tables and some can put away food as others help set up for the next activity or wash their hands.

Enriching Free-Choice Time

Children need an adequate amount of time for high-level group dramatic play and constructive play to develop during free-choice time. Short periods of time limit the complexity of play and often lead to lower levels of play, such as chase games or children wandering around uninvolved.

Children need an adequate amount of time for high-level group dramatic play and constructive play to develop during free-choice time.

To encourage high-level dramatic play, the classroom schedule should allow for a minimum of 30 minutes of free choice time; however, 45 minutes to an hour is best (Christie & Wardle 1992). This extended period of time allows children to recruit others to join, negotiate roles and rules, agree on a storyline, and so on. In constructive play, children also need time to plan, assemble materials, and build elaborate structures, which over time often become part of dramatic play.

Free-choice time is an opportunity for teachers to talk with individuals or small groups of children about their chosen activities. An engaged adult can help children build on and extend their learning by first observing what the children are doing and saying and then offering specific comments or questions to extend children's thinking and vocabulary.

To make the most of free-choice time in your classroom,

- arrange the schedule so that children have free-choice time both indoors and out;
- avoid scheduling free play solely as a before-school transition; plan another time in the day when children have 45 minutes to an hour of free play;
- provide opportunities for children to explore and use materials at their own developmental level and pace throughout the day;
- make sure there are enough materials for all children to be engaged;
- move around the room and observe each child's choices;
- participate as a play partner, starting by observing and listening to children;
- follow children's leads in play and problem solving;
- give children time to solve problems and offer support if needed;
- get down on children's level and match the complexity of their play;
- offer suggestions for extending play, staying within the play theme;
- ask questions sparingly and make them thought provoking and relevant to what the children are doing;
- allow children time to think and respond;
- introduce new, meaningful vocabulary;
- acknowledge individual work and ideas;
- provide information and examples that help families understand the importance of play and free-play time in supporting children's learning.

Conclusion

The IEA Preprimary Project's findings confirm that, despite the diversity of children's experiences in early childhood settings in different countries, there are common classroom practices that lead to desirable child outcomes. The findings emphasize the importance of child-initiated activities and deemphasize whole group instruction. In addition, they highlight the significance of teacher education. Every country should consider requiring teachers and caregivers to have as much schooling as is feasible.

Although a limited number of countries participated in the longitudinal study and many cultures and regions were not represented, the IEA Preprimary Project is the largest study of its kind ever conducted. Its findings are consistent with the developmentally appropriate practices and active learning long advocated by NAEYC and others (Head Start Bureau 1984; Bredekamp 1987; Isenberg & Quisenberry 1988; European Commission 1995; Bredekamp & Copple 1997). We hope that teachers and caregivers can use the practical information in this article to enhance the time they spend with young children and enrich learning.

References

Bredekamp, S. 1987. *Developmentally appropriate practice in early childhood programs serving children from birth through age 8.* Washington, DC: NAEYC.

Bredekamp, S., & C. Copple, eds. 1997. *Developmentally appropriate practice in early childhood programs.* Rev. ed. Washington, DC: NAEYC.

Christie, J.F., & F. Wardle. 1992. How much time is needed for play? *Young Children* 47 (3): 28–32.

Dickinson, D.K. 2001a. Large-group and free-play times. In *Beginning literacy with language*, eds. D.K. Dickinson & P.O. Tabors, 223–55. Baltimore: Brookes.

Dickinson, D.K. 2001b. Putting the pieces together. In *Beginning literacy with language*, eds. D.K. Dickinson & P.O. Tabors, 257–87. Baltimore: Brookes.

European Commission. 1995. *Pre-school education in the European Union—Current thinking and provision.* Luxembourg: Office for Official Publication of the European Communities. ERIC document ED 439975.

Hart, B., & T.R. Risley. 1995. *Meaningful differences in the everyday experience of young American children.* Baltimore: Brookes.

Head Start Bureau. 1984. *Head Start Performance Standards.* DHHS Publication No. ACF 92-31131. Washington, DC: Department of Health and Human Services.

Isenberg, J., & N. Quisenberry. 1988. Play: A necessity for all children. A position paper of the Association for Childhood Education International. Olney, MD: ACEI. Online: http:www.acei.org/playpaper.htm.

Montie, J.E., Z. Xiang, & L.J. Schweinhart. 2006. Preschool experience in 10 countries: Cognitive and language performance at age 7. *Early Childhood Research Quarterly* 21: 313–31.

Montie, J.E., Z. Xiang, & L.J. Schweinhart. 2007. *The role of preschool experience in children's development: Longitudinal findings from 10 countries.* Ypsilanti, MI: High/Scope Press.

Olmsted, P.P., & J. Montie. 2001. *Early childhood settings in 15 countries: What are their structural characteristics?* Ypsilanti, MI: High/Scope Press.

Siraj-Blatchford, I., K. Sylva, S. Muttock, R., Gilden, & D. Bell. 2002. *Researching effective pedagogy in the early years.* Research Brief No. 356. London: Department for Educational Studies, Oxford University. Online: www.dfes.gov.uk/research/data/uploadfiles/RB356.pdf.

Weikart, D.P., P.P. Olmsted, & J. Montie. 2003. *A world of preschool experience: Observations in 15 countries.* Ypsilanti, MI: High/Scope Press.

JEANNE E. MONTIE, PhD, is a senior research associate at the High/Scope Educational Research Foundation in Ypsilanti, Michigan. For more than a decade she has served as part of the team coordinating the IEA Preprimary Project. E-mail: jmontie@highscope.org. JILL CLAXTON, MA, is a senior research assistant at High/Scope. She has served as a classroom teacher, project trainer, data collection coordinator, instrument developer, and data manager. E-mail: jclaxton@highscope.org. SHANNON D. LOCKHART, MA, is a senior early childhood specialist with High/Scope. She has served as a national and international researcher, curriculum developer and trainer, teacher, and educational consultant in the United States and abroad. E-mail: slockhart@highscope.org.

The Power of Documentation in the Early Childhood Classroom

A parent eyes something on the wall in the hallway near her child's classroom. She stops and looks across the entire wall, as if trying to determine where to start. She moves to the left a bit and scans the bulletin board posted farther down. At one point she nods as if in agreement and mouths a yes. Another parent approaches and turns to see what is on the wall. He too is mesmerized by the documentation of what one child discovered about pussy willows by using an I-scope lens.

HILARY SEITZ

Early childhood educators might ask, "What is documentation?" or "Is this documentation?" They sometimes wonder, "Can my bulletin board be documentation?"

What Is Documentation?

Knowing what is documentation is the first stage of understanding the process. Katz and Chard offer this explanation: "Documentation typically includes samples of a child's work at several different stages of completion: photographs showing work in progress; comments written by the teacher or other adults working with the children; transcriptions of children's discussions, comments, and explanations of intentions about the activity; and comments made by parents" (1996, 2).

Effective Communication

An effective piece of documentation tells the story and the purpose of an event, experience, or development. It is a product that draws others into the experience—evidence or artifacts that describe a situation, tell a story, and help the viewer to understand the purpose of the action.

When used effectively, consistently, and thoughtfully, documentation can also drive curriculum and collaboration in the early childhood classroom setting.

Formats That Work

A bulletin board can be a form of documentation, but there are any number of other possible formats, including a presentation board containing documentation artifacts and/ or evidence (documentation panels), class books, portfolios, slide shows, movies, and other creative products.

The format that documentation takes can be as varied as the creator's mind permits. Because documentation should provide evidence of a process with a purpose, whatever the format, it should fully explain the process, highlighting various aspects of the experience or event.

Audience and Purposes

Successful documentation formats reflect the intended audience and purposes. In addition, the format selected will depend on the individual preparing the documentation and how the children are involved in the experience.

For example, if one teacher wants to highlight for families and administrators how the class is meeting a particular math or science standard, she would use examples of children participating in experiences that align with the standard. As evidence, she might include photographs of children measuring plant stems with a ruler, children's comments about measuring the stems, background information about how the children learned about measurement (or plants), and the specific learning standard the children are meeting by participating in this experience. To best combine all of these elements, the teacher may choose a documentation panel as the format to help the audience understand how children are learning.

If children in the class are the intended audience, however, and the purpose of the documentation is to help children reflect on their math and science learning and connect them to future lessons, then the teacher would select different artifacts and evidence. A documentation panel could again be appropriate, but different artifacts and evidence might include a web of children's ideas: for instance, why an elephant should not live at the Alaska Zoo, children's comments about the elephant, and questions for further exploration, such as, "Where should an elephant live?" Add related photographs and work samples.

Again, an explanation about where the learning began and where it is intended to go will help any audience better

Documentation Artifacts and Evidence

- Teacher's description and overview of an event/experience/skill development, such as photographs and descriptions of a field trip
- Photographs of children at work—for example, conducting a science experiment
- Samples of children's work, like a writing sample from the beginning of the year
- Children's comments, such as "All the rocks have sparkles in them," in writing or as recorded by the teacher
- Teacher or parent comments about a classroom event—for instance, "It was really fun helping the children measure the ingredients for playdough"
- Teacher transcriptions of conversations during small group time when children are exploring a new topic, such as why snow melts indoors
- Important items or observations relating to an event/experience/development, such as "Johnny can now write his own name on his work"

Possible Topics to Document

- Individual child growth and development, such as language development progression
- Expected behaviors (at group time, in using a certain toy, while eating together)
- Curriculum ideas or events (field trips, presentations, special activities, celebrations)
- Curriculum projects, such as learning about plant life cycles
- Families and relationships (different types of family structures and characteristics of the families in the classroom community)
- Evidence of meeting learning standards (by posting work samples)
- Questions and answers of the children, teachers, and families about such topics as classroom routines (like how to wash your hands)

understand the documentation. In both cases, the quality of the end product will depend on the teacher's understanding of children, the curriculum, and the standards, along with his or her effective use of technology and observation.

What Should We Document?

A variety of experiences and topics are appropriate to document, but documentation should always tell a complete story. To stay on track, carefully select one topic and explore it to the fullest rather than trying to do a little of everything. For example, if the class is learning about plants (and studying plant parts, how to grow particular plants, types of plants, and so on), it would be best to document fully just one aspect of children's learning.

To stay on track, carefully select one topic and explore it to the fullest rather than trying to do a little of everything.

Choosing a Focus

The teacher might choose to document only the children's study of plant parts, for example, and could start by providing a learning spark, such as a new plant in the classroom (Seitz 2006). As children comment on the plant parts, the teacher can create a web to record what they know and to help them formulate questions. The children might also draw and label the various plant parts.

Presenting the Topic and Learning

The teacher can combine all of these pieces to make a documentation panel. This panel would illustrate the children's knowledge and understanding more thoroughly than a panel displaying every child's worksheet on plant parts, all of their water-color paintings of a plant, and every brainstormed list of vegetable plants. Offering specific examples of how children came to their understandings about just one aspect of a lesson—in this case, plant parts—achieves more than offering an overview of several experiences.

Showing Developmental Progress

One important and common topic for documentation is individual child growth and development. As previous examples have shown, the documenter is a researcher first, collecting as much information as possible to paint a picture of progress and outcomes. Documenting individual growth requires a great deal of research, as the teacher must observe each child in a variety of areas of development (such as social-emotional, cognitive, language, and motor) over a substantial length of time. Only then can the teacher create a documentation piece that tells an accurate story about each child.

The documenter is a researcher first, collecting as much information as possible to paint a picture of progress and outcomes.

A teacher should be careful to avoid displaying private or confidential information in public forums. There are times when documentation may be more appropriately shared in other, more private venues, such as a portfolio.

Portfolios used for individual assessment of children make a particularly good format for documenting developmental progress. Teachers select several domains to research. They then collect evidence of a child's interaction with other children (photographs and written observations), record the child's reflections about their friendships and cognitive abilities in interviews or group discussions, collect work samples, and tie the documentation together by writing a narrative describing the child's abilities (not deficits) in the selected domains. Even though the portfolio focuses on a child's abilities, teachers may want to consider sharing the documentation/portfolio in a private setting, such as a parent/child/teacher conference, so that parents do not feel compelled to compare their child to others in the class.

Why Should We Document?

There are several important reasons for using documentation in early childhood classrooms.

Showing Accountability

Accountability is one reason for documentation. Teachers are accountable to administrators, families, community members, and others, and documentation helps to provide evidence of children's learning. In addition, documentation can improve relationships, teaching, and learning. Use of this tool helps educators get to know and understand children, and it allows them to reflect on the effectiveness of their teaching practices (Kroeger & Cardy 2006).

Extending the Learning

Consider the following example of how one thoughtful teacher could use documentation to prolong and extend an unexpected learning opportunity. A group of children finds some miscellaneous nuts and bolts on a playground, and their teacher, noting their curiosity, carefully observes their responses and listens to and documents their conversations (by using written notes, photographs, and video). She listens to learn what the children know about the items and what they wonder, such as "Where do these come from?" Then she facilitates a conversation with the children to learn more about their ideas and theories behind the purpose of the nuts and bolts and how they came to be on the playground.

Later the teacher incorporates the initial comments, the photographs, and the conversations in a documentation source (panel, notebook, PowerPoint, or other creative product). The children and teacher revisit the encounter through the documentation and reflect on the experience, which helps the children continue their conversation and drives forward their interest. This back-and-forth examination of the documentation helps the teacher and children negotiate a curriculum that is based on the children's interests (Seitz 2006).

Making Learning Visible

When expected to provide evidence that children are meeting learning standards, documentation is a natural way to make learning visible. Helm, Beneke, and Steinheimer (1998) call this idea "windows on learning," meaning that documenting offers an insight into children's development and learning. Moreover, they observe, "When teachers document children's learning in a variety of ways, they can be more confident about the value of their teaching" (1998, 24).

How Should We Document?

The documentation process is best done in collaboration with other teachers, parents, and, in some cases, children soon after the experience. The information and product become richer when two or more teachers, children, and parents work together to understand an event. Collaboration also helps build a classroom community, which is important because it engages teachers, parents, and children in thinking about the process of learning.

The documentation process is best done in collaboration with other teachers, parents, and, in some cases, children soon after the experience.

When two or more people discuss an event, each brings a different perspective and a new level of depth. The photo below shows two teachers discussing a possible change to the classroom environment. They have discussed aspects that are necessary and that work and things they would like to change based on the children's needs, such as repositioning the furniture. Together they share how they have observed young children using the space. This environment plan would look very different if just one individual had created it. Carlina Rinaldi discusses this notion of working together and building community: "To feel a sense of belonging, to be part of a larger endeavor, to share meanings—these are rights of everyone involved in the educational process, whether teachers, children, or parents . . . working in groups is essential" (1998, 114).

Stages of the Documenter

First and foremost, documentation is a process that is learned, facilitated, and created in stages. I would even go so far as to say that documenters go through their own stages as they learn more about documenting and using documentation to support their ideas. Many early childhood educators already document children's development and learning in many ways, and most communicate a variety of messages in diverse formats to families (Brown-DuPaul, Keyes, & Segatti 2001).

There are six stages that most early childhood educators, including college students and practicing teachers, move through both individually and collaboratively (see "Stages of Documenter Experience"). Educators who collaborate to learn more about documentation tend to have more positive experiences than those who work on their own.

Stages of Documenter Experience

Stage	Experience	Value
1. Deciding to document	Documenters ask, "What should I document?" They collect artwork from every child but at first tend to create busy bulletin boards with too much information. Concerned with equity, many include every item rather than being selective.	Documenters show pride in the children's work.
2. Exploring technology use	Documenters explore how to use equipment and photographs from various events and experiences. Most of the photos are displayed on bulletin boards or inserted in photo albums. The video clips are placed in slideshows or movies and shown to children and parents.	Documenters work hard to learn more about technology. They show pride in the children's actions by displaying photos and video clips.
3. Focusing on children's engagement	Documenters learn to photograph specific things and events with the intent of capturing a piece of the story of children engaged in learning.	Documenters become technologically competent and able to focus on important learning events and experiences.
4. Gathering information	Documenters title the photographs, events, and experiences and begin to write descriptions that tell the story of children's learning.	Documenters begin to connect children's actions and experiences.
5. Connecting and telling stories	Documenters combine work samples, photographs, descriptions, and miscellaneous information in support of the entire learning event. They tell the whole story with a beginning, middle, and an end, using supporting artifacts.	Documenters continue to use documentation artifacts to connect children's actions and experiences to curriculum and learning standards.
6. Documenting decision making	Documenters frame questions, reflect, assess, build theories, and meet learning standards, all with the support of documentation.	Documenters become reflective practitioners who document meaningful actions/events, explain why they are important, and push themselves and others to continue thinking about these experiences.

Conclusion

Documentation can be a rewarding process when educators understand the value associated with collecting evidence and producing a summary presentation, whether in a bulletin board, panel, video, or other format. To become a documenter, one must first understand what to observe and what to do with the information collected. It takes time and practice to learn which experiences support effective documentation and how to collect artifacts and evidence.

Next, as documenters learn why the information is important, they begin to understand the value of documentation for different audiences and come to recognize why certain aspects of child development are important to assess. In addition, documenters learn that administrators and parents value this information, yet it also has value to the children and the teacher in planning authentic curriculum that meets children's needs.

Often the documentation provides insights into children's thinking and helps drive the future curriculum.

Finally, the documenter learns how best to interpret and display the information gathered. Often the documentation provides insights into children's thinking and helps drive the future curriculum. Deepening children's learning is the ultimate reward of documentation.

References

Brown-DuPaul, J., T. Keyes, & L. Segatti. 2001. Using documentation panels to communicate with families. *Childhood Education* 77 (4): 209–13.

Helm, J.H., S. Beneke, & K. Steinheimer. 1998. *Windows on learning: Documenting young children's work.* New York: Teachers College Press.

Katz, L.G., & S.C. Chard. 1996. The contribution of documentation to the quality of early childhood education. ED 393608. www.eric-digests.org/1996-4/quality.htm

Kroeger, J., & T. Cardy. 2006. Documentation: A hard-to-reach place. *Early Childhood Education Journal* 33 (6): 389–98.

Rinaldi, C. 1998. Projected curriculum construction through documentation—*Progettazione.* In *The hundred languages of children: The Reggio Emilia approach—Advanced reflections,* 2nd ed., eds. C. Edwards, L. Gandini, & G. Forman, 114. Greenwich, CT: Ablex.

Seitz, H. 2006. The plan: Building on children's interests. *Young Children* 61 (2): 36–41.

Further Resources

Chard, S.C. 1998. *The Project Approach: Making curriculum come alive.* New York: Scholastic.

Curtis, D., & M. Carter. 2000. *The art of awareness: How observation can transform your teaching.* St. Paul, MN: Redleaf.

Edwards, C., L. Gandini, & G. Forman, eds. 1998. *The hundred languages of children: The Reggio Emilia approach—Advanced reflections.* 2nd ed. Greenwich, CT: Ablex.

Fraser, S., & C. Gestwicki. 2002. *Authentic childhood: Exploring Reggio Emilia in the classroom.* Albany, NY: Delmar/Thomson Learning.

Fu, V.R., A.J. Stremmel, & L.T. Hill. 2002. *Teaching and learning: Collaborative exploration of the Reggio Emilia approach.* Upper Saddle River, NJ: Merrill.

Gandini, L., & C.P. Edwards, eds. 2001. *Bambini: The Italian approach to infant/toddler care.* New York: Teachers College Press.

Hill, L.T., A.J. Stremmel, & V.R. Fu. 2005. *Teaching as inquiry: Rethinking curriculum in early childhood education.* Boston: Pearson/Allyn & Bacon.

Jones, E., & J. Nimmo. 1994. *Emergent curriculum.* Washington, DC: NAEYC.

Katz, L.G., & S.C. Chard. 2000. *Engaging children's minds: The project approach,* 2nd ed. Greenwich, CT: Ablex.

Oken-Wright, P. 2001. Documentation: Both mirror and light. *Innovations in Early Education: The International Reggio Exchange* 8 (4): 5–15.

Reed, A.J., & V.E. Bergemann. 2005. *A guide to observation, participation, and reflection in the classroom.* 5th ed. Boston: McGraw-Hill.

Shores, E.F., & C. Grace. 2005. *The portfolio book: A step-by-step guide for teachers.* Upper Saddle River, NJ: Pearson.

Wurm, J. 2005. *Working the Reggio way: A beginner's guide for American teachers.* St. Paul, MN: Redleaf.

HILARY SEITZ, PhD, is the early childhood coordinaptor in the Department of Teaching and Learning at the University of Alaska in Anchorage. Her wide range of early childhood experiences includes teaching in child care centers, a public preschool, and elementary schools. hilary@uaa.alaska.edu

UNIT 7
Curricular Issues

Unit Selections

41. **Preschool Curricula: Finding One That Fits,** Vivian Baxter and Karen Petty
42. **Got Standards?: Don't Give up on Engaged Learning!,** Judy Harris Helm
43. **The Plan: Building on Children's Interests,** Hilary Jo Seitz
44. **Constructive Play: A Value-Added Strategy for Meeting Early Learning Standards,** Walter F. Drew and James Christie
45. **Using Picture Books to Support Young Children's Literacy,** Janis Strasser and Holly Seplocha
46. **Calendar Time for Young Children: Good Intentions Gone Awry,** Sallee J. Beneke, Michaelene M. Ostrosky, and Lilian G. Katz

Key Points to Consider

- What are some questions teachers need to ask when deciding which curriculum model they might use in their classroom?

- What changes could be made to a traditional calendar time to make it more child-centered and appropriate for young children?

- How can teachers use an emergent curriculum planning approach to plan their work?

- Can teachers support prosocial development, and if so, how?

- What information should teachers send parents about their children's early literacy experiences?

- Give some reasons for why picture books should be a big part of children's learning.

Student Website
www.mhhe.com/cls

Internet References

Action for Healthy Kids
www.actionforhealthykids.org

Awesome Library for Teachers
http://www.awesomelibrary.org/teacher.html

The Educators' Network
http://www.theeducatorsnetwork.com

The Family Involvement Storybook Corner
http://www.gse.harvard.edu/hfrp/projects/fine.html

Grade Level Reading Lists
http://www.gradelevelreadinglists.org

Idea Box
http://theideabox.com

International Reading Association
http://www.reading.org

Kid Fit
http://www.kid-fit.com

The Perpetual Preschool
http://www.perpetualpreschool.com

Phi Delta Kappa
http://www.pdkintl.org

Teacher Quick Source
http://www.teacherquicksource.com

Teachers Helping Teachers
http://www.pacificnet.net/~mandel

Technology Help
http://www.apples4theteacher.com

Increasingly, preschool teachers are becoming aware of the tremendous responsibility to plan learning experiences that are aligned with state and national standards to allow children to develop a lifelong love of learning along with the necessary skills they will need to be successful. There are typically two camps into which teachers fall as they begin to plan for the young children in their classroom. First are those who use a curriculum model that may be used at thousands of preschool programs across the country, and in some cases the world, and second, those teachers who choose to develop curriculum based on standards and input from the children to develop an emergent child-centered curriculum that does not follow a set approach. Both approaches can lead to outstanding learning experiences for young children. The selection of the appropriate approach depends on teachers being confident in their beliefs of how young children best learn. "Preschool Curricula: Finding One That Fits" by Vivian Baxter and Karen Petty describes some of the more popular preschool curriculum models available for teachers.

"Got Standards?: Don't Give up on Engaged Learning!" addresses early learning standards. Standards help guide teachers as they plan appropriate activities that will allow their students to gain the necessary skills to continue to learn as they move through school. It is the responsibility of any teacher of young children to be very familiar with standards. If you are unaware of where to start, try your state Department of Education, many of which have standards for programs serving preschool children. Become familiar with the standards and incorporate them into your planning.

There is a major difference between eating frozen dinners every night vs. meals that have been prepared using the freshest local ingredients. The same holds true for planning curriculum. The "generic one-curriculum-package for all classrooms" approach allows for little, if any, local flavor. Curriculum that is jointly developed by the teachers and students brings the best of the children's interest coupled with what is happening in their world for meaningful, authentic learning. Teachers who carefully observe and listen to their children and know the events of their local community will find plenty of possibilities for topics of investigation. Young children are most interested in authentic curriculum that is meaningful to their lives. We wouldn't want to eat frozen dinners every night for the rest of our lives; neither would we want to teach from a prepackaged curriculum that does not meet the needs of our students at all. Get out there and choose some local flavor and spice up the teaching and learning experience in your classroom.

"Using Picture Books to Support Young Children's Literacy" by Janis Strasser and Holly Seplocha provides the reader with additional information on this most important of early childhood skills. The article includes suggestions for shared book experiences, emergent writing, and conversations with children in a variety of settings.

The unit ends with "Calendar Time for Young Children: Good Intentions Gone Awry." The traditional calendar time, where children sit for long periods of time as phrases, dates, or songs that are often meaningless to young children are repeated, is

in desperate need of updating. Learning experiences should be meaningful and applicable to the lives of children. Children simply parroting back to the teacher the full date including day of the week, month, date, and year has little application to young children. They instead could benefit from tracking the weather, counting the number of days until important events, or using vocabulary that will be relevant to their daily lives.

A number of the articles in Unit 7 provide opportunities for the reader to reflect on the authentic learning experiences available for children. How can they investigate, explore, and create while studying a particular area of interest? Make children work for their learning or, as noted early childhood author Lilian Katz says, "Engage their minds." As a teacher of young children, acquaint yourself with the importance of firsthand experiences. Teachers often confuse first-hand and hands-on experiences but they are very different. First-hand experiences are those where the children have a personal encounter with an event, place, or activity. First-hand experiences include a visit to a firehouse, looking for life at the end of a small pond, and touring a local art gallery. After children have these firsthand experiences they are then able to incorporate them into their play, investigating and exploring in the classroom. Hands-on experiences allow the children to actually use their hands and manipulate materials as they learn about the activity such as making a batch of play-dough, building a garage with the blocks, or investigating bubbles in the water table.

This unit is full of articles addressing different curriculum areas. Active child involvement leads to enhanced learning. Suggestions for project-based activities in literacy, movement, and technology are also included. Again, the theme runs deep. Hands On=Minds On!

Professional organizations, researchers, and educators are reaching out to teachers of young children with a clear message that what they do in classrooms with young children is extremely important for children's future development and learning capabilities. Of course, the early childhood community will continue to support a hands-on experiential learning environment, but teachers must be clear in their objectives and have standards that will lead to future school success firmly in mind. Only when we are able to effectively communicate to others the importance of what we do and receive proper recognition and support for our work will the education of young children be held in high regard. We are working toward that goal, but need adults who care for and educate young children to view their job as building a strong foundation for children's future learning. Think of early childhood education as the extremely strong and stable foundation for a building that is expected to provide many decades of active service to thousands of people. If we view our profession in that light, we can see the importance of our jobs. Bring passion and energy to what you do with young children and their families and you will be rewarded ten times over. Enjoy your work, for it is so important.

Preschool Curricula: Finding One That Fits

VIVIAN BAXTER AND KAREN PETTY

What are your beliefs about how children should be educated? Do you think play is important? Is play more important than academics? Do you believe children should be allowed to explore and construct on their own with little instruction, or do you believe that they should be "taught" everything?

Knowing your values and beliefs about education can make you a more effective and efficient teacher.

Knowing your values and beliefs about education can make you a more effective and efficient teacher. It can also help you explain your program to parents.

With Information, you will be able to find a curriculum that fits your values and beliefs.

This article offers a brief look at different preschool curriculum models. Within each model, there will be an overview and an explanation of the child's role and the teacher's role. With information, you will be able to find a curriculum that fits your values and beliefs.

Direct Instruction

Overview. The direct instruction model is academically based and teacher-centered. It is a highly structured instructional approach, designed to help at-risk students accelerate their learning (American Federation of Teachers 1998).

The main feature of the DI approach is the classroom scripts: The teacher presents activities, and the children respond to them. Classroom activities are continuous academic lessons that elicit positive reinforcements with correct responses (Schweinhart and Weikart 1998). The wording is designed to ensure consistency across the lessons and to guarantee that all students will comprehend the information presented (Association for Direct Instruction 2007).

The preschool design is to provide intensive academic instruction in reading, language, and math for at-risk students. The DI model is based on the premises that teachers can increase the amount of children's learning in the classroom by carefully planning the details of the student's interaction with their environment, and that the rate and the quality of children's learning is a function of environmental events (Jensen 2005).

Child's role. The child in a DI classroom is a recipient of learning instead of a participant in learning. Children are expected to meet the demands of the workload and work at a fast pace. Correct verbal responses are required, proper replies are expected, and children are questioned until appropriate answers are given. Children are grouped by ability as a means of allowing teachers to maintain the pace and the progress of the scripted material (Jensen 2005).

Teacher's role. The teacher is an authoritative figure, meaning that it is the teacher who plans and carries out the activities. It is the teacher who is responsible for determining what is being learned each day. The teacher works at a fast pace, giving lessons on various levels of difficulty at different times of the day. To motivate children and to keep them motivated, the teacher uses a system of rewards and praise (Jensen 2005).

Developmental-Interaction/ Bank Street

Overview. This is a child-centered approach focused on individual development. It stresses the importance of the whole child, and it recognizes the importance of both the cognitive and social parts of development.

The educational emphasis is the child's developmental progress toward competence (being capable in thought and action/ movement), individuality (letting the child be unique and accepting that uniqueness), socialization (helping children learn to control their impulses and govern their own actions), and integration (helping children merge personal and impersonal experiences) (Goffin and Wilson 2001).

Developmental-interaction schools empower children to deal effectively with their environments. The school is an active community, connected to the community around it, so it is not just an isolated place for learning (Roopnarine and Johnson 2005).

This model uses a play-based approach to early childhood education with goals of nurturing the ego development and overall mental health of the child (Frost et al. 2008).

Child's role. The child is a curious being actively engaged in the social and physical environment through sensorial exploration and experimentation (Jensen 2005; Roopnarine and Johnson 2005).

Teacher's role. The teacher is an observer (to watch the children and observe their progress), questioner (to ask questions to help children develop language skills), and planner (to plan opportunities for experiences that meet the needs of every child as an individual). The teacher facilitates and guides the children through activities that are initiated by the child and promotes play as a source of learning (Jensen 2005).

High/Scope

Overview. The High/Scope curriculum is play-based (Frost et al. 2008) and views children as active learners who create their own knowledge of the world (Samuelsson et al. 2006; High/Scope Educational Research Foundation 2007). Active learning means that the children have direct hands-on experiences with people, objects, events, and ideas, and they construct their own knowledge with these experiences (Epstein 2007).

Children take the first steps in the learning process by making choices and following through on their plans. After the children have made their plans, they experiment with their ideas. Teachers support the children in their endeavors by asking questions, providing the background support, guiding the planning process, and commenting on the children's progress (Frost et al. 2008; Samuelsson et al. 2006; Schweinhart and Weikart 1998; Walsh and Petty 2006). After the children have had time to experiment with their plans and ideas, they share and discuss their findings with their teachers and peers (Samuelsson et al. 2006).

Child's role. The child in a High/Scope classroom is an active learner, experimenter, and explorer. Children develop a sense of self as they interact with significant people in their environment.

Teacher's role. The teacher follows the children and their interests and does not impose ideas and beliefs on them. The teacher shares control with the child by following the child's lead in activities and play and by interacting on the child's level of understanding, and encouraging the child to achieve success (Jensen 2005). In this way, teachers are also active learners because they do not have a precise script. Instead, they listen closely to the child and then actively work with the child to extend activities to more challenging levels (Roopnarine and Johnson 2005).

Montessori

Overview. The Montessori method is a developmental, child-centered, hands-on approach to education. Although play was not central to Maria Montessori's view of education and development, some aspects of the curriculum are related to play. Children are allowed to choose materials and "play" with them. As children grow and develop, they no longer "play" with materials but instead prepare for lessons that refine the senses and create order (Frost et al. 2008).

In a Montessori classroom, children have the freedom to explore and construct knowledge by their participation in learning and by making their own choices and experiences. Montessori believed children have the power to teach themselves and the ability to develop freely if their minds are not oppressed by adults who may limit them (Tzuo 2007).

The classroom or environment contains a few essential materials to promote self-discovery and social development. Children learn to respect the work of others as they wait to use materials their peers are using (Walsh and Petty 2006).

Montessori classrooms are filled with children of mixed ages on the belief that children of different ages help one another. The younger children see what the older ones are working on and ask for explanations. Montessori believed that there are many things that the teacher cannot "convey to a child of three, but that a child of five can do with the utmost ease" (1995, 226). She also felt that "a child of three will take an interest in what a five-year-old is doing, since it is not far removed from their own powers," therefore making the older children heroes and teachers and the younger children their admirers (1995, 226).

Child's role. The children in a Montessori classroom are active learners who construct their own knowledge and understanding of the world and have the ability to control their focus and actions. Children are given freedom within a carefully prepared environment and have the opportunity for active involvement to develop according to their own developmental timetables and tendencies.

Teacher's role. The teacher or *directress* facilitates as opposed to teaching directly. The main responsibility of the directress is to prepare the environment to meet the needs of the children and to be an observer of the children's development (Jensen 2005). Teachers refrain from interfering with children while they are absorbed in their work and do not prevent the children's free expansion. The directress does, however, intervene in the negative behaviors of children and guides them toward the right track (Tzuo 2007).

Waldorf

Overview. The Waldorf education model seeks to educate the whole child: the head, heart, and hands (Chauncey 2006; Walsh and Petty 2006). This means that young children are working to develop their physical bodies and their will through activities that are hands-on instead of academic (Roopnarine and Johnson 2005).

The Waldorf model supports children in an aesthetic environment where creative play and artistic activities are frequent. This allows the children to learn about their world through movement (Walsh and Petty 2006).

A Waldorf classroom is designed to be an extension of the home (Roopnarine and Johnson 2005) on the belief that children relate what they learn to their own experiences and therefore are then deeply engaged and can readily integrate what they learn (Chauncey 2006).

This model is also concerned with the moral education of children, emphasizing that improving a child's sense of morality is of

Overview of Preschool Curriculum Models

Name	Teacher-Centered vs. Child-Centered	Approach	Child Groupings	Child's Role	Teacher's Role
Direct Instruction	teacher	provides intensive instruction in reading, language, and math, often for at-risk students	by ability	receives the learning	determines and presents the learning activities
Developmental Interaction/ Bank Street	child	focuses on the whole child as an individual with emphasis on intellectual and social-emotional skills	by age	actively engages in the social and physical environment	observes and guides children through learning
High/Scope	child	provides hands-on experiences to allow children to construct knowledge on their own	by age	actively experiments and explores	follows the children's lead and actively works to extend learning
Montessori	child	provides a carefully prepared environment in which children become actively involved and learn according to their own timetables	mixed ages	participates in learning by making choices and respecting others	prepares the environment to meet children's needs and facilitates learning
Waldorf	child	seeks to educate the whole child through a balance of head, heart, and hands in a family-like environment	mixed ages	learns through imaginary play and oral language	provides literacy-rich experiences
Reggio Emilia	child and family	provides play experiences and collaborative projects focusing on relationships with others	mixed ages	follows natural curiosity and engages in creative expression	learns alongside children and collaborates with other teachers to nurture and guide learning

Based on "Preschool curricula: Finding one that fits" by Vivian Baxter and Karen Petty, *Texas Child Care*, Fall 2008.

high importance as part of a child's well-being and development of educational abilities (Woodward 2005).

Waldorf classrooms are of mixed ages to promote a family-like atmosphere so that children become much like siblings. The younger children watch and imitate the older children, and the older children look out for and nurture the younger children (Roopnarine and Johnson 2005).

Child's role. The child learns through imaginary play, oral language, and hands-on experiences (Edwards 2002).

Teacher's role. The teacher provides language and literacy-rich experiences through stories, songs, and poems (Roopnarine and Johnson 2005).

Reggio Emilia

Overview. Reggio Emilia is a play-based approach centered on the child, the family, and the community. Families are made to feel welcome, and in return parents get an environment that supports their children's relational, aesthetic, and intellectual needs (New 2007).

In Reggio, play is considered essential and one of the "hundred languages." What or how the children play is not the main focus, rather it is the relationships that occur within the play experiences that are given greater attention. Teachers listen closely to children's conversation and work with them as equals in the development of learning activities and projects in the classroom (Fraser 2007). Reggio classrooms are designed to promote all areas of development, not just play.

Children spend much of their time in small or large groups collaborating on projects and play activities (Frost et al. 2008). Projects are at the center of the Reggio curriculum, but the teacher does not plan them in advance. Instead, the projects and the teacher follow the direction of the children's understanding and knowledge—giving rise to an "emergent curriculum." This approach also places a heavy emphasis on art as a means for children to express themselves (Judd 2007).

Child's role. The child's role or image in the Reggio classroom is that of being resourceful, curious, imaginative, and inventive (Gilman 2007). In the Reggio classroom, children are viewed as citizens of the community with the right to be taken seriously, respected for their intelligence and feelings, and valued for their lives (Goffin and Wilson 2001).

Teacher's role. The teacher is a nurturer, guide, and facilitator. Teachers work as a team to provide materials for open-ended discovery and problem solving and listen to and observe the children. By these methods, teachers are able to uncover children's thoughts, theories, and curiosities (Gilman 2007). Teachers encourage the children to explore and extend their own ideas and theories but do not give immediate answers (Judd 2007).

Mixed Methods

Many preschools have developed their own curriculum based on trial and error over time. These preschools have pulled ideas from various methods and theorists such as Montessori, Piaget, Vygotsky, and Gesell. Their idea is to reach the whole child. They reason that it is necessary to pull from different theorists because using just one theory may reach only part of the child. These approaches can be based on play or academics or they can be mixture of both.

Many religion-sponsored schools use a faith-based curriculum that emphasizes religious principles and may be combined with one or more of the approaches above.

Know Yourself

As a preschool educator, it is important to know how you want to teach. Do you want to guide education as you follow the child, or do you want to be in the front of the room "teaching" what the children are to learn? Whatever your beliefs, it is important to know them so you can find a school with the same educational beliefs. Knowing what kind of teacher you want to be and which curriculum fits you can help you to be the most effective and efficient teacher you can be.

References

American Federation of Teachers. 1998. Direct instruction. In *Six Promising School Wide Reform Programs*. www.aft.org/pubs-reports/downloads/teachers/six.pdf.

Association for Direct Instruction. 2007. General FAQ's. http://adihome.org/index.php?option=com_content&task=view&id=12&Itemid=31.

Chauncey, B. 2006. The Waldorf model and public school reform. *ENCOUNTER: Education for Meaning and Social Justice* 19(3): 39–44.

Edwards, C. P. 2002. Three approaches from Europe: Waldorf, Montessori, and Reggio Emilia. *Early Childhood Research and Practice* 4 (1), http://ecrp.uiuc.edu/v4n1/edwards.html.

Epstein, A. S. 2007. All about High/Scope FAQ's. *High/Scope Educational Research Foundation*. www.highscope.org/Content.asp?ContentId=291.

Fraser, S. 2007. Play in other languages. *Theory into Practice* 46(1): 14–22.

Frost, Joe L., Sue C. Wortham, and Stuart Reifel. 2008. *Play and Child Development* (3rd ed.). Upper Saddle River, NJ: Pearson.

Gilman, S. 2007. Including the child with special needs: Learning from Reggio Emilia. *Theory into Practice* 46(1): 23–31.

Goffin, Stacie G. and Catherine G. Wilson. 2001. *Curriculum Models and Early Childhood Education* (2nd ed.). Upper Saddle River, NJ: Merrill Prentice Hall.

High/Scope Educational Research Foundation. 2007. *Active Learning*. www.highscope.org/Content.asp?ContentId=217.

Jensen, M. K. 2005. Development of the early childhood curricular beliefs inventory: An instrument to identify preservice teachers' early childhood curricular orientation. PhD dissertation, Florida State University. *Dissertation Abstracts International,* publ. nr. AAT 3156224, DAI-A 65/12 (Jun 2005): 4458.

Judd, J. 2007. The conversation: Reggio Emilia preschools. *The Times Educational Supplement* 4764: 24.

Montessori, Maria. 1995. *The Absorbent Mind*. New York: Henry Holt and Company.

New, R. S. 2007. Reggio Emilia as cultural activity theory into practice. *Theory into Practice* 46(1): 5–13.

Roopnarine, Jaipaul L., and James E. Johnson. 2005. *Approaches to Early Childhood Education* (4th ed). Upper Saddle River, NJ: Merrill Prentice Hall.

Samuelsson, I. P., S. Sheridan, and P. Williams. 2006. Five preschool curricula—Comparative perspective. *International Journal of Early Childhood* 38(1): 11–30.

Schweinhart, L. J., and D. P. Weikart. 1998. Why curriculum matters in early childhood education. *Education Leadership* 55(6): 57–60.

Tzuo, P. W. 2007. The tension between teacher control and children's freedom in a child-centered classroom: Resolving the practical dilemma through a closer look at related theories. *Early Childhood Education Journal* 33(1): 33–39.

Walsh, B. A., and K. Petty. 2006. Frequency of six early childhood education approaches: A 10-year content analysis of early childhood education journal. *Early Childhood Education Journal*. 34(5): 301–305.

Woodward, J. 2005. Head, heart and hands: Waldorf education. *Journal of Curriculum and Pedagogy* 2(2): 84–85.

VIVIAN BAXTER is a doctoral student in child development at Texas Woman's University in Denton. She has a master's degree emphasizing Montessori education and has been working in Montessori education since 2003. **KAREN PETTY** is an associate professor in the Department of Family Sciences at Texas Woman's University. Her interests lie in furthering the professional development of doctoral students, especially in the area of publications in peer-reviewed journals.

Got Standards?
Don't Give up on Engaged Learning!

Judy Harris Helm

As the children enter the kindergarten classroom, they gleefully pull pairs of shoes from their backpacks for a project on shoes. There are big shoes and small ones, sneakers and ballet slippers, galoshes and flip-flops. There are new shoes and old shoes, shiny shoes and dull shoes. One child has even brought in dog shoes! The children become more excited with each pair that is added to the class collection. When the teacher gathers the group for morning meeting, the children cry out: "Our shoes are all different sizes!" "Jason brought Nikes!" "We've got boys' shoes and girls' shoes!" "When can we play with our shoes?" The teacher explains that they have to do their math lesson and reading work first, and then they can decide what to do with the shoes. The children look longingly at the shelf of shoes.

The teacher sighs inwardly. She loves the interest and curiosity generated by projects and rich thematic units, but she feels the pressure of covering curriculum and meeting kindergarten standards. "If only I could be sure they would learn what they need to know, I could harness this enthusiasm."

Like many early childhood teachers today, this kindergarten teacher is overwhelmed by early learning standards and the required curriculum experiences and commercial programs that have accompanied the standards movement into early childhood education. Faced with a literacy program and a math program with prescribed time allocations, she feels challenged to "get it all in the day." She is hesitant to engage children in integrated learning experiences because she wants to be sure they are acquiring the knowledge and skills she is responsible for teaching.

The Importance of Integrated Learning

Even in classrooms in which standards and required curriculum are prominent, there is still a place for rich, integrated learning experiences that truly engage children, such as projects. When children are engaged they are excited, curious, and intensely involved in learning experiences that are meaningful to them

(Jones et al. 1994); they take responsibility for their own learning and feel energized. They develop and practice strategies for learning and become collaborative. Engagement increases the ability of the brain to remember; adrenaline created through emotional involvement activates the amygdala, a part of the brain that decides which information is important enough to retain. Over time, a stronger and more lasting memory is created when the brain is emotionally involved (McGaugh 2003). Engagement is a valid criterion for selecting learning experiences to include in the young child's day.

Learning is easier for children when new information is connected to what they already know, not taught in isolation.

Learning is easier for children when new information is connected to what they already know, not taught in isolation. Research in early cognition indicates that by the time children are 4 years old, they have developed a complex, interconnected knowledge base about the world and how it works. Catherwood (1999), in a review of early cognition research, concludes that the task of early educators supporting cognitive development may be to help children articulate their knowledge and link that knowledge to verbal expression. For example, before reading a book about puppies, a teacher might ask the children if they have a puppy or know someone who does. If a child doesn't know about puppies but does know something about dogs, this could be the focus. A discussion about puppies and dogs will activate those parts of the brain where the children have stored knowledge and vocabulary from previous experiences. This discussion will help children connect what they already know with the new information they will gain. Experiences that support a child in making connections, according to Catherwood, "enhance the richness of neural networks in the child's brain" (1999, p.33).

For children in the early years of schooling, teachers can provide engaged and integrated learning experiences through the *project approach,* a three-phase structure for in-depth investigation of a topic that interests children (Katz & Chard 2000; Helm & Katz 2001). Integrated learning experiences, such as projects, enable children to connect the knowledge and skills specified in standards (such as counting or reading and writing) to their world. Through project work children see the value of new skills and have opportunities to practice them as they investigate topics of interest to them. Learning experiences in project work are authentic (real world) and integrative, both characteristics of engaged learning (Jones et al. 1994). Engagement and integration increase when children have an opportunity to investigate something of great interest to them and have a say in what they want to learn about the topic.

The Role of Child Initiative and Decision Making

Effective early childhood teachers use many different approaches to teaching knowledge and skills. One way to think about these approaches is to place them on a continuum of how child initiated they are, meaning how much of a role children have in determining the direction of study.

All approaches on the continuum are valuable and valid ways to teach young children. The approach used may be determined by the content to be taught. For example, when teaching children how to cross the street (to meet a standard on "knowing and using safety rules"), it is best if the teacher determines the content and the most efficient way for children to learn this valuable information. Children can easily learn knowledge about and skills for "collecting and using data to answer questions" during project work, when they will find these skills useful in completing their work. Sometimes the choice of approach is based on how much time is available to teach the concept or skill.

Teachers most often combine approaches to curriculum as they plan their week. For example, a teacher may plan for a unit on magnets in the science area; a lesson on learning how to stop, drop, and roll during large group time; and independent child choice time during which children may choose to continue their work on a project on turtles. These events may occur in the classroom during the same week, the same day, or even the same hour. By using multiple approaches, teachers introduce children to much knowledge and many skills and offer children opportunities to practice and extend their learning.

Even though all approaches are valuable, teaching approaches on the left side of the continuum (teacher-determined content, narrow units and instruction in single skills and concepts) should not be the only ones used in prekindergarten and primary classrooms. Spending too little time on the child-initiated side of the continuum may actually be harmful. When learning experiences never venture into directed inquiry or project work, children are less likely to develop the higher-level thinking skills of analyzing, hypothesizing, predicting, and problem solving (Katz & Chard 2000). Teacher-centered approaches can limit children's vocabulary development. These approaches can also be less motivating for children learning and practicing academic skills. For example, a child who wants to know how many children have shoes with Velcro fasteners versus shoes with laces is motivated to count and write numerals. A child who is making a model of a drink machine is motivated to identify words that indicate the kinds or brands of drinks and to copy and practice reading those words. These experiences not only motivate but provide an opportunity and an authentic reason to practice counting, reading, and writing. Unfortunately, teaching on the single-concept, teacher-centric side of the continuum is often recommended, and in some cases mandated, by school district administrators or directors of early childhood programs.

> **Even for learning to read, which requires mastering many specific skills, research supports the importance of a balanced approach that emphasizes children's engagement.**

Exclusive use of teacher-directed teaching approaches is especially problematic for children at risk. Martin Haberman (2004) labels these teacher-controlled approaches *directive pedagogy,* part of an ineffective *pedagogy of poverty* that focuses teachers on compliance and low-level thinking skills, which limit children's achievement and thirst to learn. Research also suggests that formal, didactic instruction in basic skills may produce more positive results on standardized measures in the short term compared to approaches that give children more initiative and choice, but will not produce higher school achievement in the long term (Marcon 1995, 2000; Golbeck 2001). Even for learning to read, which requires mastering many specific skills, research supports the importance of a balanced approach that emphasizes children's engagement (Cummins 2007).

Most teachers understand that children need learning experiences all along the continuum. Unfortunately today's emphasis on standards and required curriculum is resulting in squeezing most of the children's day into the left side of the continuum.

Integrating Standards into Engaged Learning

It is possible to teach required content and skills through project work and other child-initiated learning experiences such as a shoe project. For example, the shoes need to be sorted so they can be placed on the shelves of a pretend shoe store created by the class. As the children discuss and decide how to label the shelves, how to arrange shoes on the shelves, and where to place each pair of shoes, they learn and practice the math skills of sorting, classifying, and reading numerals. If the teacher has anticipated and prepared for the experience by providing photos of the aisles of a shoe store and shoe catalogs and flyers for children to use as resources, they will also be engaged in literacy. The teacher can take the first step to rich integration of standards and required curriculum into engaging learning experiences by making sure he has a clear understanding of *what* children need to learn and then anticipating *how* they might learn these in the learning experience.

Anticipating the opportunities for integration enables teachers to be prepared with introductory lessons, materials, and supplies and also to interact supportively with children as they do their project work. For example, while children are looking at and talking about the shoes in their shoe collection, the teacher can extend vocabulary by introducing names for the parts of shoes, encouraging children to compare parts of shoes, encouraging children to compare parts of shoes on different models, or even spontaneously showing children how they could create a chart comparing shoe parts. These supportive interactions are more likely to occur if the teacher has anticipated vocabulary and skills possible in the project.

There are specific strategies that teachers who do project work have found helpful in doing this anticipatory planning. The strategies described below can be helpful for rich thematic units or teacher-directed inquiry also.

Know the Content, Skills, and Dispositions You Are Supposed to Teach—Make a List

A first step in anticipating opportunities for integration is to analyze curriculum goals and standards and make a comprehensive list of the knowledge, skills, and dispositions children need to develop. Often teachers do not have a clear understanding of exactly what children need to learn and what they are to teach. There may be learning standards (from the state), a teacher's manual for a math or literacy program, and sometimes another list from the report card.

Often standards are global but children's progress is assessed using a checklist that is more specific. For example, there may be a global standard ("Use concepts that include number recognition, counting, and one-to-one correspondence," from the Illinois Early Learning Standards—Kindergarten), but children will be evaluated on a report card including items to be checked, such as "Recognizes and writes numerals 1–30" and "Can make sets." Sometimes a content program (such as a math book or reading book) may contain additional knowledge and skills that are not required to be taught in every local program. Textbook publishers include everything they feel that any school might want so that their books are applicable to a large number of schools. Sometimes topics in a required curriculum program are introduced to build awareness; mastery is not expected. Just because there is a page on reading pie charts in the manual, this doesn't mean that a teacher is responsible for teaching it or that all children must master that concept at this time.

A teacher who finds herself in a program that has manuals for required curriculum materials, a separate list of standards, and an assessment system with another list of goals (which may or may not be coordinated) will find it less frustrating and more effective to work with a consolidated comprehensive list. For example, a teacher might find that a state standard indicates that children "Count with understanding and recognize

'how many' in sets of objects." However, a curriculum guide may indicate that 4-year-olds should be able to count 10 items before entering kindergarten. A list distributed to families of incoming kindergartners may indicate that children should be able to count to 10. The teacher can make one consolidated list of all math requirements and their sources and then seek assistance from supervisors to clarify discrepancies. This list will be very helpful as the teacher integrates standards and required curriculum goals into engaged learning. A clear understanding of what is to be taught is essential. Training on integration of standards may be available for teachers, or they may find published tables that correlate required curriculum programs with local or state standards. Such resources will help with this consolidation task.

Align the Introduction of Skills and Concepts with Children's Engagement

Once teachers know what children need to learn and do, they can look at their curriculum guides and see if there is a particular sequence for the introduction of concepts. In multiage early childhood classrooms, this is not usually an issue. Kindergarten and primary curriculum guides, however, are usually arranged chronologically. Look to see if the knowledge or skill has to be introduced in a particular sequence. Often the order is flexible so teachers may introduce skills when they are most meaningful to children instead of following the order in the manual.

Often the order is flexible so teachers may introduce skills when they are most meaningful to children instead of following the order in the manual.

For example, in the shoe project, measuring feet to determine the correct shoe size is relevant to the children. If learning how to use standard units of measurement (such as inches) or even nonstandard units (such as Unifix cubes or straws) is a curriculum goal, then this is a perfect opportunity to teach the skill. Anticipating what skill might be needed, then teaching it at the time children must use it maximizes the children's engagement. Even when the skill requires explicit teaching, you can teach it during more formal times of your day, then use the project work as the "practice time" for integration and application of the newly developed or previously taught skill. As teachers create the comprehensive list of what they are supposed to teach, they can note what knowledge and skills will require explicit teaching or must be introduced in sequence and those that can be moved to take advantage of children's engagement.

Create an Anticipatory Planning Web That Includes Knowledge and Skills from Your List of Standards and Required Curriculum Goals

Creating anticipatory planning webs when preparing for project work makes it easier to integrate required curriculum in response to children's interests and lessens the chance that teachers will miss opportunities for skill building and practice. Teachers or teaching teams create planning webs in anticipation of all the possible opportunities for curriculum integration.

To Make an Anticipatory Planning Web

Write the main study topic in the center of a blank page using a marker. In the same color add *concepts about the topic* in a web format. For example, for the topic *shoes,* concepts might include "Shoes have parts," "Shoes come in different sizes," "Shoes are bought" (see "Step 1: Concepts about Shoes"). Keep your focus on concepts about shoes; do not list activities for children to do with the shoes. If this is difficult, imagine a book titled *All about Shoes* for elementary-age children, and think of the concepts you might find in that book. The book would not include activities to do with shoes, only content about the world of shoes.

Review your comprehensive list of knowledge and skills related to the standards and required curriculum goals; compare with your concept web. Determine which concepts would *naturally* and *authentically* provide opportunities for children to learn specific knowledge or skills. For example, the world of shoes is a natural topic in which children would use numeral recognition ("Use concepts that include number recognition," from Illinois Early Learning Standards—Prekindergarten). Learning opportunities could include reading the shoe sizes printed in the shoes and on the boxes or the prices of shoes shown in store ads or signs in shoe stores.

It is important to use this stage of the webbing to discover the most authentic and meaningful opportunities for children to

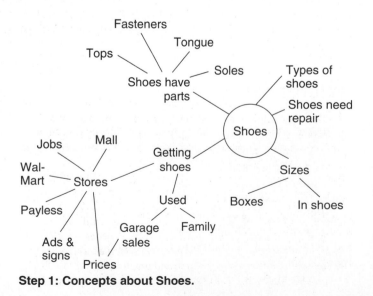

Step 1: Concepts about Shoes.

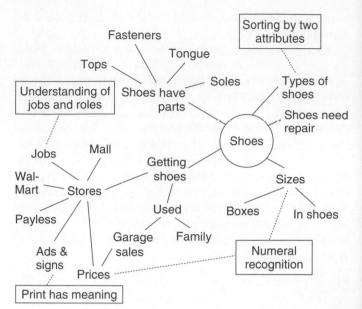

Step 2: Opportunities to Learn Required Knowledge and Skills.

learn; do not start thinking of teacher-directed activities. Write an abbreviated version of the appropriate standard (skill or knowledge) next to the concepts for which a learning opportunity is likely to occur. For example, next to "Prices" you would write "Numeral recognition" (see "Step 2: Opportunities to Learn Required Knowledge and Skills").

Keep your focus on situations in which children might see the value of relevant knowledge and skills or times when they might naturally practice their application. Do not write possible lessons or learning experiences. The goal of this step is to find authentic intersections between the topic concepts and the knowledge and skills you are to teach. In the next step you will begin to think of possible learning experiences.

Look at the web, which now has *concepts* in one color and *knowledge* and *skills* in *another*. Select an area where a concept and a standard or goal come together, such as "Sizes" and "Numeral recognition." Think of a possible authentic learning experience for children that combines these two. For example, you could show children where sizes are located on shoes, and they could then sort the shoes by sizes as they would be in a store. This is an authentic, or real, task performed in shoe stores. This activity shows children the usefulness of numerals and motivates them to learn. They are likely to repeat the activity at home, gaining additional practice with numerals. The task is highly engaging for children.

Contrast this with a shoe theme activity that is not authentic. A teacher prepares construction paper cutouts of pairs of shoes. On one shoe in each pair she places dots. On the other shoe in the pair she writes a numeral. She asks the children to make pairs of shoes by matching numerals and dots. This activity fails to engage the children in the same way, does not demonstrate the value of learning numerals or using them in the real world, and requires teacher monitoring for children to complete the task.

Look at each place on your web where concepts and knowledge and skills come together. Make a list of possible engaging learning experiences.

Choose one or two possible learning experiences from the list you have generated. The children may create a shoe store in the classroom, visit a shoe store, collect shoes, or even dissect shoes. As children become more involved with the experiences, you can easily integrate the appropriate knowledge and skills because you have anticipated the opportunities to do so. You will be prepared to "teach on the fly," incorporating content or extending learning as children become more involved with the topic. For example, you might teach children how they can use a graph to record data in response to a child's observation that there are almost as many slip-on shoes as shoes with Velcro fasteners.

Identify which concepts are of the most interest to the most children by observing children's involvement in the initial learning experiences. If children appear to be more interested in *shoe repair* than *shoe stores* or *where shoes come from,* then shoe repair can become the topic of the project, maximizing the children's initiation, engagement, and decision making. You can cut out that section of the planning web that addresses shoe repair and move it to the center of the web to remind everyone of the new topic. Instead of the *shoe* project, the children are participating in the *shoe repair* project (see "Step 5: Maximizing Engagement by Adjusting Topic Focus,".

When you cut out and move the repair section to the center of the knowledge and skills web, many of the concepts and useful and meaningful applications of the knowledge and skills will remain applicable to this new, more narrow topic. Other concepts or applications will be replaced, dropped, or moved to another, newly added concept. Selecting the topic to match the children's engagement and then encouraging children to develop questions and find answers to their questions increases

child decision making and engagement and moves the learning experience to the right on the continuum to teacher-guided inquiry or project work.

As the learning experience progresses, you can determine whether to introduce knowledge and skills before children need them or during an experience, or whether the learning experience itself will provide mainly practice. For some children each of these methods must be used; you must introduce the knowledge or skill before the child will use it, demonstrate and provide coaching at the time it will be used, and then allow the child plenty of time for practice.

Plan for Documentation

It is important for teachers to keep track of which ideas they have introduced to children and what children are and are not learning. Just because a learning experience occurs does not mean that a particular child will be engaged in it or learn the knowledge and skills you have planned to teach. As in all learning experiences, both teacher-directed and child-directed, the teacher must observe to see if each child is meeting the standards. The use of observation notes and photographs, plus the collection of children's work, enables the teacher to be sure that anticipated learning becomes actual learning, that children master knowledge and skills, and that each individual child is participating in some way and moving toward the required curriculum goals or standards (Helm & Beneke 2003; Helm, Beneke, & Steinheimer 2006). Anticipatory planning should also include preparing materials for documentation.

Making Time for Engagement

As the kindergarten teacher at the beginning expressed, time is an important issue when deciding to include engaging learning experiences like the shoe project. However, if a teacher plans what children should know and should be taught, anticipates opportunities to integrate and organize explicit teaching, and documents each child's achievement, then she can be confident that children are achieving standards and learning required knowledge and skills. Teaching time previously reserved for directly teaching these skills becomes free for more active learning experiences. Children can once again be excited about what they are learning in school.

References

Catherwood, D. 1999. New views on the young brain: Offerings from developmental psychology to early childhood education. *Contemporary Issues in Early Childhood Education* 1 (1). www.wwwords.co.uk/rss/abstract.asp?j=ciec&aid=1501

Cummins, J. 2007. Pedagogies for the poor? Realigning reading instruction for low-income students with scientifically based reading research. *Educational Researcher* 36 (9): 564–72.

Golbeck, S. L. 2001. Instructional models for early childhood: In search of a child-regulated/teacher-guided pedagogy. In *Psychological perspectives on early childhood education: Reframing dilemmas in research and practice,* ed. S.L. Golbeck, 153–80. Mahwah, NJ: Erlbaum.

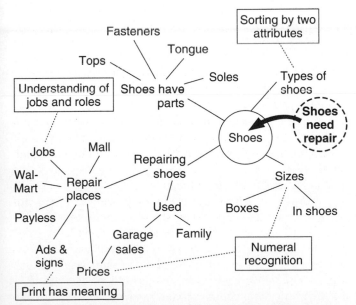

Step 5: Maximizing Engagement by Adjusting Topic Focus.

Haberman, M. 2004. *Star teachers: The ideology and best practice of effective teachers of diverse children and youth in poverty.* Houston, TX: Haberman Educational Foundation.

Helm, J.H., & S. Beneke, eds. 2003. *The power of projects: Meeting contemporary challenges in early childhood classrooms—Strategies and solutions.* New York: Teachers College Press.

Helm, J.H., S. Beneke, & K. Steinheimer. 2006. *Windows on learning: Documenting young children's work.* New York: Teachers College Press.

Helm, J.H., & L.G. Katz. 2001. *Young investigators: The project approach in the early years.* New York: Teachers College Press.

Jones, B., G. Valdez, J. Nowakowski, & C. Rasmussen. 1994. *Designing learning and technology for educational reform.* Oak Brook, IL: North Central Regional Educational Laboratory.

Katz, L.G., & S.C. Chard. 2000. *Engaging children's minds: The project approach.* 2nd ed. Stamford, CT: Ablex.

Marcon, R. 1995. Fourth-grade slump: The cause and cure. *Principal* 74 (5): 17–20.

Marcon, R. 2000. Impact of preschool models on educational transitions from early childhood to middle-childhood and into early adolescence. Poster session at the Conference on Human Development, Memphis, TN, April 16.

McGaugh, J. L. 2003. *Memory and emotion: The making of lasting memories.* New York: Columbia University Press.

JUDY HARRIS HELM, EdD, provides consultation and professional development to school districts and early childhood centers. She is the author of seven books on the project approach and documentation and provides training on integrating standards and engaged learning. judyhelm@bestpracticesinc.net. This article is available online in *Beyond the Journal,* July 2008, at www.journal.naeyc.org/btj/200807.

The Plan

Building on Children's Interests

HILARY JO SEITZ, PhD

During outdoor playtime four-year-old Angela discovers a loose metal nut about half an inch in diameter. She shows the nut to her teacher.

Angela: Look what I found. It looks just like the big one on our workbench.

Teacher: Yes, it sure does, Angela. It's called a nut.

Angela: I wonder where it came from.

Teacher: Where do you think it may have come from?

Angela: Well, actually it is the same as the ones in the workbench inside.

Teacher: This nut looks very similar to the nuts and bolts inside. I think this nut might be bigger than the nuts and bolts we have inside.

Angela: Maybe it came off of something out here.

Teacher: What do you think it is from?

Angela: Umm, I don't know—something out here.

Teacher: Maybe you should check

Angela: Okay.

Holding the nut tight in her fist, Angela walks around, stopping to examine the play equipment, the tables, the parked trikes, and anything else she thinks might have a missing nut. She can find only bolts with nuts on the trikes. She spies a large Stop sign, puts her special treasure in her pocket so other children cannot see it, and sets up a roadblock for the busy trike riders so she can check the nuts and bolts on their trikes.

Edmund stops and asks her what she is doing, and she explains. Edmund says he needs to see the nut. When Angela shows it to him, he gets off his trike and starts helping her inspect the other trikes. They eventually find the one that is missing the nut. Other children, curious, crowd around.

While incidents such as this are common in early childhood settings, teachers may not listen for them, seize upon them, and build on them. When teachers do pay attention, these authentic events can spark emergent curriculum that builds on children's interests. This kind of curriculum is different from a preplanned, "canned" thematic curriculum model. In emergent, or negotiated, curriculum, the child's interest becomes the key focus and the child has various motivations for learning (Jones & Nimmo 1994). The motivations are intrinsic, from deep within, meaningful and compelling to the child. As such, the experience is authentic and ultimately very powerful.

This article outlines a plan that teachers, children, and families can easily initiate and follow to build on children's interests. It is a process of learning about what a child or a class is interested in and then planning a positive authentic learning experience around and beyond that interest. Teachers, children, and parents alike are the researchers in this process. All continuously observe and document the process and review the documentation to construct meaning (Edwards, Gandini, & Forman 1998). Documentation is the product that is collected by the researchers. It may include work samples, children's photos, children's dialogues, and the teacher's written interpretations.

The Plan

"The Plan," as it became known in my classroom, is a simple four-step process of investigation, circular in nature and often evolving or spinning off into new investigations. (See diagram) The Plan consists of

1. **Sparks** (provocations)—Identify emerging ideas, look at children's interests, hold conversations, and provide experiences. Document the possibilities.
2. **Conversations**—Have conversations with interested participants (teachers, children, and parents), ask questions, document conversations through video recordings, tape recordings, teacher/parent dictation, or other ways. Ask "What do we already know? What do we wonder about? How can we learn more? What is the plan?"
3. **Opportunities and experiences**—Provide opportunities and experiences in both the classroom and the community for further investigation. Document those experiences.
4. **More questions and more theories**—Think further about the process. Document questions and theories.

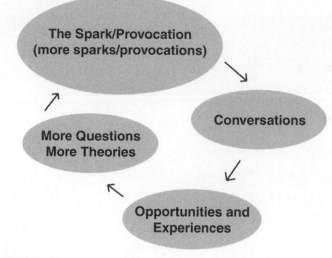

Figure 1

In other words, teachers, children, and parents identify something of interest; we discuss what we know about it or what we want to know about it; we experience it or have opportunities to learn about the idea; and then we discuss what we did and either ask more questions or make new theories. We document our understandings throughout the whole process.

The initial spark can come from anywhere or anything. For example, we might overhear children talking about the lawn-mower at the park. The class, or sometimes a smaller group of children, then sits down and devises a plan with the help of interested adults.

Step 1: Sparks

Sparks can be things, phenomena, conversations—anything that provokes deeper thought. The sparks are what trigger a child (and adult) to want to know more, to investigate further. These sparks can occur at any time. They can be as simple as finding a pebble in one's shoe, grabbing an idea or story line from a book, or finding a nut on the playground. Young children have these sparks of interest all day long.

Sparks can be things, phenomena, conversations—anything that provokes deeper thought.

How Do Teachers See/Catch These Sparks?

I often hear teachers say, "How can I learn what the children are interested in?" or "How do we find out what the children want to know?" My response is always, Talk with the children, listen to them, and observe. For some teachers, it can be difficult to sit back and trust that ideas will naturally emerge. But once teachers become familiar with the process, they begin noticing how easily sparks appear.

Teachers in preschools, Head Start programs, and public school classrooms are expected to meet state standards or curriculum content goals. It is possible (although sometimes challenging) to integrate these standards and goals into emergent themes. Teachers who know and understand the "big picture" of standards and goals are more likely to *fit* a topic or emerging idea/plan into the curriculum. They document the process of The Plan (through photographs as well as descriptive narrative) to provide evidence of meeting standards and content goals.

Can We Provoke the Sparks?

Triggering sparks is sometimes helpful and can have exciting implications. Teachers can provoke children's thinking by suggesting ideas through stories, specific items, or experiences. Again, when a teacher is knowledgeable about standards and content goals, she knows when to provide appropriate sparks. For example, reading a book such as *If You Give a Moose a Muffin*, by Laura Numeroff, may trigger thinking and conversations about several different ideas (moose and what they eat and where they live, baking, puppet shows, painting, and others) as well as support literacy development. Owocki, in discussing teachable moments in literacy development, says, "Teachable moment strategies involve knowledgeably observing children and seeking out relevant opportunities to help them extend their understandings" (1999, 28).

Introducing an item into the classroom is another way of triggering sparks of thought. Watch children's eyes light up when you place a large beetle on a table or pluck an unfamiliar stringed instrument.

Finally, we can trigger sparks by offering experiences such as a neighborhood walk or a visit to the grocery store. Authentic experiences with meaningful things interest children (Fraser & Gestwicki 2001). The following is an excerpt of an observation from an early childhood classroom.

Teachers can provoke children's thinking by suggesting ideas through stories, specific items, or experiences.

A small group of four-year-olds and their teacher prepare to visit the park across the street. The teacher locks the gate and turns toward the children. She leans down and says, "Please stay on the sidewalk." Pointing to the nearby intersection, she adds, "We are going to walk over there to the crosswalk." The teacher holds hands with one child while the others pair off and walk behind her.

Kayla: What's a crosswalk?

José: It's over there.

Teacher: At the corner, we are going to walk inside the lines of the crosswalk. The lines show people where to walk. That way, cars know to stop. It is safer for us to cross in the crosswalk than in the middle of the street.

Tiana: My mom and me always cross over there by our car.

José: That's the middle of the street.

Michael (*motioning*): See that red sign? It says STOP, so you gotta stop at it.

As the small group negotiates the crosswalk and heads down the sidewalk on the other side of the street, José points out three more signs (a No Parking sign, a street name sign, and a Caution sign). The children are puzzled by the Caution sign and stop to try to figure it out.

The teacher documents this interest in street signs and crosswalks in writing and by drawing a sketch of the situation. Later, back in the classroom with the whole class, she brings up the subject of signs. The topic stirs interest and lots of conversation—triggering a new classroom investigation and the beginning of a new plan.

Step 2: Conversations and Writing a Plan

Formal meetings, built into the daily classroom routine, are ideal times for children, teachers, and family volunteers to have large group conversations about forming and writing a plan. In these routine meetings, children already know what to expect; they understand the process as well as the expectations. Our class meetings generally include a variety of fairly predictable experiences (reading stories, singing songs, conversations). Depending on the time of the meeting, we always discuss what has happened earlier or what is about to happen. While one teacher facilitates this meeting, another adult (teaching assistant or parent) writes down ideas, questions, and thoughts about the conversations. The adults later review this documentation to help plan and provide appropriate experiences.

Conversations also take place in settings such as activities or mealtimes. Small group conversations can be very meaningful to children and adults alike. Here is one snack time conversation:

Five girls, ages three and four, are seated at a small table, eating crackers. One child mentions going to the state fair the night before with her family. Two of the other children had been to the fair the previous week, so the teacher considers where to go with this spark of interest.

Kamie: It was cold at the fair, but the animals weren't cold 'cause they got fur on them.
Stacy: I touched the goats and the baby pig!
Kamie: Me too!
Karla: I went on a ride, but next time I'm gonna see the animals.
Teacher: Where are the animals?
Stacy: They are in this big tent, and you gotta wait real long to go inside. But you can put a penny or a dollar in the machine to get food, then you can feed the goats and pigs.
Teacher: What do they eat?
Kamie: They eats lots of stuff.
Karla: Yeah, like rice and leaves.
Stacy: The pony has big teeth and a tongue. It gets your hand sticky.
Teacher: Do all the animals eat the same food? (Kamie nods yes.) Maybe we could go to the petting zoo and feed the goats and sheep.
All the girls: Yes!
Teacher: Let's make a plan.

Karla and Stacy jump out of their seats to get a big sheet of paper and markers. Kamie reminds them to bring a clipboard too.

The teacher writes THE PLAN at the top of the paper. She prints the five girls' names under it. Then she begins writing a list, speaking the words at the same time she writes them.

1. Goats and pigs and ponies eat food.
2. What do they eat?

Karla: Where do they sleep? (The teacher makes this No. 3.)

4. Go to library to get books.
5. Go to petting zoo and talk to zoo keeper.

The Plan is set and displayed on the wall. As a form of documentation, it is revisited frequently and adjusted to meet the needs of the children (Project Zero & Reggio Children 2001). Children, teachers, and families continuously reassess The Plan to guide inquiries. Often children and teachers add revisions to the plan.

Formal Planning

Teachers should also prepare a more formal lesson plan. This planning process works best when teachers, teaching assistants, and parents have opportunities to discuss ideas together. The teacher, who usually assumes the role of facilitator, needs to be prepared. She should know and understand standards and content goals; gather documentation, including photographs, observational records, and work samples; and guide the process of creating the formal plan.

The group discusses why the emerging ideas are important and how to further the investigations. Lesson plans should include the children's questions or inquiries as well as the teacher's; both are integrated into a formal plan.

Step 3: Opportunities and Experiences

Essential in a good plan is providing, facilitating, and initiating *meaningful* and *authentic* opportunities and experiences to help children further understand ideas. The word *meaningful* is the critical element here. Significant experiences create a sense of purpose for the child. John Dewey cautioned, "Attentive care must be devoted to the conditions which give each present experience a worthwhile meaning" (1938, 49).

One way to promote meaningful experiences is to find opportunities for authentic experiences that allow young children to see, negotiate, and participate in the real world. The experiences should be based on ideas that emerge from conversations or the written plan. For example, when the children initiated the conversation about street signs, their authentic experience of seeing and learning about street signs prompted a written plan for deeper understanding. The class began to take walks to explore different signs. Several children created a map showing where the street signs were located. Another group drew all the street signs they saw. Back in the classroom, everyone shared their information. Two children created signs and posted them in the classroom. There was a Stop sign and one that looked like a stop sign but read Quiet in the Library. At the sink, a yellow sign said Wash Hands.

One way to promote meaningful experiences is to find opportunities for authentic experiences that allow young children to see, negotiate, and participate in the real world.

The children also decided they needed road signs on the trike paths in the outdoor play area. Some confusion arose during this phase of the experience. Children began arguing about where signs should be placed and if they had to follow the direction on the signs. This discomfort led to the next phase of the plan (see Step 4).

Several content goals were acknowledged in the above experience. Children drew and created maps of a familiar setting; they practiced writing letters and putting together sounds; they used their knowledge of street signs to create classroom rules. In all, the children experienced authentic, meaningful learning.

Step 4: More Questions, More Theories

During this phase, the teacher carefully outlines the theories and documents new questions. As children raise new questions, they are forced to deepen their thinking about the situation. These thoughts become new sparks or provocations for future plans.

In the continuing sign investigation, the teacher called a large group meeting when the arguing about the trike signs and rules persisted. She posted a large piece of paper on the wall and said, "I noticed some confusion on the trike roads today. Jacob, tell me your plan with the signs." She was careful to focus the conversation on the plan rather than encouraging a blame game ("So-and-so went the wrong way"). Jacob expressed his concern of following the sign rules for safety. The teacher wrote on the paper, "If we follow the street signs, we will stay safe." Kayla added another theory: "People who make the signs get to

make the rules, but they have to write them out." Another child brought up additional safety issues, such as wearing helmets and keeping the trikes on the path. The children and teacher decided to post several signs on the roadway to direct traffic in a clockwise pattern.

Summary

Young children learn best through active participation and experience. When helped, allowed, and encouraged to follow an interest and construct a plan to learn more, children are empowered and become intrinsically motivated. They fully engage in the experience when it is their own (Jones & Nimmo 1994). Meaningful ideas are intrinsically motivating.

A caring, observant teacher can easily promote motivation by facilitating the planning process. As the four-step process described here becomes more familiar to children, teachers, and families, The Plan gets easier. Through collaboration, they document, reflect, and interpret ideas to form deeper meanings and foster lifelong learning.

References

Dewey, J. 1938. *Experience and education.* New York: Collier.

Edwards, C., L. Gandini, & G. Forman. 1998. *The hundred languages of children: The Reggio Emilia approach—Advanced reflections.* 2nd ed. Westport, CT: Ablex.

Fraser, S., & C. Gestwicki. 2001. *Authentic childhood: Experiencing Reggio Emilia in the classroom.* Albany, NY: Delmar.

Jones, E., & J. Nimmo. 1994. *Emergent curriculum.* Washington, DC: NAEYC.

Owocki, G. 1999. *Literacy through play.* Portsmouth, NH: Heinemann.

Project Zero & Reggio Children. 2001. *Making learning visible: Children as individual and group learners.* Reggio Emilia, Italy: Project Zero.

HILARY JO SEITZ, PhD, is an assistant professor at University of Alaska, Anchorage. She has worked in early childhood settings for the past 18 years as a teacher, administrator, and instructor.

From *Young Children*, March 2006, pp. 36–41. Copyright © 2006 by National Association for the Education of Young Children. Reprinted by permission.

Constructive Play

A Value-Added Strategy for Meeting Early Learning Standards

WALTER F. DREW ET AL.

This was one of the children's first days using turkey basters in water play. We try to add only one new thing at a time. The children started hooking the funnel to the turkey baster and found ways to fill the baster and squirt out water. They were so excited to discover they had made a fountain. They named it Water Spout. We had read the book *I Wish that I Had Duck Feet,* and the children remembered the water spout in the story.

—Trisha McCunn, Preschool Teacher

Constructive play involves building and making things no one has ever seen before. As young children fiddle with, sort, and arrange materials, ideas and imagination begin to flow. Questions arise naturally. They wonder: What will happen if I put this here? How tall will it go? Where did the bubble come from? In this way, constructive play serves to focus the minds of children through their fingertips and leads them to invent and discover new possibilities, to fulfill their sense of purpose.

Play in a Standards-oriented World

In many early childhood programs across the country, time for play is dwindling away. The field of early childhood education is in the midst of a major shift in orientation toward a standards base. Early learning standards specify what young children should know and be able to do in academic areas such as science, literacy, and mathematics. These standards have rapidly become an integral part of state systems of early childhood education. All the states plus the District of Columbia have approved early learning standards for preschoolers. As a structural element of education reform, early learning standards shape the content of instructional curriculum, set the goals of professional development, and establish the focus of outcomes assessment. Standards are increasingly seen as a powerful lever for improving preschool instruction and children's school readiness.

This rise of state early learning standards has alarmed many early childhood educators, especially advocates of play-based approaches to teaching and learning. Play has long had a central role in early childhood education, where it has been viewed as an effective means for promoting all aspects of child development. Many early childhood teachers are concerned that the standards movement and its narrowing of educational goals are pushing aside classroom learning through play in favor of more didactic forms of instruction.

Reconciling Play and Standards

In this article, we take a more positive, pragmatic approach and propose to reconcile constructive play with the standards movement. Recognizing that standards have become an integral part of early education, we believe that mature forms of play, such as the examples presented in which children are focused and intentional, can be effective strategies for helping children learn academic skills stressed in state standards (Kagan & Lowenstein 2004; Van Thiel & Putnam-Franklin 2004; Christie & Roskos 2006). Mature play is mindful make-believe and reasonably self-regulated.

Our proposals are based on field research, observations, interviews, and vignettes focused on constructive play that uses a variety of open-ended materials to promote learning and development. We share educators' stories, experiences, and ideas around principles of constructive play and include specific suggestions for practice.

Three Principles for Using Constructive Play to Meet Early Learning Standards

We identify three key principles that explain why developmentally appropriate constructive play is an ideal instructional strategy for meeting early learning standards. These principles are derived from our own experiences as play researchers and teacher educators.

1. During the preschool years, constructive play merges with exploration and make-believe play and becomes a mature form of play that allows children to strengthen inquiry skills and build conceptual understanding.

Constructive play is organized, goal-oriented play in which children use play materials to create or build something (Johnson, Christie, & Wardle 2005). It often begins during the toddler years and becomes increasingly complex with age. Constructive play involves open-ended exploration, gradually becoming more functional in nature, then evolving to make-believe transformations. Four- and 5-year-olds often switch back and forth between constructive and dramatic play, and it can be difficult to distinguish between the two forms of play. According to Bodrova and Leong (2004), the type of mature play that promotes learning and development has three critical components: imaginary situations, explicit roles, and implicit rules.

Mature play has three critical components: imaginary situations, explicit roles, and implicit rules.

We typically think of constructive play as building with blocks and other three-dimensional materials. Building a road or castle with wooden blocks, shaping a ball out of clay, constructing a spaceship with recycled materials, and putting a puzzle together are all examples of constructive play. But how is the water play, described at the beginning of this article, constructive play (see "Water Play" below)?

Trisha McCunn, a teacher of 3- to 5-year-olds at Lollipop Pre-School in rural Iowa, uses *Exploring Water with Young Children,* the Young Scientist series, and records observations of the children:

> The children discovered that a little squeeze of a water-filled baster made the water bubble, but with a big squeeze the water shot up with great force. They had made water play rules, and one was that the water had to stay in the water table. For today, we decided to set aside the rule because the water could be wiped up. Everyone wiped up water most of the afternoon, but how exciting it was to make a fountain in preschool.

> When I added clear plastic hoses, the children discovered that if they pushed the hose into the water and stuck their thumbs or fingers on the top end, they could make a bubble go up and down inside by moving the hose up or down like a steering wheel. One boy exclaimed, "Look, I'm driving a car!" He drove the car for 20 minutes, pretending the moving air bubble was the road and imagining he was following it.

For Ms. McCunn and the children in her class, constructive play is a form of hands-on inquiry, a way of meeting early learning standards. She knows the children have an innate need to understand their worlds, physically explore, and manipulate materials, and she values the exploring, inventing, and discovering they do together.

Inquiry is a way of looking at the world, according to Parker (2007), a questioning stance we take when we seek to learn something we don't yet know. And when we are truly into inquiring about something, whatever it may be, we drive ourselves to learn more and more because we seek answers to our own questions. This definition captures the very heart of inquiry-based learning and aptly relates what the children in Trish's class are doing.

Water Play

. . . is about physical science, the study of fluid dynamics. Understanding how the water spout works involves design technology, which is part of the construction of simple systems. It requires a different kind of knowledge than constructing with blocks.

If children have a goal in mind in relation to water flow, they are motivated to learn about forces of gravity, water pressure, and fluids in motion to be successful at what they are doing.

When teachers encourage children to explore and think about what they are doing and talk and plan together, there is potential for skill development in a lot of areas . . . language, science, social competence, as well as positive dispositions toward learning and learning how to learn.
—Ingrid Chalufour, Young Scientist Series Author

Believing that all children have the desire and capacity to explore and better understand their worlds is the foundation of constructive play and inquiry-based teaching in early childhood.

Trisha McCunn provided the kinds of simple constructive play materials that appeal to the children's natural desire to question and find out things for themselves. She set the stage in a way that encouraged children to construct new knowledge and thus initiated the learning process.

According to Chouinard (2007), humans' ability to seek out information from one another seems to give us a particular evolutionary advantage and allows us to learn efficiently. Chouinard's research also substantiates the belief that children need to take an active role in the questioning and information-gathering process. When children are actively involved, they remember the information they gather better than information simply given to them. Children build knowledge through active questioning and information gathering combined with hands-on experiences and direct personal-social interactions. This process of active learning and acquisition of knowledge occurs during play with materials, play with ideas, and play with others.

Vygotsky and other well-known theorists have stressed the importance of play in the learning process of young children (Bodrova & Leong 2004). Play provides an intrinsically motivating context in which children come together to understand their world. Constructive play, with its emphasis on hands-on inquiry, is ideally suited for helping children learn the academic skills and concepts found in states' early learning standards (see "Connections between Arizona Early Learning Standards and Constructive Play").

2. Teachers who are knowledgeable about the purposeful use of materials, the process of constructive play, and intentional strategies for interacting with children succeed in helping children develop essential concepts and skills in all content areas.

Making things is an activity that is key to successful learning for young children. They combine the dexterity of their little fingers with the power of their brains to develop a knack for

Connections between Arizona Early Learning Standards and Constructive Play

Early Learning Standards (Arizona)	Constructive Play, Research Supported
Language and Literacy	
Strand 2: Pre-Reading Processes, **Concept 5:** Vocabulary Development—The child understands and uses increasingly complex vocabulary.	Research by Cohen (2006) shows that children learn new vocabulary words as they socially interact with partners and in groups during constructive play.
Strand 2: Pre-Reading Processes, **Concept 1:** Print Awareness—The child knows that print carries meaning.	Literacy-enriched play centers contain theme-related reading and writing materials. For example, a block center might contain pencils, pens, materials for making signs, storage labels (for large blocks, Legos), and so on. Research indicates that when children play in print-enriched settings, they often learn to read play-related print (Neuman & Roskos 1993; Vukelich 1994).
Strand 3: Pre-Writing Processes, **Concept 1:** Written Expression—The child uses writing materials to communicate ideas.	Research by Pickett (1998) shows that adding writing materials to block centers results in a large increase in emergent writing, including making signs to identify function and ownership, regulate behavior, and communicate messages.
Mathematics	
Strand 4: Geometry and Measurement, **Concept 1:** Spatial Relationships and Geometry—The child demonstrates an understanding of spatial relationships and recognizes attributes of common shapes.	Recent research by Miyakawa, Kamii, and Nagahiro (2005) confirms that block building can help children learn important spatial relationships.
Social-Emotional	
Strand 2: Social Interactions with Others, **Concept 2:** Cooperation—The child demonstrates the ability to give and take during social interactions.	Creasey, Jarvis, and Berk (1998) contend that a two-way relationship exists between group play and social development: the social environment influences children's play, and play acts as an important context in which children acquire social skills and social knowledge needed to engage in group play. Children learn attitudes and skills needed for this play from their parents, teachers, and other children. At the same time, play with others has a key role in social development by providing a context in which children can acquire many important social skills, such as turn taking, sharing, and cooperation, as well as the ability to understand other people's thoughts, perceptions, and emotions.
Strand 4: Approaches to Learning, **Concept 5:** Problem-solving—The child demonstrates the ability to seek solutions to problems.	Bruner (1972) proposes that play contributes to children's ability to solve problems by increasing their behavioral options and suggests that block play encourages inventive thinking and logical reasoning while constructing three-dimensional patterns. Copely and Oto (2006) find that young children demonstrate considerable problem-solving knowledge during block play.

Source: Arizona Early Learning Standards, www.azed.gov/earlychildhood/downloads/EarlyLearningStandards.pdf.

representation and the capacity for creative visual symbolizing. It is interesting to consider this as the ability to imagine the future. The ability to physically construct new connections between thoughts and objects is the act of innovation and change. Teachers who understand and encourage this process of learning help children develop a very important talent.

By taking known elements and creating new connections, children demonstrate the lifelong process of accommodation and improvisation. In this regard, current research emphasizes the importance of school readiness factors covering all developmental domains and including active approaches to learning (Bowman & Moore 2006). Child-focused inquiry learning that involves constructive play with an array of three-dimensional materials, fosters positive learning, such as enthusiasm, resilience, creativity, decision making, and persistence in completing tasks (Day 2006).

For optimal learning to occur through play, children need support, time, and open-ended materials that stimulate the brain to think imaginatively. The materials teachers choose to bring into the classroom reveal the choices they have made about knowledge and what they think is important for children to learn, including the content of applicable learning standards.

Pauline Baker, a cooperating early childhood resource teacher in the Tucson Unified School District, supports the constructive play of 4-, 5-, and 6-year-olds who come to her studio.

I pick up interesting materials all the time . . . sticks, stones, wire, wood, and use them all with the children.

I organize materials by color and keep them in baskets, bins, boxes, and lettuce trays. Some materials are organized by "circleness," both man-made and nature-made.

Quality early childhood programs reflect the knowledge of teachers, like Ms. Baker, who understand their roles during children's constructive play and learning and routinely allocate ample time for children to choose and engage in a wide variety of play-related activities, including constructive play with different types of blocks and other open-ended materials (Drew & Rankin 2004).

By age 4, children begin to move from sorting, lining up, stacking, and pushing blocks to constructing and symbolically representing a tree house, for instance, as in the classroom description. As children practice building, their constructions become more detailed, more complex, more coordinated, and balanced.

In addition, constructions are more likely to be used in dramatic pretense. Children may use foam blocks to make a forest of trees, while using other materials to represent people and animals that have adventures in the forest. Constructive play becomes more popular with age, accounting for more than 50 percent of play activity in pre-school settings (Rubin, Fein, & Vandenberg 1983).

Linda Vinson, a pre-K teacher of children with disabilities in Brevard County, Florida, offers a variety of materials to the children in her class.

The eight 2- to 4½-year-olds in my class are socially and emotionally developmentally delayed. At the beginning of the year they did not know how to play. I put something in their hands to get them started.

Gradually, I've offered more open-ended and natural materials to help the children express their thinking through words and actions and gain a sense of competence. Now the children have wooden blocks, foam rectangles, purple cylinders, stretchy fabric scraps, soft wire, cardboard tubes, colorful plastic caps, and mat board, all collected from our local reusable resource center. The materials are arranged in straw baskets that add a homelike atmosphere to my classroom.

Yesterday, after reading the Three Little Pigs, we talked about the wolf and the forest and the different houses the pigs built. The children retold the story, using stuffed animals and puppets. Afterwards, they went to the shelves of materials and began building. Kevin made a tree house of foam rectangles. He built it up and knocked it down 15 or 20 times—each time confidently building it a little higher, laughing as it toppled, and exclaiming, "I can build anything all the way to the sky!"

In construction play activities, children do both science and mathematics.

Linda Vinson's account of the children's play shows the opportunity for conceptual understanding in the area of structural engineering as Kevin makes his tree house. He explores the forces of gravity, compression, tension, and the relationship between the characteristics of materials and successful design to achieve balance, stability, and even aesthetic sensibility. During construction play, Kevin discovers the science of quantity (arithmetic) and shape (geometry) in the making and testing of different design patterns. In short, in construction play activities, children do both science and mathematics. Ms. Vinson is aware of the value-added benefits that come from joyful play—like Kevin's feeling a sense of personal power, competence, and a positive disposition about himself and learning.

3. Professional development experiences that feature hands-on constructive play with open-ended materials help early childhood educators extend and deepen their understanding of constructive play as a developmentally appropriate practice for meeting early learning standards.

Providing professional development opportunities that supply rich, hands-on play experiences using a variety and abundance of open-ended materials, time for reflection on those experiences, and guidance in applying new insights to teaching practice is a powerful strategy for helping teachers develop deeper understandings of developmentally appropriate practice and the essential role of constructive play in quality early childhood programs. Adults who engage in active inquiry and construct knowledge through creative exploration with materials are more positively disposed to encouraging children to do the same. In this way teachers come to understand and appreciate how play helps children develop character virtues, such as tenacity, flexibility, creativity, courage, and resilience—all are characteristics practiced in constructive play, by child and adult.

The adults' hands-on experience is consistent with recommended developmentally appropriate practices for young children. Just as with children, constructive play stimulates an inner dialogue between the teacher and the materials. Ideas, feelings, questions, and relationships begin to take form. The teacher becomes the protagonist—exploring, assuming control through objects, creatively inventing, and becoming the empowered initiator of inquiry and self-discovery.

In *The Ambiguity of Play,* play scholar Brian Sutton-Smith describes play not only as about learning important concepts and skills but also as about playing with interpreting one's own feelings and thoughts instead of primarily representing the external world. He says, "What is adaptive about play, therefore, may be not only the skills that are a part of it but also the willful belief in acting out one's own capacity for the future" (2001, 198). Teachers and children who are most likely to succeed are the ones who believe in possibilities—optimists, creative thinkers, people who have flexibility along with a sense of power and control. Adult constructive play helps to inform teachers of the kinds of insights, issues, and feelings children experience during their play. Teachers discover new ways of thinking about play and compelling new insight into children's learning. Constructive play becomes an effective self-reflective professional practice that stimulates the creativity of teachers to construct new play strategies to meet early learning standards.

In *Teaching Adults Revisited: Active Learning for Early Childhood Educators,* Betty Jones reminds us that, "Wherever they are in their educational journey, teachers of young children need to tell their stories, hear other stories, and practice reflective thinking about children's development—over and over again" (2007, ix).

Conclusion

Professional development activities in which teachers play together using construction materials can foster a deeper understanding of how to employ materials and engage young children in positive constructive play. Play can be a bridge to school readiness and academic success for all children. Three key principles in using constructive play to meet early learning standards are interrelated in this way.

Players are active agents in learning, imagining, and creating together. This kind of mature or quality play involves imaginary situations, explicit roles, and implicit rules and is recognizable by its persistence and tendency to become more elaborate over time.

Social interaction and shared imaginings often emerge in the context of constructive play, adding values over and above the benefits of reaching academic standards. These extra benefits include creativity, imagination, problem solving, eagerness to learn, ability to cooperate and stay on task, and learning how to self regulate and be more responsible overall for one's own learning and development in general.

Finally, setting up and supporting positive constructive play in the early educational setting rests on teachers' creativity, sound judgments, and wise decisions. Although constructive play involves objects, good teachers do not focus on these per se but instead on the actions that take place and especially on the children playing. Learningful play, or "play learning" as it is called by some (Pramling-Samuelsson 2007), occurs when children have teachers who are empathic, playful, and intentional. Open-ended, fluid, and natural materials for creative constructive play are important. In addition, teachers must guide exploration and play, helping children as needed, stepping in and out at the right times, and scaffolding in appropriate ways during constructive play episodes.

Constructive play must connect to other kinds of play and activities and be networked with different aspects of the curriculum to maximize its value. To be sure, for the benefit of young children, we must see clearly the value-added connection between constructive play and meeting early learning standards. The challenges are great, as is the reward. Teachers will be helping to restore play to its proper place in early education.

References

Bodrova, E., & D. Leong. 2004. Observing play: What we see when we look at it through "Vygotsky's eyes"? *Play, Policy and Practice Connections* 8 (1–2).

Bowman, D., & E.K. Moore, eds. 2006. *School readiness and social-emotional development: Perspectives on cultural diversity.* Washington, DC: National Black Child Development Institute.

Bruner, J. 1972. The nature and uses of immaturity. *American Psychologist* 27: 687–708.

Chouinard, M.N. 2007. Children's questions: A mechanism for cognitive development. Serial no. 286. *Monographs of the Society for Research in Child Development* 73 (1).

Christie, J., & K. Roskos. 2006. Standards, science, and the role of play in early literacy education. In *Play = learning: How play motivates and enhances children's cognitive and social-emotional growth,* eds. D. Singer, R. Golinkoff, & K. Hirsh-Pasek, 57–73. Oxford, UK: Oxford University Press.

Cohen, L. 2006. Young children's discourse strategies during pretend block play: A sociocultural approach. PhD diss., Fordham University, New York.

Copely, J., & M. Oto. 2006. An investigation of the problem-solving knowledge of a young child during block construction. www.west.asu. edu/cmw/pme/resrepweb/PME-rr-copley.htm

Creasey, G., P. Jarvis, & L. Berk. 1998. Play and social competence. In *Multiple perspectives on play in early childhood education,* eds. O. Sara-cho & B. Spodek, 116–43. Albany: State University of New York Press.

Day, C.B. 2006. Leveraging diversity to benefit children's social-emotional development and school readiness. In *School readiness and social emotional development: Perspectives on cultural diversity,* eds. D. Bowman & E.K. Moore, 23–32. Washington, DC: National Black Child Development Institute.

Drew, W., & B. Rankin. 2004. Promoting creativity for life using open-ended materials. *Young Children* 59 (4): 38–45.

Johnson, J., J. Christie, & F. Wardle. 2005. *Play, development, and early education.* New York: Allyn & Bacon.

Jones, E. 2007 *Teaching adults revisited: Active learning for early childhood educators.* Washington DC: NAEYC.

Kagan, S.L., & A.E. Lowenstein. 2004. School readiness and children's play: Contemporary oxymoron or compatible option? In *Children's play: The roots of reading,* eds. E. Zigler, D. Singer, & S. Bishop-Josef, 59–76. Washington, DC: Zero to Three Press.

Miyakawa, Y., C. Kamii, & M. Nagahiro. 2005. The development of logico-mathematical thinking at ages 1–3 in play with blocks and an incline. *Journal of Research in Child Development* 19: 292–301.

Neuman, S., & K. Roskos. 1993. Access to print for children of poverty: Differential effects of adult mediation and literacy-enriched play settings on environmental and functional print tasks. *American Educational Research Journal* 30: 95–122.

Parker, D. 2007. *Planning for inquiry: It's not an oxymoron!* Urbana, IL: National Council of Teachers of English.

Pickett, L. 1998. Literacy learning during block play. *Journal of Research in Childhood Education* 12: 225–30.

Pramling-Samuelsson, I. 2007. A research-based approach to preschool pedagogy: Play and learning integrated. *Play, Policy, and Practice Connections (*Newsletter of the Play, Policy, & Practice Interest Forum of NAEYC) 10 (2): 7–9.

Rubin, K., G. Fein, & B. Vandenberg. 1983. Play. In *Socialization, personality, and social development,* vol. 4, *Handbook of child psychology,* ed. E. Hetherington, series ed. P. Mussen, 693–774. New York: Wiley.

Sutton-Smith, B. 2001. *The ambiguity of play.* Cambridge, MA: Harvard University Press.

Van Thiel, L., & S. Putnam-Franklin. 2004. Standards and guidelines: Keeping play in professional practice and planning. *Play, Policy, and Practice Connections* 8 (2): 16–19.

Vukelich, C. 1994. Effects of play interventions on young children's reading of environmental print. *Early Childhood Research Quarterly* 9 (2): 153–70.

WALTER F. DREW, EdD, is executive director of the Institute for Self-Active Education and cofounder of the Reusable Resources Association. He chairs the Play Committee for the Early Childhood Association of Florida and is creator of Dr. Drew's Discovery Blocks. drdrew@cfl.rr.com. **JAMES CHRISTIE,** PhD, is a professor of curriculum and instruction at Arizona State University in Phoenix. He is past president of the Association for the Study of Play and a member of the board of directors of Playing for Keeps. jchristie@asu.edu. **JAMES E. JOHNSON,** PhD, is professor-in-charge of early childhood education at Penn State University in University Park. He is the current series editor of *Play and Cultural Studies* and the former president of the Association for the Study of Play. **ALICE M. MECKLEY,** PhD, professor in early childhood education at Millersville University, Pennsylvania, researches the social play of young children. She is a member of the NAEYC Play, Policy, and Practice Interest Forum's Research Group and TASP (The Association for the Study of Play). Alice.Meckley@millersville.edu. **MARCIA L. NELL,** PhD, is assistant professor in the Elementary and Early Childhood Department at Millersville University. Marcia has been a public school teacher for 25 years in kindergarten through second grade classrooms.

Using Picture Books to Support Young Children's Literacy

JANIS STRASSER AND HOLLY SEPLOCHA

Five-year-old Levi is listening to his teacher read *Why Epossumondas Has No Hair on His Tail* (Salley, 2004). This richly woven and engaging tale includes several unfamiliar words, like "lollygagging," "skedaddle," and "persimmon." It also contains phrases that Levi has never heard before, including "my sweet little pattootie" and "no sirree." Because the art and text so beautifully express the joy of eating a persimmon, Levi asks questions about the fruit once the teacher has finished the story. The next day, the teacher brings several persimmons to class. As the children examine them, cut them, and taste them, they recall the events in the story, sing the song that is part of the story, and remember such rich descriptive terms as "powder-puff tails." Later, in the art area, Levi draws a sketch of a persimmon and tries to write the word, coming up with "PRSMN." The children ask to sing the song about persimmons for the next several days. The teacher suggests that they change the words to create their own version. She writes their version on large chart paper. In the library area, two weeks after the initial whole-group story reading, three children are making the "RRRRRR" sound of Papapossum's stomach as they point to the text in the book that matches the sound. Two of them decide to go into the art area and make puppets to act out the story. As the teacher watches them glue wiggly eyes and a tail made out of yarn onto a large oval shape they have cut out from cardboard, she asks, "What do you think are some good things about not having hair on your tail?"

This example shows the multiple ways in which a picture book can support literacy in the classroom. Literacy skills can be embedded when using an engaging children's picture book, as in the example above, instead of focusing on skills in isolation (as in "letter of the week" types of activities).

Literacy skills can be embedded when using an engaging children's picture book instead of focusing on skills in isolation.

How Do Picture Books Support Literacy?

The benefits of storybook reading are well documented (Aram & Biron, 2004; Neuman, 1999; Neuman, Copple, & Bredekamp, 2000; Strickland & Morrow, 1989). As preschoolers, children should be active participants in picture book reading—chiming in on the refrain of predictable books, dramatizing stories they love, and reciting the text of books "so familiar that they have been committed to memory" (Jalongo, 2004, p. 91).

A joint position paper issued by the National Association for the Education of Young Children and the International Reading Association (cited in Neuman, Copple, & Bredekamp, 2000) states, "The single most important activity for building . . . understandings and skills essential for reading success appears to be reading aloud to children" (p. 8). Neuman (1999) explains how storybook reading helps children gain general knowledge, practice cognitive thinking, and learn about the rhythms and conventions of written language.

Vygotskian theory supports the notion that through interaction with text (written by other authors or themselves), "children transfer the understandings and skills they have gleaned from dialogues with others to their own literacy-related discourse . . . they converse not just with themselves but also with the text narrative" (Berk & Winsler, 1995, p. 115). Creating opportunities for young children to explore literature, individually and in small groups, helps this discourse to flourish. Through such activities as looking through new books, rereading (or "pretend reading") stories that the teacher has read, imagining new endings for popular stories, or creating artistic renderings of favorite stories, young children can interact with text in meaningful ways. In considering extension activities for literature, teachers should consider whether the activity grows naturally out of the literature, encourages students to thoughtfully reexamine the book, and/or demonstrates something the reader has gained from the book (Routman, 1991, p. 87).

Definition of a Picture Book

A picture book is different from a children's book that contains illustrations. In a picture book, both the picture and text are equally important. There exists "a balance between the pictures and text . . . neither of them is completely effective without the other" (Norton, 1999, p. 214). They contain at least three elements: what is told with words, what is told through the pictures, and what is conveyed from the combination of the two (Jalongo, 2004). A fourth element is the child's personal association with the book. Anyone who has read a good picture book has experienced the unique magic and beauty of this relationship. The story line is brief (about 200 words) and straightforward, with a limited number of concepts; the text is written in a direct, simple style; illustrations complement the text; and the book is usually 32 pages long (Jalongo, 2004). Classic picture books that fit these criteria include Keats' *The Snowy Day* (1962), Numeroff's *If You Give a Mouse a Cookie* (1985), and Ringgold's *Tar Beach* (1996). They are more than "cute little books" or useful teaching tools, however; they "also exist as an art form that transcends the functions of informing, entertaining and providing emotional release" (Jalongo, 2004, p. 13). They can be fiction or nonfiction and the illustrations can be photographs as well as drawings, paintings, or collage.

Language Learning with Picture Books

Picture books not only expose young children to words and pictures, they also provide the following experiences that support the dispositions and feelings in learning how to read (Jalongo, 2004):

- Holding Attention: with powerful, vivid illustrations
- Accommodating Difference: within the developmental differences of individual children
- Giving Pleasure: within an intellectually stimulating context
- Challenging the Brain: as the brain seeks patterns out of the complexity of stimulation from text and illustrations at the same time
- Provoking Conversation: hearing stories increases children's vocabulary
- Connecting Experiences: from home and family to stories

Oral language is a key area of literacy development in early childhood. The components of language skills include: Communication, Forms and Functions, Purposeful Verbal Interactions, and Play With Language (Isenberg & Jalongo, 2001). In one classroom of 3-year-olds, the teacher has read Vera B. Williams' *"More More More" Said the Baby* (1997) to individual children and small groups many times, at their request, over a two-week period. She has documented the ways in which the children have practiced the four components of language skills as they connect with elements of the picture book (about the ways that three families show their love for the children in their family):

- Communication: The children pretend to be mommies, grandmothers, and uncles putting their babies to bed, singing to them and kissing them goodnight.

- Forms and Functions: Some children scold the "babies" when they don't go right to sleep, others sing in a gentle voice, and some pretend to laugh as they tickle the "babies."
- Purposeful Verbal Interaction: In their play, the children problem solve how to undress the "baby" and put her in the cradle quietly, as she has fallen asleep while the "grandma" sang to her. Two other children figure out what materials to use to make a blanket when they can't find the blanket that used to be in the dramatic play area.
- Play With Language. The children make up funny names for the babies (with reference in their play to one of the babies in the book who was called "Little Bird"). They call the babies "Little Quacky Duck" and "Puppy Poo Poo."

Picture books should be a part of every day in the early childhood years. Reading to children and engaging them in activities that encourage the use of expressive language, phonological awareness, and high-level thinking is critical for the development of the skills and dispositions that are necessary for reading and writing.

In another classroom, the teacher supported one child's language and cognitive development after reading Ehlert's *Eating the Alphabet* (1993). She watched the child begin to create "vegetables" by cutting orange, brown, and green pieces of foam and gluing them onto her paper. The child then said to the teacher, "When you do this, you have to use your imagination." The teacher responded, "That's very true when creating art. I like how you used the word 'imagination.' " The child then went over and brought back Sendak's *Where the Wild Things Are* (1998) and said, "This is an imagination book, because you can see in the pictures that his room changes. It's pretend." The child was clearly responding to the illustrations and text of the two books, and synthesizing the information in her conversation. The classroom environment had supported this learning through its accessible art area, rich selection of books, flexibility allowing children to bring books into the art area, and the scaffolding conversation between the child and the adult.

Rich Vocabulary

A preschool teacher is reading *Giraffes Can't Dance* (Andreae, 1999) to her class of 4-year-olds. The lavish, colorful illustrations help to illuminate the rich text describing animals dancing in a contest. Verbs like "prance" and "sway" and phrases like "buckled at the knees" and "swishing round" are new for the children. Rhyme and alliteration appear throughout the book; for example:

The warthogs started waltzing and the rhinos rock'n'rolled.

The lions danced a tango

That was elegant and bold.

When the children ask about the waltz and tango, the teacher downloads these two types of music from the computer for the children to listen to during center time. She puts the book into the music center so that the children can look at the illustrations of the warthogs, rhinos, and lions dancing as they listen to different types of music. She stays in the music center for a while so that she can explain which type of music is played for each type of dance. Her questions invite the children to compare and contrast the two different styles. They don't have to ask about "buckled at the knees." The illustration clearly shows what this means.

The fact that reading to young children supports language development is clearly evidenced in the literature (Aram & Biron, 2004; Bus, van IJzendoorn, & Pelligrini, 1995; Hargrave & Senechal, 2000; Koralek, 2003; Schickedanz, 1999). When the story reading includes explanations of particular words, dialogue about new vocabulary, high-level questions, and other active participation by children, that language development is further enhanced (Hargrave & Senechal, 2000).

Although such wordless picture books as *Good Dog, Carl* (Day, 1989) do not fit the traditional definition of a picture book, they are a wonderful way to encourage children to use expressive language, as they use visual literacy and knowledge of story sequence to become the author of the story (Owocki, 2001). Teachers can audiotape children's voices as they "read" the story to their friends and keep the tape in the listening area with the book.

Phonological and Phonemic Awareness

Phonological awareness is "the ability to hear, identify and manipulate the sounds of spoken language (hearing and repeating sounds, separating and blending sounds, identifying similar sounds in different words, hearing parts of syllables in words)" (Seplocha & Jablon, 2004, p. 2). It includes "the whole spectrum[,] from primitive awareness of speech sounds and rhythms to rhyme awareness and sound similarities and, at the highest level, awareness of syllables or phonemes" (Neuman, Copple, & Bredekamp, 2000, p. 124).

As children listen to songs, nursery rhymes, poems, and books with repetitive words and phrases, they begin to play with language. For example, when chanting alliterative phrases, such as, "Splash, splosh, splash, splosh, splash, splosh" to describe the river and "Squelch, squerch, squelch, squerch, squelch, squerch" to describe the "thick, oozy mud" in Rosen's *We're Going on a Bear Hunt* (1997), children revel in the sounds and begin to want to create their own descriptive, playful phrases. Teachers can begin by reading the book, inviting children to join in the repetitive parts with their voices while slapping their knees to the rhythm, and helping them to create their own versions of the story (hunting other animals in other environments). A perfect companion to this book is Axtell's *We're Going on a Lion Hunt* (1999). This version, situated in the jungle, also contains lots of alliteration and rhythm as the suspense builds to a crescendo. Using both books, followed by a compare and contrast discussion, encourages higher order thinking and promotes ample use of rich descriptive language, as well as analysis and attention to phonological awareness.

Children learn to pay attention to the sounds in spoken language through rhymes, chants, nonsense words, and poetry. Many picture books, such as the Dr. Seuss books, contain predictable rhymes, rhythms, alliteration, and a great deal of word play that invite children to complete lines, make up nonsense words, and engage in other types of phonological-based activities, when these types of activities are promoted by the teacher.

Phonemes are the building blocks of words. They are "perceivable, manipulable units of sound; they can be combined and contrasted with one another in ways that matter to language users, that is, in ways that make possible the production and perception of words" (McGee & Richgels, 2004, p. 20). The ability to hear phonemes (i.e., words that begin or end with the same sounds) is called phonemic awareness. It is more finite, more related to specific letters and sounds, and usually develops later than phonological awareness. It is a critical skill for reading and writing. It usually does not develop spontaneously, but is supported as teachers plan activities and interactions that draw attention to the phonemes in spoken words (Neuman, Copple, & Bredekamp, 2000).

As mentioned above, phonological and phonemic awareness can be supported when teachers choose books to read aloud that focus on sounds. Many picture books are based on songs that children love to sing. Among them are *Miss Polly Has a Dolly* (Edwards, 2003), *The Itsy Bitsy Spider* (Trapani, 1997), and *Miss Mary Mack* (Hoberman, 1998). Reading/singing these books, and making up new words to the familiar tunes, promote the development of phonological and phonemic awareness.

In a mixed-age class (3- to 5-year-olds), 3-year-old Jacob runs over to his teacher, bringing a piece of paper that is colored with red marks and taped to two Popsicle sticks. He says, "Look, I made a stop sign for our bus." His older friend Deshawn says, "No. You have to put S on the sign and some other letters if you want it to be a real stop sign." Deshawn shows him where and how to add the letters SDP. The teacher had read *Don't Let the Pigeon Drive the Bus* (Willems, 2003) several days earlier, and some of the children were making "things that go" in various areas of the classroom. The main character of the story, the pigeon, is just like a 3-year-old: impulsive, easily frustrated, and seeing the world only from his own perspective. The children, like the pigeon, wish they could really drive. So, they make a three-dimensional bus from a dishwasher crate that the teacher placed in the art area (after moving around some furniture), an airplane from some chairs in the dramatic play area, and a train in the block area. The teacher had suggested that 5-year-olds Rebecca and Devone write instructions for how to drive their train. They are writing on large chart paper taped to the wall in the block area. They are figuring out how to write "Don't Go Too Fast." Devone says, "Don't starts like Devone, with D." They make some other marks on the paper, followed by FS and an exclamation mark. Their teacher had pointed out the many exclamation marks contained in the book. She draws their attention to the page on which the pigeon describes the sound of the bus as "Vroom-vroom, vroomy-vroom!," and suggests they try to figure out how to write some noises that their train makes. Five-year-old Aisha decides to write "CHKU CHKU CHU! CHU!" on a separate piece of paper. The exclamation mark was used in this picture as well as on the large chart made by the children. This example shows how easily the children transfer the phonemic and phonological awareness skills linked to prior knowlcdgc, cngaging picture books, and play.

Teachers can support language development and cognitive thinking through such activities as reading multiple versions of the same folktale (e.g., a traditional version of "The Three Little Pigs," Lowcll's *The Three Little Javelinas* (1992), and Scieszka's *The True Story of the Three Little Pigs!* (1989)) and asking children to compare and contrast the versions. Creating new endings to favorite stories and/or planning open-ended art projects that synthesize knowledge (e.g., a mural depicting metamorphosis, as explained in Eric Carle's *The Very Hungry Caterpillar* (1981), helps children learn to synthesize information. Assembling diverse collections of subjects of interest from particular books, such as *Bread, Bread, Bread* (1993) or *Hats, Hats, Hats* (1993), both by Ann Morris, and charting which are the favorites, help children learn to evaluate and discuss others' opinions.

Print-Rich Environments

Research has shown that when additional literacy props and tools are added to various centers in preschool classrooms, children's conversations and understanding of written language are enhanced (Neuman & Roskos, 1991; Schickedanz, 1999). Literacy props include the types of things that would naturally occur in each of the centers, such as recipe cards, coupons, cookbooks, pencils, and notepads in the kitchen area. Using picture books to support these literacy tools makes play scenarios even richer. For example, one teacher read *The Little Red Hen Makes a Pizza* (Sturges, 2002). The book contains funny and interesting ingredients from the hen's kitchen, such as pickled eggplant, anchovies, and blue cheese. The teacher saw how eager the children were to make their own shopping lists, copying words from the labels of the variety of strange and interesting items that the teacher brought into the kitchen area (marinated artichokes, hearts of palm, Kalamata olives, etc). The children and teacher ultimately made real individual pizzas, choosing their own toppings.

In order for children to extend the experiences they read about in books, they must have many other literacy tools to do so. Art areas with open-ended materials from which children can choose, writing/drawing tools and other implements, a variety of types of paper, paint, three-dimensional materials, and long periods of time to work on independent or collaborative projects are important. For example, one kindergarten teacher always finds several of her children engaged in book-making activities after she reads high-quality picture books. After reading *The Napping House* (Wood, 1994), some of the children made felt figures of the characters in the book in order to reenact the story with their flannel board. Additionally, the children made their own version of the book, called "The Kindergarten Napping House," in which each child contributed a page with various texts, according to their writing abilities and interests.

Picture books focused on writing, such as *Click, Clack, Moo: Cows That Type* (Cronin, 2000), offer a perfect vehicle through which teachers can introduce writing for a purpose. Just as the cows type their complaints to the farmer, children can voice their opinions in print on issues related to classroom problems or concerns.

Exploring picture books and creating lists of the types of literacy tools (or making prop boxes) that would support the content of specific books is a valuable exercise. Additionally, thinking about which books should be included in *each* of the early childhood interest areas (changed regularly, to allow for changes in children's interests, themes, etc.) is important.

Teachers also should consider the needs and interests of specific children when considering which books to read to individuals. One teacher noted that Quincy was having difficulty creating rhymes. So, she read Trapani's (1998) *The Itsy Bitsy Spider* to him. Then, using a flannel board, Quincy acted out the song with a flannel spider and other props. The next day, the teacher extended this activity even further. She put other felt animals next to the flannel board and invited Quincy and Fatima to change the animals and make up a new song. Together, the two children giggled as they sang, *"The itsy bitsy kitty went up the water spout. Down came the water and cried the kitty out. Out came the sun and the kitty cried away and the itsy bitsy spider went out the day-de-day."*

Conclusions

The text and illustrations of high-quality picture books weave rich stories that can excite and surprise children, make them laugh, make them wonder, and make them think. Turning each page brings another element to the magic. Whether the pictures are photographs, black-and-white line drawings, unusual designs, paintings, woodcuts, or collage, the visual art form excites the young audience. Whether the text is factual, fictional, historical, readily identifiable to the listener, or something from another culture, the stories fill young children with a multitude of ideas, words, and questions.

Using the wealth of classic and new picture books available, adults can support literacy in ways that are engaging to children. Picture books should be a part of every day in the early childhood years. Reading to children and engaging them in activities that encourage the use of expressive language, phonological awareness, and high-level thinking is critical for the development of the skills and dispositions that are necessary for reading and writing.

In the picture book *Book!* (George, 2001), a preschool child opens a present and falls in love with his new picture book. He typifies the relationship young children can have with books when he says:

I'll take you on a wagon ride to my secret place, Where both of us can hide.
After that, we'll find an empty lap before I take my nap.
We'll read you warm and snug, Book!
I'll give you a hug, Book!
Open wide.
Look inside.
Book!

References

Andreae, G. (1999). *Giraffes can't dance.* New York: Orchard Books.

Aram, D., & Biron, S. (2004). Joint storybook reading and joint writing interventions among low SES preschoolers: Differential contributions to early literacy. *Early Childhood Research Quarterly, 19,* 588–610.

Axtell, D. (1999). *We're going on a lion hunt.* New York: Henry Holt and Company.

Berk, L. E., & Winsler, A. (1995). Scaffolding children's learning: *Vygotsky and early childhood education.* Washington, DC: National Association for the Education of Young Children.

Bosschaert, G. (2000). *Teenie bird and how she learned to fly.* New York: Harry N. Abrams, Inc.

Bus, A. G., van IJzendoorn, M. H., & Pelligrini, A. D. (1995). Joint book reading makes for success in learning to read: A meta-analysis on intergenerational transmission of literacy. *Review of Educational Research, 65,* 1–21.

Carle, E. (1981). *The very hungry caterpillar.* New York: Philomel Books.

Cronin, D. (2000). *Click, clack, moo: Cows that type:* New York: Simon & Schuster.

Day, A. (1989). *Good dog, Carl.* New York: Simon & Schuster.

Edwards, P. D. (2003). *Miss Polly has a dolly.* New York: Penguin Young Readers Group.

Ehlert, L. (1993). *Eating the alphabet.* New York: Harcourt Brace Company.

George, K. O. (2001). *Book!* New York: Clarion Books/Houghton Mifflin.

Hargrave, A. C., & Senechal, M. (2000). A book reading intervention with preschool children who have limited vocabularies: The benefits of regular reading and dialogic reading. *Early Childhood Research Quarterly, 15,* 75–90.

Hoberman, M. A. (1998). *Miss Mary Mack.* Hong Kong: Little Brown.

Isenberg, J. P., & Jalongo, M. R. (2001). *Creative expression and play in early childhood.* Upper Saddle River, NJ: Merrill.

Jalongo, M. R. (2004). *Young children and picture books* (2nd ed.). Washington, DC: National Association for the Education of Young Children.

Keats, E. J. (1962). *The snowy day.* New York: Viking Juvenile.

Koralek, D. (Ed.). (2003). *Spotlight on young children and language.* Washington, DC: National Association for the Education of Young Children.

Lowell, S. (1992). *The three little javelinas.* Flagstaff, AZ: Rising Moon.

McGee, L. M., & Richgels, D. J. (2004). *Literacy's beginnings: Supporting young readers and writers.* New York: Pearson, Allyn and Bacon.

Morris, A. (1993). *Bread, bread, bread.* New York: HarperCollins.

Morris, A. (1993). *Hats, hats, hats.* New York: William Morrow & Company.

Neuman, S. B. (1999). Books make a difference: A study of access to literacy. *Reading Research Quarterly, 34,* 286–311.

Neuman, S. B., Copple, C., & Bredekamp, S. (2000). *Learning to read and write: Developmentally appropriate practices for young children.* Washington, DC: National Association for the Education of Young Children.

Neuman, S. B., & Roskos, K. (1991). Peers as literacy informants: A description of young children's literacy conversations in play. *Early Childhood Research Quarterly, 6,* 23–248.

Norton, D. E. (1999). *Through the eyes of a child: An introduction to children's literature* (5th ed.). Columbus, OH: Merrill.

Numeroff, L. J. (1985). *If you give a mouse a cookie.* New York: HarperCollins.

Owocki, G. (2001). *Make way for literacy: Teaching the way young children learn.* Portsmouth, NH: Heinemann & Washington, DC: National Association for the Education of Young Children.

Ringgold, F. (1996). *Tar beach.* New York: Dragonfly.

Rosen, M. (1997). *We're going on a bear hunt.* New York: Simon and Schuster Children's Publishing Division.

Routman, R. (1991). *Invitations: Changing as teachers and learners K-12.* Portsmouth, NH: Heinemann.

Salley, C. (2004). *Why Epossumondas has no hair on his tail.* New York: Harcourt.

Schickedanz, J. A. (1999). *Much more than the ABC's: The early stages of reading and writing.* Washington, DC: National Association for the Education of Young Children.

Scieszka, J. (1989). *The true story of the three little pigs.* New York: Penguin Group.

Sendak, M. (1998). *Where the wild things are.* San Diego: HarperCollins.

Seplocha, H., & Jablon, J. (2004). *New Jersey early learning assessment system: Trainer's box.* Trenton, NJ: New Jersey Department of Education.

Strickland, D.S., & Morrow, L. M. (1989). *Emerging literacy: Young children learn to read and write.* Newark, DE: International Reading Association.

Sturges, P. (2002). *The little red hen makes a pizza.* New York: Puffin.

Trapani, I. (1997). *The itsy bitsy spider.* New York: Charlesbridge.

Williams, V. B. (1997). *"More more more," said the baby.* New York: HarperCollins.

Willems, M. (2003). *Don't let the pigeon drive the bus!* New York: Scholastic.

Wood, A. (1994). *The napping house.* New York: Harcourt.

JANIS STRASSER is Associate Professor of Early Childhood Education and **HOLLY SEPLOCHA** is Associate Professor of Early Childhood Education, Willam Paterson University, Wayne, New Jersey.

Thank you to Darcee Chaplick, Christina Komsa, Lisa Mufson, Joe Murray, and Sage Seaton for sharing their experiences with children.

Calendar Time for Young Children
Good Intentions Gone Awry

Sallee J. Beneke, Michaelene M. Ostrosky, and Lilian G. Katz

W hy do the children struggle to answer Ms. Kelsey correctly, when they have participated in this routine for months? What is the long-term impact on children when they engage regularly in an activity they do not fully understand? Here is a fresh look at calendar time in light of what we know about child development and best practices.

Young Children's Development of a Sense of Time

Adults use calendars to mark and measure time, such as scheduling appointments, remembering birthdays, and anticipating upcoming special events (spring break, a basketball tournament). However, if we look at the development of children's understanding of time (sometimes referred to as *temporal understanding*), there is little evidence that calendar activities that mark extended periods of time (a month, a week) are meaningful for children below first grade (Friedman 2000). However, there *are* some temporal concepts that preschoolers can grasp in the context of their daily activities—concepts such as *later, before,* and *after.*

Barriers to Meaningful Participation

To participate meaningfully in calendar activities, young children must understand that time is sequential. The sequences include yesterday, today, and tomorrow; morning, afternoon, and evening; Sunday, Monday, Tuesday, and so on. Children also must be able to conceptualize *before* and *after* and think about future and past events. Three-year-olds typically "have established object permanence and can recall past events, even though they do not understand the meaning of the words 'yesterday,' 'today,' or 'tomorrow'" (CTB/McGraw-Hill 2002, 9). Thus, young children can talk about things that have happened or will happen, but they cannot yet understand or talk about these events in terms of units of time (days, weeks) or sequence. This child development knowledge draws into question the usefulness of calendar activities for children under age 6.

Heather, a student teacher, watches as Ms. Kelsey begins calendar time with the 4-year-olds seated in a semicircle on the rug. "What day is it today?" Ms. Kelsey asks, gesturing toward the large calendar on an easel next to her. When no one responds, she asks, "Well, what day was it yesterday?" The children show little enthusiasm for the exercise, but finally Mindy offers, "Yesterday was Friday!" Ms. Kelsey says, "No, it wasn't Friday, Mindy. Does someone else know what day it was yesterday?" Terrance suggests, "Wednesday?" to which Ms. Kelsey responds, "Right! And if it was Wednesday yesterday, then what day is it today?" Several wrong guesses later, the correct answer emerges.

Ms. Kelsey then asks Terrance to cross out the corresponding date on the calendar. When he hesitates, she prompts, "Just look at the date we crossed out yesterday." Terrance still seems confused, so Ms. Kelsey points to a box and says, "That's the one for today." Although the children are quite restless and appear indifferent to the solution to the date problem, Ms. Kelsey succeeds in getting them to say in unison, "Today is Thursday, February 15th."

Shortly after large group time, Heather meets with her faculty supervisor, who suggests that when helping the children get ready to go home, Heather might casually ask them what day it will be when they get home. She also suggests that when a child gives the correct answer, Heather should ask, "Are you sure?"

Later, following this advice, Heather finds that about a third of the children do not know what day it will be when they get home. Among those who get the day right, about half are unsure of their answer. Heather wonders about the calendar activity. After all, it is February, and calendar time has been part of the children's daily routine since September.

Young children can talk about things that have happened or will happen, but they cannot yet understand or talk about these events in terms of units of time or sequence.

Distance in Time

Calendar use requires children to understand not only concepts such as *before* and *after* but also the relative lengths of time or distance of past or future events from the present (Friedman 2000). For example, how far away is October 30 when today is October 5? How long is the weekend? Preschoolers cannot usually judge such distances or lengths of time. A 4-year-old who learns that there will be a field trip in five days will not judge the temporal distance of this event any differently than if he were told it is in eight days. In fact, it is difficult for preschoolers to judge length of time within a given day (with hours as the unit of time), such as "in two hours" versus "in four hours." Perhaps this is the reason children on a car trip repeatedly ask, "How long until we get there?"

According to Friedman (2000), the ability to judge the relative time from a past event or until a future event in terms of the calendar year is not in place until sometime between 7 and 10 years of age. The following anecdote about 6-year-olds' attempts to understand time concepts associated with birthdays and age illustrate Friedman's point.

As Joey's grandparents arrive for his birthday, Joey runs to greet them, saying, "I can't believe I'm gonna be 6." "So, you're going to be 6. Six what?" his grandmother asks. Joey responds, "It's my birthday. I'm gonna be 6." "Yes, I know," she replies, "but six what? You're not six books." At that point Joey's 9-year-old brother whispers in his ear, "You're gonna be 6 years old, dummy!" and Joey says, "I'm gonna be 6 years old."

Three days later, as Joey's friends assemble for the traditional noisy birthday party, a discussion begins about who is already 6 and who is not. Marta states, "Well, I'm 6½." Joey asks her, "Six-and-a-half what?" Marta responds, "I don't know." Another child says to 6½-year-old Marta, "Wait a minute. When were you a baby?" She hesitates and then answers, "I don't know, maybe 10 years ago."

True understanding of dates and the calendar comes with maturity. Given the above information on the level of thinking required to grasp the time concepts of the calendar and the developmental abilities of young children, teachers may want to reconsider the calendar routine and their expectations for young children's comprehension.

Teaching Using the Calendar—or Not?

Early childhood educators may use the calendar to teach concepts other than time, including numeracy, vocabulary (*month, year, weekend*), sequencing (yesterday, today, tomorrow), and patterning (Monday, Tuesday, Wednesday). Additionally, as children attend to the visual calendar, teachers may hope they will learn numeral recognition and one-to-one correspondence. Early childhood specialists have cited numbers, spatial reasoning, patterning, logical relations, measurement, and early algebra as key components of young children's mathematical

growth (for example, Greenes 1999; NCTM 2000). However, most 4-year-olds are not ready to grasp the complex concepts involved in dates (Etheridge & King 2005).

Math Concepts

Learning experiences that center on mathematical concepts should not only be enjoyable and meaningful but also direct children's thinking toward, and focus it on, important mathematical ideas (Trafton, Reys, & Wasman 2001). Giving preschool children opportunities to explore and experiment individually with math concepts, using concrete materials with a responsive adult to question and guide learning, is likely to be more meaningful and beneficial than having young children participate in a whole group discussion of such concepts centered on the calendar.

For example, a teacher can help children notice patterns in the environment and in their work and explain the process of patterning both at circle time and individually. A teacher might join a child who is stringing beads and say, "I think I will make a pattern with my beads. My pattern is blue, yellow, red; blue, yellow, red. What kind of pattern can you make with your beads?" These approaches can help children build their own patterning abilities.

Other Knowledge and Skills

Many teachers use calendar time to teach skills unrelated to math, such as colors, letters, emergent writing, and social skills. While each of these concepts and skills is important for young children to learn, the calendar routine is not the most useful format for teaching them. For example, it is difficult for teachers to individualize instruction to meet the diverse needs of young learners during a large group activity such as calendar time.

Better Alternatives at Group Time

If focusing on the calendar is not an appropriate way to introduce young children to time concepts, numeracy, and the other concepts mentioned above, then what are some better ways?

The following evidence-based practices are likely to be more effective than calendar activities in presenting time concepts to young children.

Picture Schedules

Although young children have difficulty judging the length of time between events (for example, how long the time between snack and outside play will be), they can understand a sequence of events (for example, snack comes after circle time). Young children generally have a strong sense of narrative and the way a story progresses. Pictures illustrating the schedule of class activities are often recommended for children with particular disabilities. Similarly, a poster with illustrations or photos of the day's activities in sequence can be helpful for all young children.

A poster with illustrations or photos of the day's activities in sequence can be helpful for all young children.

Classroom Journal

Using a digital camera, the teacher can take frequent photographs of classroom events, projects, or field trips, then invite the children to help select photos for a classroom journal. Attach the photos to a dated page (one photo per page or multiple photos on a page) or tuck them into a plastic sleeve. Post or display them in a designated place—on a wall or bulletin board or in a binder—to clearly reflect the sequence of activities: "On Tuesday, we went to the park, we made pancakes, and we read *Pancakes, Pancakes!* by Eric Carle." As the children add new pictures chronicling recent events, they can revisit and discuss past shared events.

Along these same lines, the teacher can collect samples of children's work in a notebook as a visual record of shared events. Children can take turns contributing work to this community notebook. When teachers encourage children to tell peers or their families the story of their project, the children strengthen their understanding of the way an event unfolds, with the various activities taking place in a time sequence.

Documentation Displays

Displaying documentation of shared class events can lead to meaningful discussions that involve time-linked vocabulary. For example, when looking at a documentation display about the class construction of a giant papiermâché butterfly, one child said, "See, there's the butterfly we made that other time." Her teacher responded, "Yes, we made the giant butterfly two weeks ago. Here [pointing to a photograph on the display] is a picture of the frame we built the first day, and the picture next to it shows you adding the papiermâché on the second day."

Linear Representations

Linear representations also can help children begin to understand and conceptualize that a day is a unit of time and talk about it with increasing clarity. For example, to count the number of days they have been in kindergarten, children can add a link to a paper chain each day, or number a pattern of colored Post-it notes and place them on the classroom wall, or add a Unifix cube to a stack of cubes. The teacher can emphasize time-linked vocabulary, such as *before, after, later, earlier,* as the children add the new link. Unlike calendars, linear representations do not require the left-to-right orientation.

Games

Games are another way for children to begin to get a feel for the length of various units of time and the vocabulary associated with them. For example, children might guess how many seconds it takes to walk from one side of the playground to the other, and the teacher or another child can time it with a watch. Or a teacher might ask the children to guess how many minutes it will take for a snowball to melt indoors and then time it with a clock. They might guess how many hours it will be until story time, tally the hours as they pass, and then compare the result with their estimate. These experiences with units of time

(seconds, minutes, hours) can lead to discussions about points in time during the school day and the relative distance in the future of these points in time. For example, the teacher might say, "We are going to the library at nine o'clock, and we will go outside at ten o'clock. Where are we going first?"

Project Work

Project work, in which children actively engage in ongoing investigations of events and phenomena around them, is another way to give children opportunities to acquire many concepts and skills related to time (Helm & Beneke, 2003). In project work, calendar concepts are useful rather than ritualistic in nature. Project work lends itself to planning future events and keeping a record of events that happen over time. For example, in a mixed-age preschool, the children investigated eggs. They incubated mallard duck eggs, and each day they added to a tally of days until the ducklings would hatch. As children plan for investigation and reflect on what they have learned and when they learned it in the meaningful context of a project, they naturally begin to develop a sense of the relative lengths of time in the past and future.

> **Project work lends itself to planning future events and keeping a record of events that happen over time.**

Intellectual Development and Calendar Time

A teacher's actions can enhance or inhibit young children's learning. Communication, classroom support, activities, and interactions all play a part. If young children participate frequently in activities they do not really understand, they may lose confidence in their intellectual powers. In this case, some children may eventually give up hope of understanding many of the ideas teachers present to them. Certainly all children will experience some degree of not fully understanding activities at some point. However, in such cases it is helpful for the teacher to reassure learners that fuller understanding will come and that it often takes practice to master a concept, and to indicate in other ways that feeling "out of it" happens to us all sometimes and will be overcome. "Curriculum goals must be both challenging and achievable for all children . . . one size does not fit all. Children will learn best if curriculum content connects with what they already know and have experienced, while introducing them to important new ideas and skills" (Hyson 2000, 61).

In a joint position statement on best practices in early childhood mathematics learning, NAEYC and the National Council of Teachers of Mathematics (NCTM) (2002) stated,

> It is vital for young children to develop confidence in their ability to understand and use mathematics—in other words, to see mathematics as within their reach. In addition, positive experiences with using mathematics

to solve problems help children to develop dispositions such as curiosity, imagination, flexibility, inventiveness, and persistence that contribute to their future success in and out of school. (p. 5)

Lengthy daily calendar sessions in which a teacher expresses the expectation that young children will understand the workings of a calendar run counter to this position. Teachers who intend to keep calendar a part of their daily classroom routine will be more effective if they develop ways to incorporate the calendar that require little time and reflect young children's limited development of time concepts.

Conclusion

As teachers reflect on their practice, they may experience an inner conflict in terms of what they believe about children's development and how and what they teach. Understanding how children learn should enable teachers to focus on calendar-related constructs such as patterning, sorting, and seriating during more natural and appropriate routines. In fact, many teachers will likely realize they already address these fundamental concepts during other parts of the classroom day.

As we return to the opening vignette, considering the information in this article, the discussion Ms. Kelsey has with her class might look something like this:

As Heather watches, Ms. Kelsey addresses the 4-year-olds seated on the rug in front of her: "It's time for us to add another link to our chain. Who would like to attach the link that stands for today?" Mindy volunteers, and Ms. Kelsey says, "Wonderful! Pick someone for your partner, and you two can take care of that." Mindy holds out her hand to Ginelle, and Ginelle joins her in attaching the latest link.

"Now, let's look at our picture chart. Who can tell me what we are going to do after circle time?" Terrance offers, "We're going to the library." Ms. Kelsey responds, "Right! Does anyone remember what are we going to do after that?" Althea enthusiastically states, "We're going out for recess!" Ms. Kelsey cheerfully responds, "Yes, that's right, Althea."

Ms. Kelsey then says, "Mindy and Ginelle have added a link for today to the paper chain. How far does the chain reach, now?" Ginelle responds, "It's almost to the window. It's really getting long." Many of the children voice their agreement.

Not long after circle time, Heather's faculty supervisor suggests that when she helps the children get ready to go home, she might ask them what they are going to

tell their parents they did that day at school. Most of the children plan to tell their parents about the day's sequence of activities, and when Heather prompts them with, "Are you sure?" several children refer to the picture chart to verify their statements.

References

CTB/McGraw-Hill. 2002. *Pre-kindergarten standards: Guidelines for teaching and learning.* Executive summary. www.ctb.com/media/articles/pdfs/resources/PreKstandards_summary.pdf

Etheridge, E.A., & J.R. King. 2005. Calendar math in preschool and primary classrooms: Questioning the curriculum. *Early Childhood Education Journal* 32 (5): 291–96.

Freidman, W.J. 2000. The development of children's knowledge of the times of future events. *Child Development* 71 (4): 913–32.

Greenes, C. 1999. The Boston University-Chelsea project. In *Mathematics in the early years,* ed. J.V. Copley, 151–55. Washington, DC: NAEYC.

Helm, J.H., & S. Beneke. 2003. *The power of projects.* New York: Teachers College Press.

Hyson, M. 2000. "Is it okay to have calendar time?" Look up to the star—Look within yourself. *Young Children* 55 (6): 34–36.

NAEYC & NCTM (National Council of Teachers of Mathematics). 2002. Early childhood mathematics: Promoting good beginnings. A joint position statement of NAEYC and NCTM. www.naeyc.org/about/positions/mathematics.asp

NCTM (National Council of Teachers of Mathematics). 2000. *Principles and standards for school mathematics.* Reston, VA: Author.

Trafton, P., B.J. Reys, & D.G. Wasman. 2001. Standards-based mathematics curriculum materials: A phrase in search of a definition. *Phi Delta Kappan* 8 (3): 259–64.

SALLEE J. BENEKE is the author and coauthor of several books on the project approach. She is a doctoral student in the Department of Special Education at the University of Illinois and provides professional development for school districts and child care centers. **MICHAELENE M. OSTROSKY**, PhD, is on faculty in the Department of Special Education at the University of Illinois at Urbana-Champaign. She collaborates with other faculty in the Center on Social and Emotional Foundations for Early Learning and is involved with The Autism Program in Illinois. Micki is involved in research on social interaction interventions, naturalistic language interventions, social-emotional competence, challenging behavior, and transitions. ostrosky@uiuc.edu. **LILIAN G. KATZ**, PhD, is codirector of the Clearinghouse on Early Childhood and Parenting and professor emerita at the University of Illinois, Urbana-Champaign. Lilian served as vice president and president of NAEYC in the 1990s. She has lectured in more than 60 countries and served as visiting professor in a half dozen countries.

From *Young Children*, May 2008, pp. 12–16. Copyright © 2008 by National Association for the Education of Young Children. Reprinted by permission.

Test-Your-Knowledge Form

We encourage you to photocopy and use this page as a tool to assess how the articles in *Annual Editions* expand on the information in your textbook. By reflecting on the articles you will gain enhanced text information. You can also access this useful form on a product's book support website at *http://www.mhhe.com/cls*.

NAME:

DATE:

_____

TITLE AND NUMBER OF ARTICLE:

_____

BRIEFLY STATE THE MAIN IDEA OF THIS ARTICLE:

_____

LIST THREE IMPORTANT FACTS THAT THE AUTHOR USES TO SUPPORT THE MAIN IDEA:

_____

WHAT INFORMATION OR IDEAS DISCUSSED IN THIS ARTICLE ARE ALSO DISCUSSED IN YOUR TEXTBOOK OR OTHER READINGS THAT YOU HAVE DONE? LIST THE TEXTBOOK CHAPTERS AND PAGE NUMBERS:

_____

LIST ANY EXAMPLES OF BIAS OR FAULTY REASONING THAT YOU FOUND IN THE ARTICLE:

_____

LIST ANY NEW TERMS/CONCEPTS THAT WERE DISCUSSED IN THE ARTICLE, AND WRITE A SHORT DEFINITION:

We Want Your Advice

ANNUAL EDITIONS revisions depend on two major opinion sources: one is our Advisory Board, listed in the front of this volume, which works with us in scanning the thousands of articles published in the public press each year; the other is you—the person actually using the book. Please help us and the users of the next edition by completing the prepaid article rating form on this page and returning it to us. Thank you for your help!

ANNUAL EDITIONS: Early Childhood Education 10/11

ARTICLE RATING FORM

Here is an opportunity for you to have direct input into the next revision of this volume.
We would like you to rate each of the articles listed below, using the following scale:

1. **Excellent: should definitely be retained**
2. **Above average: should probably be retained**
3. **Below average: should probably be deleted**
4. **Poor: should definitely be deleted**

Your ratings will play a vital part in the next revision.
Please mail this prepaid form to us as soon as possible.
Thanks for your help!

RATING	ARTICLE	RATING	ARTICLE
	1. Invest in Early Childhood Education		26. Developmentally Appropriate Practice in the Age of Testing
	2. A Foundation for Success		27. What Research Says about . . . Grade Retention
	3. Joy in School		28. Back to Basics: Play in Early Childhood
	4. Early Education, Later Success		29. Scripted Curriculum: Is It a Prescription for Success?
	5. The Changing Culture of Childhood: A Perfect Storm		30. Using Brain-Based Teaching Strategies to Create Supportive Early Childhood Environments That Address Learning Standards
	6. No Child Left Behind: Who's Accountable?		
	7. Preschool Comes of Age: The National Debate on Education for Young Children Intensifies		31. Successful Transition to Kindergarten: The Role of Teachers and Parents
	8. Class Matters—In and Out of School		32. The Looping Classroom: Benefits for Children, Families, and Teachers
	9. Early Childhood School Success: Recognizing Families as Integral Partners		33. Beyond *The Lorax*?: The Greening of the American Curriculum
	10. Meeting of the Minds		
	11. Making Long-Term Separations Easier for Children and Families		34. Play: Ten Power Boosts for Children's Early Learning
	12. Fast Times		35. Ready or Not, Here We Come: What It Means to Be a Ready School
	13. Whose Problem Is Poverty?		
	14. How to Support Bilingualism in Early Childhood		36. "Stop Picking on Me!": What You Need to Know about Bullying
	15. Learning in an Inclusive Community		37. Developmentally Appropriate Child Guidance: Helping Children Gain Self-Control
	16. Young Children with Autism Spectrum Disorder: Strategies That Work		
	17. Including Children with Disabilities in Early Childhood Education Programs: Individualizing Developmentally Appropriate Practices		38. Fostering Positive Transitions for School Success
			39. A Multinational Study Supports Child-Initiated Learning: Using the Findings in Your Classroom
	18. Play and Social Interaction in Middle Childhood		
	19. Twelve Characteristics of Effective Early Childhood Teachers		40. The Power of Documentation in the Early Childhood Classroom
	20. Health = Performance		41. Preschool Curricula: Finding One That Fits
	21. Which Hand?: Brains, Fine Motor Skills, and Holding a Pencil		42. Got Standards?: Don't Give up on Engaged Learning!
			43. The Plan: Building on Children's Interests
	22. Keeping Children Active: What You Can Do to Fight Childhood Obesity		44. Constructive Play: A Value-Added Strategy for Meeting Early Learning Standards
	23. The Truth about ADHD		
	24. When Girls and Boys Play: What Research Tells Us		45. Using Picture Books to Support Young Children's Literacy
	25. Enhancing Development and Learning through Teacher-Child Relationships		46. Calendar Time for Young Children: Good Intentions Gone Awry

213

BUSINESS REPLY MAIL
FIRST CLASS MAIL PERMIT NO. 551 DUBUQUE IA

POSTAGE WILL BE PAID BY ADDRESSEE

McGraw-Hill Contemporary Learning Series
501 BELL STREET
DUBUQUE, IA 52001

NO POSTAGE
NECESSARY
IF MAILED
IN THE
UNITED STATES

ABOUT YOU

Name

Date

Are you a teacher? ☐ A student? ☐
Your school's name

Department

Address   City   State   Zip

School telephone #

YOUR COMMENTS ARE IMPORTANT TO US!

Please fill in the following information:
For which course did you use this book?

Did you use a text with this ANNUAL EDITION? ☐ yes ☐ no
What was the title of the text?

What are your general reactions to the Annual Editions concept?

Have you read any pertinent articles recently that you think should be included in the next edition? Explain.

Are there any articles that you feel should be replaced in the next edition? Why?

Are there any World Wide Websites that you feel should be included in the next edition? Please annotate.

May we contact you for editorial input? ☐ yes ☐ no
May we quote your comments? ☐ yes ☐ no

NOTES

NOTES

NOTES

NOTES